Advanced Cisco Router Configuration

Laura Chappell, Editor

Macmillan Technical Publishing
201 West 103rd Street
Indianapolis, Indiana 46290 USA

Advanced Cisco Router Configuration

Laura Chappell, Editor

Copyright © 1999 Cisco Systems, Inc.

Cisco Press logo is a trademark of Cisco Systems, Inc.

Published by:
Macmillan Technical Publishing
201 West 103rd Street
Indianapolis, IN 46290 USA

Printed in the United States of America   5 6 7 8 9 0

Library of Congress Cataloging-in-Publication Number 98-85495

ISBN: 1-57870-074-4

Warning and Disclaimer

This book is designed to provide information about Cisco router configuration. Every effort has been made to make this book as complete and as accurate as possible, but no warranty or fitness is implied.

The information is provided on an "as is" basis. The author, Macmillan Technical Publishing, and Cisco Systems, Inc., shall have neither liability nor responsibility to any person or entity with respect to any loss or damages arising from the information contained in this book or from the use of the discs or programs that may accompany it.

The opinions expressed in this book belong to the author and are not necessarily those of Cisco Systems, Inc.

Feedback Information

At Cisco Press, our goal is to create in-depth technical books of the highest quality and value. Each book is crafted with care and precision, undergoing rigorous development that involves the unique expertise of members from the professional technical community.

Readers' feedback is a natural continuation of this process. If you have any comments regarding how we could improve the quality of this book, or otherwise alter it to better suit your needs, you can contact us at ciscopress@mcp.com. Please make sure to include the book title and ISBN in your message.

We greatly appreciate your assistance.

Associate Publisher	Jim LeValley
Executive Editor	John Kane
Cisco Systems Program Manager	H. Kim Lew
Managing Editor	Caroline Roop
Acquisitions Editor	Brett Bartow
Development Editor	Kezia Endsley
Project Editor	Tim Tate
Technical Editors	John Berry
	Dan Farkas
	Randall Fischer
	Gary Rubin
	Doug MacBeth
	Scott Morris
Copy Editor	Jill Bond
Team Coordinator	Amy Lewis
Indexer	Kevin Fulcher
Production and Design	Argosy

Trademark Acknowledgments

All terms mentioned in this book that are known to be trademarks or service marks have been appropriately capitalized. Macmillan Technical Publishing or Cisco Systems, Inc., cannot attest to the accuracy of this information. Use of a term in this book should not be regarded as affecting the validity of any trademark or service mark.

Acknowledgments

Special thanks to Carol Lee for her tremendous commitment to content organization and development of this title. Thanks also to Jill Poulsen, of ImagiTech, Inc., for her assistance with the coordination of this project on behalf of Ms. Chappell. Our appreciation to the ImagiTech, Inc., clients for their assistance and support in our internetworking ventures.

This book is the product of many contributors within the Cisco education department including, but not limited to, Cisco course developers, course editors, and instructors. We would like to acknowledge the efforts of Ilona Serrao, Certified Curriculum Planner, and Kevin Calkins, Cisco Instructor.

Thanks also to John Berry, Dan Farkas, Randall Fischer, Gary Rubin, and Scott Morris for their time and efforts on technical review of this material.

John Berry, CCIE #3162, is a Cisco certified trainer and course developer working for Azlan Training, a Cisco training partner in Europe.

Dan Farkas, CCIE #3800, is a Certified Cisco Systems Instructor teaching classes for Cisco, USWest, and Ascolta. He also delivers seminar presentations on Internet, switching, remote access, and other network solutions.

Gary Rubin, president of Information Innovation, Inc., is a data network consultant and Certified Cisco Systems Instructor. He currently teaches courses for Cisco's Engineering and Marketing Departments. He taught the ACRC class for five years and provided feedback to Cisco on several versions of the course.

Randall Fischer is a certified instructor for Cisco and International Network Services. He has created courseware on network design, switching fundamentals, and voice and data integration.

We are grateful for the efforts of Macmillan Technical Publishing in developing this title and bringing it to press. Specifically, we would like to thank John Kane, Caroline Roop, Brett Bartow, Kezia Endsley, Thomas Cirtin, Tim Tate, Jill Bond, and Amy Lewis.

Contents

Introduction

With the dramatic increase in network size and complexity, harnessing the power and potential of internetworking devices becomes essential to ensuring the health and longevity of the network. As the premier internetworking company, Cisco understands how internetworking device configurations affect network performance.

This book is designed, structured, and written based on Cisco's highly successful "Advanced Cisco Router Configuration" course, which is offered worldwide and is considered one of the premier courses on internetworking LANs and WANs using Cisco routers. This book is the follow-up work to the Cisco Press title *Introduction to Cisco Router Configuration*.

This book provides details on how to manage traffic and network access for the most popular internetworking protocols today, such as TCP/IP and Novell's IPX/SPX. You'll learn the difference between link-state and distance vector routing protocols and decide which routing method is best suited in various configurations. This book also focuses on WAN configurations and the methods for controlling WAN traffic and ensuring access security.

Each chapter ends with a test to evaluate your understanding of the concepts in each of the chapters and your ability to apply the configuration techniques available for Cisco routers.

WHO SHOULD READ THIS BOOK

This book contains a broad range of technical details on routing protocols, configurations, access methods, security, traffic control, and management. As an advanced title, this book can be used as a general reference for anyone designing, implementing, or supporting an internetwork with TCP/IP or IPX/SPX over a LAN or WAN. As well, this book provides in-depth study for Cisco certification candidates who are studying for their ACRC exams.

Even if you're not using Cisco routers, this book can increase your awareness of the underlying technologies affecting network communications and security and provide you with the simple rules for defining internetworking configurations.

VERSION INFORMATION

This book is based on the Cisco "Advanced Cisco Router Configuration" course which covers IOS v11.3. Although some references are made to earlier versions of IOS, the examples shown throughout this course are based on IOS v11.3. For more information on Cisco router configuration options and commands, refer to the Cisco documentation maintained online at www.cisco.com.

PART I: OVERVIEW OF SCALEABLE INTERNETWORKS

This section provides the foundation knowledge required to characterize scalable networks.

Chapter 1, "Overview of Scalable Internetworks," examines the three levels of internetworking that connects the local offices with the corporate backbone and campus internetwork. Readers are provided with the configuration considerations that should be taken into account when setting up internetworking devices.

PART II: INTRODUCTION TO MANAGING TRAFFIC AND ACCESS

This section examines the elements of internetwork traffic and access that should be considered when configuring network devices. It will examine the two most popular network protocols, TCP/IP and IPX/SPX, to see how network access should be managed.

Chapter 2, "Introduction to Managing Traffic and Congestion," focuses on network congestion and access control. In this chapter, you'll learn the affects of network congestion and how to reduce the drain on network bandwidth and device resources by controlling network traffic.

Chapter 3, "Managing IP Traffic," looks specifically at IP traffic patterns and the methods used to control the IP traffic patterns. Standard and extended IP access lists, virtual terminal restrictions, and helper addresses are defined and used as examples and options to help preserve precious network bandwidth.

Chapter 4, "Managing Novell IPX/SPX Traffic," delves into the specific methods available for managing NetWare's IPX/SPX traffic. Traffic filtering, IP tunneling, and access lists are shown as possible traffic management methods.

Chapter 5, "Configuring Queuing to Manage Traffic," defines how to provide Quality of Service (QOS) traffic flows through traffic prioritization. This chapter defines weighted fair queuing, priority queuing, and custom queuing techniques.

PART III: CONFIGURING SCALABLE ROUTING PROTOCOLS

This section will focus on the actual steps required to configure scaleable routing protocols such as OSPF and IGRP. It will examine the basic characteristics of a scalable routing protocol and explain how to extend IP addressing using variable-length subnet masking and configure OSPF routers within a single area or to interconnnect multiple areas. Finally, we examine Cisco's IGRP routing protocol as another option for scalable routing.

Chapter 6, "Routing Protocol Overview," defines the fundamentals of routing protocols and a provides a brief comparison between common routing protocols.

Chapter 7, "Extending IP Addresses Using VLSMs (Variable-Length Subnet Masks)," lists some of the issues that occur with restrictive IP addresses and the methods used to extend IP addresses using variable-length subnet masks. This chapter will look at several sample network configurations to see how these VLSMs help resolve IP addressing problems.

Chapter 8, "Configuring OSPF in a Single Area," examines the basic design of OSPF routing and provides details on how to configure OSPF within a single area. Finally, this chapter provides details on verifying OSPF configurations.

Chapter 9, "Interconnecting Multiple OSPF Areas," defines how to create multiple OSPF areas and configure OSPF operations across multiple areas. Finally, you'll learn how to verify and validate your OSPF configuration.

Chapter 10, "Configuring Enhanced IGRP," examines the advantages and uses of enhanced IGRP, as well as the configuration and verification of EIGRP configurations.

Chapter 11, "Optimizing Routing Update Operation," focuses on how to control routing update traffic and mixing routing protocols on a single network segment. This chapter also defines routing information redistribution techniques.

Chapter 12, "Connecting Enterprises to an Internet Service Provider," shows how Cisco BGP can be used to connect an internetwork to the Internet.

PART IV: CONFIGURING DIALUP CONNECTIVITY

This section focuses on various WAN connectivity options and encapsulation protocols. It will look at how to configure ISDN dial-on demand routing and PPP connections and multilink PPP connections.

Chapter 13, "WAN Connectivity Overview," will look at encapsulation methods for providing single-protocol WAN communications.

Chapter 14, "Configuring Dial-on Demand Routing," defines the elements of ISDN communication and how DDR routing is configured. It will also look at dialer profiles as a method of customizing ISDN connections.

Chapter 15, "Customizing DDR Operation," defines methods to change the default operation of DDR links including multilink PPP configuration and setting up snapshot routing. This section also details options available for IPX DDR routing.

PART V: INTEGRATING NONROUTED SERVICES

This section moves down the OSI stack to the data link layer by providing details on bridging operations and configurations. It examines transparent and source-route bridging operations and internetwork designs.

Chapter 16, "Bridging Overview," provides the technical details of bridging and routing functionality and defines when one operations is preferred over the other.

Chapter 17, "Configuring Transparent Bridging and Integrated Routing and Bridging," covers simple transparent bridging operations and how to set up a hybrid type of device that can perform bridging and routing simultaneously.

Chapter 18, "Configuring Source-Route Bridging," examines the operations of source routing and defines how to verify current SRB configurations.

APPENDIXES

The appendixes include the chapter test answer key and details on managing AppleTalk traffic, configuring NLSP (NetWare Link Services Protocol), T1/E1 and ISDN options, and an SMDS configuration overview. A comprehensive glossary is also included for your reference.

COMMAND CONVENTIONS

The conventions used to present commands in this book are the same conventions used in the IOS Command Reference. The Command Reference describes these conventions as follows:

- Vertical bars (|) separate alternative, mutually exclusive, elements.

- Square brackets [] indicate optional elements.

- Braces {} indicate a required choice.

- Braces within square brackets [{}] indicate a required choice within an optional element.

- **Boldface** indicates commands and keywords that are entered literally as shown.

- *Italics* indicate arguments for which you supply values.

Commands that are too long to fit on one line in the book are shown with an indented second line:

```
access-list access-list-number {permit | deny} protocol source source-wildcard
    destination destination-wildcard [log]
```

PART 1

Overview of Scalable Internetworks

CHAPTER 1

Overview of Scalable Internetworks

This chapter defines scalability and introduces methods for building a secure, responsive, and adaptable network. It also explains how a router can provide the critical elements required to build a scalable internetwork by offering varying levels of connectivity for workgroups and critical networks, such as a backbone network.

SCALING LARGE INTERNETWORKS

A *scalable network* is one that can be adjusted without major modification as time and resources require. Many of today's internetworks need to be scalable because they are experiencing phenomenal growth, primarily due to the increasing demands for connectivity in business and at home. What do scalable networks look like? What are the requirements that you, as an administrator, must be aware of when managing the growth of your scalable internetwork?

Scalable internetworks are typically described as networks that are experiencing constant growth. They must be flexible and expandable. The best-managed scalable internetworks are typically designed following a hierarchical model. This is because a hierarchical model simplifies the management of the internetwork and allows for controlled growth without overlooking the network requirements.

Figure 1–1 illustrates a typical three-layer hierarchical internetworking model. The layers are defined as follows:

- *Core layer*—The core is the central internetwork for the entire enterprise and may include LAN and WAN backbones. The primary function of this layer is to provide an optimized and reliable transport structure.

- *Distribution layer*—This represents the campus backbone. The primary function of this layer is to provide access to various parts of the internetwork, as well as access to services.

- *Access layer*—This provides access to corporate resources for a workgroup on a local segment.

Figure 1–1
An internetwork may include core, distribution, and access areas.

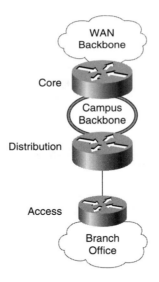

A hierarchy simplifies tasks such as addressing and device management. Using an addressing scheme that maps to the hierarchy reduces the need to redo the network addresses as a result of growth. Knowing where devices are placed in a hierarchy enables you to configure all routers within one layer in a consistent way because they all must perform similar tasks. This kind of router specialization allows the best use of the Cisco IOS features discussed in this book.

DEFINING THE ROUTER'S ROLE IN A HIERARCHY

Figure 1–2 shows a hierarchical model that provides a physical topology for building internetworks. Because the hierarchical structure uses three distinct layers that provide unique functionality, the routers placed at each layer also have unique functionality, as described in the following list:

- Core routers provide services that optimize communication among routes at different sites or in different logical groupings. In addition, core routers provide maximum availability and reliability. Core routers should be able to maintain connectivity when LAN or WAN circuits fail at this layer. A fault tolerant network design ensures that failures do not have a major impact on network connectivity.

- Distribution routers control access to resources that are available at the core layer and must, therefore, make efficient use of bandwidth. In addition, a distribution router must address the quality of service (QoS) needs for different protocols by implementing policy-based traffic control to isolate backbone and local environments. Policy-based traffic control enables you to prioritize traffic to ensure the best performance for the most time-critical and time-dependent applications.

- Access routers control traffic by localizing broadcasts and service requests to the access media. Access routers must also provide connectivity without compromising network integrity. For example, the routers at the access point must be able to detect whether a telecommuter dialing in is legitimate, yet require minimal authentication steps required by the telecommuter.

You should know where the router is located in the hierarchy and what the key needs are for a given layer so that the router can be configured to meet the specific needs of the layer. Although some needs are common to all layers, other needs are unique, or more critical to certain layers, as in the following example:

- Core routers must be reliable because they carry information about all the routes in an internetwork. If one of these routers goes down, it affects routing on a larger scale than when an access router goes down.

- Distribution routers need to be able to select the best path to different locations in order to make efficient use of bandwidth.

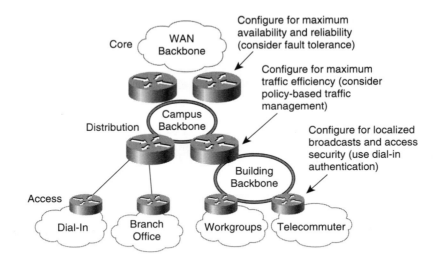

- Access routers are typically where you provide security and filtering. Access routers reduce the amount of overhead by keeping unnecessary traffic out of the core of the network.

- Examples of Cisco routers that can be used at each layer of the hierarchy are as follows:

  - *Core*—Cisco 7000 and 12000 series routers

  - *Distribution*—Cisco 4000 series routers

  - *Access*—Cisco 1000 and 2500 series routers

TIPS

Many companies are currently implementing switched backbones. A *switched backbone* is a network backbone that resides within a switch, with critical devices, such as servers and routers, connected directly to the switch ports, instead of a backbone network cable. A network that supports a switched backbone design is often referred to as a *flattened network*. For example, rather than using routers at the core layer, they are using ATM switches at the core, with routers connecting in at the distribution and access layers. There are benefits and drawbacks to this method. The benefits include a more streamlined, dedicated communication path and error filtering through the switch. The drawbacks can be the centralized nature of the cabling design required to configure a switched backbone.

KEY CHARACTERISTICS OF SCALABLE INTERNETWORKS

This book presents features and technologies that can be used to respond to the following key scalability requirements:

- *Reliable and available*—This includes being dependable and available 24 hours a day, 7 days a week (24×7). In addition, failures need to be isolated and recovery must be invisible to the end user.

- *Responsive*—This includes managing the QoS needs for the different protocols being used without affecting a response at the desktop. For example, the internetwork must be able to respond to latency issues common for Systems Network Architecture (SNA) traffic, but still allow for the routing of desktop traffic, such as IPX, without compromising QoS requirements.

- *Efficient*—Large internetworks must optimize the use of resources, especially bandwidth. Reducing the amount of overhead traffic, such as unnecessary broadcasts, service location, and routing updates, results in an increase in data throughput without increasing the cost of hardware or the need for additional WAN services.

- *Adaptable*—This includes being able to accommodate disparate networks and interconnect independent network clusters (or islands), as well as to integrate *legacy* technologies, such as those running SNA.

- *Accessible but secure*—This includes the capability to enable connections into the internetwork using dedicated, dialup, and switched services while maintaining network integrity.

Each of these characteristics is discussed in more detail in the following sections.

Making the Network Reliable and Available

The internetwork should be reliable and available at all layers, but most critically at the core layer. Recall that core routers must be reliable because they carry information about all the routes in an internetwork. If one of these routers goes down, it affects routing on a large scale.

Core routers are reliable when they can accommodate failures by rerouting traffic and respond quickly to changes in the network topology. Some protocols that enhance network reliability and availability that the Cisco IOS supports are scalable routing protocols, tunnels, and dial backup.

- *Scalable protocols*—These include Open Shortest Path First (OSPF), NetWare Link Services Protocol (NLSP), and Enhanced IGRP (EIGRP). These protocols provide the following features:

  - Reachability—Scalable networks, even those using a hierarchical design, can have a large number of reachable networks or subnetworks. These networks can be subject to reachability problems due to metric limitations of distance vector routing protocols. Scalable routing protocols, such as OSPF, NLSP, and EIGRP, use metrics that expand the reachability potential for routing updates because they use cost, rather than hop count, as a metric.

  - Fast convergence time—*Convergence time* is defined as the amount of time required to propagate new route information from one end of the internetwork to the other end of the internetwork. Scalable protocols can converge quickly because of the router's capability to detect failure rapidly and because each router maintains a network topology map. Routers also forward network changes quickly to all routers in the network topology.

  - Congestion control—Scalable routing protocols generally add less traffic overhead to the network for carrying routing information by providing summarizations of network information.

- *Alternate paths*—Scalable protocols, such as EIGRP and OSPF, enable a router to maintain a map of the entire network topology, so when a failure is detected the router can reroute traffic by looking at the network topology and finding another path. Enhanced IGRP is also a feasible solution because it keeps a record of alternate routes in case the preferred route goes away.

- *Load balancing*—Because scalable protocols have a map of the entire network topology, and because of the way in which they maintain their routing tables, they are able to transport data simultaneously across multiple paths to a given location, as shown in Figure 1–3.

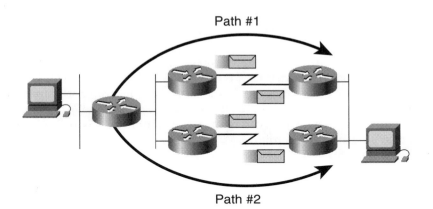

Path #1

Path #2

Figure 1–3
Load balancing enables two or more paths to be used for communication.

- *Tunnels*—Software tunnels can provide communication across WAN links into network areas that were previously unreachable. Tunnels allow you to configure a *point-to-point link* between two discontiguous networks running a given protocol, such as IPX, without configuring the entire cloud for IPX. Not only does this provide availability, but it also eliminates the overhead associated with running an additional routing protocol over the link.

- *Dial backup*—On WAN connections, you can configure backup links when you need to perform the following tasks:

  - Make the primary WAN connection more reliable by configuring one or more on backup connections.

  - Increase availability by configuring the backup connections to be used when a primary connection is experiencing congestion.

Making the Network Responsive

End users should not experience delays in computing responsiveness as the internetwork grows. In addition, as an administrator, you need to be aware of the latency issues that are unique to each protocol operating in the internetwork. *Latency* is the delay experienced by traffic as it crosses a network. Some protocols may timeout when the latency is too great. Routers are responsive when they can accommodate the latency needs of each protocol, without affecting response time at the desktop.

The main Cisco IOS feature that supports responsiveness on slow wide-area links is queuing. *Queuing* is the reordering of traffic packets after their arrival and dispatching them in the new order, favoring desirable traffic. Cisco supports three forms of queuing: weighted fair queuing, which is on by default on slow WAN links, and priority and custom queuing, which can be manually optimized. Cisco IOS features that support responsiveness are as follows:

- *Weighted fair queuing*—An automated method that provides fair bandwidth allocation to all network traffic. It ensures that high-bandwidth conversations do not consume all bandwidth.

- *Priority queuing*—A particular traffic type is prioritized higher than all other traffic types; thus it is allowed to go through before all other types. In this way, the priority traffic is assured of getting through, but other types of traffic may not get through in a timely manner.

In Figure 1–4, for example, the router prioritizes the traffic to enable SNA packets through before IP and IPX traffic.

Figure 1–4
Queuing enables different types of traffic to share bandwidth on a priority or nonpriority basis.

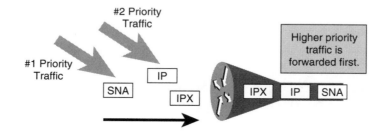

- *Custom queuing*—Each traffic type gets a share of the available bandwidth; thus certain types of traffic can be allocated larger or smaller amounts of bandwidth, depending on such things as sensitivity to latency.

Cisco IOS Release 11.2 and later includes the following additional features that can make your network more responsive:

- *Frame Relay Traffic Shaping*—Provides a mechanism for you to be able to perform rate enforcement and backward explicit congestion notification (BECN) support on a per-VC basis, and priority, custom, and weighted fair queuing at the VC level. *Rate enforcement* measures the amount of allowable traffic on a congested link and ensures that lower priority traffic is dropped when congestion occurs. BECN identifies the traffic type along a path and can request that higher-level protocols take flow control action as appropriate when the network becomes congested.

- *Generic Traffic Shaping (GTS)*—Provides a mechanism to help control the amount of traffic allowed onto the network from particular hosts or applications. GTS works in coordination with interfaces to a variety of Layer 2 data-link technologies (for example, Frame Relay, SMDS, or Ethernet) to detect and alleviate congestion on the network.

- *Random Early Detection (RED)*—Helps eliminate network congestion during peak traffic loads by using the characteristics of robust transport protocols, such as TCP, to reduce transmission volume at the source when traffic volume threatens to overload a router's buffer resources.

Refer to the *Cisco Connection Documentation, Enterprise Series* CD-ROMs for more information on these technologies.

Making the Network Efficient

Optimizing your network at all layers of an internetwork hierarchy is critical because it can reduce potential costs in additional hardware or WAN services. In this book, the focus is on optimizing your bandwidth. Bandwidth optimization is normally done by reducing the amount of update traffic on the LAN over a WAN connection, without dropping essential routing information, to increase data traffic throughput.

Cisco IOS features that can help optimize bandwidth use are as follows:

- *Access lists*—Can be used to permit or deny (drop) protocol update traffic, data traffic, and broadcast traffic, as shown in Figure 1–5. Access lists are available for IP, IPX, and AppleTalk and can be tailored to meet the needs for each protocol. An access list, for example, can be defined by Transmission Control Protocol (TCP) port or by IPX network number, depending on the situation.

Figure 1–5
Access lists are defined to deny unwanted traffic from propagating further onto a network.

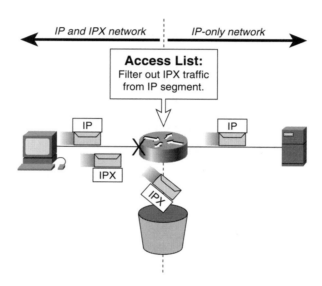

- *Snapshot routing*—Allows peer routers to exchange full distance vector routing information upon initial connection, and then on a predefined interval. Typically used with ISDN, this feature can reduce WAN costs when using distance vector protocols because routing information is exchanged at an interval you define. Between update exchanges, the routing tables for the distance vector protocols are kept frozen. Snapshot routing is only for distance vector protocols such as IP RIP. If you are using link-state protocols, other options are available, such as OSPF for On Demand Circuits. This feature is not discussed in this book, but performs a similar function as snapshot routing.

- *Compression over WANs*—Several compression techniques can be used to reduce traffic that is crossing a WAN connection. Cisco supports TCP/IP header compression and data (payload) compression. In addition, you can configure link compression, which compresses header and data information into packets that cross point-to-point connections (leased lines). Compression is accomplished by software within the router before the frame is placed on the appropriate media for transmission.

- *Dial-on-demand routing (DDR)*—Connections for infrequent traffic flow can be accomplished using DDR. In DDR, active links are created only after "interesting traffic" is detedcted by the router, as shown in Figure 1–6. This "only as required" service replaced dedicated circuits that you pay for even when that link is idle.

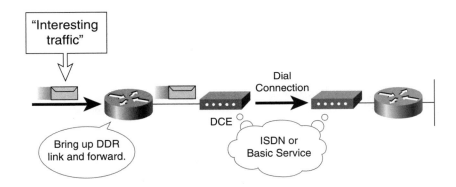

Figure 1–6
Dial-on-deman d routing brings up a link only when "interesting" traffic is seen.

- *Switched access*—Packet-switched networks, such as X.25 and Frame Relay, offer the advantage of providing global connectivity through a large number of service providers with established circuits to most major cities. Packet-switched networks enable multiple nodes to share a common network typically referred to as a "cloud." This concept allows the customers to be free of concern with the particulars of every step to get packets from point A to point B.

- *Reduce the number of routing table entries*—You can reduce the number of router processing cycles by reducing the overall number of routing entries in a router's routing table. This can be done using the following Cisco IOS features:

  - Route summarization—The number of entries in a routing table can be reduced by using route aggregation or, as it is more commonly known, *route summarization*. Summarization of routes occurs at major network boundaries for most routing protocols by simply finding the common bits or bytes of addresses that a router advertises. Instead of advertising all the routes, the router only advertises the common bits or bytes (or summary) of the routes. Some IP routing protocols, such as OSPF and Enhanced IGRP, allow manual summarization on arbitrary boundaries within the major network. Careful planning and address allocation is required for route summarization to be most effective.

o Incremental updates—Protocols such as Enhanced IGRP and OSPF make more efficient use of bandwidth than distance vector protocols by sending only topology changes rather than the entire routing table contents at fixed intervals.

Making the Network Adaptable

Because scalable internetworks experience change frequently, they must be able to adapt to changes, such as the following:

- *Mixing routable and nonroutable protocols*—A network delivering both routable and nonroutable traffic has some unique problems. Routable protocols can be forwarded from one network to another based on a network-layer address (such as an IP address). Non-routable protocols do not contain any network-layer address and cannot be forwarded by routers. Most nonroutable protocols also lack a mechanism to provide flow control and are sensitive to delays in delivery. Any delays in delivery or packets arriving out of order can result in session loss.

- *Integrating "islands" of networks*—Many companies are integrating islands of networks that are typically using different protocols in their hierarchical design. In this case, you can add any protocols used by the network islands to the core layer, or create a tunnel in the backbone that will connect the network islands but not add new protocol traffic to the core backbone.

- *Meet the varying requirements for each protocol in the internetwork*—When multiple protocol traffic is present, the network must be balanced between the special needs of each protocol.

Cisco IOS features that focus on network adaptability are as follows:

- *EIGRP*—A routing protocol that supports IP, IPX, and AppleTalk traffic.

- *Redistribution*—You can exchange routing information between networks that are using different routing protocols. Route redistribution is a key feature in Cisco routers. Mastering the usage of route redistribution is important to enable different protocols to communicate with each other successfully.

- *Bridging mechanisms*—You can integrate your legacy systems into your network using transparent, source-route bridging and integrated routing and bridging (IRB). Transparent bridging forwards packets based on the MAC address table learned by the router. Source-route bridging forwards packets based on the route information that is placed inside a packet by a source routing station. IRB can be a useful feature if you are connecting bridged networks to routed networks. IRB lets you bridge the protocol in from the bridged network and route it out through the routed interface.

Making the Network Accessible but Secure

The network should be accessible, particularly at the access layer. Access routers need to connect to a variety of WAN services, yet be secure, as shown in Figure 1–7.

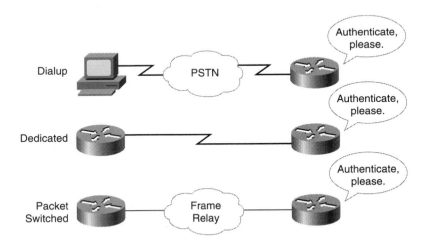

Figure 1–7
Access routers need to connect to a variety of WAN services.

Support for a variety of WAN technologies is important because the technologies are not all available throughout the world. In many cases, not only is usage a consideration when selecting a WAN technology, but so is geographical availability.

IP access routers must also allow telecommuters to dial in, but be able to differentiate between legitimate and hostile connection attempts. Cisco IOS features that support access are as follows:

- *Dedicated and switched WAN support*:

  ○ Dedicated access—Cisco routers can be directly connected to basic telephone service or digital services such as T1/E1. This means that you can create a core WAN infrastructure for heavy traffic loads, and then use other access services for sporadic traffic requirements.

  ○ Switched access—Cisco routers support Frame Relay, X.25, SMDS, and ATM. With this variety of support, you can determine which switched service, or combination of switched services, to use, based on cost, location, and traffic requirements.

- *Exterior protocol support*—Cisco IOS supports several exterior protocols, including Exterior Gateway Protocol (EGP) and Border Gateway Protocol (BGP). EGP is an older exterior gateway protocol that provides connection between separate autonomous systems. BGP is often used by Internet Service Providers (ISPs) and by organizations that want to connect to ISPs. For more information on BGP configuration, refer to Chapter 12, "Connecting Enterprises to an Internet Service Provider."

Features that support network security are as follows:

- *Access lists*—Access lists, which are lists containing information about which type of traffic should be forwarded, can be defined to prevent user traffic from accessing portions of the network. Access lists can also assist in providing security because when they block user traffic effectively, the users themselves are being denied access to sensitive areas of the network. Access lists can be used to filter access to certain locations, but this is not a security feature. Cisco does not market access lists as security mechanisms; rather, these lists assist in making the network more secure. Chapter 2, "Introduction to Managing Traffic and Congestion," discusses access lists in more detail.

- *Authentication protocols*—These are protocols that authenticate a user before allowing access to data. On WAN connections using PPP, you can configure authentication protocols such as Password Authentication Protocol (PAP) or Challenge Handshake Authentication Protocol (CHAP).

As shown in Figure 1–8, the central site router participates in an authentication process with the dial-in user. If authentication fails, the user is denied access.

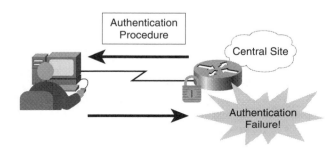

Authentication
Procedure

Central Site

Authentication
Failure!

Figure 1–8
*Authentica-
tion failures
effectively
lock out
untrusted con-
nections.*

Lock and Key Security and Network Layer Encryption are two additional Cisco IOS security features, as described here:

- *Lock and Key Security*—This is a Cisco IOS feature that defines dynamic access lists, which grant access per user on a specific source/destination host basis through a user authentication process. It is typically recommended that Lock and Key Security be used in conjunction with a TACACS+ server. TACACS (The Terminal Access Controller Access Control System) provides a way to centrally validate users attempting to gain access to a router or access server.

- *Network Layer Encryption*—In Cisco IOS Release 11.2 and later, Network Layer Encryption enables you to protect the confidentiality and integrity of network data traveling between cooperating (peer) encrypting routers because it allows for the authentication of the peer routers and encrypts data between these routers using the Diffie-Hellman encryption algorithm. The Diffie-Hellman encryption method allows two hosts to create and share a secret key for encryption and decryption purposes.

Refer to the *Cisco Connection Documentation, Enterprise Series* CD-ROMs for details about Lock and Key Security and Network Layer Encryption.

The key characteristics of a scalable network are reliability and availability, responsiveness, efficiency, adaptability, and being accessible but secure.

Key Concept

SUMMARY

This chapter has defined scalability and provided examples of Cisco IOS features that enable you to grow your network successfully. You learned, for example, that knowing where the router is located in the hierarchy and what the key needs are for a given layer make it easier for you to configure the router to meet the specific needs of the layer.

Recall that the key characteristics of a scalable network are reliability and availability, responsiveness, efficiency, adaptability, and being accessible but secure. You will see these same concepts discussed again and again as you make your way through this book. Chapter 2 talks in more detail about addressing and access lists.

Chapter One Test
Overview of Scalable Internetworks

Estimated Time: 15 minutes

Complete all the exercises to test your knowledge of the materials contained in this chapter. Answers are listed in Appendix A, "Chapter Test Answer Key."

Question 1.1

Complete the table by assigning to each network problem one of the five following requirements. Then list one or more Cisco IOS features that can be used to correct each network problem.

- Reliable and available

- Responsive

- Efficient

- Adaptable

- Accessible but secure

Network Problem	Key Requirement	Cisco IOS Feature(s)
Connectivity restrictions		
Single paths available to all networks		
Too much broadcast traffic		
Application sensitivity to traffic delays		

Network Problem	Key Requirement	Cisco IOS Feature(s)
Convergence problems with metric limitations		
Competition for bandwidth		
Illegal access to services on the internetwork		
Single WAN links available to each remote site		
Expensive tariffs on WAN links that do not get much use		
Very large routing tables		
Integrate networks using legacy protocols		

PART 2

Introduction to Managing Traffic and Access

Introduction to Managing Traffic and Congestion

This chapter outlines the causes of network congestion and provides high-level solutions available using the software shipped with the Cisco router. The chapter also provides an introduction to traffic congestion as a preface to the next four chapters, which cover the details about traffic management and security for IP, IPX, and different queuing methods.

CONGESTION OVERVIEW

Congestion occurs when the amount of network traffic transmitted on a particular medium exceeds the bandwidth of that medium, as shown in Figure 2–1. This leads to lost data packets and timeouts. The users of the network perceive the network to be "slow," but they may not understand the cause of the "slowness."

Temporary congestion can be expected in every network. Periodic congestion often occurs because of the *bursty* nature of today's network applications. Bursty traffic transitions from lots of packets per second to very few packets per second, based on the tasks being performed. Causes of chronic congestion, however, should be identified and remedied. *Chronic congestion* is defined as congestion that occurs regularly or as a result of daily or regular use of the network, and not congestion that occurs at unusually heavy times. If chronic congestion causes packet loss, the network should be examined to determine the possible cause.

Figure 2–1
Congestion occurs when the data traffic exceeds the data-carrying capacity of the link.

Network Traffic

Bandwidth of the Link

Congestion anywhere in the path
results in delays for user applications.

Serial lines are generally where congestion is experienced most often because their available bandwidth is typically much smaller than LAN bandwidth. When LAN-to-LAN traffic crosses a WAN link, it is most often the WAN link that is the bottleneck.

TIPS

You can use a network analyzer to determine your network's current bandwidth utilization. This information is typically presented as a percentage of the total possible bandwidth. For example, an analyzer may indicate your average bandwidth utilization at 10 percent on a 10BaseT network. This indicates that your average traffic level is 1 Mbps (10 percent of 10 Mbps).

So where does all this traffic that causes congestion come from? Understanding the source of the traffic can enable you to reconfigure the network to control the traffic flow based on the type of traffic and its source and ultimate destination. Traffic sources in IP networks, IPX networks, and other multiprotocol networks are discussed next.

Traffic in an IP Network

An IP network has many sources of data traffic and overhead traffic, as follows:

- *User applications*—Data traffic is usually generated by user applications. These applications initiate file transfers using the File Transfer Protocol (FTP) and Trivial File Transfer Protocol (TFTP). Electronic mail is another common source of data traffic; it uses the Simple Mail Transfer Protocol (SMTP).

- *Routing protocol updates*—Routing protocols send updates periodically or when routing information changes.

- *Encapsulated protocol transport*—Noncontiguous (or dissimilar) networks can be joined by encapsulating the network traffic in IP packets and sending that traffic across the IP network. If the two noncontiguous networks generate large amounts of traffic, slow links in the IP network could become congested.

- *Broadcasts*—Overhead traffic is generated by a variety of broadcast traffic. This can include token ring explorer packets, address resolution protocol (ARP) packets, RIP and IGRP routing packets, or a workstation's DHCP requests. Any application that needs to address the entire network will do so with a broadcast packet that is sent to every station within a shared medium, which can utilize a large portion of bandwidth. Depending on the applications (and operating systems) running on a particular network, the specifics and quantity of broadcasts may differ greatly. Cisco terms a network "healthy" in which total broadcasts do not exceed 20% of total utilization.

Traffic in an IPX Network

An IPX network has many sources of data traffic and overhead traffic, as follows:

- *User services*—Users accessing NetWare servers and printers, especially over serial links, can cause network congestion.

- *Routing protocol updates*—Periodic routing updates can add to network congestion.

- *Service Advertising Protocol (SAP) announcements*—SAP is the protocol used to announce network services, such as file, print, and directory services. Much of the traffic in an IPX network is inherent to NetWare support of client services. SAP traffic is overhead but is required for announcements about service availability. SAP traffic can congest the serial line. This congestion can result in the loss of SAPs, which can cause intermittent service interruptions.

- *Client/server keepalive updates*—NetWare clients and servers use keepalive traffic (watchdog traffic) to verify that connections are active.

Other Traffic in a Multiprotocol Network

A multiprotocol network has several protocol suites active at the same time, as shown in Figure 2–2. All user data traffic for the different protocols is active at the same time, and many concurrent data transfers are taking place. In addition, the overhead traffic for each protocol requires a portion of the bandwidth.

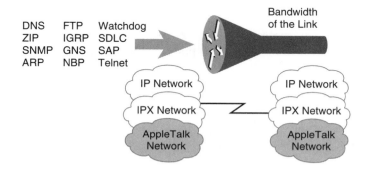

Figure 2–2
Increased traffic due to multiprotocol support may also congest a link.

Although it was not mentioned earlier, there is some underlying traffic on the media associated with the lower layers of the OSI reference model. All of the following require some portion of the medium's data-carrying capacity:

- Address Resolution Protocol (ARP) to resolve logical-to-physical addressing issues (except IPX since the host address is typically the MAC address already)

- Layer 2 keepalives to maintain connectivity

- Tokens for accessibility on a token ring network

- Time To Live updates that periodically indicate the remaining lifetime of distributed information

MANAGING TRAFFIC CONGESTION

Network congestion results from too much traffic at one time. To resolve congestion, the traffic either must be reduced or rescheduled. The following methods, discussed in detail in the following sections, can be used to manage congestion:

- Filtering user and application traffic (access lists)

- Filtering broadcast traffic (placement of routers, choice of routing protocols)

- Adjusting timers on periodic announcements (configuration of routing protocols)

- Providing static entries in routing tables (*ip route* statements)

- Prioritize traffic (queueing techniques)

Filtering User and Application Traffic

You can use standard and extended access lists to filter user and application traffic. Traffic filters can keep some traffic from reaching critical links.

Filtering Broadcast Traffic

If your broadcast traffic levels become excessive, you can filter broadcasts in areas where they are not required. On IP networks, you can manage network segments and routing protocol choice. On IPX networks, you can filter Netware SAP broadcasts, and manage RIP broadcasts.

Adjusting Timers on Periodic Announcements

Some periodic broadcasts, such as SAP packets, have configurable transmission timers to lengthen the interval between broadcasts.

Lengthening the timers reduces the overall traffic load on the link. For example, you can lengthen the time between SAP updates to minimize traffic load by the periodic SAP broadcasts.

Providing Static Entries in Routing Tables

Using *static entries* (entries which are locally defined, not dynamically learned) in a routing table can eliminate the need to dynamically advertise network routes across that link. This technique is very effective for reducing congestion on serial lines.

Prioritizing Traffic

Traffic that uses a slow link, such as a serial line, can be prioritized to ensure that critical applications do not time out. You can reorder the application's traffic from its first-come, first-served order to give some traffic preference. You can also control bandwidth on serial lines using *queuing techniques,* which enable you to specify which traffic is forwarded first through the router.

Key Concept   **The basic steps to controlling congestion are filtering traffic, adjusting timers, using static entries, and prioritizing traffic.**

SUMMARY

In summary, traffic congestion can be caused by a number of factors common to growing internetworks, including broadcast updates, an increase in user activity, and more bandwidth-intensive applications. There are, fortunately, many possible methods for controlling congestion. You learned the basic principles for controlling congestion in this chapter—filtering traffic, adjusting timers, using static entries, and prioritizing traffic. The next four chapters provide more details on managing this traffic through the use of traffic filters and various other traffic-controlling options. Chapter 3, "Managing IP Traffic," starts with an in-depth discussion of managing IP traffic.

Chapter Two Test
Introduction to Managing Traffic and Congestion

Estimated Time: 15 minutes

Complete all the exercises to test your knowledge of the materials contained in this chapter. Answers are listed in Appendix A, "Chapter Test Answer Key."

Use the information contained in this chapter to answer the following questions:

Question 2.1

What types of communications can cause traffic congestion?

A. _____

B. _____

C. _____

D. _____

E. _____

Question 2.2

What methods can be used to control traffic congestion?

A. _____

B. _____

C. _____

Managing IP Traffic

This chapter covers the configuration tasks necessary to deal with managing traffic and controlling access in an IP network. You learn details about the use and placement of both standard and extended access lists, as well as alternative methods, including null interfaces and helper addresses, to control IP traffic in the network.

TIPS

In Cisco IOS Release 11.3, TCP intercept was introduced. It is a feature that protects TCP servers from TCP SYN-flooding attacks, also known as *denial-of-service attacks*. The TCP intercept feature helps prevent denial-of-service attacks by tracking and optionally intercepting and validating TCP connection requests. This feature uses access lists to identify which TCP packets to watch for. For more information on TCP intercept, refer to www.cisco.com.

TRAFFIC MANAGEMENT TECHNIQUES

Integral to the task of managing IP traffic is eliminating unwanted traffic while still allowing appropriate user-access to necessary services. For many protocols, *broadcasting* is the primary method for locating services. Broadcasting is a technique used to address all devices by sending packets to the broadcast address. Because routers inherently do not forward broadcasts, it is frequently necessary to help these broadcasts become forwarded onto the appropriate subnet where the server is located.

The Cisco IOS software provides mechanisms for reducing unwanted traffic, for restricting network use to only authorized users, and for enabling broadcasts to be forwarded beyond the local router to the desired server (see Figure 3–1). Access lists limit traffic and restrict network use, and helper addressing enables broadcast forwarding. Both access lists and helper addressing are covered in this chapter.

Figure 3–1
There are different ways to eliminate unwanted traffic.

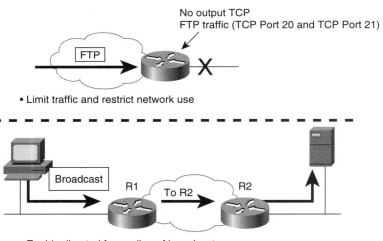

IP Access Lists

An *IP access list* is a sequential collection of permit and deny conditions that apply to IP addresses or upper-layer IP protocols. The following table shows the types of access lists and the available list numbers for IP:

Type of Access List	Range
IP standard	1–99
IP extended	100–199
Bridge type-code	200–299
IPX standard	800–899
IPX extended	900–999
IPX SAP	1000–1099

Refer to the Cisco Press title *Introduction to Cisco Router Configuration* (ISBN: 1-57870-076-0), for introductory details on access lists.

IP access lists come in two formats. Standard access lists filter based on source address only. Extended access lists offer more control by filtering based on source address, destination address, or protocol characteristics. Access lists are a fundamental tool for managing IP traffic.

Access lists can be applied to a network interface or virtual terminal line, as shown in Figure 3–2.

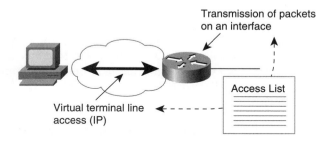

Figure 3–2
Access lists can be used to limit the transmission of packets through an interface and limit virtual terminal line access.

Use access lists primarily to limit network traffic and thereby to realize a performance increase in the network. Access lists are not necessarily secure when used by themselves; however, they may be used as part of a network security strategy.

Access lists are applied to one or more interfaces and can filter inbound traffic or outbound traffic depending on the configuration. The choice of inbound or outbound access lists will depend greatly on your traffic and control requirements at the time of configuration. If a direction is not specified when applying an access list to an interface, outbound is assumed by the router.

Access lists are used to define input traffic to other technologies, such as priority and custom queuing and dial-on-demand routing (DDR), as well. Traffic priority and custom queuing is covered in detail in Chapter 5, "Configuring Queuing to Manage Traffic."

Access lists serve many purposes, as shown in the following list:

- To control the transmission of packets on an interface

- To select the interesting traffic that initiates a DDR connection

- To restrict contents of routing updates

This chapter deals with using access lists to manage IP traffic. The other uses are covered later in this book.

Helper Addressing

Routers block broadcasts and prevent *broadcast storms*—a situation in which a single broadcast triggers an onslaught of other broadcasts, ultimately leading to a disruption in network services. Large flat networks are notorious for their bouts with broadcast storms.

What if a client needs to reach a server and does not know the server's address? In these situations, the client broadcasts to find the server. If a router separates the client and server, the broadcast will not get through. *Helper addresses* facilitate connectivity by forwarding these broadcasts directly to the target server.

CONFIGURING IP STANDARD ACCESS LISTS

Standard access lists allow filtering based only on the source address. The allowable range of standard access lists is 1 to 99. Standard access lists can also be used in other ways such as to limit virtual terminal connectivity into networking devices. Virtual terminal connectivity is used to attach to the router in a nonphysical way (such as through serial links).

In Figure 3–3, for example, the router examines only the source address 10.0.0.3 to see whether the packet is restricted by a standard access list.

Figure 3–3
Standard access lists permit or deny packets based only on the source IP address of the packet.

Standard access lists are a quick way of limiting traffic; however, they are not as robust as extended access lists. Consider a LAN that is producing a storm of packets and about to take out the whole network. In this case, you might not know which machine is at fault and you might not have time to perform a diagnosis before losing your network. You could instead configure standard access lists for fault isolation and analyze the problem with only a local impact.

CAUTION

The Cisco IOS Release 10.3 introduced substantial additions to IP access lists. These extensions are backward-compatible. Migrating from existing releases to the Release 10.3 or later image will convert your access lists automatically. Previous releases, however, are not upwardly compatible with these changes. Thus, if you save an access list with the Release 10.3 or later image and then use older software, the resulting access list will not be interpreted correctly. This incompatibility can cause security problems. Save your old configuration file before booting Release 10.3 (or later) images in case you need to revert to an earlier version.

Inbound Access List Processing

An access list is a sequential collection of permit and deny conditions that applies to IP addresses. The router tests addresses against the conditions in an access list one by one. The first match determines whether the router accepts or rejects the packet. Because the router stops testing conditions after the first match, the order of the conditions is critical. If no conditions match, the router rejects the packet.

For inbound standard access lists, after receiving a packet, the router checks the source address of the packet against the access list. If the access list permits the address, the router exits the access list and continues to process the packet. If the access list rejects the address, the router discards the packet and returns an Internet Control Message Protocol (ICMP) "Host Unreachable" message.

Note that in Figure 3–4 when no more entries are found in the access list, the packet is denied, which illustrates an important concept to remember when creating access lists. The last entry in an access list is what is known as an implicit "deny any." All traffic not explicitly permitted will be implicitly denied.

Figure 3–4
Standard IP access list inbound processing.

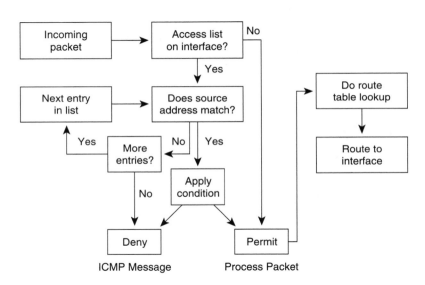

Key Concept When configuring access lists, order is important. Make sure that you list the entries in order from specific to general. To filter a specific host address, and then permit all other addresses, for example, make sure your entry about the specific host appears first.

Outbound Access List Processing

As shown in Figure 3–5, for outbound standard IP access lists, after receiving and routing a packet to an interface with an outbound access list, the route checks the source address of the packet against the access list. If the access list premits the address, the router transmits the packet. If the access list denies the address, the router will discard the packet and may return an ICMP "Host Unreachable" message.

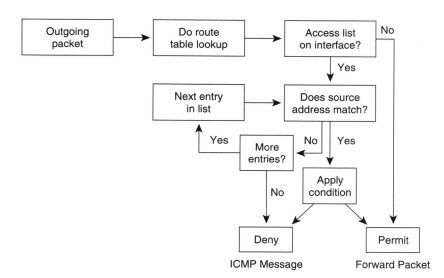

Figure 3–5
Standard IP access list outbound processing.

The primary difference between a standard access list and an extended access list is that the latter may continue to check other information in the packet against the access list after a matching source address has been found. When configuring outbound access lists, order is important (just as it is with inbound access lists). Make sure you list the entries in order from specific to general.

IP Addressing Review

As shown in Figure 3–6, the IP address is 32 bits in length and is made up of the following two parts:

- Network number

- Host number

The address format is known as dotted-decimal notation. An example address is 131.108.122.204. Each bit in an octet (a byte) has a binary weight, such as (128,...4,2,1). The minimum value for an octet is 0; it contains all zeros. The maximum value for an octet is 255; it contains all ones.

Figure 3–6
*IP address
review.*

High-Order Bits	First Octet	Class	Standard Mask
0	1-126	A	255.0.0.0
10	128-191	B	255.255.0.0
110	192-223	C	255.255.255.0

Figure 3–6 *IP address review.*

Class B subnets

0	255.255.0.0
~~1~~	~~255.255.128.0~~
2	255.255.192.0
3	255.255.224.0
4	255.255.240.0
5	255.255.248.0
6	255.255.252.0
7	255.255.254.0
8	255.255.255.0
9	255.255.255.128
10	255.255.255.192
11	255.255.255.224
12	255.255.255.240
13	255.255.255.248
14	255.255.255.252
~~15~~	~~255.255.255.254~~

Class C subnets

0	255.255.0.0
~~1~~	~~255.255.128~~
2	255.255.192
3	255.255.224
4	255.255.240
5	255.255.248
6	255.255.252
~~7~~	~~255.255.254~~

The *first octet* rule enables you to recognize the network classes on sight. Class A: 1–126. Class B: 128–191. Class C: 192–223. Class D: 224.0.0.0—used for multicast. Class E: 240.0.0.0—used for experimentation. Multicast communications are addressed to a group of devices.

The allocation of addresses is managed by a central authority. Network numbers and domain names are administered by the Internet Network Information Center (InterNIC). The NIC was also the main Request For Comments (RFCs) repository until mid 1998—now it just manages network numbers and domain name assignments.

The numbers in Figure 3–6 with the line through them represent a "not-recommended" or an invalid number of bits of subnetting for the Class B or Class C address space shown. One bit of subnetting gives a 0 and a 1, but has no valid range of host addresses. The early Internet specifications recommend against the use of subnet 0, but with the *ip subnet-zero* command (available since IOS 10.0), Cisco routers will support it. Beginning with RFC 950 (August, 1985), and the introduciton of Classless Inter-Domain Routing (CIDR) and Variable Length Subnet Mask (VLSM), there has been an increased use of subnet-zero as a means to increase the number of populated networks, and reduce the waste of address space. Be aware that working with some non-Cisco equipment may cause conflicts.

Access Lists Use Wildcard Mask

Both standard and extended IP access lists use a wildcard mask. Like an IP address, a *wildcard mask* is a 32-bit quantity written in dotted-decimal format. Address bits corresponding to wildcard mask bits set to 1 are ignored in comparisons; address bits corresponding to wildcard mask bits set to 0 are used in comparisons. This may feel quite backwards from the operation used in subnet masking (see Figure 3–7).

Address	Mask	Matches
0.0.0.0	255.255.255.255	any address
131.108.0.0/16	0.0.255.255	network 131.108.0.0
131.104.7.11/16	0.0.0.0	host or subnet address
255.255.255.255	0.0.0.0	local broadcast
131.111.8.0/21	0.0.7.255	only subnet 131.111.8.0*

* Assuming subnet mask of 255.255.248.0

Mask: 0 bit = must match bits in address; 1 bit = no need to match bits in addresses

Figure 3–7
A 0 bit in mask means it must match bits in address; a 1 bit in mask means no need to match bits in addresses.

An alternative way to think of the wildcard mask is as follows:

- If a 0 bit appears in the mask, the corresponding bit location in the access list address and the same location in the packet address must match (either both 0 or both 1).

- If a 1 bit appears in the mask, the bit location in the packet will match whether it is 0 or 1, and the bit location in the access list address is ignored. For this reason, 1 bits in the mask are sometimes called "don't care" bits.

An access list can contain an indefinite number of actual and wildcard addresses. A wildcard address has a non-zero address mask and thus potentially matches more than one actual address. Remember that the order of the access list statements is important because the access list is no longer processed after a match is found.

An access list is a sequential list of "access-list" entries, not necessarily just one entry.

Access List Configuration Tasks

Whether you are creating a standard or extended access list, you need to complete the following tasks:

1. Create an access list in global configuration mode by specifying an access list number and access conditions.

2. Define a standard IP access list using a source address and wildcard.

3. Define an extended access list using source and destination addresses, as well as optional protocol-type information for finer granularity of control.

4. Apply the access list in interface configuration mode to interfaces or terminal lines. After an access list is created, you can apply it to one or more interfaces. Access lists can be applied on either outbound or inbound interfaces.

Standard Access List Commands

There are two standard access list commands:

-   access-list

-   ip access-group

The access-list Command

Use the **access-list** command to create an entry in a standard traffic filter list (numbered 1–99).

```
access-list access-list-number {permit | deny} source [source-wildcard] any
```

access-list Command	Description
access-list-number	Identifies the list to which the entry belongs; a number from 1 to 99.
permit | deny	Indicates whether this entry allows or blocks traffic from the specified address.

access-list Command	Description
source	Identifies source IP address.
source-wildcard	(Optional) Identifies which bits in the address field are matched. It has a 1 in positions indicating "don't care" bits, and a 0 in any position that is to be strictly followed. If this field is omitted, the mask 0.0.0.0 is assumed.
any	Uses address 0.0.0.0 and source wildcard 255.255.255.255 to match any address.

IP access-group Command

Use the **ip access-group** command to link an existing access list to an interface. Each interface may have both an inbound and an outbound access list.

The lines are associated with each other by the access list number, forming the access list.

The lines are maintained in the configuration file in order of entry. New lines are always appended to the bottom of the list. This means that it is not possible to insert or remove lines from the access list. Because of this, you may want to configure your access lists using a separate text editor rather than through the router interface. You will, however, want to know how to use the router interface for access list configuration in an emergency, such as during fault isolation, where you identify the source of a communication problem. Because of this, you may want to configure your access lists using a text editor on a separate device and cut and paste it to the router rather than configuring directly through the router interface.

You can eliminate the entire list by typing **no access-list** *access-list-number* or you can unapply the list by typing the **no ip access-group** *access-list-number* command.

The list is applied to an interface by referring to the access list number in the **ip access-group** interface configuration command. The **in** keyword configures the access list for inbound traffic and the **out** keyword is used for outbound traffic. *It is highly recommended that you include notes and code this parameter for clarity.* (The default for Cisco IOS Release 11.0 is **out.**)

An interface can have one access list active per network-layer protocol per direction. For example, the interface can have one input and one output IP access list, either standard or extended, one IPX access list, one AppleTalk access list, and so on.

A single access list may be applied to more than one interface at a time.

More than one interface can be included in the group described by the **ip access-group** command. All designated interfaces in the group will permit or deny packets based on tests in the access list statements.

ip access-group *access-list-number* {**in** | **out**}

ip access-group Command	Description
access-list-number	Indicates the number of the access list to be linked to this interface.
in | **out**	Process packets arriving on/leaving from (default) this interface.

When you enable outbound access lists, you automatically disable autonomous switching for that interface. When you enable inbound access lists on any cBus or CxBus interface, you automatically disable autonomous switching for all interfaces. A Silicon Switch Processor (SSP) configured with standard access lists can still switch packets on outbound, and in Release 11.0 (3), SSP switching of inbound access lists is also supported.

Implicit Masks

Implicit masks are masks that are implied based on the current mask set. They reduce typing and simplify configuration. For example, if you permit one, it is implied that you deny all others.

Figure 3–8 shows three examples of implicit masks. The first line is an example of a specific host configuration. For standard access lists, if no mask is specified, the mask is assumed to be 0.0.0.0. The implicit mask makes it easier to enter a large number of individual addresses. When the symbolic name **any** is used, the mask 255.255.255.255 is implied.

When a packet does not match any of the configured lines in an access list, the packet is denied by default because there is an invisible line at the end of the access list that is equivalent to **deny any**. Denying any is the same as configuring 0.0.0.0 255.255.255.255, so the last two lines are not needed.

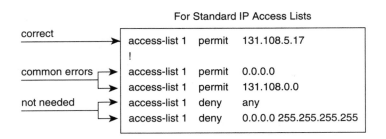

Figure 3–8
Omitted masks are assumed to be 0.0.0.0.

Common errors are found in the following other access list lines:

- *The second line*—**permit 0.0.0.0** would exactly match the address 0.0.0.0 and then permit it. In most cases, this address is illegal so this list would prevent all traffic from getting through (the implicit **deny any**).

- *The third line*—**permit 131.108.0.0** is probably a configuration error. The intention is probably 131.108.0.0 0.0.255.255. The exact address 131.108.0.0 is reserved to refer to the network and would never be assigned to a host. Network and subnets are represented by explicit masks. As a result, nothing would get through with this list, again due to the implicit **deny any**.

- *The fourth and fifth lines*—**deny any** and **deny 0.0.0.0 255.255.255.255** are unnecessary to configure because they duplicate the function of the default deny that occurs when a packet fails to match all of the configured lines in an access list.

Although not necessary, you may want to add one of these entries for record-keeping purposes.

Configuring Principles for Access Lists

The following four general principles help ensure that the access lists you create have the intended results:

- *Top-down processing*

  Organize your access list so that more specific references in a network or subnet appear before more general ones.

  Place more frequently occurring conditions before less frequent conditions to optimize performance.

- *Implicit deny any*

  Unless you end your access list with an explicit permit any, it will deny by default all traffic that fails to match any of the access list lines.

- *New lines added to the end*

  Subsequent additions are always added to the end of the access list.

  You cannot selectively add or remove lines when using numbered access lists, but you can when using IP-named access lists (a Cisco IOS Release 11.2 feature; see www.cisco.com).

- *Undefined access list means permit any*

  If you apply an access list with the **access-group** command to an interface before any access list lines have been created, the result will be permit any. The list is "live," so if you enter only one line, it goes from a permit any to a "deny most" (because of the implicit deny any) as soon as you press Return. For this reason, create your access list before you apply it to an interface.

Note that this usage changed with Release 10.3. In previous releases, an undefined access list caused everything to be denied. This is because they interpreted an undefined access list as an actual access list with no entries, and therefore had only an implicit "deny any" at the end.

TIPS

One way to change an access list is to configure the new or revised access list with a different access list number. Use the **ip access-group** command and assign the new access list a different number. The new access list replaces the old one. For a few seconds (or microseconds), you will not have protection on the interface while the router replaces the old access list with the new. If you are working in a secure environment where this kind of security breach is unacceptable, use the **ip shutdown** command to disable the interface for IP packets during the changeover, as in the following example:

```
interface serial 0
ip shutdown
ip access-group 2
no ip shutdown
```

Standard Access List Example

Figure 3–9 shows an example of a standard access list permitting a specific host on a subnet while denying all other hosts on that subnet, permitting all other hosts on the same network, and denying the outside world (Internet).

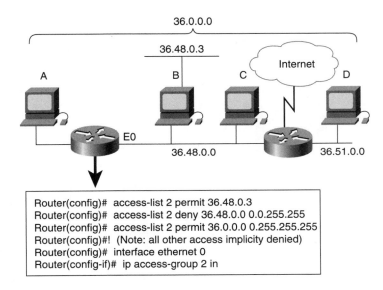

Figure 3–9
*Who can con-
nect to A?*

So, who can connect to A? Answer the following questions:

- Can host B communicate with host A? Yes. Permitted by the first line, which uses an implicit host mask.

- Can host C communicate with host A? No. Host C is in the subnet denied by the second line.

- Can host D communicate with host A? Yes. Host D is on a subnet that is explicitly permitted by the third line.

- Can users on the Internet communicate with host A? No. Users outside of this network are not explicitly permitted, so they are denied by default (implicit **deny any**).

Location of Standard Access Lists

Access list location can be more of an art than a science, but there are some general guidelines that you can discover by looking at the example shown in Figure 3–10.

Figure 3–10
On which router should the access list be configured to deny host Z access to network 10.20.0.0?

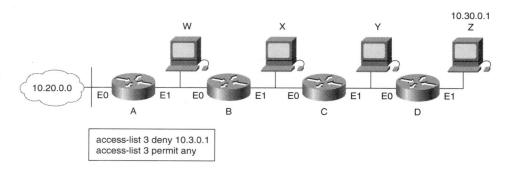

If the policy goal is to deny host Z access to host V, and not to change any other access policy, on which router should the access list shown in Figure 3–10 be configured and on which interface of that router? The access list would be placed on router A. The reason is that the standard access list can only specify the source address. Wherever in the path the traffic is denied, no hosts beyond can connect.

The access list could be configured as an outbound list on E0, but it may be configured as an inbound list on E1 so that packets to be denied would not have to be routed first.

What would be the effect of placing the access list on other routers?

- Router B: Host Z could not connect with hosts V and W.

- Router C: Host Z could not connect with hosts V, W, and X.

- Router D: Host Z could not connect with hosts V, W, X, and Y.

TIPS

For standard access lists, place them as close to the destination router as possible in order to exercise the most control.

RESTRICTING VIRTUAL TERMINAL ACCESS

Standard and extended access lists will block packets from going through the router. They are not designed to block packets that originate within the router. An outbound Telnet extended access list does not prevent router-initiated Telnet sessions, by default.

For security purposes, users can be denied virtual terminal (vty) access to the router, or users can be permitted vty access to the router but denied access to destinations from that router. Restricting virtual terminal access is less a traffic control mechanism than one technique for increasing network security.

vty access is accomplished using the Telnet protocol to make a non-physical connection to the router. As a result, there is only one type of vty access list.

How to Control vty Access

Just as there are physical ports or interfaces, such as E0 and E1 on the router, there are also virtual ports. These virtual ports are called virtual terminal lines. There are five such virtual terminal lines, numbered vty 0 through 4, as shown in Figure 3–11.

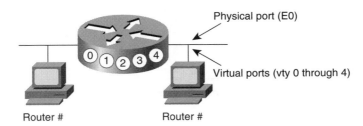

Physical port (E0)

Virtual ports (vty 0 through 4)

Router #   Router #

Figure 3–11
There are five virtual terminal lines (0 through 4).

You should generally set identical restrictions on all virtual terminal lines because you cannot control on which virtual terminal line a user will connect.

TIPS

Some experts recommend that you configure the last vty terminal line (line vty 4) differently than the others. This way, you will have a "back door" into the router. This works because the connection will use the first line available at the moment at the lowest unused number.

Virtual Terminal Line Commands

There are two new commands used to configure vty access:

- line
- access-class

The line Command

Use the **line** command to place the router in line configuration mode.

`line {vty-number | vty-range}`

line Command	Description
vty-number	Indicates the number of the line to be configured
vty-range	Indicates the lower and upper limits of the lines to which the configuration will apply

The access-class Command

Use the **access-class** command to link an existing access list to a terminal line or range of lines.

`access-class  access-list-number {in | out}`

access-class Command	Description
access-list-number	The number of the access list to be linked to a terminal line. This is a decimal number from 1 to 99.
in	Prevents the router from receiving incoming connections from the addresses in the access list.
out	Prevents the router from initiating a connection to the addresses in the access list.

Virtual Terminal Access Example

Consider the sample configuration that follows:

```
access-list 12 permit 192.89.55.0 0.0.0.255
!
line vty 0 4
access-class 12 in
```

In this example, you are permitting any device on network 192.89.55.0 to establish a virtual terminal (Telnet) session with the router. Of course, the user must know the appropriate passwords to enter user mode and privileged mode.

Notice that identical restrictions have been set on all virtual terminal lines (0–4) because you cannot control on which virtual terminal line a user will connect.

The implicit **deny any** still applies in an alternative application, such as limiting virtual terminal access.

CONFIGURING EXTENDED ACCESS LISTS

Standard access lists offer quick configuration and low overhead in limiting traffic based on the source address within a network. Extended access lists provide a higher degree of control by enabling filtering based on the session-layer protocol, destination address, and application port number. These features make it possible to limit traffic based on the uses of the network.

In Figure 3–12, if the requirement is to restrict network access based on department, standard access lists would work fine. You could create a list that allowed only Accounting (and deny every other department) to talk to Sales and Sales to talk only to Manufacturing (and deny every other department). If, however, Manufacturing had a database of inventory levels that could be accessed via Telnet, and you wanted to allow Sales only Telnet access to Manufacturing, standard access lists would not suffice. Similarly, if Sales had the latest price list on a server accessible via Telnet, and you wanted Accounting to have only Telnet access to Sales, extended access lists are required for this degree of control. With extended access lists, you can filter based not only on the source address, but also on the destination address or application port number.

Figure 3–12
Extended access lists enable you to control traffic by application, not just by address.

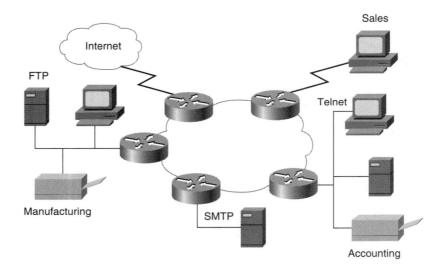

Note that a router cannot be a full firewall solution, although routers are important components of firewalls.

Extended Access List Processing

Figure 3–13 shows the decision process used with extended access lists.

Every condition tested must match for the line of the access list to match and the permit or deny condition to be applied. As soon as one parameter or condition fails, the next line in the access list is compared.

The extended access list checks source address, protocol, and destination address. Depending on the protocol configured, there may be more protocol-dependent options tested. For example, a TCP port may be checked, which allows routers to filter at the application layer.

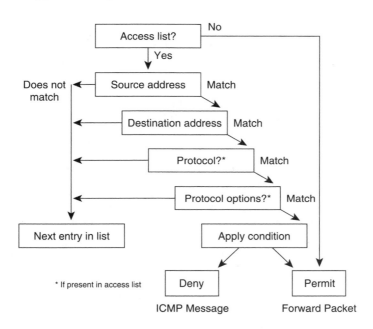

Figure 3–13
Every condition is tested during packet processing.

IP permits fragmentation to allow large packets to be split up into smaller ones (fragments) in order to cross networks that support smaller packet sizes. With extended access lists, nonfragmented packets are tested against the access list. The initial fragment of a fragmented packet set is tested against the access list. Subsequent fragments are permitted without being tested against the access list. This may be a problem if you are using access lists as a security mechanism.

Extended IP Access List Command

Use the **access-list** command to create an entry in a complex traffic filter list, as follows:

```
access-list access-list-number {permit | deny}
    {protocol | protocol-keyword}
    {source source-wildcard | any}
    {destination destination-wildcard | any}
    [protocol-specific-options] [log]
```

```
access-list access-list-number {permit | deny} protocol source
    source-wildcard destination destination-wildcard [log]
```

access-list Command	Description
access-list-number	A number from 100 to 199.
permit | deny	Whether this entry is used to allow or block the specified address(es).
protocol	**ip, tcp, udp, icmp, igmp, gre, igrp, eigrp, ospf, nos,** or a number in the range of 0 through 255. To match any Internet protocol, use the keyword **ip**. Some protocols have more options that are supported by an alternate syntax for this command.
source and *destination*	IP addresses.
source-wildcard and *destination-wildcard*	Wildcard masks of address bits that must match. 0s indicate bits that must match, 1s are "don't care."
any	Use this keyword as an abbreviation for a *source* and *source-wildcard*, and *destination* and *destination-wildcard* of 0.0.0.0 255.255.255.255.
log	(Optional) Causes informational logging messages about the packet that matches the entry to be sent to the console. Exercise caution when using this keyword because it consumes CPU cycles.

The extended access list has so many options that it is helpful to divide the options by protocol and to examine them as alternate syntax cases. The syntax shown is the generic command syntax that you use to configure an extended access list for the IP protocol. Alternate syntaxes follow in the next pages.

Mask Keywords

The following two keywords can be used to define IP addresses with masks:

- any

- host

The keyword **any** in either the source or destination position matches any address and is equivalent to configuring 0.0.0.0 255.255.255.255:

```
access-list 101 permit ip 0.0.0.0 255.255.255.255 0.0.0.0 255.255.255.255
!(alternate configuration)
access-list 101 permit ip any any
```

The keyword **host** in either the source or destination position causes the address that immediately follows it to be treated as if it were specified with a mask of 0.0.0.0:

```
host 131.108.5.17 = 131.108.5.17 0.0.0.0
access-list 101 permit ip 0.0.0.0 255.255.255.255 131.108.5.17 0.0.0.0
!(alternate configuration)
access-list 101 permit ip any host 131.108.5.17
```

ICMP Command Syntax

Use the **access-list icmp** command to create an entry in a complex traffic filter list. The protocol keyword **icmp** indicates that an alternate syntax is being used for this command and that protocol-specific options are available.

```
access-list  access-list-number {permit | deny} icmp
    {source source-wildcard | any}
    {destination destination-wildcard | any}
    [icmp-type [icmp-code] | icmp-message]
```

access-list icmp Command	Description
access-list-number	A number from 100 to 199.
permit | **deny**	Whether this entry is used to allow or block the specified address(es).
source and *destination*	IP addresses.
source-wildcard and *destination-wildcard*	Wildcard masks of address bits that must match. 0s indicate bits that must match, 1s are "don't care." The keyword **any** used in place of either the source and destination, or wildcard masks can be used as a shortcut to typing 0.0.0.0 255.255.255.255.
icmp-type	(Optional) Packets can be filtered by ICMP message type. The type is a number from 0 to 255.

access-list icmp Command	Description
icmp-code	(Optional) Packets that have been filtered by ICMP message type can be further filtered by ICMP message code. The code is a number from 0 to 255.
icmp-message	(Optional) Packets can be filtered by a symbolic name representing an ICMP message type or a combination of ICMP message type and ICMP message code. The list of names is provided in the "ICMP Message and Type Names" section.

Packets can also be filtered by precedence level, specified by a number from 0 to 7. A list of names can also be used in the precedence field: critical, flash, flash-override, immediate, Internet, network, priority, routine. Packets can also be filtered by type-of-service level specified by a number from 0 to 15.

Both of these filtering options are rarely used. Historically, precedence was rarely used outside the military, but it may become of greater importance because it affects *weighted fair queuing*. This queuing system is discussed in Chapter 5. Refer also to www.cisco.com.

ICMP Message and Type Names

Cisco IOS Release 10.3 and later versions provide symbolic names that make configuration and reading of complex access lists easier. With symbolic names, it is no longer critical to understand the meaning of message 8 and message 0 in order to filter the **ping** command. Instead, the configuration would use **echo** and **echo-reply**.

The following list indicates the symbolic names you can define in extended access lists:

```
administratively-prohibited        alternate-address
conversion-error                   dod-host-prohibited
dod-net-prohibited                 echo
echo-reply                         general-parameter-problem
host-isolated                      host-tos-redirect
host-tos-unreachable               host-unknown
host-unreachable                   information-reply
mask-reply                         mask-request
```

```
mobile-redirect              net-redirect
net-tos-redirect             net-tos-unreachable
net-unreachable              network-unknown
no-room-for-option           option-missing
packet-too-big               parameter-problem
port-unreachable             reassembly-timeout
redirect                     router-advertisement
router-solicitation          source-quench
source-route-failed          time-exceeded
traceroute                   ttl-exceeded
unreachable
```

TIPS

Use the context-sensitive help feature by entering **?** in the Cisco IOS user interface to verify available names and proper command syntax.

RFC 1812 says that traffic denied by filtering (that is, that hits a deny rule) should cause an ICMP Administratively Prohibited message to the sender, using the sender's address as destination and the filtering router's interface's address as source. Many security authorities prefer not to send this message back to external users because the fact that there is filtering implies there is something worth protecting. To enforce such a policy, you would want to deny ICMP Administratively Prohibited messages outbound at the external user interface.

TCP Syntax

Use the **access-list tcp** command to create an entry in a complex traffic filter list. The protocol keyword **tcp** indicates that an alternate syntax is being used for this command and that protocol-specific options are available.

```
access-list  access-list-number {permit | deny} tcp
    {source source-wildcard | any}
    [operator source-port | source-port]
    {destination destination-wildcard | any}
    [operator destination-port | destination-port]
        [established]
```

access-list tcp Command	Description
access-list-number	A number from 100 to 199.
permit | **deny**	Whether this entry is used to allow or block the specified address(es).
source and *destination*	IP addresses.
source-wildcard and *destination-wildcard*	Wildcard masks of address bits that must match. 0s indicate bits that must match, 1s are "don't care."
operator	(Optional) A qualifying condition. Can be **lt = less than; gt = greater than; eq = equal to; neq = not equal to.**
source-port and *destination-port*	(Optional) A decimal number from 0 to 65535 or a name that represents a TCP port number. In previous versions of Cisco IOS, only destination ports could be filtered. Starting with Cisco IOS Release 10.3, both source and destination ports can be used as criteria. The port follows its respective address and wildcard in the command syntax.
established	(Optional) A match occurs if the TCP datagram has the ACK or RST bits set. Use this if you want a telnet or another activity to be established in one direction only.

The **established** optional parameter can only be used with TCP because this is the only connection-oriented IP protocol currently supported.

When **established** is configured, a match occurs only if the TCP ACK (acknowledge) or RST (Reset) bits are set. This means that it matches an already established connection, which can then be permitted. The SYNchronize message to establish a new connection can then be explicitly or implicitly denied.

Without the **established** keyword, TCP timeouts may occur. With it, you can permit sessions to be initiated in one direction but not the other. In earlier versions of the Cisco IOS software, the established parameter can only be configured on **tcp access list** statements without specific port numbers. In 10.3 and later versions, the established command can be configured on statements with ports specified.

Access lists with the **established** keyword are typically used on inbound access lists assigned to an outside-link interface. Programming your access lists in this fashion, the initial SYN (first establishing packet) must originate from within your network.

CAUTION

Source-port filtering is not secure because a hacker could change a source port. *Source-port filtering* is the procedure of filtering data upon the source identifying port of a process. A hacker could easily create a packet with a different source port (perhaps using a dynamic source port number) which would fall through the filter.

The TCP Connection Process

Consider the following TCP connection process:

```
Host A   ----------------> SYNchronize   Host B
Host A   ACK SYNchronize <--------------  Host B
Host A   ------------------------> ACK    Host B
```

The goal is to stop B from initiating connections with A while permitting A to initiate connections with B. If you configure an access list to block messages from B, it will stop B-initiated sessions. A session initiated from A will also be blocked because the acknowledge message from B will never make it back.

This is further complicated because the message being blocked is coming from host B, so there is no way for the router to send an ICMP message to host A. Therefore, host A will appear to hang and will eventually get a TCP timeout.

This situation can be handled with the **established** parameter, as follows:

```
access list 101 permit tcp host B host A established
access list 101 deny tcp host B host A
```

where "host B" and "host A" are replaced by the host IP addresses.

TCP Port Names

The following list defines some of the TCP port names that can be used to make extended access list coding easier.

```
bgp                             chargen
daytime                         discard
domain                          echo
finger                          ftp-control
ftp-data                        gopher
hostname                        irc
klogin                          kshell
lpd                             nntp
pop2                            pop3
sunrpc                          syslog
tacacs-ds                       talk
telnet                          time
uucp                            whois
```

www

Use the **?** in place of the port number when entering the command in order to verify the port numbers associated with these protocol names. Other port names can be found in the "Assigned Numbers" RFC (1700).

UDP Syntax

The **access-list udp** command creates an entry in a complex traffic filter list. The protocol keyword **udp** indicates that an alternate syntax is being used for this command and that protocol-specific options are available.

The configuration for UDP is similar to TCP. Because UDP is not a connection-oriented protocol, there is no **established** parameter as there is in TCP.

```
access-list  access-list-number {permit | deny} udp
    {source source-wildcard | any}
    [operator source-port | source-port]
    {destination destination-wildcard | any}
    [operator destination-port | destination-port]
```

access-list udp Command	Description
access-list-number	A number from 100 to 199.
permit | **deny**	Whether this entry is used to allow or block the specified address(es).
source and *destination*	IP addresses.
source-wildcard and *destination-wildcard*	Wildcard masks of address bits that must match. 0s indicate bits that must match, 1s are "don't care."
any	Use this keyword as an abbreviation for a source and source-wildcard, and destination and destination-wildcard of 0.0.0.0 255.255.255.255.
source-port and *destination-port*	(Optional) A decimal number from 0 to 65535 or a name that represents a UDP port number.
operator	(Optional) A qualifying condition. Can be **lt = less than; gt = greater than; eq = equal to; neq = not equal to.**

UDP Port Names

UDP port names can be used to simplify extended access list configurations. The following is a partial list of defined UDP port names:

```
biff                    bootpc
bootps                  discard
dns                     dnsix
echo                    mobile-ip
nameserver              netbios-dgm
netbios-ns              ntp
rip                     snmp
snmptrap                sunrpc
syslog                  tacasds-ds
talk                    tftp
time                    whois
xdmcp
```

Use the **?** in place of the port number when entering the command in order to verify the port numbers associated with these protocol names.

Extended Access List Examples

The next sections show various extended access list examples, one providing Internet mail to a network device and another extended access list providing DNS and ping (ICMP echo requests and ICMP echo replies).

Providing Internet Mail

In Figure 3–14, Ethernet interface 1 is part of a Class B network with the address 128.88.0.0, and the mail host's address is 128.88.1.2. The keyword **established** is used only for the TCP protocol to indicate an established connection. A match occurs if the TCP datagram has the ACK or RST bits set, which indicate that the packet belongs to an existing connection. If the ACK is not set, and the SYN is set, someone on the Internet is initializing the session, in which case the packet is denied.

Figure 3–14
Extended access list example #1.

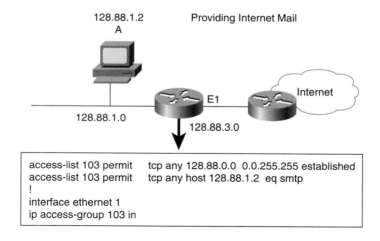

```
access-list 103 permit    tcp any 128.88.0.0  0.0.255.255 established
access-list 103 permit    tcp any host 128.88.1.2  eq smtp
!
interface ethernet 1
ip access-group 103 in
```

Providing DNS and Ping

Figure 3–15 also permits name/domain server packets and ICMP echo and echo-reply packets.

The first line permits any connections that are already established. The second and third lines permit UDP and TCP domain name services. The last two lines allow ICMP echo and echo-reply messages. These are the messages used for the **ping** command.

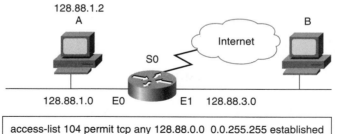

Figure 3–15
*Extended
access list
example #2.*

```
access-list 104 permit tcp any 128.88.0.0  0.0.255.255 established
access-list 104 permit tcp any host 128.88.1.2  eq domain
access-list 104 permit udp any eq domain any
access-list 104 permit icmp any any echo
access-list 104 permit icmp any any echo-reply
!
interface serial 0
ip access-group 104 in
```

The Domain Name Services (DNS) uses a UDP transport for typical hostname or host IP lookup. TCP can be used where large quantities of information is being returned, typically between DNS servers providing secondary support. For this reason, the filter shown explicitly permits DNS over both UDP and TCP.

CONFIGURING NAMED ACCESS LISTS

CAUTION

Named access lists are not recognized by any software release prior to Cisco IOS Release 11.2.

You can identify IP access lists with an alphanumeric string (a name) rather than with a number (1 to 199). This feature allows you to configure more than 99 standard IP and 100 extended IP access lists in a router.

The key advantages of using named access lists are a) the name can be meaningful for documentation and maintenance and b) you can selectively delete specific lines within a named access list, making it more flexible.

If you identify your access list with a name rather than a number, the mode and command syntax are slightly different. Currently, only packet and route filters can use a named list.

Implementation Considerations

Consider the following before configuring named access lists:

- Access lists specified by name are not compatible with older releases.

- Not all access lists that accept a number will accept a name. Access lists for packet filters and route filters on interfaces can use a name.

- A standard access list and an extended access list cannot have the same name.

Numbered access lists are also available, as described in the preceding section.

To create a standard access list, perform the following tasks beginning in global configuration mode:

Task	Command
Define a standard IP access list using a name.	**ip access-list standard** *name*
In access-list configuration mode, specify one or more conditions allowed or denied.	**deny** {*source* [*source-wildcard*] | **any**}
This determines whether the packet is passed or dropped.	or **permit** {*source* [*source-wildcard*] | **any**}
Exit access-list configuration mode.	**exit**

To create an extended access list, perform the following tasks beginning in global configuration mode:

Task	Command
Define an extended IP access list using a name.	**ip access-list extended** *name*
In access-list configuration mode, specify the conditions allowed or denied. Use the **log** keyword to get access list logging messages, including violations.	{**deny** | **permit**} *protocol source source-wildcard destination destination-wildcard* [**precedence** *precedence*][**tos** *tos*][**established**][**log**]
Define an extended IP access list using an abbreviation for a source and source wildcard of 0.0.0.0 255.255.255.255, and an abbreviation for a destination and destination wildcard of 0.0.0.0 255.255.255.255.	{**deny** | **permit**} *protocol* **any any**

Named Access List Example

The following configuration creates a standard access list named Internet_filter and an extended access list named marketing_group:

```
interface Ethernet0/5
 ip address 2.0.5.1 255.255.255.0
 ip access-group Internet_filter out
 ip access-group marketing_group in
...
ip access-list standard Internet_filter
 permit 1.2.3.4
 deny any
ip access-list extended marketing_group
 permit tcp any 171.69.0.0 0.0.255.255 eq telnet
 deny tcp any any
 permit icmp any any
 deny udp any 171.69.0.0 0.0.255.255 lt 1024
 deny ip any any log
```

Location of Extended Access Lists

Because extended access lists can filter on more than the source address, location is no longer a constraint. Frequently, policy decisions and goals are the driving force behind extended access list placement.

If your goal is to minimize traffic congestion and maximize performance, you might want to push the access lists close to the source to minimize cross traffic and host unreachable messages. If your goal is to maintain tight control over access lists as part of your network security strategy, you might want to have them more centrally located. Notice how changing network goals will affect access list configuration.

The following guidelines should be used for extended access list placement:

- Minimize distance traveled by traffic that will be denied (and ICMP unreachable messages).

- Keep denied traffic off the backbone.

- Select router to receive CPU overhead from access lists.

- Consider which interfaces are affected.

- Consider access list management and security.

- Consider network growth impacts on access list maintenance.

VERIFYING ACCESS LIST CONFIGURATIONS

Use the following four commands to view previously configured access lists:

- **show access-list**

- **show ip access-list** [*access-list-number*]

- **clear access-list counters** [*access-list-number*]

- **show line**

Use the **show access-list** command to display access lists from all protocols.

Use the **show ip access-list** command to display IP access lists.

show ip access-list Command	Description
access-list-number	(Optional) Shows a specific list. If this option is not specified, all IP access lists are displayed.

The system counts how many packets pass each line of an access list; the counters are displayed by the **show access-list** command. Use the **clear access-list counters** command in EXEC mode to clear the counters of an access list.

Use the **show line** command to display information about terminal lines.

The output from the **show ip access-lists** command displays the contents of previously defined IP access lists.

For example, consider the following results:

```
p1r1#show access-lists
Extended IP access list 100
    deny tcp host 10.1.1.2 host 10.1.1.1 eq telnet (3 matches)
    deny tcp host 10.1.2.2 host 10.1.2.1 eq telnet
    permit ip any any (629 matches)
```

Notice that three packets have matched the filter defined for telnet sessions, whereas 629 packets have been allowed to pass through.

Access lists have overhead, especially if the list is long and is placed on busy backbone routers. Such access lists could become performance concerns. Although the underlying technology of access list processing is efficient, in a few cases an alternative can be used to avoid access lists altogether. The next section covers such an alternative.

USING AN ALTERNATIVE TO ACCESS LISTS

Access lists require CPU resources. Although the access list is optimized for router operation, there are still some cases in which the processing overhead can be diminished further. One way to eliminate access list overhead is to avoid using them. This section looks at the null interface as a suitable alternative to access lists.

Configuring Null Interface

Access lists are processor-intensive. The router processes every line of an access list until a match is found. There is an alternative to using access lists if the policy is for unwanted traffic to a certain destination to be discarded every time. The alternative is to configure a null interface. A null interface saves CPU cycles.

The *null interface* is a software-only interface that functions similarly to a "null" device used by operating systems. Message traffic that is not required is directed to the null interface using a static route, where it is effectively "dropped," as shown in Figure 3–16. Static routes are covered later in this book in Chapter 11, "Optimizing Routing Update Operation."

Figure 3–16
Route to nowhere saves valuable CPU cycles.

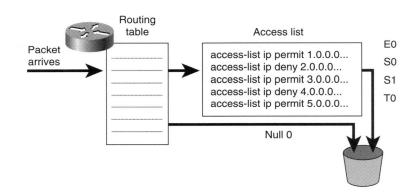

Note that it is important to consider the location of the null interface because anytime a packet comes into the router to the defined destination, it will be dropped.

Null Interface Command

Use the **ip route** command to establish static routes and to specify the null interface (always null 0), as follows:

```
ip route address mask null 0
```

ip route Command	Description
address	IP address of the target network, subnet, or host
mask	Network mask that lets you mask network, subnetwork, or host bits

Figure 3–17 shows the following:

ip route 201.222.5.0 255.255.255.0 null 0 Command	Description
201.222.5.0. 255.255.255.0	The destination IP address and the mask
null 0	The null interface to which traffic is "forwarded"

Note that this mask is a subnet mask with the ones on the left, and not an access list wildcard mask with the ones on the right.

The static route forwards traffic for network 201.222.5.0 to the null interface, which drops it.

Consider the example shown in Figure 3–17.

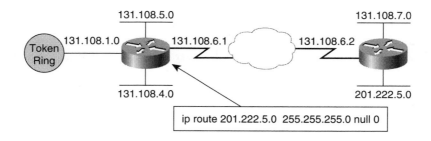

Figure 3–17
This configuration eliminates traffic for 201.222.5.0 from the WAN.

Valid traffic is allowed through the WAN cloud if it is destined for the subnet where the network management station is located. Traffic to the Class C network 201.222.5.0 is blocked before it enters the WAN cloud. In Figure 3–17, access list processing is avoided on the left router by routing unwanted traffic to the null interface.

You do not care about network 201.222.5.0, so you simply pretend it is directly connected. The static route will always give you a better path than any routing protocol will find. Then you route the packet to nowhere and drop it.

USING HELPER ADDRESSES

Recall that routers block broadcasts and prevent *broadcast storms*—a situation in which a single broadcast triggers an onslaught of other broadcasts ultimately leading to a disruption in network services. Large flat networks are notorious for their bouts with broadcasts storms.

An example of broadcasting is when a client sends a broadcast to find a server. If the server is not on the same network, the broadcast will not get through to the server. *Helper addresses* facilitate connectivity by forwarding these broadcasts directly to the target server.

Client hosts interact with a variety of network support servers, such as a domain name server (DNS), BOOTP/Dynamic Host Configuration Protocol (DHCP) server, or TFTP server. At startup time, the clients often do not know the IP address of the server, so they broadcast to find it. Sometimes the clients do not know their own IP address, so they use BOOTP or DHCP to obtain it. If the client and server are on the same network, the server will respond to the client's broadcast request. From these replies, the client can glean the IP address of the server and use it in subsequent communication.

But what if the server is not on the same physical medium as the client? Remember that a destination IP address of 255.255.255.255 is sent in a link-layer broadcast (FFFFFFFFFFFF). By default, routers will never forward such broadcasts and you would not want them to. A primary reason for implementing routers is to localize broadcast traffic. You do, however, want clients to be able to reach the appropriate server(s). You use helper addresses for this purpose.

Helper commands change broadcast addresses to a unicast address (an address of a single device on the network) so that the broadcast message can be routed to a specific destination, rather than everywhere. It is important to note that every broadcast (as specified or defaulted in the configuration you will see later) is sent to all helpers, whether or not the helper will actually be able to help for a certain port. Helper commands forward UDP broadcasts directed to ports for DNS, NTP (time), TACACS, TFTP, BOOTP, DHCP, NBNAME and NBDATAGRAM.

Consider the design shown in Figure 3–18. The client boots up and sends a broadcast to locate the server. The broadcast is stopped at the router. The router then reissues the broadcast as a unicast that is directed to the BOOTP server.

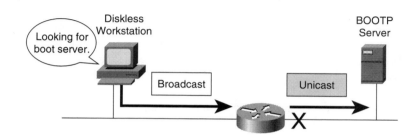

Figure 3–18
Helpers change broadcasts to unicasts to reach server.

	Router-Broadcast Handling from RFC 1812
Background information on router-broadcast handling from RFC 1812, *Requirements for IPv4 Routers*:	

Background information on router-broadcast handling from RFC 1812, *Requirements for IPv4 Routers*:

5.3.4 Forwarding of Link Layer Broadcasts

A router *must not* forward any packet that the router received as a Link Layer broadcast, unless it is directed to an IP Multicast address. In this latter case, one would presume that link layer broadcast was used due to the lack of an effective multicast service.

A router *must not* forward any packet which the router received as a Link Layer multicast unless the packet's destination address is an IP multicast address.

A router *should* silently discard a packet that is received via a Link Layer broadcast but does not specify an IP multicast or IP broadcast destination address.

When a router sends a packet as a Link Layer broadcast, the IP destination address *must* be a legal IP broadcast or IP multicast address.

See the RFC (1812) for the complete text.

Server Location

It is important to consider how you want to get the broadcast, in a controlled way, to the appropriate server(s). Such considerations depend on the location of the server(s). In practice, there are several ways that server location is implemented (see Figure 3–19):

- *A single server on a single remote medium*

  Such a medium may be directly connected to the router that blocks the broadcast, or might be several routing hops away. In any case, the all-ones broadcast needs to be handled at the first router it encounters and sent to the server.

- *Multiple servers on a single remote medium, sometimes called a "server farm"*

  Different kinds of servers (for example, DNS and TFTP for Cisco AutoInstall) could exist on the same medium. Or perhaps redundant servers of the same type are installed on the same medium. In either case, you want a directed broadcast on the server farm subnet so the multiple devices can see it.

- *Multiple servers on multiple remote media*

  Here, a secondary DNS server could exist on one subnet and the primary DNS server on another subnet. For fault tolerance, client requests need to reach both servers.

IP Helper Address Commands

Two commands are used to configure helper addresses:

- **ip helper-address**

- **ip forward-protocol**

The ip helper-address Command

Use the **ip helper-address** command to configure an interface where broadcasts are expected or can be received. The specified address can be the unicast address of a remote server or a directed broadcast address.

```
ip helper-address address
```

If an **ip helper-address** is defined, forwarding for eight default UDP ports is enabled automatically. The default ports are TFTP (69), DNS (53), Time (37), NetBIOS name service (137), NetBIOS datagram service (138), BOOTP/DHCP server (67), BOOTP/DHCP client (68), and TACACS (49).

These same eight ports are automatically forwarded if you define an **ip helper-address** and **ip forward-protocol udp.**

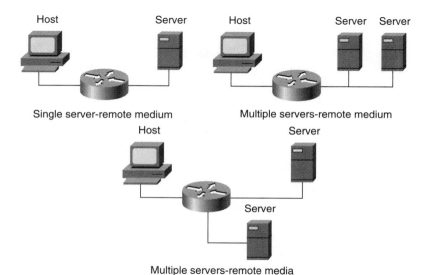

Single server-remote medium

Multiple servers-remote medium

Multiple servers-remote media

Figure 3–19
Several server placement configurations affect broadcast handling.

The ip forward-protocol Command

Use the **ip forward-protocol** command to specify which type of broadcast packet is forwarded.

```
ip forward-protocol {udp [port] | nd | sdns}
```

ip forward-protocol Command	Description
udp	User Datagram Protocol (UDP); the transport-layer protocol.
port	(Optional) When UDP is specified, port numbers for the UDP destination port may be used.
nd	Network disk; an older protocol used by diskless Sun workstations.
sdns	Secure Data Network Service.

To forward only one UDP port (whether a default-forwarded port, another UDP port, or a custom port), you must use **ip forward-protocol udp** [*port*] for the port(s) you want to forward and then specify **no ip forward-protocol udp** [*port*] for the default ports you do not want forwarded.

There really is no easy way to forward all UDP broadcasts. Essentially, you would need to specify all the UDP ports in the **ip forward-protocol** command.

Helper Address Examples

The following examples show how helper addresses can be used when connecting to remote networks with one or more servers.

Single Server-Remote Medium

In Figure 3–20, where a single server is on a single remote medium, a helper address allows the router to perform the desired function of forwarding a client request to a server.

The basic **ip helper-address** statement must be placed on the router interface that receives the original client broadcast. It causes the router to convert the 255.255.255.255 (all-ones) broadcast to a unicast or a directed broadcast. A directed broadcast is a local broadcast within a particular subnet.

In Figure 3–20, the **ip helper-address** statement placed on interface Ethernet 0 causes the default eight UDP broadcasts sent by all hosts to be converted into unicasts with a destination address of the Boot Server—144.253.2.2. These unicasts then will be forwarded to the boot server.

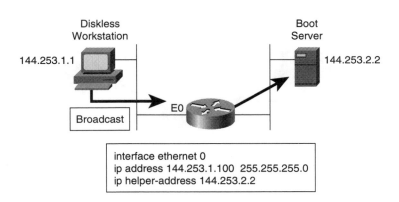

Figure 3–20
*Forwarding
default UDP
broadcasts.*

Note that additional helper addresses are not required on the router in the middle of Figure 3–20 because the router has modified the destination address. The modification of the destination address from broadcast to unicast or directed broadcast lets the packet be routed, over several hops if necessary, to its final destination.

Single Server-Remote Medium

You may not want to forward all default UDP broadcasts to the server, but only those of a protocol type supported on that server. Use the **ip forward-protocol** command followed by the keyword **udp** and port number or protocol name for those UDP broadcasts that are *not* automatically forwarded. Turn off any automatically forwarded ports with the **no ip forward-protocol udp *port*** or *port name* command.

In Figure 3–21, in addition to the default UDP broadcasts, the forwarding of a custom application using UDP port 3000 has been enabled. Because the server does not support TFTP requests, the administrator has disabled the automatic forwarding of port 69.

Multiple Servers-Remote Medium

To handle forwarding broadcasts to multiple servers on the same remote medium, you can use a directed broadcast into the subnet instead of using several unicast helpers.

As shown in Figure 3–22, configuring a directed broadcast address, the broadcast address changes into a directed broadcast.

Figure 3–21
Forwarding default and other broadcasts.

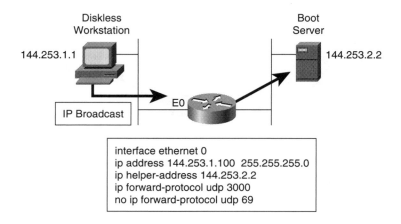

```
interface ethernet 0
ip address 144.253.1.100  255.255.255.0
ip helper-address 144.253.2.2
ip forward-protocol udp 3000
no ip forward-protocol udp 69
```

Figure 3–22
Directed broadcast into subnet.

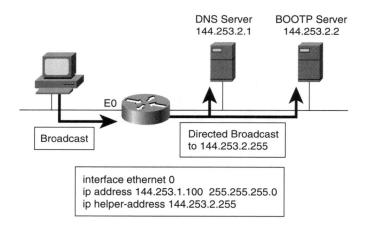

```
interface ethernet 0
ip address 144.253.1.100  255.255.255.0
ip helper-address 144.253.2.255
```

Multiple Servers-Remote Media

The most general case is when multiple servers are located on different remote media, as shown in Figure 3–23. This case can be handled by a combination of multiple helper statements, some with a unicast and some with a directed-broadcast address. The helper statements can be used to address individual servers on different media, whereas the directed broadcast can be used to address sets of servers that reside together on a common medium.

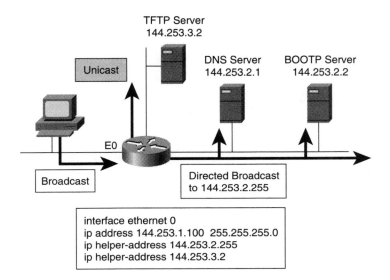

Figure 3–23
Directed broadcast and unicast.

The TCP intercept feature implements software to protect TCP servers from TCP SYN-flooding attacks, which are a type of denial-of-service attack.

TCP Intercept

A *SYN-flooding attack* occurs when a hacker floods a server with a barrage of requests for connection. Because these messages have unreachable return addresses, the connections cannot be established. The resulting volume of unresolved open connections eventually overwhelms the server and can cause it to deny service to valid requests, thereby preventing legitimate users from connecting to a Web site, accessing e-mail, using FTP service, and so on.

The TCP intercept feature helps prevent SYN-flooding attacks by intercepting and validating TCP connection requests. In intercept mode, the TCP intercept software intercepts TCP synchronization (SYN) packets from clients to servers that match an extended access list. The software establishes a connection with the client on behalf of the destination server, and if successful, establishes the connection with the server on behalf of the client and knits the two half-connections together transparently. Thus, connection attempts from unreachable hosts will never reach the server. The software continues to intercept and forward packets throughout the duration of the connection.

In the case of illegitimate requests, the software's aggressive timeouts on half-open connections and its thresholds on TCP connection requests protect destination servers while still allowing valid requests.

TCP Intercept

When establishing your security policy using TCP intercept, you can choose to intercept all requests or only those coming from specific networks or destined for specific servers. You can also configure the connection rate and threshold of outstanding connections.

You can choose to operate TCP intercept in watch mode, as opposed to intercept mode. In watch mode, the software passively watches the connection requests flowing through the router. If a connection fails to become established in a configurable interval, the software intervenes and terminates the connection attempt.

TCP options that are negotiated on handshake (such as RFC 1323 on window scaling) will not be negotiated because the TCP intercept software does not know what the server can do or will negotiate.

To enable TCP intercept, perform the following tasks in global configuration mode:

Task	Command
Define an IP extended access list	**access-list** *access-list-number* {**deny** | **permit**} **tcp any** *destination destination-wildcard*
Enable TCP intercept	**ip tcp intercept list** *access-list-number*

You can define an access list to intercept all requests or only those coming from specific networks or destined for specific servers. Typically the access list will define the source as **any** and define specific destination networks or servers. That is, you do not attempt to filter on the source addresses because you don't necessarily know from whom to intercept packets. You identify the destination in order to protect destination servers.

If no access list match is found, the router allows the request to pass with no further action. For more information on TCP Intercept, refer to www.cisco.com.

SUMMARY

In this chapter, you have learned about the configuration tasks necessary to deal with managing traffic in an IP environment—using access lists and using helper addressing. You've learned about the difference between standard and extended access lists and you have seen example configurations of each type of access list. In turn, you learned about the four configuring principles for access lists. You also discovered how a network can be protected from denial-of-service attacks based on the TCP connection establishment process. In the next chapter, you learn how to manage Novell IPX/SPX traffic.

Chapter Three Test
Managing IP Traffic

Estimated Time: 15 minutes

Complete all the exercises to test your knowledge of the materials contained in this chapter. Answers are listed in Appendix A, "Chapter Test Answer Key."

Use the information contained in this chapter to answer the following questions.

Question 3.1

Examine the network shown in Figure 3–24.

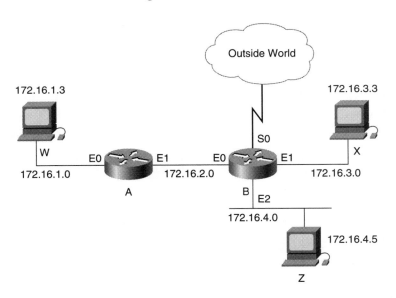

Figure 3–24
IP standard access list exercise.

Create a standard access list and place it in the proper location to satisfy the following requirements:

- Prevent all hosts on subnet 172.16.1.0/24 except host 172.16.1.3 from accessing subnet 172.16.4.0.

- Prevent the outside world from accessing subnet 172.16.4.0.

- Allow all other hosts on all other subnets of network 172.16.0.0 (subnet mask 255.255.0.0) to access 172.16.4.0.

- Prevent host 172.16.3.3 from accessing subnet 172.16.4.0.

Write your configuration in the space that follows. Be sure to include the router name (A or B), interface name (E0, E1, or E2), and access list direction (in or out).

Question 3.2

Consider the following access list:

```
access-list 12 permit 192.89.55.0 0.0.0.255
!
line vty 0 4
```

access-class 12 in

Mark the following statements as true or false:

T   F   Only device 192.89.55.0 is allowed to establish a vty connection with the router.

T   F   This access list uses illegal characters.

T   F   This access list affects all virtual terminal lines.

T   F   This access list controls unbound traffic.

Question 3.3

What command should you use to view access lists applied to vty ports?

Question 3.4

Consider the following extended access list:

```
access-list 103 permit tcp any 128.88.0.0 0.0.255.255
access-list 103 permit tcp any host 128.88.1.2 eq smtp
!
interface ethernet 1
ip access-group 103 in
```

What command should be added to ensure that new TCP connections are not allowed through this router?

_____   _____

Question 3.5

How can the router identify a device that is trying to obtain a TCP connection?

_____   _____

Question 3.6

What command can you use to verify access list commands for all protocols?

_____   _____

Question 3.7

Consider the graph shown in Figure 3–25.

Figure 3–25
*Access list
alternatives
exercise.*

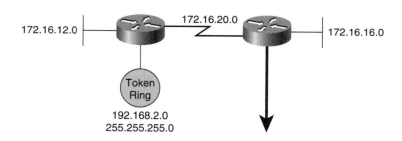

Write the configuration that sends all traffic bound for 192.168.2.0 to the null interface.

_____   _____

Question 3.8

Consider the graph shown in Figure 3–26.

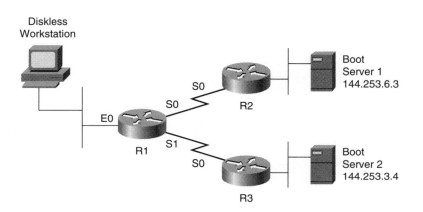

Figure 3–26
*IP helper
address
exercise.*

Write a configuration that allows the default UDP broadcasts sent by the diskless workstation to reach both boot servers. Be sure to include the router's name (R1, R2, or R3) and interface name in the space provided.

Router _____

interface _____

ip address 144.253.1.10 255.255.255.0

_____

_____

Managing Novell IPX/SPX Traffic

This chapter covers the configuration tasks necessary to deal with congestion in an IPX network using access lists. Access lists are presented in more detail as filters for special IPX broadcasts, such as Service Advertising Protocol (SAP) and Get Nearest Server (GNS) requests. SPX spoofing and watchdog spoofing are also covered as methods to help control NetWare traffic on WAN links. A software-only tunnel interface is also presented as a means to connect IPX networks.

For additional information on IPX/SPX configuration, refer to the "Configuring Novell IPX" chapter in the Cisco IOS configuration guides and command references or to the related sections on the Documentation CD-ROM (formerly UniverCD), or refer to www.cisco.com.

NOVELL IPX/SPX OVERVIEW

Novell's IPX/SPX-based NetWare is a proprietary protocol stack derived from the Xerox Network Systems (XNS) protocol. Novell NetWare has several important components, as shown in Figure 4–1.

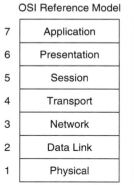

Figure 4–1
*The IPX/SPX
protocol stack.*

OSI Reference Model		Netware 3.x/4.x Protocols					
7	Application	NCP	Novell SAP	Novell RIP NLSP	NetBIOS	Applications	7
6	Presentation						6
5	Session						5
4	Transport	Internetwork Packet eXchange (IPX)				SPX	4
3	Network						3
2	Data Link	Medium Access Protocols (Ethernet, Token Ring, WAN, Others)					2
1	Physical						1

Component	Description
IPX	Novell Internetwork Packet Exchange (IPX) is a connectionless datagram protocol. IPX is NetWare's network-layer service. IPX provides network-layer addressing and is a routable protocol.
SPX	Novell Sequenced Packet Exchange (SPX) is a Novell proprietary connection-oriented transport-layer protocol.
NCP	NetWare Core Protocol (NCP) is an upper-layer protocol used for client/server connection requests, file system requests, print, security, and other network services. Get Nearest Server (GNS) requests are NCP broadcasts used to locate a NetWare server.
SAP	Devices use Service Advertising Protocol (SAP) to locate and advertise NetWare services.
RIP/NLSP	Novell Routing Information Protocol (RIP) and NetWare Link Services Protocol (NLSP) are NetWare-based routing protocols.

Note that NetWare also supports NetBIOS emulation in order to run NetBIOS-based applications.

IPX Addressing

An IPX network address consists of a network number and a node number, expressed in the *network.node* format, such as 0D2D.033A.0000.1B24.2345, where 0D2D.033A is the network portion and 0000.1B24.2345 is the node portion of the address.

The *network number* is a four-byte (32-bit) number that identifies a logical network. The network number is expressed in hexadecimal (0000.4a1d) and must be unique throughout the entire IPX internetwork. When configuring an IPX network number, you can omit leading zeros.

The *node number* identifies a single device on the network. It is a 48-bit number, expressed by dotted triplets of four-digit hexadecimal numbers (0000.0c56.de33, for example). The node number is normally taken from the MAC address of the NetWare node or router interface. You can configure the IPX node address on a Cisco router with the **ipx routing** command. The node address must be set if the router does not have any interfaces with MAC addresses, such as Ethernet, Token Ring, or FDDI.

As Figure 4–2 shows, the router's interfaces have the following IPX addresses:

Interface	IPX Address	Network Number	Node Number
E0	4a1d.0000.0c56.de33	4a1d	0000.0c56.de33
E1	3f.0000.0c56.de34	3f	0000.0c56.de34
S0	2c.0000.0c56.de33	2c	0000.0c56.de33

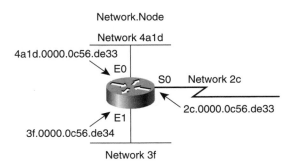

Figure 4–2
Node addresses are based on the MAC address of a device.

An IPX internal network number identifies a 3.1*x* and 4.*x* and 5.*x* NetWare server and is made up of a network address and the 0000.0000.0001 node address. A Novell Server is in fact a router, and the services are connected to a "virtual" internal network which therefore has no network card and hence no MAC address, so 000.000.000.001 is used.

The serial interface does not have a MAC address. It uses the default Novell node address, which is the MAC address of first activated interface in the order of Ethernet, and then Token Ring, and finally FDDI.

Several IPX networks can exist on the same media segment. These networks must each use a different encapsulation method. The **ipx network secondary** command configures additional networks after the primary network.

Managing IPX/SPX Traffic

Novell NetWare is a networking operation system that uses several services that periodically broadcast updates across the network, as shown in Figure 4–3. These periodic broadcasts facilitate network use and management. In small LANs, the traffic generated by these updates does not generally consume a significant portion of the LAN's bandwidth.

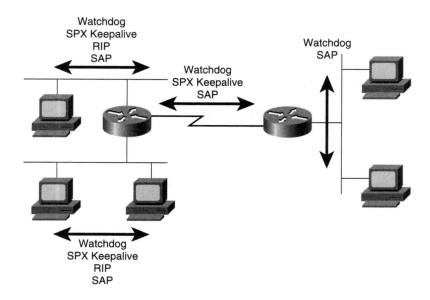

Figure 4–3
NetWare's periodic broadcast traffic can affect WAN performance.

As IPX internetworks grow, slower and more expensive WAN links are incorporated into the internetwork. NetWare broadcast traffic can use a significant portion of the available WAN bandwidth.

TIPS

Incidentally, EIGRP's support of reliable SAP updates (RSUP) is a powerful and flexible tool for managing SAP traffic. EIGRP is covered in Chapter 10, "Configuring Enhanced IGRP." If RSUP is enabled, the EIGRP routing updates are suspended and RIP is used instead.

IPX internetwork managers may want to prevent access to network resources for security reasons or to save internetwork bandwidth. Cisco IOS software offers the following several tools to manage IPX internetworking:

- *Traffic filtering*—You can use access lists to filter traffic based on a source and destination network address or socket.

- *IPX broadcast filtering*—You can use access lists to restrict SAP and RIP broadcasts.

- *WAN connectivity*—You can tunnel IPX traffic through an IP network.

- *Periodic update spoofing for WAN links*—You can manage broadcasts to use circuit-switched WAN services effectively.

- *GNS filtering*—You can use access lists to configure GNS replies from a router.

In Figure 4–3, SAP, RIP watchdog, and SPX keepalive traffic is shown. IPX watchdog is part of the NetWare Control Protocol stack and is used to verify connections from NetWare servers to clients. Watchdog packets are maintained for each NCP connection and login per MAC address, so if a user is using resources (established a connection) from two separate NetWare servers, there will be two separate IPX watchdog packets each time.

SPX keepalive traffic is generated by NetWare applications, such as RCONSOLE, RPRINTER, and NetWare for SAA. Cisco IOS supports SPX keepalive and watchdog spoofing to control traffic on WAN connections.

IPX TRAFFIC FILTERING

Novell NetWare typically generates large amounts of broadcast and service-oriented traffic. Filtering this traffic can help conserve network bandwidth and control access to NetWare services.

IPX Traffic Filtering Overview

Novell NetWare is a client/server networking environment. As IPX internetworks grow, management of client/server traffic and administrative broadcasts can become critical for network administrators. You can use standard and extended IPX access lists to manage traffic on a Novell NetWare internetwork. In Figure 4–4, the access list on router A can prevent clients of networks aa and cc from accessing servers on network bb.

Key Concept Recall that standard access lists filter based on source address only. Extended access lists offer more control by filtering based on source address, destination address, or protocol characteristics.

Figure 4–4
IPX access lists restrict traffic.

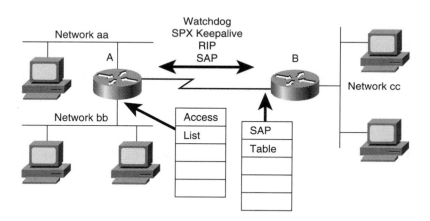

SAP filters let you block SAP traffic by prohibiting the router from advertising services learned from NetWare servers. Input SAP filters (**input-sap-filter**) prevent the addition of SAP advertisements to the router's SAP table. Output SAP filters (**output-sap-filter**) prevent the router from advertising the SAP service. You can configure SAP filters to block SAP traffic from specific servers or all servers on a network. SAP filters are configured as a specific range of access lists.

The following table shows the types of access lists and the available list numbers for IPX:

Type of Access List	Range
IPX standard	800–899
IPX extended	900–999
IPX SAP	1000–1099
NLSP route aggregation	1200–1299

Enhanced IGRP sends SAP updates over serial lines only when the SAP table changes. This feature is a straightforward method for controlling SAP traffic. This is the default operation, and the function can be enabled or disabled on any media.

IPX Access List Commands

You use the **access-list** and **ipx access-group** commands, both discussed in the following sections, to configure IPX access lists.

The access-list Command

Use the **access-list** command to filter traffic in an IPX network. Using filters on the outgoing router interface allows or restricts different protocols and applications on individual networks. You can apply an input or output filter.

```
IPX standard access list:
access-list access-list-number {permit | deny} source-network [.source-node
    [source-node-mask]]
    [destination-network[.destination-node [destination-node-mask]]]
```

access-list Command	Description
access-list-number	Access list number for an IPX standard filter list from 800 to 899.
source-network	Source network number, expressed in eight-digit hexadecimal.
.source-node	Node number on the source network. Represented as a 48-bit value shown in a dotted triplet of four-digit hexadecimal numbers, such as 0000.1B12.3456.
source-node-mask	A mask that can be applied to the source-node address.
destination-network	Network number to which the packet is being sent.
.destination-node	Node on the destination network to which the packet is being sent.
destination-node-mask	A mask that can be applied to the destination-node address.

The ipx access-group Command

Use the **ipx access-group** command to link an IPX traffic filter to an interface.

```
ipx access-group access-list-number [in | out]
```

ipx access-group Command	Description
access-list-number [**in** | **out**]	Access list number for an IPX filter list from 800 to 999. **in:** Filter is placed on incoming traffic; filtered information is not placed in the router's tables. **out:** filter is placed on outgoing traffic. The following IPX protocol numbers have been defined and may be used in extended access lists:

- *–1*—Wildcard. This Cisco **access-list** command option matches any packet type in 900 lists.

- *0*—Could be an undefined protocol. Refer to the socket number to determine the packet type.

- *1*—RIP

- *2*—Cisco-specific echo packet (ping)

- *3*—Error packet

- *4*—IPX

- *5*—SPX

- *17*—NCP

- *20*—IPX NetBIOS

The following IPX socket numbers have been defined:

- *0*—All sockets

- *451*—NCP process

- *452*—SAP process

- *453*—RIP process

- *455*—Novell NetBIOS packet

- *456*—Novell diagnostic packet

- *457*—Novell serialization socket

- *4000–7FFF*—Dynamic sockets; used by workstations for interaction with file servers and other network servers

- *8000FFFF*—Sockets assigned by Novell

- *85BE*—IPX Enhanced IGRP

- *9001*—NLSP

- *9004*—IPXWAN/IPXWAN2

- *9086*—IPX official ping

Use the **access-list** command with the keywords that appear in the following command definition to create an extended to IPX filter.

```
IPX extended access lists:
Access-list access-list-number {permit | deny} protocol [source-network]
    [[[.source-node]source-node-mask] | .source-node
    source-network-mask.source-node-mask]] [source-socket]
    [destination.network] [[[.destination-node] destination-node-mask] |
    [.destination-node destination-network-mask.destination-node-mask]]
    [destination-socket] [log]
```

Following are some of the more useful keyword definitions:

access-list Command	Description
access-list-number	Access list number for an IPX extended filter list from 900 to 999 for IPX extended access lists.
protocol	Number of the protocol type. Can be 0=any protocol, 1=RIP, 4=IPX, 5=SPX, 17=NCP, 20=IPX NetBIOS.
source-network	Source network number, expressed in eight-digit hexadecimal.
.source-node	Node number on the source network. Represented as a 48-bit value shown in a dotted triplet of four-digit hexadecimal numbers.
source-socket	Socket name or number (hexadecimal) from which the packet is being sent.
destination-network	Network number to which the packet is being sent.
.destination-node	Node on the destination network to which the packet is being sent.
destination-socket	Socket number to which the packet is being sent, expressed in hexadecimal. For example, socket number 452=SAP.

IPX SAP Overview

NetWare service-providing devices, such as NetWare file servers, print servers, and gateway servers, use SAP broadcasts to advertise their services and addresses (see Figure 4–5). Each server on the IPX internetwork broadcasts a SAP update at startup and every 60 seconds during operation, by default.

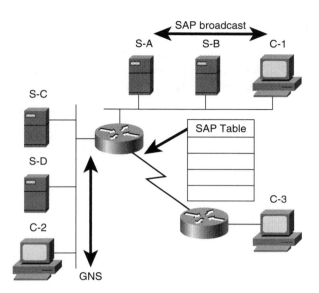

Figure 4–5
*SAPs synchro-
nize the list of
available ser-
vices.*

On large internetworks, these SAP broadcasts can consume a large portion of available network bandwidth. Cisco routers do not forward each SAP broadcast that they receive. Instead, the router maintains a SAP table and broadcasts this table every 60 seconds.

Clients then use this information to determine which services are available on the network and to obtain the internetwork addresses of servers.

If the router passed a SAP every time it received a SAP broadcast, the WAN link would be flooded with small SAP packet traffic. Instead, the router builds a SAP table and advertises this information every 60 seconds with up to seven entries per packet. **Key Concept**

GNS requests are NetWare client-based SAP broadcasts. When a NetWare client starts up, it broadcasts a GNS request to locate a server.

Routers maintain a SAP table that contains service information received from servers on the network. The router propagates this routing table to other networks that it is connected to.

SAP Operation

SAP broadcasts are essential to NetWare networking operation. As a result, routers must forward the SAP information. The router compiles the SAP information into the SAP table and transmits the appropriate SAP updates out each interface.

In internetworks with large numbers of IPX servers, the SAP updates can consume a large portion of the WAN link. For example, a SAP update frame can contain only up to seven 64-byte service entries (448 bytes) plus 40 bytes of WAN-link header information, for a maximum of 488 bytes per packet. If 500 services are advertised, 72 frames are sent over the WAN link every minute.

TIPS

Over a Cisco-to-Cisco WAN link, the SAP interval can be changed. When communicating with any non-Cisco devices that do not support different SAP update intervals, the SAP interval must be left at 60 seconds. Use the **ipx sap-interval** *interval* command to change the update frequency, where *interval* is the number of minutes between updates.

If you assume 72 480-byte packets, transferred over a 5600-bps line, transmission of these packets would take 4.9 seconds: 72 * 480 * 8 / 56000 = 4.9 seconds, where

- 72 is the number of packets

- 480 is the number of bytes per packet

- 8 is used to convert bytes to bits

- 56000 is the number of bits per second that the line can transmit

On a 56-kbps link, the transfer of these 72 frames would take approximately 5 seconds to complete. During those 5 seconds of each minute, other services would not have access to the serial line.

Key Concept   SAP filtering lets you control SAP updates from network segments or from specific servers.

This calculation does not include the MAC-layer information added to each packet. A SAP packet contains the following fields:

- SDLC/PPP header—5 bytes

- IPX header—30 bytes

- Up to seven SAP entries—448 bytes

- SLDP trailer information—3 bytes

SAP Filters

SAP filtering uses access lists to control SAP updates. To configure SAP filtering, do the following:

1. Define an access list for filtering SAP traffic.
2. Enable the SAP access list on an interface.

When a SAP input filter is in place, the number of services entered into the router's SAP table is reduced, as shown in Figure 4–6. The propagated SAP updates represent the entire table, but contain only a subset of all services.

When a SAP output filter is in place, the number of services propagated from the table is reduced. The propagated SAP updates represent a portion of the table contents and are a subset of all the known services.

SAP filters are created using the **access-list** command with the **access-list**-*number* in the range of 1000 to 1099. After creating the access list, apply the access list to an input or output interface.

SAP Filter Configuration

The following three commands can be used to define a SAP filter:

- **access-list**

- **ipx input-sap-filter**

- **ipx output-sap-filter**

Figure 4–6
*Input and out-
put
filters affect
the router's
SAP table, as
well as the
SAP traffic on
the
network.*

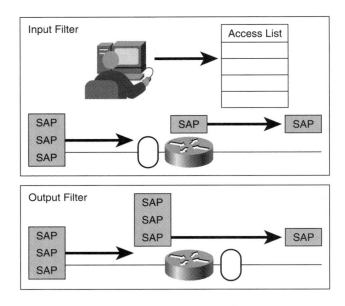

You do not need both an input and output filter, although they can both be used on a single access list if desired.

The access-list Command

The **access-list** command creates a SAP filter entry. Important arguments are the *service-type* and *server-name* arguments. Server names are limited to 31 characters. You can use SAP filters to limit the servers from which you learn information, as well as the types of services that will be advertised by the router.

access-list *access-list-number* {**deny** | **permit**} *network* [*.node*] [*network-mask node-mask*] [*service-type* [*server-name*]]

access-list Command	Description
access-list-number	Number from 1000 to 1099; indicates a SAP filter list.
network [*.node*]	Novell source network with optional node number; –1 means all networks.
network-mask *node-mask*	Mask to be applied to the network and node. Place 1s in the positions to be masked.

access-list Command	Description
service-type	SAP service type to filter. Each SAP service type is identified by a hexadecimal number. Some common examples are: 4-File server 7-Print server 24-Remote bridge-server (router)
server-name	Name of the server providing the specified service type.

The ipx sap-filter Command

The **ipx sap-filter** command applies the specified list to the interface. There are three choices for the kind of SAP filter applied to the interface:

- **input**—Filters SAP entries before building the SAP table

- **output**—Filters SAP table entries prior to generating the next SAP update

- **router**—Defines from which router(s) SAP updates will be accepted

Only one of the three types of SAP filters can be active on an interface.

```
ipx input-sap-filter access-list-number
ipx output-sap-filter access-list-number
```

The **ipx input-sap-filter** and **ipx output-sap-filter** commands place a SAP filter on an interface. The use of **input** or **output** determines whether SAPs are filtered before entry into the SAP table, or whether the SAP table contents are filtered during the next update.

SAP table content can be filtered on input by using the **ipx router-sap-filter** command, which identifies from which router SAP advertisements can be received. The syntax for this command is **ipx router-sap-filter** *access-list-number,* where the source router's address is defined in an access list.

SAP Filtering Examples

The following two examples show you how SAP filters can be implemented to block advertisement of specific types of services.

Example 1: Filtering Print Service Information

In Figure 4–7, router A denies print server SAPs on the interface serial 0. Router B permits only NetWare server SAPs to be transmitted from the interface serial 0.

Figure 4–7
Denying print services.

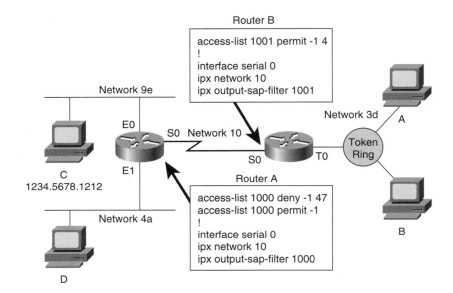

The router A configuration shown in Figure 4–7 is detailed below.

access-list 1000 deny –1 47 Command	Description
1000	An access list number in the Novell SAP filter range.
deny	SAP services matching selected parameters will be blocked.
–1	Source network number. –1 means all networks.
47	Type of SAP service; advertising print server.

access-list 1000 permit –1 Command	Description
1000	Access list number is 1000.

access-list 1000 permit –1 Command	Description
permit	SAP services matching parameters will be forwarded.
–1	Source network number. –1 means all networks.

ipx output-sap-filter 1000 Command	Description
1000	Places list 1000 on interface serial 0 as an output SAP filter.

In this example, router A permits all services except print services on interface serial 0.

The **access-list 1001 permit –1 4** command configures router B to allow all NetWare file servers on its interface serial 0. Other services, such as print servers, are denied. Common SAP service numbers include the following:

- 4—File server

- 7—Print server

- 47—Advertising print server

- 107—RCONSOLE

- 278—NetWare NDS server

Example 2: Filtering File Service Information

In Figure 4–8, services from NetWare server C are blocked on router A's S0 interface. As a result, users on network 3d do not see server C.

File server advertisements from server 2e.0000.0000.0001 will not be forwarded on interface serial 0. All other SAP services from any source will be forwarded on interface serial 0.

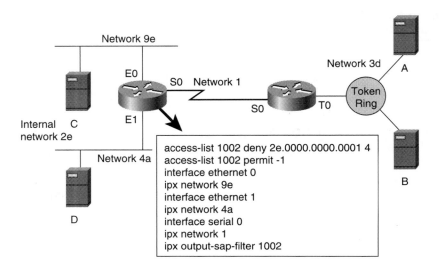

Figure 4–8
File services from Novell server C not advertised on A or B.

```
access-list 1002 deny 2e.0000.0000.0001 4
access-list 1002 permit -1
interface ethernet 0
ipx network 9e
interface ethernet 1
ipx network 4a
interface serial 0
ipx network 1
ipx output-sap-filter 1002
```

Command	Description
access-list 1002 deny 2e.0000.0000.0001 4	
1002	An access list number in the Novell SAP filter range.
deny	SAP services matching selected parameters will be blocked.
2e.0000.0000.0001	Source network address of SAP advertisement. The address is the NetWare server's internal network number 2e and 0000.0000.0001 that represents the MAC address for the internal network number.
4	Type of SAP service. Advertises file service.
access-list 1002 permit –1	
1002	Access list number is 1002.
permit	SAP services matching parameters will be forwarded.
–1	Source network number. **–1** means all networks.
ipx output-sap-filter 1002	Places list 1002 on interface serial 0 as an output SAP filter.

TIPS

When configuring SAP filters for NetWare 3.*x*, 4.*x*, and 5.*x* servers running the bindery emulation, use the NetWare server's internal network and the 0000.0000.0001 node number as its address in the access list command. Do not use the network.node address of the particular interface.

Filtering RIP Traffic

Figure 4–9 shows how you can use RIP filters to stop specific network information from propagating through an internetwork.

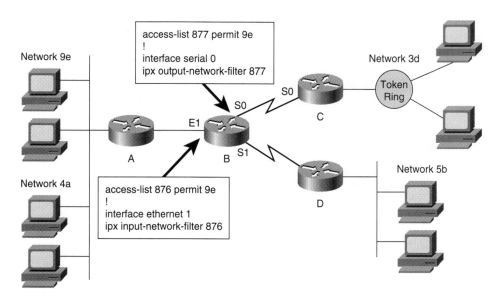

Figure 4–9
The ipx input-network-filter command controls which networks are added to the routing tables.

The **ipx input-network-filter** command uses the following syntax:

```
ipx input-network-filter access-list-number
```

Filtering RIP traffic keeps routing updates from consuming the bandwidth of WAN links. You can also use RIP filtering to hide networks.

Use the **ipx input-network-filter** command to control which networks are added to the router's routing table. This command controls adding routing table updates based on networks learned on the configured interface.

In Figure 4–9, input RIP filter 876 allows only network 9e into router B's RIP table. Only Network 9e is advertised out the serial 0 interface.

The **ipx output-network-filter** command filters routing updates sent out on an interface. In this case, only network 9e is advertised from router B's S0 interface. As a result, users on network 3d see network 9e.

If desired, another IPX output network filter can be applied to router B's S1 interface to block advertisements from network 9e. In that case, users on network 5b would not see network 9e.

SAP/GNS Operation

GNS (Get Nearest Server) requests are used by NetWare clients to locate network services. Three commands can be used to change the way a Cisco router responds to GNS queries from NetWare clients:

- **ipx gns-reply-disable**

  Use this command to completely disable the router from sending replies to IPX GNS queries.

- **ipx gns-response-delay**

  Use the **ipx gns-response-delay** command to change the time that the router waits before sending a Get Nearest Server response. The default is 0 milliseconds, which indicates no delay. As a result, the router responds immediately to GNS requests. If a server is on the local network, however, the router does not reply to the GNS response, which allows the server to respond to the GNS request.

The **ipx gns-response-delay** command is both a global and an interface command; it can be applied at each interface to tune different segments, depending on the server type and desired performance. It also can be used globally to affect all interfaces.

- **ipx gns-round-robin**

  Use the **ipx gns-round-robin** command, as shown in Figure 4–10, to configure the router to answer successive GNS requests for a particular type of server by providing the address of the next server available. This approach helps distribute work among servers.

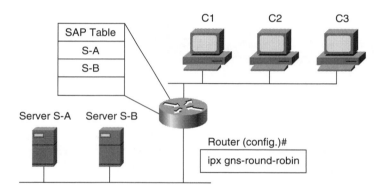

Figure 4–10
The router acts like a server by building the SAP table.

Older versions of Cisco IOS software had GNS round-robin on by default; however, this condition has the undesirable side effect of allocating remote servers when closer ones are available. In current versions of Cisco IOS software, this feature is off by default. Cisco IOS 11.2 software responds to GNS requests with the most recently known available server of the type requested.

Round-robin server allocation treats all servers equally. If the **gns-round-robin** command is not used, the router responds with the servers specified in the **output-gns-filter**. The router chooses the server with the best metric in the SAP table. If several servers have the same best metric, the router broadcasts the most recently received best-metric router. You can see the top entry in the SAP table with the command **show ipx server unsorted**.

The router handles SAPs just like a server. It listens to SAP messages and builds a SAP table. If there is another device advertising a service with a better metric than the servers listed in the router's SAP table, the router does not respond to the GNS.

Note that SAPs are split-horizoned, based on the IPX route back to the server's internal network number.

Limiting GNS Responses

The **ipx output-gns-filter** command is used with the **access-list** command to control which servers are included in GNS responses.

In Figure 4–11, only the S-D server is included in GNS responses sent out on the E1 interface. As a result, the C-1 client receives a GNS response from S-D.

Figure 4–11
You can link a GNS filter to an interface where GNS requests are expected.

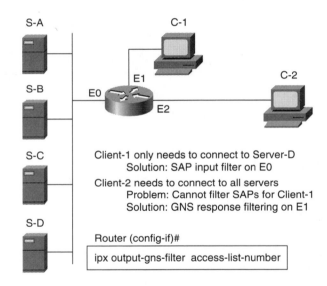

Client-1 only needs to connect to Server-D
Solution: SAP input filter on E0

Client-2 needs to connect to all servers
Problem: Cannot filter SAPs for Client-1
Solution: GNS response filtering on E1

Router (config-if)#

```
ipx output-gns-filter  access-list-number
```

Clients attached to the network connected to the E2 interface receive GNS responses from the router for all servers.

You can use an IPX access list on interface E1 to filter servers S-A, S-B, and S-C so that only S-D responds to client C-1's login request.

Static SAP Table Entries Configuration Example

Novell NetWare 3.x and 4.x servers using the bindery emulation advertise their services via SAP broadcast packets. Cisco IOS software stores this information in the SAP table, as shown in Figure 4–12. As the router receives new SAP updates, this table is updated.

The syntax for the **ipx sap** command is as follows:

```
ipx sap service-type name network.node socket hop-count
```

Parameter	Description
service-type	SAP service type number
name	Name of the server that provides this service
network.node	Network number and node address of the server
socket	Socket number for this service
hop-count	Number of hops to the server

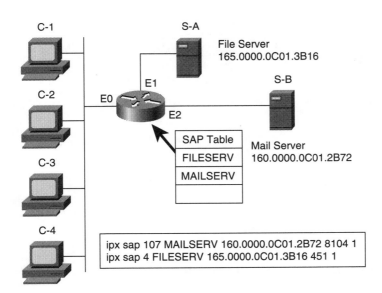

Figure 4–12
MAILSERV and FILESERV are static SAP table entries.

You can explicitly add entries to the SAP table so that clients always use a particular server's service. Static SAP assignments always override any identical entries in the SAP table that are learned dynamically, regardless of hop count.

ipx sap 107 MAILSERV 160.0000.0C01.2B72 8104 1 Command	Description
107	Identifies the SAP service-type number, in this case mail service.
MAILSERV	Identifies the name of the mail server.
160.0000.0C01.2B72	Represents the network number and node address of the server.
8104	Represents the socket number for this service.
1	Identifies the number of hops to the server.

ipx sap 4 FILESERV 165.0000.0C01.3B16 451 1 Command	Description
4	Identifies the SAP service-type number, in this case file service.
FILESERV	Identifies the name of the file server.
160.0000.0C01.3B16	Represents the network number and node address of the server.
451	Represents the socket number of this service.
1	Identifies the number of hops to the server.

The router will not announce a static SAP entry unless it has a route to that network. In Figure 4–12, the S-A file server's services and the S-B mail server's services have been statically entered in the SAP table.

SAP Interval Configuration Example

Use the **ipx sap-interval** command to configure less frequent SAP updates. You can use this feature to save bandwidth on slow links. It is important when using this command that the interval on the routers and IPX servers is consistent. Otherwise, the devices may determine that one or the other has gone down just because SAPs age. If an interval on one device (for example, a server) is longer than on another device (for example, a router), the router may consider the server down, because its entry about that server will age out before the server sends an update.

Setting the interval at which SAP updates are sent is most useful on limited-bandwidth, point-to-point links. NetWare 4.11 and later versions of NetWare enable you to change this update interval. On earlier versions of NetWare (such as NetWare 2.x and 3.x), however, you could not change it. This means that the interval should not be changed for networks that have these servers. It is also possible to use static SAP entries on routers to keep availability while reducing update traffic on a slow link.

In Figure 4–13, the **ipx sap-interval** command reduces the number of SAP updates over the serial link by increasing the time between SAP updates. Because the routers receive SAP updates from the NetWare nodes on the local LAN segments, the routers maintain accurate service information from servers and workstations connected on the LAN segments.

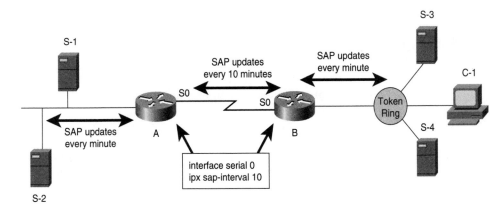

Figure 4–13
Routers A and B exchange SAP updates every 10 minutes.

If the S-1 server on one side of the WAN link goes down, the C-1 client might not receive the update for up to 15 minutes.

CAUTION

Setting the **ipx sap-interval command** to 0 means that periodic SAP updates are never sent. It is not recommended to do this because clients cannot use the services unless static SAP entries are defined.

CONNECTING IPX NETWORKS USING IP TUNNELS

Novell NetWare is commonly used in office environments. As the number of noncontiguous NetWare workgroups grow, it is often desirable to connect these IPX networks. If the core network is IP-based, the network designer/manager can add IPX to the core network or can tunnel IPX traffic across the IP intranetwork.

Tunnels can connect noncontiguous networks. A tunnel can be used to connect IPX networks that are physically separated and connected only by an IP WAN or backbone. Tunneling has the following three primary components:

- A passenger protocol, in this case IPX

- Carrier encapsulation, if going across a WAN link

- A transport protocol, in this case IP

Configuring an IP Tunnel Interface

Software-only tunnel interfaces permit traffic from isolated hosts to be carried through an intermediate internetwork, as shown in Figure 4–14.

Protocol traffic is encapsulated within a WAN *carrier protocol*; the use of different encapsulations allows interoperability with vendor equipment. The tunnel is created by specifying a source and destination IP address. Using an IP network as the transport mechanism provides reliability through its dynamic route selection for traffic passing through the tunnel.

Note that, although this chapter introduces tunneling in the context of IPX, a tunnel interface can also transport other protocols, such as AppleTalk.

Figure 4–14
A tunnel interface creates a point-to- point link between isolated hosts.

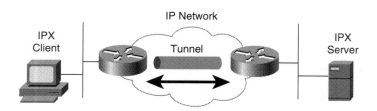

To set up a tunnel, perform the following steps:

1. Use the **interface tunnel** command to create a tunnel interface to carry the protocol traffic. You must specify a tunnel interface number. The **interface tunnel** command creates a software interface. The range is 0 to 2147483647.

2. Use the **ipx network** address to define an IPX address for the tunnel.

3. Define the tunnel's source interface with the **tunnel source** command. The **tunnel source** command can be specified either by an actual address or by an interface port name.

4. Use the **tunnel destination** command to specify a tunnel interface's destination. The **tunnel destination** command can be specified either by an actual address or by a name previously defined in a static name table using the **ip host** command.

5. Set the encapsulation mode for the tunnel interface with the **tunnel mode gre ip** command.

   The **tunnel mode** command supports several encapsulation methods. The following encapsulations are available:

   - *AURP*—AppleTalk Update Routing Protocol. Allows Cisco routers to communicate with Apple Internetwork Routers (AIRs). Added in Release 10.2.

   - *Cayman*—A proprietary protocol used to transmit AppleTalk over IP. Allows Cisco to communicate with Cayman GatorBox devices.

   - *EON*—A standard for carrying CLNP/CLNS over IP networks.

   - *GRE IP*—Generic routing encapsulation (GRE). Cisco proprietary multiprotocol carrier protocol. Transport is via IP networks. GRE IP is the default.

   - *NOS*—KA9Q/NOS IP-compatible IP using the popular KA9Q program.

A direct connection is not required between the source and destination when establishing a software tunnel.

IP Tunnel Configuration Example

In Figure 4–15, a tunnel interface is configured on the S0 physical interface of router A.

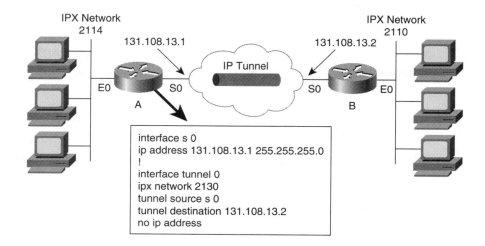

Figure 4–15
The tunnel defines GRE IP as the encapsulation type.

interface s 0
ip address 131.108.13.1 255.255.255.0
!
interface tunnel 0
ipx network 2130
tunnel source s 0
tunnel destination 131.108.13.2
no ip address

Command	Description
interface tunnel 0	Specifies creation of tunnel interface 0.
ipx network 2130	Defines the IPX network number assigned to the tunnel.
tunnel source serial 0	Specifies that traffic entering the tunnel uses interface serial 0.
tunnel destination 131.108.13.2	Specifies traffic leaving the tunnel arrives at the specified address.
tunnel mode gre ip	Specifies GRE IP as the encapsulation method used to carry traffic within the tunnel. Note that this is the default, therefore it does not appear in the configuration output.
no ip address	Defines that the tunnel itself does not have an IP address.

IPX traffic for network 2110 will use the GRE IP tunnel that starts on interface S0 and terminates at IP address 131.108.13.2 (S0 of the right router). The tunnel is assigned an IPX address to allow it to route IPX out the interface and pass it to IPX RIP. Although the tunnel uses existing IP links to deliver encapsulated traffic, the tunnel itself does not require an IP address to function properly. A tunnel interface must also be configured for router B.

VERIFYING IPX TRAFFIC OPERATION

It is important to verify the IPX configuration after you have set it up. Verifying IPX includes the following:

- Verifying the status of interfaces that are routing IPX traffic by using the **show ipx interface** EXEC command

- Viewing the IPX routing table by using the **show ipx route** EXEC command

- Verifying the IPX fast-switching cache by using the **show ipx cache** EXEC command

- Displaying the available IPX servers by using the **show ipx servers** EXEC command

- Verifying IPX traffic by using the **show ipx traffic** user EXEC command

The following **show** commands provide important information for verifying IPX traffic operation:

- The **show ipx interface** command displays information on the IPX address of the interface, IPXWAN status, IPX helper information, and SAP and access list filtering.

- The **show ipx route** command displays information on the following types of routers: connected primary network, internal network, static, floating static, IPXWAN, RIP, Enhanced IGRP, NLSP, and external, and aggregate.

- The **show ipx cache** command shows the routes that are cached.

- The **show ipx servers** command displays the type of service, the name of the servers, the network address of the server, and the distance in hops and ticks to the server. This is, in fact, displaying the router's SAP table.

- The **show ipx traffic** command shows the number of packets transmitted and received. This information includes broadcast, SAP, routing, and watchdog information.

SUMMARY

In this chapter, you learned how to manage IPX traffic through traffic filters, SAP filters, and GNS filters. You have also seen how to configure a tunnel to place IPX traffic inside other transport mechanisms. Finally, you learned how to verify IPX traffic operation using the various **show** commands. In the next chapter, you learn about the various queuing mechanisms available for handling traffic to ensure fair or preferential access to the network.

Chapter Four Test
Managing Novell IPX/SPX Traffic

Estimated Time: 15 minutes

Complete all the exercises to test your knowledge of the materials contained in this chapter. Answers are listed in Appendix A, "Chapter Test Answer Key."

Use the information contained in this chapter to answer the following questions

Question 4.1

Use your understanding of IPX/SPX traffic to indicate whether the following statements are true or false.

T   F   SPX, NCP, and SAP are NetWare services or protocols.

T   F   IPX is an OSI Layer 5 connection-oriented protocol.

T   F   You can filter traffic based on the IPX source or destination address.

T   F   SAP broadcasts are transmitted periodically.

T   F   A Cisco router can filter SAP broadcasts.

Question 4.2

Examine the graphic shown in Figure 4–16.

Configure an IPX SAP output filter to filter printer advertisements, allowing other IPX traffic over the S0 interface. Use 2b for the serial interface's IPX network number.

Set the SAP interval between the routers to five minutes.

Figure 4–16
*SAP filter
exercise.*

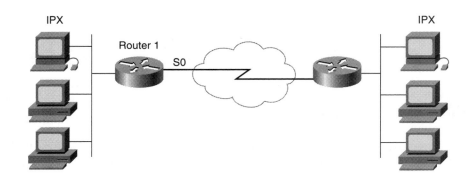

Write the SAP filter configuration in the space provided.

_____

_____

_____

_____

_____

_____

_____

Question 4.3

Examine the graphic shown in Figure 4–17.

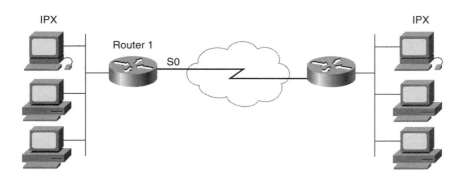

Figure 4–17
*Tunnel inter-
face exercise.*

Configure an IPX tunnel interface on router 1's S0 interface. Use the following settings:

- 131.108.99.1 for the source IP addresses

- 131.108.99.2 for the destination IP address

- 2b IPX network

- The default encapsulation method

Write the tunnel interface configuration in the space provided.

_____

_____

_____

_____

_____

_____

Configuring Queuing to Manage Traffic

This chapter covers the three queuing techniques Cisco supports: weighted fair queuing, priority queuing, and custom queuing. *Queuing,* which is the process of allowing certain traffic to be delivered before others, controls traffic congestion in an internetwork. Queuing is especially critical on low-bandwidth serial links when some multiprotocol traffic, such as video/audio traffic, is more time-critical than other types of traffic.

QUEUING OVERVIEW

Traffic arriving at a router interface is handled by a protocol-dependent switching process. The switching process includes delivery of traffic to an outgoing interface buffer. *First-in, first-out (FIFO) queuing* is the classic algorithm for packet transmission. With FIFO, transmission occurs in the same order as messages are received. Until IOS version 11.1, FIFO queuing was the default for all router interfaces. If user needs require traffic to be reordered, the department or company must establish a queuing policy other than FIFO queuing.

If the interface buffers fill up in FIFO queuing, the router is indiscriminate about which packets are dropped. By implementing a new queuing method, the network manager decides which packets are dropped (in the case of priority or custom queuing) or allows the router to decide (in the case of weighted fair queuing). For example, in Figure 5–1, you can see three packets arrive at the router's buffer. Because the administrator has configured SNA and IP traffic with higher priorities than IPX traffic, they will be handled by the router before IPX traffic.

Figure 5–1
*Changing the
queuing oper-
ation can reor-
der packets.*

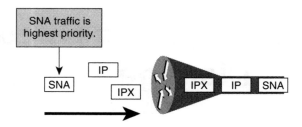

Cisco IOS software offers the following three queuing options as alternatives to FIFO queuing:

- *Weighted fair queuing (WFQ)* prioritizes interactive traffic over file transfers in order to ensure satisfactory response time for common user applications.

- *Priority queuing* ensures timely delivery of a specific protocol or type of traffic because that traffic is transmitted before all others.

- *Custom queuing* establishes bandwidth allocations for each different type of traffic.

The need for queuing stems from the need to prioritize traffic, so the next section discusses what traffic prioritization is all about.

Traffic Prioritization

The need to prioritize packets arises from the diverse mixture of protocols and their associated behaviors found in today's data networks. Different types of traffic that share a data path through the network can impact each other.

Depending on the application and overall bandwidth, users may or may not perceive any real performance degradation. For example, in order to satisfy users, delay-sensitive interactive, transaction-based applications may require a higher priority than a file transfer.

The classic interactive application is the telnet-based terminal server or terminal emu-lator running on a personal computer. Interactive traffic is essentially random, per-haps because humans typing on keyboards do so erratically and randomly. Such applications generally accumulate characters for a short period and then transmit them to the peer application. The peer application acknowledges the characters, often by sending the same traffic back. This method is called *echoplex* transmission.

Because new transmissions wait until an outstanding transmission has been acknowl-edged, this type of application is very sensitive to delay. Desktop videoconferencing requires a specified amount of bandwidth to perform acceptably. If your network is designed so that multiple protocols share a single data path between routers, priori-tization may be a requirement.

Prioritization is most effective on WAN links where the combination of bursty traffic and relatively lower data rates can cause temporary congestion. Prioritization is most effective when applied to links at T1/E1 (1.544 Mpbs/2.048 Mbps) bandwidth speeds or lower.

If there is no congestion on the WAN link, there is no reason to implement traffic pri-oritization because traffic prioritization adds overhead to the router's operation. Therefore, implementing queuing on a uncongested link reduces overall performance.

If a WAN link is constantly congested, traffic prioritization may not resolve the problem. Adding bandwidth might be the appropriate solution. Use a WAN analyzer to determine what the average bandwidth utilization is on the WAN link. If the link averages 80 percent or greater utilization, you should consider adding bandwidth to accommodate the traffic needs.	**Key Concept**

For information on how traffic prioritization becomes more effective as the average packet size increases, see "Performance Measurements of Advanced Queuing Tech-niques in the Cisco IOS" at www.cisco.com.

Establishing a Queuing Policy

A queuing policy helps network managers meet two challenges: to provide an appro-priate level of service for all users and to control expensive WAN costs.

Typically, the corporate goal is to deploy and maintain a single enterprise network even though the network supports disparate applications, organizations, technolo-gies, and user expectations. Consequently, network managers are concerned about providing all users with an appropriate level of service while continuing to support mission-critical applications, and at the same time having the capability to integrate new technologies.

Because the major cost of running a network is related also to WAN circuit charges, network managers must strike the appropriate balance between the capacity and cost of these WAN circuits and the level of service provided to their users.

To meet these challenges, queuing allows network managers to prioritize, reserve, and manage network resources and to ensure the seamless integration and migration of disparate technologies without unnecessary costs.

For example, in Figure 5–2, a priority has been set on the router queue to ensure that IPX traffic has the best access to an overloaded WAN link.

Figure 5–2
A queuing policy can be used to allow certain traffic access to an overloaded interface.

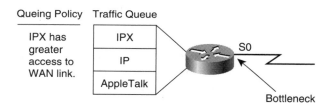

After the need to prioritize traffic has been determined and the queuing policy has been decided and agreed upon, the next step is to determine which queuing option is appropriate for your network.

Choosing a Cisco IOS Queuing Option

Determining the best Cisco IOS queuing option for your traffic needs involves adhering to the following general guidelines (also outlined in Figure 5–3):

1. Determine whether the WAN is congested.

2. If traffic does not back up, there is no need to sort the traffic—it is serviced as it arrives. If the offered load exceeds the transmission capacity for periods of time, however, then there is an opportunity to sort the traffic with one of the Cisco IOS queuing options.

3. Decide whether strict control over traffic prioritization is necessary and whether automatic configuration is acceptable. One option for automatic configuration is *weighted fair queuing*. This queuing method does not require

configuration of queue lists to determine the preferred traffic on a serial interface. Instead, the fair queue algorithm dynamically sorts traffic into messages that are part of a conversation.

Proper queuing configuration is a nontrivial task. To effectively perform this task, the network manager must study the types of traffic using the interface, determine how to distinguish them, and decide their relative priority. This done, the manager must install the filters and test their effect on the traffic. Traffic patterns change over time, so the analysis must be periodically repeated.

4. Establish a queuing policy.

A queuing policy results from the analysis of traffic patterns and the determination of relative traffic priorities discussed in step 2.

5. Determine whether any of the traffic types identified in the traffic pattern analysis can tolerate a delay.

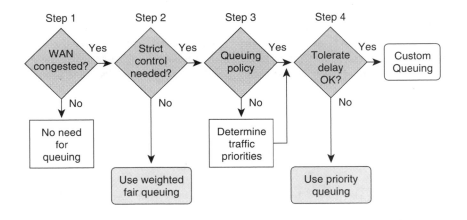

Figure 5–3
Queuing decision flow chart.

For most networks, the default weighted fair queuing is probably appropriate.

Key Concept

Determine whether strict control in necessary in your queuing and whether you want to define specific traffic as higher priority. Also consider the delay tolerance of the protocol that you are prioritizing. For example, perhaps you have a network that supports multiple protocols. The e-mail traffic is running over IPX, but file transfer is being performed over IP. You may want to assign the IP file transfer traffic from one interface as higher priority than the IPX-based e-mail traffic from another interface using priority queuing. If, however, the e-mail communications consistently time out during processing, consider allowing the e-mail traffic to have fair access by using weighted fair queuing.

Primary Differences Between the Queuing Options

The primary distinction between custom queuing and priority queuing is that custom queuing guarantees some level of service to all traffic, whereas priority queuing guarantees that one type of traffic will get through, possibly at the expense of all others. As a result, a low queue can be starved out and never be allowed to transmit if there is a limited amount of available bandwidth or if the transmission frequency of the critical traffic is too high.

Weighted fair queuing differs from priority and custom queuing in several ways. Priority and custom queuing must be explicitly enabled on an interface, whereas weighted fair queuing is enabled by default. Weighted fair queuing does not use queue lists to determine the preferred traffic on a serial interface. Instead, the fair queue algorithm dynamically sorts traffic into messages that are part of a conversation. The messages are queued for low-volume conversations, usually interactive traffic, and are given priority over high-volume, bandwidth-intensive conversations, such as file transfers. When multiple file transfers are occurring, the transfers are given comparable bandwidth.

Table 5–1 shows these queuing options side by side.

Table 5–1
Cisco IOS queuing options.

Weighted Fair Queuing	Priority Queuing	Custom Queuing
No queue lists	4 queues	16 queues
Low volume given priority	High queue serviced first	Round-robin service
Conversation dispatching	Packet dispatching	Threshold dispatching
Interactive traffic gets priority	Critical traffic gets through	Allocation of available bandwidth
File transfer gets balanced access	Designed for low-bandwidth links	Designed for higher-speed, low-bandwidth links
Enabled by default	Must configure	Must configure

The following sections cover the queuing options in detail so you can better understand and choose the right queuing option for your circumstances.

WEIGHTED FAIR QUEUING OVERVIEW

Weighted fair queuing guarantees that high-bandwidth conversations do not consume all bandwidth. Unlike other queuing techniques, weighted fair queuing requires no configuration. Weighted fair queuing is most useful on low-bandwidth serial interfaces.

Weighted fair queuing is an automated method that provides fair bandwidth allocation to all network traffic. Weighted fair queuing provides traffic priority management that dynamically sorts traffic into messages that make up a conversation. Weighted fair queuing then breaks up the "train" of packets within each conversation to ensure that bandwidth is shared fairly between individual conversations.

Weighted fair queuing overcomes an important limitation of FIFO queuing. When FIFO queuing is in effect, traffic is transmitted in the order received without regard for bandwidth consumption or the associated delays, as shown in Figure 5–4. As a result, file transfers and other high-volume network applications often generate series of packets of associated data. These related packets are known as *packet trains*. Packet trains are groups of packets that tend to move together through the network. These packet trains can consume all available bandwidth and starve out other traffic.

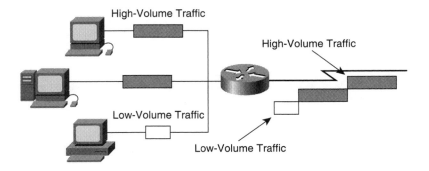

Figure 5–4
FIFO queuing gives the low-volume interactive packet "less fair" bandwidth access and makes it the last member of the data train.

Weighted fair queuing breaks up packet trains to ensure that low-volume traffic is transferred in a timely fashion. Weighted fair queuing gives low-volume traffic, such as telnet sessions, priority over high-volume traffic, such as FTP sessions. It also gives concurrent file transfers balanced use of link capacity.

Weighted fair queuing is enabled by default for physical interfaces with bandwidth less than or equal to 2.048 Mbps and with interfaces that do not use Link Access Procedure, Balanced (LAPB), X.25, compressed PPP, or Synchronous Data Link Control (SDLC) encapsulations. Weighted fair queuing is not an option for these protocols. Because weighted fair queuing gives low-volume traffic priority over high-volume traffic, it is not used on higher bandwidth networks where it could possibly inflict undue restrictions on heavy conversations. Custom queuing was designed for higher speed links.

Weighted Fair Queuing Operation

The weighted fair queuing algorithm arranges traffic into conversations. The discrimination of traffic into conversations is based on packet header addressing. Common conversation discriminators are as follows:

- Source/destination network address

- Source/destination MAC address

- Source/destination port or socket numbers

- Frame Relay data-link connection identifier (DLCI) value

- Quality of service/type of service (QoS/ToS) value

In Figure 5–5, for example, the weighted fair queuing algorithm has identified three conversations.

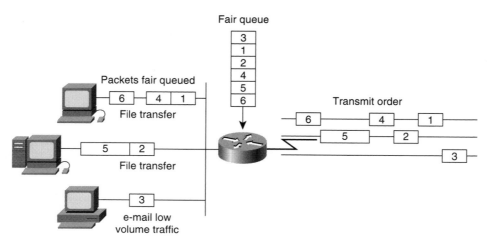

The weighted fair queuing algorithm places packets of the various conversations in the fair queue before transmission. The order of removal from the fair queue is determined by the virtual time of the delivery of the last bit of each arriving packet.

Small, low-volume packets are given priority over large, high-volume conversation packets. After low-volume conversations have been serviced, high-volume conversations share the remaining link capacity fairly and interleave or alternate transmission time slots.

In Figure 5–5, high-volume conversation packets are queued in order of arrival after the low-volume packet. The queuing algorithm ensures the proper amount of bandwidth for each message. With weighted fair queuing, two equal-size file transfers get equal bandwidth, rather than the first file transfer using the majority of the link's capacity.

In Figure 5–5 for example, packet 3 is queued before packets 1 or 2 because packet 3 is a small packet in a low-volume conversation.

The result of the queuing order and the transmission order is that short messages, which do not require much bandwidth, are given priority and the short messages arrive at the other end of the link first.

Weighted fair queuing automatically runs on all low-speed serial interfaces. You can configure the weighted fair queue, as you will see in the next section.

Weighted Fair Queue Example

The **fair-queue** command enables fair queuing on an interface. In Figure 5–6, serial 1 interface is attached to a Frame Relay network and is configured to operate at a 56-kbps link speed. The **fair-queue 128** command sets the congestive-discard-threshold-number to 128.

The congestive-discard-threshold-number is the number of messages creating a congestion threshold after which messages for high-volume traffic are no longer queued. Valid values are 1 to 512 inclusive. The default is 64 messages. The **fair-queue 128** command sets the congestive-discard-threshold-number to 128.

The congestive discard policy applies to only high-volume conversations that have more than one message in the queue. The discard policy tries to control conversations that would monopolize the link. If an individual conversation queue contains more messages than the congestive discard threshold, that conversation will not have any new messages queued until that queue's content drops below one-fourth of the congestive-discard value. In this case, any queue must contain fewer than 32 entries (1/4 of 128).

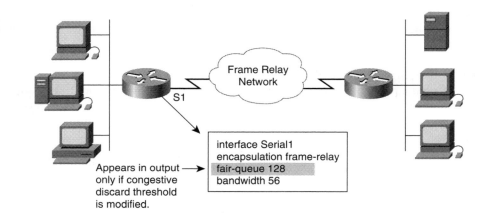

Figure 5–6
A discard threshold is set to ensure no single conversation monopolizes the 56 kbps link.

PRIORITY QUEUING OVERVIEW

Priority queuing is useful in environments in which the network administrator wants strict control over which traffic is forwarded. Before weighted fair queuing, priority queuing was typically used to prioritize interactive traffic (Telnet sessions) over batch traffic (file transfers). Now that weighted fair queuing effectively accomplishes the same task without any configuration, priority queuing is typically used in situations in which it is necessary to guarantee timely delivery of mission-critical traffic.

Priority queuing categorizes and prioritizes datagrams traveling on an interface (see Figure 5–7). Traffic can be assigned to the various queues according to protocol or TCP port number. Priority queuing controls time-sensitive traffic, such as DEC LAT, or mission-critical traffic, such as transaction processing, on low-bandwidth serial links.

A priority list selects traffic for placement into one of the queues. Priority lists are maintained manually and are linked to an interface to participate in priority queuing.

With priority queuing, the high-priority queue is always emptied before the medium-priority queue, and so on. As a result, traffic in lower-priority queues might not get forwarded in a timely manner or get forwarded at all. For this reason, priority queuing provides the network administrator the most control over deciding which traffic gets forwarded.

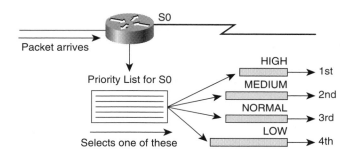

Figure 5–7
Traffic that is given high priority will always be sent before any other traffic.

TIPS

Weighted fair queuing automatically prioritizes traffic to ensure that all traffic is given fair access to bandwidth. Use priority queuing only when you must guarantee that certain types of traffic receive as much of the available bandwidth as is needed.

Priority queuing does not compensate for inadequate bandwidth. Also, this method is appropriate only for low-bandwidth serial lines. The overhead involved makes this queuing strategy unacceptable for higher-speed interfaces such as Ethernet.

Priority Queuing Operation

As shown in Figure 5–8, an incoming packet is compared with the priority list in order to select a queue. After the queue is selected, if there is room, the packet is buffered in memory and waits to be dispatched. If the queue is full, the packet is dropped. For this reason, controlling queue size is an available configuration task.

The timeout decision block on Figure 5–8 is a reminder that some protocols, such as IP, check the Time To Live (TTL) or equivalent fields before dispatching (forwarding) the packet.

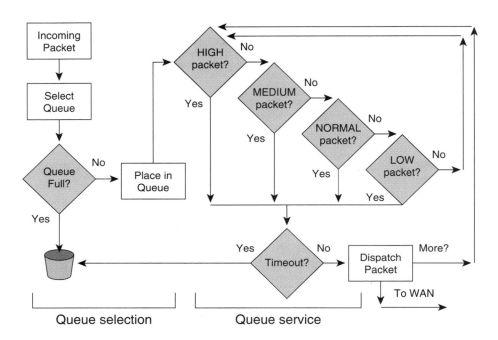

Figure 5–8
*Priority queu-
ing flow chart.*

The queuing process empties the high-priority queue before the queuing software services the medium-priority queue. The *dispatching algorithm* controls this process.
The dispatching algorithm checks a queue for a packet and then dispatches it. Therefore, the high queue must be empty before the medium queue will get any service. As
a result, mission-critical traffic in the high queue is always transmitted before traffic
in other queues.

TIPS

You must configure a default queue for traffic not identified by the priority list.

CAUTION

Be careful when defining the packets that belong in the high queue because packets in
the high queue always are processed first. If the high queue is always filled, packets in
other queues will not have a chance to be transmitted.

Priority Queuing Configuration Tasks

To configure priority queuing, perform the following tasks:

1. Create an output priority queuing list.

A priority list is a set of rules that describes how packets should be assigned to priority queues. You can establish queuing priorities based on the protocol type or based on packets entering from a specific interface. All Cisco-supported protocols are allowed. In Figure 5–9, the priority queue list is TCP (high), IPX and AppleTalk (medium), and IP (normal).

A priority list is like an access list and so only IP traffic that is not carrying TCP will fall through to the normal queue.

2. Assign a default queue.

Remember that you must explicitly assign a queue for those packets that were not specified in the priority list. In Figure 5–9, the default queue is lowest priority. DECnet traffic would be placed in the default queue.

3. Specify the queue sizes. (Optional)

You can specify the maximum number of allowable packets in each queue. In general, it is not recommended that the default queue sizes be changed, unless high-priority traffic monopolizes the link, causing timeouts for other communications.

4. Assign the priority list number to an interface.

Only one list can be assigned per interface. Once assigned, the priority list rules are applied to all traffic that passes through the interface.

Figure 5–9
*Only one pri-
ority list can
be assigned to
an interface.*

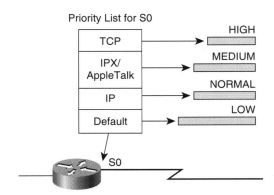

Priority List Configuration Commands

There are five configuration commands used to set up priority queuing on an interface, as follows:

- priority-list protocol

- priority-list interface

- priority-list default

- priority-list queue-limit

- priority group

Each of these commands is explained in more detail in the following sections.

The priority-list protocol Command

Use the **priority-list protocol** command to define a priority list for a protocol, as follows:

```
priority-list list-number protocol protocol-name
    {high | medium | normal | low} queue-keyword keyword-value
```

priority-list protocol Command	Description
list-number	User-specified number from 1 to 16 that identifies the priority list. In Cisco IOS releases prior to 11.2, only 10 priority lists were supported.
protocol-name	Can be **aarp, arp, apollo, appletalk, bridge** (transparent), **clns, clns_es, clns_is, compressed tcp, cmns, decnet, decnet_node, decnet_router-l1, decnet_router-l2, ip, ipx, pad, rsrb, stun, vines, xns,** or **x25.**
queue-keyword and *keyword-value* represent some of the following arguments or keywords:	
byte-count	Can be **gt**—greater than or **lt**—less than.
list	Specifies an access list for IP, AppleTalk, IPX, VINES, XNS, bridging.
tcp/udp	For IP only; can be port number or port name.
fragments	For IP only.

The priority-list interface Command

Use the **priority-list interface** command to set queuing priorities for all traffic arriving on an incoming interface, regardless of protocol, as follows:

```
priority-list list-number interface interface-type interface-number
     {high | medium | normal | low}
```

priority-list interface Command	Description
list-number	User-specified number from 1 to 16 that identifies the priority list
interface-type	Specifies the name of the interface with incoming packets
interface-number	Number of specified interface

The priority-list default Command

Use the **priority-list default** command to assign packets to a queue if no other priority list conditions are met, as follows:

```
priority-list list-number default {high | medium | normal | low}
```

The priority-list queue-limit Command

The **priority-list queue-limit** command changes the default maximum number of packets in each queue, as follows:

```
priority-list list-number queue-limit high-limit medium-limit normal-limit
    low-limit
```

priority-list queue-limit Command	Description
list-number	User-specified number from 1 to 16 that identifies the priority list
queue-limit defaults:	Default number of datagrams
high-limit	Default 20 datagrams
medium-limit	Default 40 datagrams
normal-limit	Default 60 datagrams
low-limit	Default 80 datagrams

In general, it is not a good idea to change the default queue sizes.

CAUTION

The default queue sizes have been carefully considered and are appropriate for the majority of environments. Caution should be used when changing the default queue sizes. Making the high queue limit too large could cause a long burst of high-priority traffic to monopolize the link or could cause delay-sensitive protocols such as DEC LAT to time out if the queuing delay becomes too great.

The priority-group Command

Use the **priority-group** command to link a priority list to an interface, as follows:

`priority-group list`

priority-group Command	Description
list	Arbitrary number from 1 to 16 that identifies the priority list selected by the user

Priority Queuing Example

In the configuration example shown in Figure 5–10, priority-list 1 is defined with the default queue sizes in effect and includes the following settings:

- Telnet (TCP port 23) traffic is assigned to the high-priority queue.

- AppleTalk and IPX traffic are assigned to the medium-priority queue.

- All other IP traffic is assigned to the normal-priority queue.

- All other traffic not specified in priority-list 1 is assigned to the low-priority queue.

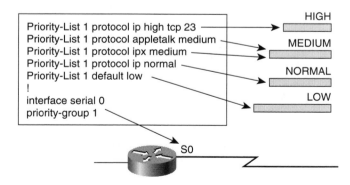

Figure 5–10
Prioritizing traffic by protocol and port number.

Priority-list 1 is linked to interface serial 0 by the **priority-group 1** command.

The order of the steps in the priority list is critical. In addition, it is important to keep the lists short; list processing creates considerable processor overhead.

In this example, interactive telnet traffic is placed in the high queue. All traffic that does not match the priority list filters is placed in the low queue.

In the configuration shown in Figure 5–11, priority-list 2 specifies the following settings:

- Telnet (TCP port 23) traffic is assigned to the high-priority queue.

- Traffic from source network 131.108.0.0 is assigned to the high-priority queue, as specified by access-list 1. The list 1 argument in the second line of the configuration specifies that access-list 1 be used to sort packets for placement in the high-priority queue.

- All traffic arriving from Ethernet interface 0 is assigned to the medium-priority queue.

- All other IP traffic is assigned to the normal-priority queue.

- All other traffic not specified in priority-list 2 is assigned to the low-priority queue.

- Queue-size limits have been changed from the default values to give more bandwidth to the low queue traffic because this network has a management discovery process running on the network periodically:

  o 15 datagrams for the high queue

  o 20 datagrams for the medium queue

  o 20 datagrams for the normal queue

  o 30 datagrams for the low queue maximum

Priority-list 2 is linked to interface serial 0 by the **priority-group 2** command.

In this example, an access list is used to sort mission-critical IP traffic from network 131.108.0.0 and place it in the high-priority queue. Traffic from the Ethernet 0 interface is placed in the medium-priority queue.

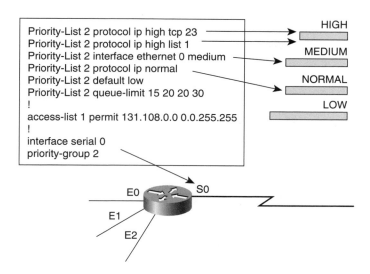

Priority-List 2 protocol ip high tcp 23
Priority-List 2 protocol ip high list 1
Priority-List 2 interface ethernet 0 medium
Priority-List 2 protocol ip normal
Priority-List 2 default low
Priority-List 2 queue-limit 15 20 20 30
!
access-list 1 permit 131.108.0.0 0.0.255.255
!
interface serial 0
priority-group 2

HIGH

MEDIUM

NORMAL

LOW

E0   S0
E1
E2

Figure 5–11
*Prioritizing
data by proto-
col, access list,
and interface.*

Note that, in general, priority list numbers and access list numbers are a different set
of numbers. In the example in Figure 5–11, the priority list uses number 2 and the
access list uses number 1. You can, if desired, use the same list number for both of
these lists.

CUSTOM QUEUING OVERVIEW

Custom queuing and priority queuing use the same filtering method of classifying
packets for placement in queues. Before a packet is placed in a queue, a set of filters
or access list entries is applied to each message. These filters inspect the packet for
attributes such as source, destination, transport protocol, or application to classify
the message. The queuing algorithm then places the packet in the appropriate queue.

Custom queuing and priority queuing use different queuing algorithms at the interface.

Custom queuing lets you guarantee bandwidth for traffic by assigning queue space to
each protocol. Custom queuing eliminates a potential priority queuing problem.
When using priority queuing, it is possible that packets from higher-priority queues
could consume all the available interface bandwidth. As a result, packets in the
lower-priority queues might not get forwarded in a timely manner or at all.

Figure 5–12
*Custom queu-
ing handles its
queues in a
round-robin
fashion.*

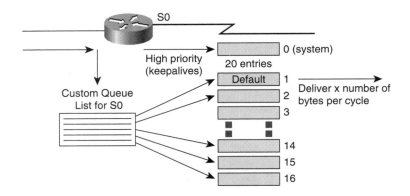

Figure 5–12
Custom queuing handles its queues in a round-robin fashion.

Custom queuing eliminates this problem. With custom queuing, you reserve a certain percentage of bandwidth for each specified class of traffic. You can use custom queuing to allocate bandwidth based on a protocol or source interface.

Using custom queuing, you can use filters to assign types of traffic to 1 of 16 possible queues. The router services each queue sequentially, transmitting a configurable quantity of traffic from each queue before servicing the next queue. As a result, one type of traffic will never monopolize the entire bandwidth. By configuring the number of bytes transmitted from a queue at one time, you can control the percentage of the interface's bandwidth that a queue consumes.

TIPS

Custom queuing is particularly important for time-sensitive protocols such as SNA that require predictable response time.

Queue 0 is a system queue that handles system packets such as keepalives. Queue 0 is emptied before the other custom queues. Specifically, the following traffic uses queue 0 for its time-critical packets:

- ISO IGRP hellos

- ESIS hellos

- ISIS hellos

- DECnet hellos

- SLARP address resolution

- EIGRP hellos

- OSPF hellos

- Router syslog messages

- Spanning tree keepalives

Because these communications are considered low-volume traffic, they would not get much bandwidth share in a priority queuing network. They would be given greater priority in the weighted fair queuing environment, however, because low-volume data receives priority.

Custom Queuing Operation

Custom queuing has the following two components:

- Traffic filtering

  The forwarding application, such as IP, IPX, or AppleTalk, applies a set of filters or access list entries to each message that it forwards. The messages are placed in queues based on the filtering.

- Queued message forwarding

  Custom queuing uses a round-robin dispatching algorithm to forward traffic. Each queue continues to transmit packets until its configured byte limit is reached, as shown in Figure 5–13. When this queue's threshold is reached or the queue is empty, the queuing software services the next queue in sequence.

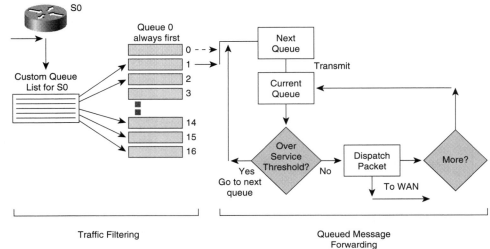

Figure 5–13
*Custom queu-
ing uses a
round-robin
dispatching
algorithm.*

Traffic Filtering   Queued Message
                                                         Forwarding

Custom Queuing Configuration Tasks

To configure custom queuing, perform the following tasks:

1. Set custom queue filtering for a protocol or for an interface.

    You can configure custom queuing to filter for an interface or a protocol. As shown in Figure 5–14, for example, you can do the following:

    - Send all traffic from Token Ring interface 0 to custom queue 1
    - Send all IP traffic to custom queue 2
    - Send all IPX traffic to custom queue 3
    - Send all AppleTalk traffic to custom queue 4

2. Assign a default custom queue. You can assign a queue for those packets that do not match the custom queue filtering.

3. Change the queue capacity. You can designate the maximum number of packets that a queue can contain. (Optional)

4. Configure the transfer rate per queue. To allocate more bandwidth to a protocol's traffic or traffic from an interface, you increase the size of a queue.

5. Assign the custom queue list to an interface. The filters of the queue list are applied to all traffic that passes through the interface.

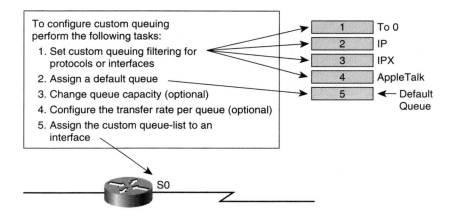

To configure custom queuing perform the following tasks:

1. Set custom queuing filtering for protocols or interfaces
2. Assign a default queue
3. Change queue capacity (optional)
4. Configure the transfer rate per queue (optional)
5. Assign the custom queue-list to an interface

Figure 5–14
Custom queuing configuration tasks.

Custom Queue Configuration Commands

There are six commands used to configure custom queuing:

- **queue-list protocol**

- **queue-list interface**

- **queue-list default**

- **queue-list queue limit**

- **queue-list queue byte-count**

- **custom-queue-list**

Each of these commands is explained in more detail in the following sections.

The queue-list protocol Command

Use the **queue-list protocol** command to specify inclusion of a protocol in a particular queue, as follows:

```
queue-list list-number protocol protocol-name queue-number queue-keyword
    keyword-value
```

queue-list protocol Command	Description
list-number	Number of the queue list from 1 to 16
protocol-name	Required argument that specifies the protocol type; can be **aarp, arp, apollo, appletalk, bridge** (transparent), **clns, clns_es, clns_is, compressed tcp, cmns, decnet, decnet_node, decnet_router-l1, decnet_router-l2, ip, ipx, pad, rsrb, stun, vines, xns,** or **x25**
queue-number	Number of the queue from 1 to 16
queue-keyword keyword-value	**gt, lt, list, tcp,** or **udp,** where **gt** means greater than and **lt** means less than

The **queue-list protocol** command *protocol* options decnet_router-l1 and decnet_router-l2 refer to DECnet level 1 and level 2. These options include the lowercase letter "l" followed by the numeral 1 or 2.

The queue-list interface Command

Use the **queue-list interface** command to establish queuing priorities on incoming interfaces:

```
queue-list list-number interface interface-type interface-number
    queue-number
```

queue-list interface Command	Description
list-number	Number of the queue list from 1 to 16
interface-type	Required argument that specifies the name of the interface

queue-list interface Command	Description
interface-number	Number of the specified interface
queue-number	Number of the queue from 1 to 16

In Cisco IOS Release 11.0, the maximum number of queues that can be used for custom queuing increased from 10 to 16.

The queue-list default Command

Use the **queue-list default** command to assign packets to a queue if no other queue list conditions are met. For example, if you define three queues to handle IP traffic, traffic from Ethernet 0, and traffic that matches an AppleTalk access list defined, what should be done when an IPX packet comes in from interface E1? Use the **queue-list default** command, as follows:

```
queue-list list-number default queue-number
```

queue-list default Command	Description
list-number	Number of the queue list from 1 to 16
queue-number	Number of the queue from 1 to 16

The queue-list queue limit Command

Use the **queue-list queue limit** command to limit the length of a particular queue. The contents of the queue must have already been specified:

```
queue-list list-number queue queue-number limit limit-number
```

queue-list queue limit Command	Description
list-number	Number of the queue list from 1 to 16
queue-number	Number of the queue from 1 to 16
limit-number	Maximum number of packets in a queue at any time. Range is 0 to 32767 entries; default is 20

The queue-list queue byte-count Command

Use the **queue-list queue byte-count** command to set the minimum byte count transferred from a given queue at a time. This value is specified on a per-queue basis:

```
queue-list list-number queue queue-number byte-count byte-count-number
```

queue-list queue byte-count Command	Description
list-number	Number of the queue list (from 1 to 16).
queue-number	Number of the queue (from 1 to 16).
byte-count-number	Specifies the minimum number of bytes the system allows to be delivered from a given queue during a particular cycle. The default is 1500 bytes.

The **queue-list queue byte-count** command sets the threshold of bytes to be transmitted from a queue. If the byte-count value is reached while transmitting a packet, the entire packet is sent. As a result, increasing the byte-count value slightly can result in a significant change to the queue's throughput.

In a situation in which most packets are 1500 bytes or fewer, if you assign three queues of 1600 bytes, 1500 bytes, and 1500 bytes, the throughput of the first queue will be significantly higher than the throughput of the second and third queues because it allows for a greater number of packets to fit into the queue before transmitting.

The custom-queue-list Command

Use the **custom-queue-list** command to link a queue list to an interface, as follows:

```
custom-queue-list list
```

custom-queue-list Command	Description
list	Number of the queue list (from 1 to 16) made available to control the interface's available bandwidth

Custom Queuing Examples

In Figure 5–15, five equal-size custom queues have been configured. These custom queues are assigned to queue list 1.

- Traffic from Ethernet interface 0 is assigned to queue 1.

- IP traffic is sent to queue 2.

- IPX traffic goes to queue 3.

- AppleTalk traffic goes to queue 4.

- Queue 5 is the default queue. Traffic that is not from Ethernet interface 0 or is not IP, IPX, or AppleTalk-based is sent to this queue.

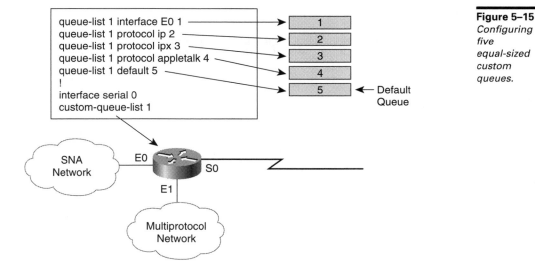

Figure 5–15
Configuring five equal-sized custom queues.

The **custom-queue-list 1** command assigns queue-list 1 to the serial 0 interface.

The next configuration example filters for FTP traffic. A more complex custom queue is also set up. Figure 5–16 illustrates several important custom queuing features.

Figure 5–16
FTP traffic (port 20) has more bandwidth than other traffic.

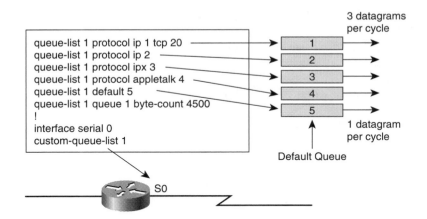

Custom queue lists create a more fair environment for protocol traffic than priority queues.

The configuration example in Figure 5–16 contains different kinds of traffic of varying sizes. The **queue-list 1 queue 1 byte-count 4500** command establishes a maximum byte count of 4500 to queue number 1. The following queue lists are set up:

- FTP traffic (TCP port 20) is assigned to queue 1.

  The **queue-list 1 protocol ip 1 tcp 20** command designates FTP data traffic by identifying TCP port 20.
- Non-FTP IP traffic is assigned to queue 2.

- IPX traffic is assigned to queue 3.

- AppleTalk traffic is assigned to queue 4.

- All other traffic is assigned to queue 5.

- FTP traffic receives more bandwidth.

The **queue-list 1 queue 1 byte-count 4500** command in Figure 5–16 allocates 4500 bytes to queue 1. This command increases queue 1's transfer capacity from the default of 1500 bytes to 4500 bytes. As a result, FTP traffic is allocated more bandwidth than any other type of traffic.

VERIFYING QUEUING OPERATION

The **show interfaces** and **show queueing** commands are helpful in monitoring queuing configuration and operation. Use the **show queueing** command to display detailed queuing information about all interfaces when fair queuing is enabled.

In the following configuration, for example, there are two active conversations (117 and 155) on interface Serial0. The **show queueing** command displays queuing status on all interfaces:

```
Router#  show queueing
Current fair queue configuration:
Interface Serial 0

    Input queue: 0/75/0 (size/max/drops); Total output drops: 0
    Output queue: 18/64/30 (size/threshold/drops)
      Conversations 2/8 (active/max active)
      Reserved Conversations 0/0 (allocated/max allocated)

      (depth/weight/discards) 3/4096/30
    Conversation 177, linktype: ip, length: 556, flags: 0x280
    source: 172.16.128.155, destination: 172.16.58.89, id: 0x1069, ttl: 59,
    TOS: 0 prot: 6, source port 514, destination port 1022

(depth/weight/discards) 14/4096/0
    Conversation 155, linktype: ip, length: 1504, flags: 0x280
    source: 172.16.128.155, destination: 172.16.58.89, id: 0x104D, ttl: 59,
    TOS: 0 prot: 6, source port 20, destination port 1554
```

You can also use the **show interfaces** command to display queuing information for the router's interfaces. (Note that the word "queuing" is spelled "queueing" in the commands and spelled "queuing" in the text.) Use the **show queueing custom** command to display custom queue information.

In the following configuration, custom queue list 3 information is displayed. The **show queueing custom** command displays information for custom queue list 3.

```
Router#  show queueing custom
Current custom queue configuration:
List   Queue   Args
3      5       default
3      1       interface Serial 3
3      3       protocol ip
3      3       byte-count 1518
```

The current custom queue configuration options are defined as follows:

Queue	Args	Description
5	default	Defines the default queue.
1	interface Serial 3	All traffic for interface Serial 3 is sent to queue 1.
3	protocol ip	IP traffic is sent to queue 3.
3	byte-count 1518	Specifies the minimum number of bytes delivered from queue 3 during a single cycle.

You can use the **show queueing priority** command to display priority queuing information and use the **show queueing fair** command to display weighted fair queuing information.

SUMMARY

In this chapter, you learned how traffic prioritization (or queuing) can preserve precious WAN bandwidth and ensure equal access to the network to support time-dependent applications. *Queuing* is the process of allowing certain traffic to be delivered before others. You learned the difference between weighted fair queuing, priority queuing, and custom queuing. Each is a valid queuing method, and which one you use depends on the needs and characteristics of your network, as you have learned.

In Chapter 6, "Routing Protocol Overview," you learn the underlying technologies used by various routing protocols, including learning the difference between distance vector and link state routing protocols.

Chapter Five Test
Configuring Queuing to Manage Traffic

Estimated Time: 15 minutes

Complete all the exercises to test your knowledge of the materials contained in this chapter. Answers are listed in Appendix A, "Chapter Test Answer Key."

Use your understanding of queuing to indicate whether the following statements are true or false.

Question 5.1

T   F   If your WAN link is congested, implementing a queuing strategy will always resolve the problem.

Question 5.2

T   F   You may need to give interactive traffic higher priority to ensure Telnet sessions receive adequate throughput.

Question 5.3

T   F   Prioritization is most effective on WAN links T1/E1 and above.

Question 5.4

T   F   Cisco IOS software supports priority and custom queuing.

Question 5.5

T   F   The fair queue algorithm dynamically prioritizes traffic by assigning different amounts of queue space to different protocols.

Question 5.6

T   F   Weighted fair queuing normally gives bandwidth-intensive traffic, such as file transfers, priority over interactive traffic.

Question 5.7

T   F   By default, weighted fair queuing is enabled on T1/E1 or slower interfaces.

Question 5.8

T   F   The discrimination of traffic into conversations is based on access list filtering.

Question 5.9

T   F   With weighted fair queuing, two equal-size file transfers get equal bandwidth.

Question 5.10

T   F   By default, the weighted fair queuing congestion threshold is 512.

Question 5.11

T   F   Custom queuing allows for up to 16 queues.

Question 5.12

T   F   Priority queuing was designed for low-bandwidth links.

Question 5.13

T   F   Custom queuing is enabled by default.

PART 3

Configuring Scalable
Routing Protocols

Routing Protocol Overview

In this chapter, you learn the key information that routers must have in order to route data. You also learn the difference between distance vector and link state routing protocols. A solid understanding of routing procedures and options enables you to select the most appropriate routing protocol for your network and configure the router for best performance.

WHAT IS ROUTING?

Routing is the process by which a packet gets from one network to another. To be able to route anything successfully across a network, a router needs to know the following key information:

- The *destination* of the packet that needs to be routed.

- A routing entry for that destination. (This can include unknown "default" route.)

The routing entry information is gathered using a *routing protocol*. A routing protocol gathers information about available networks and the distance, or cost, to reach those networks. Further, each routing protocol uses a slightly different mechanism to obtain this information. Nevertheless, the goal is the same.

This chapter discusses routing protocols in the context of how they operate to provide a router the key information listed previously. In this way, you should be able to better compare routing protocols and their application in your networking environment.

COMPARING ROUTING PROTOCOLS

Although there are numerous routing protocols, such as RIP, OSPF, IS-IS, and NLSP, they can all be classified under one of two categories, as shown in the following table.

Category	Routing Protocol
Distance vector routing protocols	IP RIP, IPX RIP, AppleTalk RTMP, IGRP
Link-state routing protocols	IP OSPF, IPX NLSP, IS-IS

Although these protocols operate slightly differently, the mechanisms they use for learning and selecting paths, for example, have their origin in either distance vector or link-state routing. *Distance-vector protocols*, the simpler of the two, were written first and designed for use in smaller network environments. *Link-state protocols* were created as a result of growing networks in order to address the limitations that distance vector protocols have when used in larger internetworks.

Distance vector routing protocols maintain a list of the distance to another network in hops (number of routers crossed). They consider all networks further than 15 hops away as too far. Link state routing protocols use a link-speed-based metric to define the distance to another network. Each link state router maintains a map of the entire internetwork, allowing it to see alternate routes or parallel paths for load balancing. For more information on distance vector and link state routing protocols, refer to *Introduction to Cisco Routing Configuration* by Cisco Press.

Key Concept   To be able to route anything, a router needs to know the following key information: the final *destination* of the information that needs to be routed, the *source* from which the router learned the paths to given destinations, possible *routes*, or paths, to intended destinations, and the *best path(s)* to the intended destinations.

The following sections discuss the differences in how each routing protocol category obtains the following key information for a router:

- Identifying neighbors

- Discovering routes

- Selecting a route

- Maintaining routing information

Using Convergence

In networks with few routers, routers can *converge* (obtain common routing information) in a reasonable amount of time, even though a downed router is not detected quickly. The delay in detecting a downed router in a large network, however, can be disastrous.

Whenever a network is not converged, there is network downtime. Two situations can cause a network to lose convergence:

- A change in the status of a router

- A change in the status of a link

Distance vector protocols have no way of detecting their neighbors. They detect changes only when three consecutive routing updates have been missed concerning a specific route. Link-state protocols detect neighbors via hello packets. Link-state protocols detect changes via both link-state advertisement packets and hello packets.

To make sure a downed router is located quickly in a large network, link-state protocols include a process for identifying neighbors and verifying periodically that the neighbors exist (see Figure 6–1).

Figure 6–1
Link-state routers send "hello" packets to establish links with neighbor link state routers.

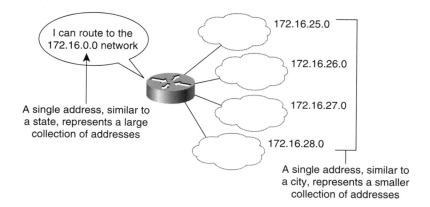

The key differences in how distance vector and link-state protocols identify neighbors are as follows:

Distance Vector	Link-State
Does not have a formal way of learning about neighbors.	Establishes a formal connection (link-state) with each directly connected neighbor. This is done using the Hello protocol, which is shown in Figure 6–2.
Detects when a network is unavailable only when the routing update is missing for a specific period of time (typically three times the update interval).	Detects when a neighbor is unavailable when three hellos in a row are not received (the *dead interval*).

Discovering Routes

In networks with few routers, distance vector protocols can send periodic updates and still maintain acceptable convergence times. Further, sending out the entire routing table in a small internetwork does not use much overhead. Consider, however, an internetwork with 100 routers. What would happen if each router sent out its entire routing table?

To reduce traffic overhead, link-state routers send information for specific links, not their entire link-state table. In addition, because the link-state information is received firsthand by each router, there is less chance for routing errors to be propagated throughout the network.

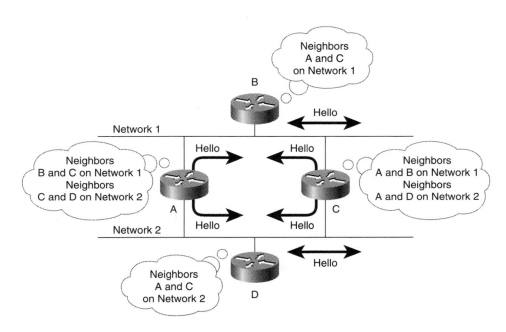

Figure 6–2
Link-state routers build a forwarding table by initially listing all available routes to all known networks.

Link-state routers build a forwarding table based on their picture of the network and the best paths determined to each network in the internetwork.

The key differences in how distance vector and link-state protocols discover the network are as follows:

Distance Vector	Link-State
Each router creates a routing table that includes its directly connected networks and sends the routing table to its directly connected neighbors. The routing table sent out by distance vector routers follows the split horizon algorithm.	Each router creates a link-state table that includes entries about the entire network. In Figure 6–3, for example, Router 1 builds its table by determining what route(s) it has to each network and selecting the best route as the preferred path.
The neighbor incorporates all received routing tables into its own routing table and sends the updated routing table to its neighbors.	Each router floods the entire internetwork with information about the links it knows about in update packets.

Distance Vector	Link-State
	Each neighboring router receives the update packet, copies the contents, and continues sending it. Note that the router does not recalculate its routing table before sending the entry to its neighbors.

Selecting a Route

The key differences in how distance vector and link-state protocols select the best path to a destination in the internetwork are as follows:

Distance Vector	Link-State
The typical metric used is to count the number of routers (hops) on the path to the destination. IPX RIP also uses a time value called a *tick (1/18th of a second)*.	The metric used is a numerical value based on the bandwidth of the link. The value is called *cost*.
The path with the lowest number of hops is the best path. The maximum number of hops is typically 15.	The path with the lowest total cost is the best path. The maximum possible cost is almost unlimited.
To determine the shortest path, the Bellman-Ford algorithm is used.	The algorithm used to determine the lowest cost is the shortest path first (SPF) algorithm.
The routing table can include multiple equal cost routes to a given destination. These can be used for load balancing or redundancy.	The routing table can include multiple equal cost routes to a given destination. These can be used for load balancing or redundancy.

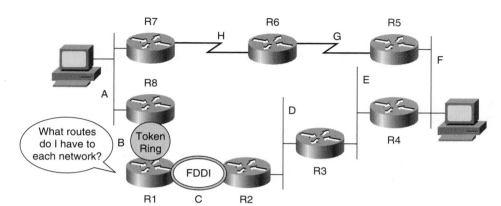

Figure 6–3
Link-state routers use a metric (typically based on available bandwidth) to determine the best path to another network.

TIPS

IGRP is an exception to the rule explained previously because it is a distance vector protocol and it takes into account bandwidth and delay when figuring the best path to a network.

Maintaining Routing Information

In a small network using a distance vector protocol, neighboring routers exchange their route information at a periodic interval, which is acceptable because a small network does not typically have much route information. In contrast, routers in large networks must manage large amounts of routing information. Exchanging large routing tables periodically could bring down a network and not allow any data traffic to flow. Link-state protocols address this issue.

The key differences in how distance vector and link-state protocols maintain routes are defined in the following table. This table defines only the basic functionality of a link-state routing protocol. For greater detail, refer to Chapter 8, "Configuring OSPF in a Single Area."

Distance Vector	Link-State
When a router learns about a change in the internetwork, the router updates its routing table with the change. This change is propagated when the router broadcasts its periodic update.	When a router learns about a change in the internetwork, it updates its link-state table and sends an update only about changed entries to all routers in the internetwork.
Neighboring routers incorporate the received routing information into their routing table (including the new information). When their next update process occurs, they broadcast this new information along with the other entries in their tables.	Each router receives the update and adds it to the link-state table.
This process continues until all routers converge.	The routers then run the SPF algorithm to select the best paths.
If there is no change in the internetwork at a periodic interval (usually 60 seconds), each router sends out its routing table to its neighbors.	If no change occurs in the internetwork, the routers will send updates only for those route entries that have not been updated periodically—from 30 minutes to two hours—depending on the routing protocol.

SUMMARY

In this chapter, you learned the key differences between distance vector and link-state routing protocols. Recall that *routing* is the process by which a packet gets from one network to another. A routing protocol, however, is used to build routing tables necessary to make the correct forwarding decisions. You also learned about the type of information received from these protocols used by network routers. Recall that distance vector protocols only know the next hop to a destination, whereas link state protocols have a map of the entire internetwork and can balance between multiple paths and identify invalid paths more quickly than distance vector protocols.

In Chapter 7, "Extending IP Addresses Using VLSMs," you learn how you can extend available IP addresses by changing the length of the network and host portion to allow for a subnetwork address.

Chapter Six Test
Routing Protocol Overview

Estimated Time: 15 minutes

Complete all the exercises to test your knowledge of the materials contained in this chapter. Answers are listed in Appendix A, "Chapter Test Answer Key."

Objective: List the key information routers need to route data.

Objective: Compare distance vector and link-state protocol operation.

Question 6.1

List the five pieces of information that a router needs to route traffic successfully across a network.

A. _____

B. _____

C. _____

D. _____

E. _____

Question 6.2

In the line to the left of each statement, identify the routing protocol by placing a *DV* for distance vector or *LS* for link-state. If a sentence describes more than one routing protocol, identify all protocols that apply.

A. _____ Sends out updates when network changes occur.

B. _____ The simplest routing protocol to configure.

C. _____ RIP and RTMP are examples of this routing protocol.

D. _____ OSPF is an example of this protocol.

E. _____ Learns about neighbors to ensure bidirectional communication.

F. _____ Some implementations of this protocol determine the best path by using the lowest hop count.

G. _____ Uses the shortest path first algorithm.

7

Extending IP Addresses Using VLSMs (Variable-Length Subnet Masks)

This chapter discusses the key components related to IP addressing, including variable-length subnet masks and route summarization. The content in this chapter is a prerequisite to understanding how to reduce routing table entries and the amount of route updates issued by routing protocols, such as OSPF (Open Shortest Path First). Knowing these IP addressing techniques enables you to define an appropriate IP address scheme for your network.

IP ADDRESS ISSUES AND SOLUTIONS

When IP addressing was first defined in 1981, it was designed as a 32-bit number that had two components: a network address and a node (host) address. Classes of addresses were also defined: class A, B, and C, and later classes D and E. Since then, the growth of the Internet has been incredible. Following are two addressing issues that have resulted from this explosion:

- *IP address exhaustion*—This is due largely to the random allocation of IP addresses by the NIC (Network Information Center). It is also due to the fact that not all IP classes are suitable for a typical network topology, as you will see later in this chapter.

- *Routing table growth and manageability*—One source indicates that in 1990 only about 5,000 routes needed to be tracked in order to use the Internet. By 1995, this number had grown to 35,000 routes. In addition to the exponential growth of the Internet, the random assignment of IP addresses throughout the world has also contributed to the exponential growth of routing tables.

IPv6 (the next-generation IP) responds to these problems by introducing a 128-bit address. In the meantime, RFCs (Requests for Comment) have been introduced to enable the current IP addressing scheme to be organized in a hierarchical manner. One particularly effective method of combating these problems is by using addressing hierarchies, as described in the next section.

Using Addressing Hierarchies

What is an addressing hierarchy, and why do you want to have it?

Perhaps the best known addressing hierarchy is the telephone network. The telephone network uses a hierarchical numbering scheme that includes country codes, area codes, and local exchange numbers, as shown in Figure 7–1. For example, if you are in San Jose, California, and call someone else in San Jose, then you dial the San Jose local exchange number, 528, and the person's telephone number, 7777. The central office, upon seeing the number 528, recognizes that the destination telephone is within its area so it looks for number 7777 and transfers the call.

Figure 7–1
Telephone number hierarchy.

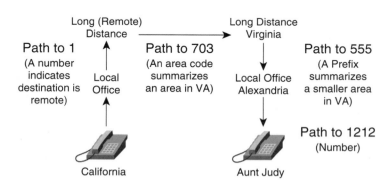

To call Aunt Judy in Alexandria, Virginia, from San Jose, dial the area code, 703, the Alexandria prefix, 555, and then Aunt Judy's local number, 1212. The central office first looks up number 703 and determines that it is not in its local area. The central office immediately routes the call to a central office in Alexandria. The San Jose central office does not know where 555-1212 is, nor does it have to. It only needs to know the area codes, which summarize the local telephone numbers within an area.

If there were no hierarchical structure, every central office would need to have every telephone number, worldwide, in its locator table. With a simple hierarchical addressing scheme, the central office uses country codes and area codes to determine how to route a call to its destination. A summary number (address) represents a group of numbers. For example, an area code, such as 408, is a summary number for the San Jose area. That is, if you dial 408 from anywhere in the United States, and then a seven-digit telephone number, the central office will route the call to a San Jose central office. This is the kind of addressing strategy that the Internet gurus are trying to work toward, and that you as a network administrator should implement in your own internetwork.

The benefits of hierarchical addressing are twofold:

- *Efficient allocation of addresses*—Hierarchical addressing enables one to optimize the use of the available addresses. because you group them contiguously. With random address assignment, you may end up wasting groups of addresses because of addressing conflicts.

- *Reduced number of routing table entries*—Whether it is with your Internet routers, or your internal routers, you should try to keep your routing tables as small as possible by using *route summarization*. Route summarization is a way of having a single IP address represent a collection of IP addresses when you employ a hierarchical addressing plan. By summarizing routes, you can keep your routing table entries manageable, which means the following:

  ○ More efficient routing

  ○ Reduced number of CPU cycles when recalculating a routing table, or when sorting through the routing table entries to find a match

  ○ Reduced router memory requirements

Slowing IP Address Depletion

Since the 1980s, several solutions have been developed to slow the depletion of IP addresses and to reduce the number of Internet route table entries by enabling more hierarchical layers in an IP address. The solutions discussed in this chapter are as follows:

- *Subnet Masking*—RFC 950 (1985); 1812 (1995). Developed to add another level of hierarchy to an IP address. This additional level allows for extending the number of network addresses derived from a single IP address. (Discussed in *Introduction to Cisco Router Configuration*, ISBN: 1-57870-076-0, by Cisco Press.)

- *Variable-Length Subnet Masks*—RFC 1009 (1987). Developed to allow the network designer to utilize multiple address schemes within a given class of address. This strategy can be used only when it is supported by the routing protocol, such as OSPF and EIGRP.

- *Address Allocation for Private Internets*—RFC 1918 (1996). Developed for organizations that do not need much access to the Internet. The only reason to have a NIC-assigned IP address is to interconnect to the Internet. Any and all companies can use the privately assigned IP addresses within the organization, rather than using a NIC-assigned IP address unnecessarily.

- *Network Address Translation*—RFC 1631 (1994). Developed for those companies that use private addressing or use non-NIC-assigned IP addresses. This strategy enables an organization to access the Internet with a NIC-assigned address without having to reassign the private or "illegal" addresses that are already in place.

- *Classless Inter-Domain Routing (CIDR)*—RFCs 1518 and 1519 (1993). This is another method used for and developed for ISPs. This strategy suggests that the remaining IP addresses be allocated to ISPs in contiguous blocks, with geography being a consideration.

Key Concept | Hierarchical addressing allows for efficient allocation of addresses and reduced number of routing table entries.

VARIABLE-LENGTH SUBNET MASKS

If you do not fully understand IP addressing and subnet masking, refer to *Introduction to Cisco Router Configuration* by Cisco Press (ISBN: 1-57870-076-0). Chapter 9, "IP Addressing," details how to establish IP addresses.

This section explains VLSMs in detail and gives an example of a VLSM.

Variable-Length Subnet Mask Overview

VLSMs (Variable-Length Subnet Masks) provide the capability to include more than one subnet mask within a class-based address, and the capability to subnet an already subnetted network address. VLSMs do this by using a portion of the host address space as a subnet address. The term *variable* is used because the subnet address field can be variable length, such as two bits, three bits, or four bits, as opposed to using a full byte for the subnet. These capabilities offer the following two benefits:

- *Even more efficient use of IP addresses*—Without the use of VLSMs, companies are locked into implementing a single subnet within a NIC number in the entire network. With VLSMs, you can create a subnet with only two hosts, for example, which is ideal for serial links.

  For example, consider that the 172.16.0.0/16 network address is divided into subnets using 172.16.0.0/24 masking and one of the subnetworks in this range, 172.16.14.0/24, is further divided into smaller subnets with the 172.16.14.0/27 masking (see Figure 7–2). These subnets range from 172.16.14.4 to 172.16.14.252. In Figure 7–2, one of the smaller subnets is further divided with the 172.16.14.128/30 subnet to be used on the WAN links.

- *Greater capability to use route summarization*—VLSMs allow for more hierarchical levels within your addressing plan, and thus allow for better route summarization within routing tables. In Figure 7–2, for example, subnet 172.16.0.0/24 summarizes subnet 172.16.14.0. Subnet 172.16.0.0/24 includes all the addresses that are further subnetted, using VLSMs, from subnets 172.16.14.0/27 and 172.16.14.128/30.

How to use route summarization is discussed in more detail later in this chapter.

Classless and Classful Updates

VLSMs can be used when the routing protocol sends a subnet mask along with each network address. The protocols that support subnet mask information include RIP2, OSPF, Enhanced IGRP, BGP, and IS-IS. Networks running these protocols are called *classless networks* because they are not constrained by the Class A, B, and C designations that indicate the boundary for network and host portions. A prefix identifies the number of bits used for the network portion. This prefix accompanies all routing exchanges.

Figure 7–2
Subnet 172.16.14.0/24 is divided into smaller subnets.

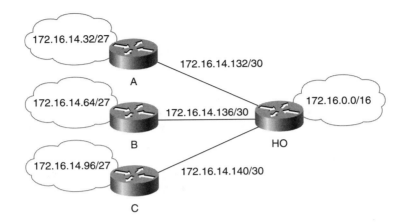

RIP1 and IGRP do not support VLSMs. RIP1 and IGRP networks support only one subnet per network address because routing updates do not have a subnet mask field. As a result, upon receiving a packet, the router does one of the following to determine the network portion of the destination address:

- If the routing update information about the same network number is configured on the receiving interface, the router applies the subnet mask that is configured on the receiving interface.

- If the router receives information about a network address that is not the same as the one configured on the receiving interface, it will apply the default (by class) subnet mask, which is why RIP1 networks are referred to as *classful networks*. RIP1 route updates do not have a subnet mask field.

In Figure 7–3, for example, in the RIP network router B is attached to network 172.5.1.0/24. Therefore, if router B learns about any network that is also a subnet of the 172.5.0.0 network, it will apply the subnet mask configured on its receiving interface (/24).

But notice how router C, which is attached to the 192.168.5.0/24 subnet, handles network address 172.5.2.0. Rather than assigning the network address the correct subnet mask (/24), it applies the default (classful) subnet mask for a Class B network address—172.5.0.0.

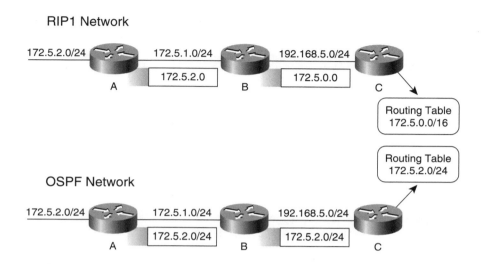

RIP1 Network

Figure 7–3
RIP1 routers cannot exchange network mask information along with route information like RIP2 and OSPF routers can.

It is impossible in this kind of environment to further subnet already subnetted IP addresses without causing confusion. Instead, VLSMs can be used only when the routing protocol sends subnet mask information along with the network address.

Calculating VLSMs

As discussed previously, VLSMs allow you to subnet an already subnetted address. Consider, for example, that you need to assign subnetted address 172.6.32.0/20 to a network that has 10 hosts (allowing 12 bits for the host portion).

With this address, however, you get over 4,000 (2^{12}-2-4094) host addresses, so you would be wasting about 4,000 IP addresses. With VLSM, you can further subnet address 172.6.32.0/20 to give you more network addresses and fewer hosts per network, which would provide more room to grow your network. If, for example, you subnet 172.6.32.0/20 to 172.6.32.0/26, you can now have up to 62 (2^6-2) subnetworks, each of which could support up to 62 (2^6-2) hosts.

VLSMs provide the capability to include more than one subnet mask within a network and the capability to subnet an already subnetted network address.

Key Concept

To further subnet 172.6.32.0/20 to 172.6.32.0/26 and gain five more network addresses, perform the following steps:

1. Write 172.6.32.0 in binary form.

2. Draw a vertical line between the 20th and 21st bits, as shown in Figure 7–4.

3. Draw a vertical line between the 26th and 27th bits, as shown in Figure 7–4.

4. Calculate the five network addresses from lowest to highest in value, as shown in Figure 7–4. If necessary, refer to the IP address calculation tables in Tables 7–1 and 7–2.

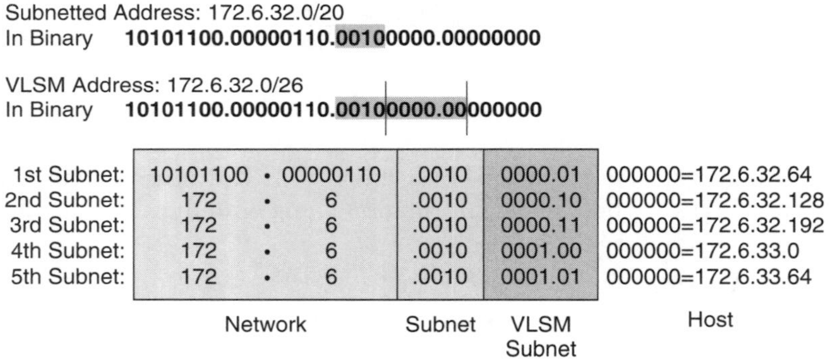

Figure 7–4
Calculating VLSMs may require binary conversions.

Subnetted Address: 172.6.32.0/20
In Binary   **10101100.00000110.0010**0000.00000000

VLSM Address: 172.6.32.0/26
In Binary   **10101100.00000110.0010**0000.00**000000**

	Network		Subnet	VLSM Subnet	Host
1st Subnet:	10101100 · 00000110	.0010	0000.01	000000=172.6.32.64
2nd Subnet:	172 · 6	.0010	0000.10	000000=172.6.32.128
3rd Subnet:	172 · 6	.0010	0000.11	000000=172.6.32.192
4th Subnet:	172 · 6	.0010	0001.00	000000=172.6.33.0
5th Subnet:	172 · 6	.0010	0001.01	000000=172.6.33.64

TIPS

There are also VLSM calculators on the Web. The following URL is for the one offered by Cisco: www.cisco.com/techtools/ip_addr.html.

In Table 7–1, the # Bits column indicates how many bits have been taken from the host address bits from the classful address. For example, the first line indicates that two bits have been masked off from the host address portion to be used as subnet bits. This creates a subnet value of 11000000 in the third byte (which has the decimal equivalent of 192).

The Mask column indicates the mask value in decimal once the subnet bits have been masked off. For example, 255.255.192.0 is the mask for a Class B address that is subnetted using two bits for the subnet portion. The Effective Subnets and Effective Hosts columns indicate how many different network and host numbers can be created with the bits masked off for the network portion and remaining host portion. Network and host numbers using all 1s or all 0s are not counted in these numbers.

# Bits	Mask	Effective Subnets	Effective Hosts	VLSM
2	255.255.192.0	2	16382	/18
3	255.255.224.0	6	8190	/19
4	255.255.240.0	14	4094	/20
5	255.255.248.0	30	2046	/21
6	255.255.252.0	62	1022	/22
7	255.255.254.0	126	510	/23
8	255.255.255.0	254	254	/24
9	255.255.255.128	510	126	/25
10	255.255.255.192	1022	62	/26
11	255.255.255.224	2046	30	/27
12	255.255.255.240	4094	14	/28
13	255.255.255.248	8190	6	/29
14	255.255.255.252	16382	2	/30

Table 7–1
Class B IP address quantities.

Table 7–2 defines the subnet options using a Class B address that typically provides three bytes for the network portion and one byte for the host portion.

# Bits	Mask	Effective Subnets	Effective Hosts
2	255.255.255.192	3	62
3	255.255.255.224	7	30
4	255.255.255.240	15	14
5	255.255.255.248	31	6
6	255.255.255.252	63	2

Table 7–2
Class C IP address quantities.

VLSM Example

Figure 7–5 shows a VLSM example used to optimize the number of possible addresses available for a network. Because point-to-point serial lines require only two host addresses, you want to use a subnetted address that will not waste scarce subnet numbers.

Figure 7–5
A VLSM internetwork.

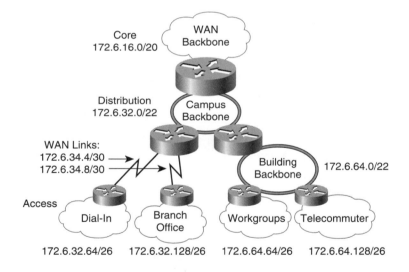

In Figure 7–5, the addresses used are those generated in the earlier section "Calculating VLSMs." Figure 7–5 illustrates where the addresses can be applied, depending on the network layer, and the number of hosts anticipated at each layer. For example, the WAN links use Class B addresses with a prefix of /30. This prefix allows for 16,382 subnets (2^{14}-2) and only two hosts (2^2-2)—just enough hosts for a point-to-point connection between a pair of routers.

ROUTE SUMMARIZATION OVERVIEW

This section discusses what route summarization is and how VLSMs maximize the use of route summarization. The concept of summarization is covered here so that its configuration can be the focus in the protocol-specific chapters that follow.

What Is Route Summarization?

In large internetworks, hundreds or even thousands of network addresses can exist. In these environments, some routers may become overwhelmed. Route summarization, also called *route aggregation* or *supernetting*, reduces the number of routes that a router must maintain because it represents a series of network numbers as a single summary address. In Figure 7–6, for example, you can either send three routing update entries or summarize the addresses into a single network number (172.16.0.0/16).

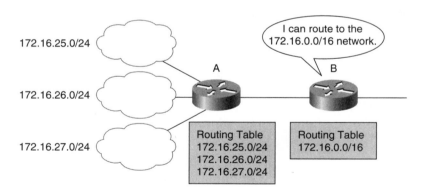

Figure 7–6
Route summa-rization reduces router B's routing table size.

Another advantage to using route summarization in a large, complex network is that it can isolate topology changes from other routers. That is, if a specific link in the 172.16.27.0/24 domain was intermittently failing, the summary route would not change, so no router external to the domain would need to keep modifying its routing table due to this problematic activity.

Route summarization is most effective within a subnetted environment when the network addresses are in contiguous (sequential) blocks in powers of two. For example, consider these two addresses:

- 130.129.0.0

- 130.192.0.0

Both addresses have nine matching bits in the beginning. If you were going to add more network addresses after you've used all numbers possible with these nine bits matching, you can dip into the next bit, the tenth bit, to define another group of addresses.

Routing protocols summarize or aggregate routes based on shared network numbers within the network. RIP2, OSPF, and Enhanced IGRP support route summarization based on subnet addresses, including VLSM addressing.

Summarization is described in RFC 1518, *An Architecture for IP Address Allocation with CIDR*.

Summarizing Within an Octet

Figure 7–6 illustrates a summary route based on a full octet—172.16.25.0/24, 172.16.26.0/24, and 172.16.27.0/24 could be summarized into 172.16.0.0/16. What if a router received updates for the following routes? How would the routes be summarized?

Consider the following list of network addresses:

- 172.108.168.0

- 172.108.169.0

- 172.108.170.0

- 172.108.171.0

- 172.108.172.0

- 172.108.173.0

172.108.168.0 =	10101100 · 01101100 .10101	000 · 00000000
172.108.169.0 =	172 · 108 .10101	001 · 0
172.108.170.0 =	172 · 108 .10101	010 · 0
172.108.171.0 =	172 · 108 .10101	011 · 0
172.108.172.0 =	172 · 108 .10101	100 · 0
172.108.173.0 =	172 · 108 .10101	101 · 0

Number of Common Bits = 21   Noncommon
Summary: 172.108.168.0/21   Bits = 11

Figure 7–7
Find the common subnet bits to summarize routes.

To determine the summary route, the router looks for the most highest-order number of bits that match. Referring to the list of IP addresses in Figure 7–7, the best summary route is 172.108.168.0/21.

To allow the router to aggregate the most number of IP addresses into a single route summary, your IP addressing plan should be hierarchical in nature. This approach is particularly important when using VLSMs, as illustrated in the next section.

In addition, you can summarize when the count is a power of two. The starting octet must be a multiple of the count. For example, you can summarize 8 bits starting with a multiple of 8, or 16 bits starting with a multiple of 16.

Route summarization, also called *route aggregation* or *supernetting*, reduces the number of routes that a router must maintain because it represents a series of network numbers as a single summary address.

Key Concept

Summarizing Addresses in a VLSM-Designed Network

A VLSM design allows for maximum use of IP addresses, as well as more efficient routing update communication when using hierarchical IP addressing. In Figure 7–8, for example, route summarization occurs at the following two levels:

- Router C summarizes two routing updates from networks 172.16.32.64/26 and 172.16.32.128/26 into a single update, 172.16.32.0/24.

- Router A receives three different routing updates, but summarizes them into a single routing update before propagating it to the Internet.

Figure 7-8
*Summariza-
tion can be
performed by
multiple rout-
ers along a
path.*

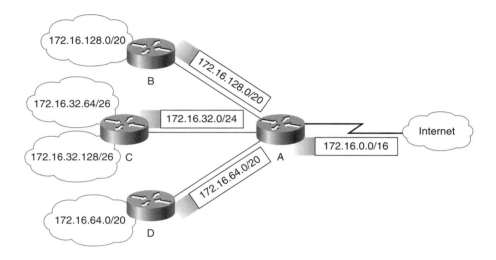

Route Summarization Implementation Considerations

Route summarization reduces memory use on routers and routing-protocol network
traffic. Requirements for summarization to work correctly are as follows:

- Multiple IP addresses must share the same high-order bits.

- Routing tables and protocols must base their routing decisions on a 32-bit IP
  address and prefix length that can be up to 32 bits.

- Routing protocols must carry the prefix length (subnet mask) with the 32-bit
  IP address.

For example, consider the binary equivalent of 172.21.134.0/16 and
172.21.138.0/16, as follows:

```
10101100.00010101.10001000.00000000
10101100.00010101.10001100.00000000
```

You can count the common high order bits at 21 and then summarize these routes as
172.21.134.0/21. The first 21 bits are common between the two addresses. The number "21" is used as the prefix.

Route Summarization Operation in Cisco Routers

This section discusses the generalities of how Cisco routers handle route summarization. Details about how route summarization operates with a specific protocol are discussed in the specific protocol chapter. For example, route summarization for OSPF is discussed in Chapter 9, "Interconnecting Multiple OSPF Areas."

Cisco routers manage route summarization in two ways:

- *Sending route summaries*—Routing information advertised out an interface is automatically summarized at major (classful) network address boundaries only for some protocols, such as IGRP and RIP. A classful network address is a traditional address that has defined standard boundaries. For example, the address 12.0.0.0 is a classful address using the first byte for the network portion (12.0.0.0/8). Specifically, this automatic summarization occurs for those routes whose classful network address differs from the major network address of the interface to which the advertisement is being sent. For protocols such as OSPF, you must configure summarization.

  Route summarization is not always a good solution. You would not want to use route summarization if you needed to advertise all networks across a boundary, such as when you have discontiguous networks (discussed next in this section). Protocols such as EIGRP and RIP2 allow you to disable automatic summarization.

- *Selecting routes from route summaries*—If more than one entry in the routing table matches a particular destination, the longest prefix match in the routing table is used. This is known as "most specific route" in Cisco terms. Several routes may get close to one destination, but the most specific one will always be chosen.

  For example, if a routing table has different paths to 172.168.0.0/16 and to 172.168.5.0/24, packets addressed to 172.168.5.99 would be routed through 172.168.5.0/24 because that address has the longest prefix match.

Summarizing Routes in a Discontiguous Network

Classful routing protocols summarize automatically at network boundaries. This behavior, which cannot be changed with RIP and IGRP, has the following important results:

- Subnets are not advertised to a different major network.

- Discontiguous subnets are not visible to each other.

In Figure 7–9, the 172.16.5.0 255.255.255.0 and 172.16.6.0 255.255.255.0 subnetworks are not advertised by RIP because RIP cannot advertise subnets. Therefore, each router advertises 172.16.0.0, which leads to confusion when routing across network 172.168.14.0 because this network receives routes about 172.16.0.0 from two different directions, so it cannot make a correct routing decision.

Figure 7–9
RIP1 and IGRP do not advertise subnets.

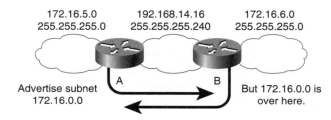

This situation is resolved by RIP2, OSPF, and Enhanced IGRP when summarization is not used because the routes could be advertised with their actual subnet masks.

Advertisements are configurable with OSPF and Enhanced IGRP. Cisco IOS software also provides an IP unnumbered feature that permits noncontiguous (or nonsequential) subnets separated by an unnumbered link. An unnumbered link does not have an address assigned to it.

Key Concept **RIP1 and IGRP do not advertise subnets or support noncontiguous subnets.**

OTHER ADDRESSING CONSIDERATIONS

This section discusses the use of *private IP addresses* (addresses that are not allowed on the public Internet because they are either reserved addresses or previously assigned) and *network address translation* (translation from one IP address to another address).

Using Private Addressing

Some organizations do not need to connect to the Internet, or any other external IP network. In other situations, some organizations may have some hosts or networks that never need to make connections external to their own network. For example, if the arrival and departure display monitors in a large airport are individually addressable via TCP/IP, these displays most likely need not be directly accessible from other networks.

In these cases, you can use private addresses, as defined in RFC 1918, *Address Allocation for Private Internets*. This RFC specifies the following IP addresses as private:

- Class A—10.0.0.0 to 10.255.255.255

- Class B—172.16.0.0 to 172.31.255.255

- Class C—192.168.0.0 to 192.168.255.255

Implementation Considerations

If you decide to use these private addresses, you do not need to coordinate them with the Internet registry because they will never be broadcast external networks. You should, however, do some planning before randomly assigning the addresses. Some implementation considerations are as follows:

- Determine which hosts do not need to have network-layer connectivity to the outside. These hosts are considered private hosts. Private hosts can communicate with all other hosts within your network, both public and private, but they cannot have direct connectivity to external hosts.

- Routers that connect to external networks should be set up with the appropriate packet and routing filters at both ends of the link in order to prevent the leaking of the private IP addresses. You should also filter any private networks from inbound routing information in order to prevent ambiguous routing situations that can occur if routes to the private address space point outside the network.

- Changing a host from private to public will require changing its address, and in most cases, its physical connectivity. In locations where such changes can be foreseen, you might want to configure separate physical media for public and private subnets to make these changes easier.

Note that private addresses can connect to external hosts through a network address translation (NAT) capable device or a proxy device.

Accessing the Internet Using Private Addresses

If a host configured with a private IP address needed to access the Internet or other external hosts, its IP address would need to be reconfigured, and the host device would most likely need to be moved physically to a network that used a public IP address. Reconfiguring and reconnecting an entire network, building, or corporation can be a very costly venture, both in time and resources. To avoid having to renumber all hosts, an RFC—RFC 1631, *The IP Network Address Translator (NAT)*—was defined.

A NAT router or host is placed on the border of a *stub domain* (an internetwork that has a single connection to the Internet—referred to as the inside network) and a public network, such as the Internet (referred to as the outside network). The NAT router translates the internal local addresses into globally unique IP addresses before sending packets to the outside network, as shown in Figure 7–10.

NAT takes advantage of the fact that relatively few hosts in a stub domain communicate outside of the domain at any given time. Because most of the hosts do not communicate outside of their stub domain, only a subset of the IP addresses in a stub domain must be translated into globally unique IP addresses when outside communication is necessary.

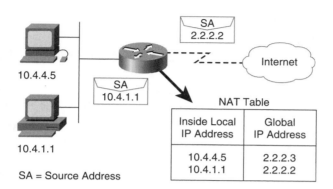

Figure 7–10
A NAT router connects a private network to the Internet.

NAT can also be used when you need to modify your internal addresses because you change ISPs. Rather than renumber your networks, use NAT to translate the appropriate addresses.

The private IP addresses, as defined by RFC 1918, are as follows:

- **Class A—10.0.0.0 to 10.255.255.255**

- **Class B—172.16.0.0 to 172.31.255.255**

- **Class C—192.168.0.0 to 192.168.255.255**

Key Concept

One disadvantage of using NAT, however, is with network management. In order to track NAT activity, you need two network management hosts on either side of the NAT router because the SNMP IP address table does not go through the NAT router correctly.

Translating Inside Local Addresses

Figure 7–11 illustrates one of several NAT (Network Address Translator) capabilities—the capability to translate addresses from inside your network to destinations outside of your network. The steps shown in Figure 7–11 are defined as follows:

1. User at host 10.4.1.1 opens a connection to host B.

2. The first packet that the router receives from 10.4.1.1 causes the router to check its NAT table.

If a translation is found because it has been statically configured, the router continues to step 3.

If no translation is found, the router determines that address 10.4.1.1 must be translated. The router allocates a new address and sets up a translation of the inside local address 10.4.1.1 to a legal global address from the dynamic address pool. This type of translation entry is referred to as a *simple entry*.

3. The router replaces the inside local IP address 10.4.1.1 with the selected inside global address (2.2.2.2) and forwards the packet.

4. Host B receives the packet and responds to 10.4.1.1 using the inside global IP address 2.2.2.2.

5. When the router receives the packet with the inside global IP address of 2.2.2.2, the router performs a NAT table lookup using the inside global address as the reference. The router then translates the address back to 10.4.1.1 and forwards the packet to the host.

6. 10.4.1.1 receives the packet and continues the conversation. For each packet, the router performs steps 2 through 5.

Figure 7–11
The private network address of 10.4.0.0 is never seen on the Internet.

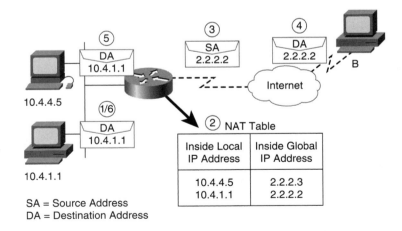

The Cisco IOS Release 11.2 and later supports the following additional NAT features:

- *Static address translation*—Establishes a one-to-one mapping between inside local and global addresses.

- *Dynamic source address translation*—Establishes a dynamic mapping between the inside local and global addresses. Dynamic mapping is done by describing the local addresses to be translated and the pool of addresses from which to allocate global addresses, and associating the two. The router will create translations as needed.

- *Address overloading*—You can conserve addresses in the inside global address pool by allowing source ports in TCP connections or UDP conversations to be translated. When different inside local addresses map to the same inside global address, each inside host's TCP or UDP port numbers are used to distinguish between them.

- *TCP load distribution*—A dynamic form of destination translation can be configured for some outside-to-inside traffic. After a mapping is set up, destination addresses matching an access list are replaced with an address from a rotary pool. Allocation is done on a round-robin basis, and only when a new connection is opened from the outside to the inside. All non-TCP traffic is passed untranslated (unless other translations are in effect).

SUMMARY

In this chapter, you learned how subnet masks, VLSMs, private addressing, and network address translation can enable more efficient use of IP addresses.

You learned that hierarchical addressing allows for efficient allocation of addresses and reduced number of routing table entries. VLSMs, specifically, provide the capability to include more than one subnet mask within a network and the capability to subnet an already subnetted network address. Proper IP addressing is required to ensure the most efficient network communications system.

In the next chapter, you learn how to configure OSPF (Open Shortest Path First) routing.

Chapter Seven Test
Extending IP Addresses Using VLSMs

Estimated Time: 15 minutes

Question 7.1

Using the network in Figure 7–12, indicate where route summarization can occur, and what the summarized address would be by completing the following table.

Figure 7–12
*Where can
route summa-
rization occur
on this
network?*

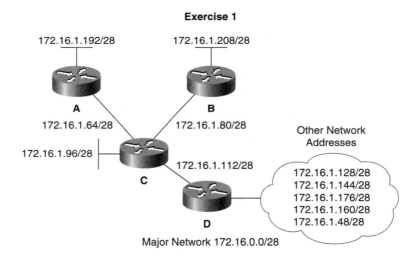

Exercise 1

172.16.1.192/28   172.16.1.208/28

A   B

172.16.1.64/28   172.16.1.80/28   Other Network
                                                 Addresses

172.16.1.96/28

                         172.16.1.112/28

C

                                            172.16.1.128/28
                                            172.16.1.144/28
                                            172.16.1.176/28
D   172.16.1.160/28
                                            172.16.1.48/28

Major Network 172.16.0.0/28

Router C Route Table Entries	Routes That Can Be Advertised to Router D from Router C
172.16.1.64/28	
172.16.1.80/28	
172.16.1.96/28	
172.16.1.192/28	
172.16.1.208/28	
172.16.1.112/28	

Question 7.2

Before implementing private addressing, what should you do?

A. _____

B. _____

C. _____

Question 7.3

What are the private IP addresses, as defined by RFC 1918?

A. _____

B. _____

C. _____

Question 7.4

Provide one example of when NAT can be used.

_____

Configuring OSPF in a Single Area

This chapter covers the use, operation, configuration, and verification of *Open Shortest Path First (OSPF)*. OSPF is a link-state routing protocol that was written for large and growing networks. It allows you to divide a large internetwork into smaller areas. This chapter discusses how OSPF operates within an area and the next chapter, Chapter 9, "Interconnecting Multiple OSPF Areas," discusses how the areas interoperate with each other. This chapter also discusses basic configuration tasks.

OSPF OVERVIEW

OSPF is a link-state technology, as opposed to a distance vector technology such as Routing Information Protocol (RIP). Link-state routers maintain a common picture of the network and exchange link information upon change. Link-state routers do not broadcast their tables periodically, like distance vector routing protocols do. OSPF was developed by the Internet Engineering Task Force (IETF) in 1988. The most recent version, known as OSPF version 2, is described in RFC 2178. OSPF was written to address the needs of large, scaleable internetworks that RIP could not. The issues it addresses are as follows:

- *Speed of convergence*—In large networks, RIP convergence can take several minutes as the routing algorithm goes through a holddown and route-aging period. With OSPF, convergence is faster because routing changes are flooded immediately and computed in parallel.

- *Support for Variable-Length Subnet Masks (VLSMs)*—RIP1 does not support VLSMs. OSPF supports subnet masking and VLSMs. (Note that RIP2 does support VLSMs by exchanging subnet mask information with network information.)

- *Network reachability*—A RIP network that spans more than 15 hops (15 routers) is considered unreachable. OSPF has virtually no reachability limitations.

- *Use of bandwidth*—RIP broadcasts full routing tables to all neighbors every 30 seconds, which is especially problematical over slow WAN links. OSPF multicasts link-state updates and sends the updates only when there is a change in the network.

- *Method for path selection*—RIP has no concept of network delays and link costs. Routing decisions are based purely on hop count, which could lead to suboptimal path selection in cases where a longer path (in terms of hop count) has a higher aggregate link bandwidth and shorter delays. OSPF uses a cost value, which is based on the speed of the connection.

Note that although OSPF was written for large networks, implementing it requires proper design and planning, which is especially important if your network has more than 50 routers. At this size, it is important to configure your network to let OSPF reduce traffic and combine routing information whenever possible.

It is important to understand the unique terms associated with OSPF and link-state routing in general. The following list introduces the various terms that will be used in this chapter and that are shown in Figure 8–1.

- *Link*—An interface on a router.

- *Link-state*—The status of a link between two routers. Also a router's interface and its relationship to its neighboring routers.

- *Cost*—The value assigned to a link. Rather than hops, link-state protocols assign a cost to a link, which is based on the speed of the media.

- *Area*—A collection of networks and routers that has the same area identification. Each router within an area has the same link-state information. A router within an area is called an *internal* router.

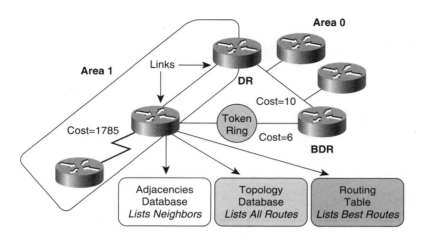

Figure 8–1
The OSPF elements.

- *Designated router (DR) and backup designated router (BDR)*—A router that is elected by all other routers on the same LAN to represent all the routers. Each network has a DR and BDR. These routers have special responsibilities that are discussed later in this chapter.

- *Adjacencies database*—A listing of all the neighbors to which a router has established bidirectional communication.

- *Link-state database* (or *topological database*)—A list of information about all other routers in the internetwork. It shows the internetwork topology. All routers within an area have identical link-state databases.

- *Routing table*—The routing table (also known as the *forwarding database*) generated when an algorithm is run on the link-state database. Each router's routing table is unique.

The OSPF protocol's benefits include no hop count limitation, the capability to multicast routing updates, faster convergence rates, and better path selection.

Key Concept

STEPS TO OSPF OPERATION

An *OSPF area* is a collection of networks and routers that has the same area identification. OSPF operations follow these steps:

Step 1 Establish router adjacencies.

Step 2 Elect a designated router and a backup designated router.

Step 3 Discover routes.

Step 4 Select appropriate routes to use.

Step 5 Maintain routing information.

Key Concept An OSPF area is a collection of networks and routers that has the same area identification.

Each of these steps is detailed in the next sections.

Step 1: Establishing Router Adjacencies

Because OSPF routing is dependent on the status of a link between two routers, neighbor routers must "recognize" each other on the network before they can share information. Neighbor routers are routers that connect to the same network, as shown in Figure 8–2. This process is done using the Hello protocol (part of the OSPF suite of protocols). This protocol enables neighbor routers to establish links (adjacencies) and to ensure bidirectional communication with each other before exchanging link-state information.

Hello packets are sent periodically out of each interface using IP multicast addresses. Multicast addresses are used to send packets to a group of devices. The information contained in a hello packet is as follows:

- *Router ID*—Used to identify a router to OSPF. The dotted-decimal IP address on an active interface is used as the router ID. This identification is important in establishing neighbor relationships and coordinating messages between OSPF routers on the network. Also, the router ID is used to break ties during the DR and BDR election processes if the priority values are equal. (DR and BDR are discussed later.)

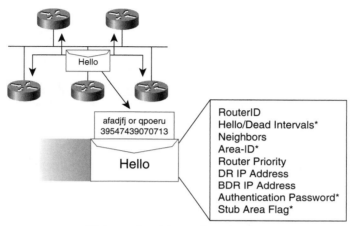

Figure 8–2
*All routers
send hello
packets that
contain router
information.*

- *Hello and dead intervals*—The hello interval specifies the frequency in seconds that a router sends hellos (10-second default on multiaccess networks), as shown in Figure 8–2. The dead interval is the time in seconds that a router waits to hear from a neighbor before declaring the neighbor router down (four times the hello interval by default). These timers must be the same on neighboring routers.

- This hello process also provides quicker detection of failed routers because hellos are exchanged every 10 seconds. Routers expect to hear from their neighbors every 10 seconds. If a router is silent for 40 seconds, its neighbors believe it is down.

- *Neighbors*—The neighbors to which adjacencies have been created. (At the initial startup point, this field is empty because the first router hasn't heard other routers send hellos.)

- *Area-ID*—To communicate, two routers must share a common network segment, have their interfaces belong to the same area on that segment, and also have the same subnet and mask. These routers will all have the same link-state database information.

- *Router Priority*—A value that indicates the priority of this router when selecting a designated DR and BDR. The default priority is 1 and can be configured to a higher number to ensure a router becomes the DR.

- *DR and BDR*—If known, the IP addresses of the DR and BDR for the specific network.

- *Authentication password*—If authentication is enabled, two routers must exchange the same password. Authentication is optional.

- *Stub area flag*—A *stub area* is a special area that has only one router which connects to another area. Stub areas are discussed in Chapter 9. Two routers must agree on the stub area flag in the hello packets.

Neighbor relationships differ based on the types of connection that exist between the routers, as follows:

- *Broadcast multiaccess*—In a typical LAN environment, the DR communicates with all other OSPF routers regarding the LAN network. That router shares learned information with other local routers. Neighbor relationships are formed based on a dynamic learning process using multicast hellos.

- *Point-to-point*—Across a serial connection, for example, neighbor relationships are formed only with the other router on the point-to-point link. Because there are only two routers on this type of connection, no DR or BDR is needed or used.

- *Nonbroadcast multiaccess*—Across a standard Frame Relay network, for example, all routers might not communicate with other OSPF routers because multicasts are not available in a nonbroadcast environment; therefore, neighbor relationships are formed by a manual configuration process.

The exchange process, when all routers are coming up on the network at the same time, uses the Hello protocol. This process is shown in Figure 8–3 and detailed in the following steps:

1. Router A is enabled on the LAN and is in an OSPF *down* state because it has not exchanged information with any other router. Router A sends a hello packet on to the network.

2. All OSPF routers with the IP multicast address enabled receive the hello packet from router A and add router A to their adjacencies database. This is the *Init* state.

3. All routers that received the packet send a unicast reply hello packet to router A with their corresponding information, as listed in step 1. A *unicast packet* is a packet addressed to one specific device on the network. The neighbor field includes all other neighboring routers, including router A.

4. When router A receives these packets, it adds all the routers that had its (router A's) router ID in their packet to its own adjacencies database. This is referred to as the *two-way* state. At this point, all routers that have each other in their adjacencies database have established bidirectional communication.

5. The routers determine who the DR and BDR will be. The DR and BDR election process is described in the next section, "Electing the DR and BDR." This process must occur before routers can begin exchanging link-state information (information about the network topology and routing devices). Link-state exchanges are discussed in the "Discovering Routes" section to follow.

6. Periodically (10 seconds by default), the routers within a network exchange hello packets to ensure communication is still working. The hello updates include the DR router ID and the list of routers whose hello packets have been received by the router sending the hello.

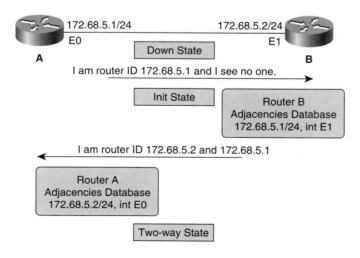

Figure 8–3
Once each router sees the other, they are in the "two-way" state.

Step 2: Electing the DR and BDR

When routers first come up on a network, they perform the hello process, as discussed earlier. In addition, they must elect a DR and BDR (designated router and backup designated router) to build the network entry in the link-state database. The DR and BDR add value to the network in the following ways:

- *Reduce routing update traffic*—The DR and BDR act as a central point of contact for link-state information exchange on a given network; therefore, each router must establish an adjacency with the DR/BDR, as shown in Figure 8–4. Instead of each router exchanging link-state information with every other router on the segment, each router sends information about itself in a link-state format to the DR and BDR. The DR sends each router's link-state information to all other routers in the network. This *flooding* process significantly reduces the router-related traffic on a segment.

- *Manage link-state synchronization*—The DR and BDR ensure that the other routers on the network have the same link-state information about the internetwork. In this way, the number of routing errors is reduced.

Figure 8–4
Each router forms adjacency with DR and BDR.

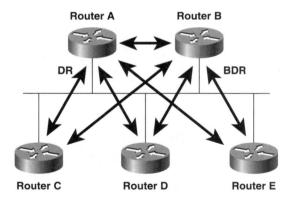

The BDR does not perform any DR functions when the DR is operating. Instead, it receives all information, but allows the DR to perform the forwarding and synchronization tasks. The BDR performs DR tasks only if the DR fails.

To elect a DR and BDR, the routers view each other's priority value during the hello packet exchange process, as shown in Figure 8–5. In Figure 8–5, the priorities are listed as P=x where x is the priority setting. The router with priority 3 is the highest priority number and will become the designated router. The router with the next highest priority (priority 2) is the BDR. Routers with a priority of 0 cannot become a designated router or a backup designated router. The following conditions are used to determine which routers are elected as DR and BDR:

- The router with the highest set priority value is the DR.

- The router with the second highest set priority value is the BDR.

- The default for the interface OSPF priority is 1. In case of a tie, the router's router ID is used as a tie breaker. The router with the highest ID number becomes the DR.

- If a router with a higher priority value is added to the network, the DR and BDR do *not* change. The only time a DR or BDR will change is if one of them goes down. If the DR goes down, the BDR takes over as the DR and a new BDR is elected. If the BDR goes down, a new BDR is elected.

- To determine whether the DR is down, the BDR sets a timer. This is a reliability feature. If the BDR does not hear the DR forwarding *link-state advertisements* (LSAs) before the timer expires, the BDR assumes the DR is out of service.

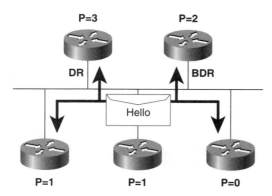

Figure 8–5
Routers with highest OSPF priority are elected DR and BDR.

In a multiaccess environment, each network segment, as shown in Figure 8–5, will have its own DR and BDR. Therefore, a router that is connected to multiple networks can be a DR on one segment and a regular router on another segment. How neighbors are perceived in other network topologies is discussed next.

Step 3: Discovering Routes

After the DR and BDR have been elected, the routers are considered to be in the *Exstart* state, as shown in Figure 8–6. They are ready to discover the link-state information about the internetwork and create their link-state databases.

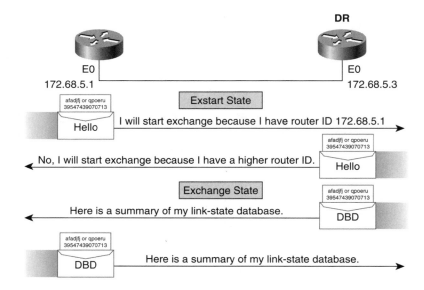

The process used to discover the network routes is called the *exchange protocol*, and is performed to get the routers to a *Full* state of communication. After adjacent routers are in a Full state, they do not redo the exchange protocol unless the Full state changes. The exchange protocol operates as follows:

1. In the Exstart state, the DR and BDR establish adjacencies with each router in the network. During this process, a master-slave relationship is created between each router and its DR/BDR. The router that has the higher router ID acts as the master.

Note that link-state information is exchanged and synchronized only between the DR/BDR and the routers to which they have established adjacencies. Having the DR represent the network in this capacity reduces the amount of routing update traffic.

2. The master and slave routers exchange one or more database description packets (DBDs or DDPs). This is referred to as the *Exchange* state.

A DBD includes the LSA (link-state advertisement) entries that appear in the master router's link-state database. The entries can be about a link or about a network. Each LSA entry includes such things as a link-state type, the address of the advertising router, the cost of the link, and the sequence number. The sequence number is a router's way of determining the "newness" of the received link-state information. The sequence number used by the adjacent routers is the one defined by the master.

3. When the slave router receives the DBD, it does the following:

- Acknowledges the receipt of the DBD by echoing the link-state entry sequence numbers in a link-state acknowledgment (LSAck) packet, as shown in Figure 8–7.

- Compares the information it received with the information it has. Remember that the initial entries put into the link-state database are from the adjacencies database. If the DBD has a more up-to-date link-state entry, then the slave router sends a link-state request (LSR) to the master router.

- The master router responds with the complete information about the requested entry in a link-state update (LSU) packet. Again, the slave router sends an LSAck when the LSU is received. The process of sending LSRs is referred to as the *Loading* state.

4. All routers add the new link-state entries into their link-state database.

5. After all LSRs have been satisfied for a given router, the adjacent routers are considered synchronized and in a Full state. The routers must be in a Full state before they can route traffic. At this point, the routers should all have identical link-state databases.

Step 4: Choosing Routes

After a router has a complete link-state database, it is ready to create its routing table so it can route traffic. Recall that distance vector protocols, such as RIP, select the best route to a destination based on a hop count metric. Distance vector routing protocols use the Bellman-Ford algorithm to determine the routes with the lowest hop count.

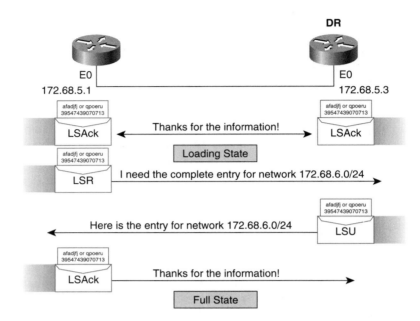

Figure 8–7
Link-state exchanges are used to build the database.

The Bellman-Ford algorithm defines the process by which routers keep routing information to ensure the least cost (based on hop count) path is the preferred path.

Link-state protocols use a cost metric to determine the best path to a destination. The default cost metric is based on media bandwidth. 10-Mbps Ethernet, for example, has a lower cost than a 56-kbps line because 10 Mbps is faster than 56 kbps.

To calculate the lowest cost to a destination, link-state protocols such as OSPF use the Dijkstra algorithm. In simple terms, the algorithm adds up the total costs between the local router (called the root) and each destination network. If there are multiple paths to a destination, the lowest-cost path is preferred. But note that OSPF keeps up to six equal-cost route entries in the routing table for load balancing.

The Dijkstra algorithm (named after its creator, Edsgar Dijkstra) requires the entire network picture to be placed in a "tree" design, with the local router appearing as the root. Touring loops are broken during this process (also known as the spanning tree protocol). The Dijkstra algorithm simply "walks" the tree from the root (local router) to the distant branches (remote networks), adding the costs associated with traversing each link. Paths are compared to ensure the least-cost paths are considered most favorable. Refer to the OSPF version 2 RFC for a detailed description of the Dijkstra algorithm. In Figure 8–8, for example, router A uses this algorithm to select the lowest-cost route to network 3.3.3.0.

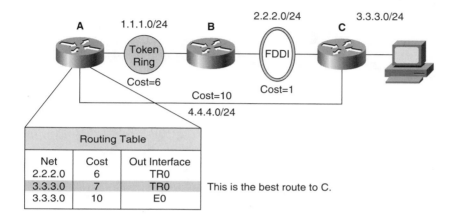

Sometimes a link, such as a serial line, will go up and down rapidly (called *flapping*), or a link-state change may affect another series of links. In these situations, a series of LSUs could be generated, which would cause routers to repeatedly recompute a new routing table. This flapping could be so serious that the routers would never converge (exchange). To minimize this problem, each time an LSU is received, the router waits for a period of time (a *holdtime*) before recalculating its routing table. The **spf holdtime** command was added to the Cisco IOS software to prevent routers from computing a new routing table until 10 seconds (default) after a route change.

Step 5: Maintaining Routing Information

When there is a change in a link-state, the router uses a *flooding* process to notify the other routers in the network of the change. In general, the flooding process is as follows:

1. A router notices a change in a link-state and multicasts an LSU packet that includes the updated LSA entry to 224.0.0.6, the "all OSPF DRs" (and BDR) address.

2. The DR acknowledges the receipt of the change and floods the LSU to others on the network using the OSPF multicast address 224.0.0.5, as shown in Figure 8–9. After receiving the LSU, each router responds to the DR with an LSAck.

Figure 8–9
The DR sends
new link-state
information to
multicast
224.0.0.5.

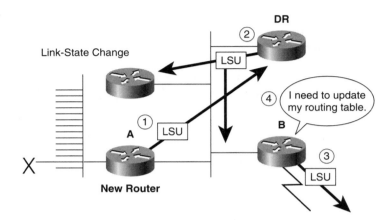

Figure 8–9
The DR sends new link-state information to multicast 224.0.0.5.

3. If a router is connected to another network, it floods the LSU to other networks by forwarding the LSU to the DR of the multi-access network, or adjacent router if in a point-to-point network. The DR, in turn, multicasts the LSU to the other routers in the network.

4. When a router receives the LSU that includes the changed LSU, the router updates its link-state database. It then computes the SPF algorithm with the new database to generate a new routing table. After a short delay, it switches over to the new routing table.

If a route already exists in a Cisco router, the routing table is used as the SPF is calculating. But if the SPF is calculating a new route, the use of the routing table occurs after the SPF calculation is complete.

Each LSA entry has its own aging timer. The default timer value is 30 minutes. After an LSA entry ages, the router that originated the entry sends an LSU to the network to verify that the link is still active. This validation method saves on bandwidth compared to distance vector routers, which frequently send their entire routing table to the broadcast address.

When each router receives the LSU, it does the following (see Figure 8–10):

- If the entry already exists and the received LSU has the same information, it ignores the LSA entry.

- If the entry already exists but the LSU includes new information, it sends an LSAck to the DR, adds the entry to its link-state database, and updates its routing table.

- If the entry already exists but the LSU includes older information, it sends an LSU with its information.

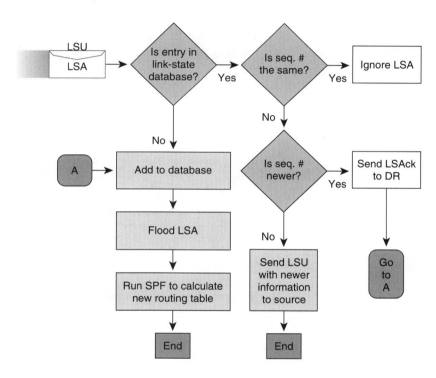

Figure 8–10
All incoming LSAs are examined to see whether they contain more recent link-state database information.

Note that there are different types of LSAs. In this chapter, the LSAs discussed are the *router link LSA*, which is an LSA about a link and its status, and the *network LSA*, which the DR sends out. The network LSA describes all the routers attached to a multiaccess segment. The next chapter discusses other LSA types.

CONFIGURING OSPF ON ROUTERS WITHIN A SINGLE AREA

In this section, you learn how to configure OSPF on routers within a certain area.

Basic Configuration Steps

To configure OSPF, you must enable OSPF on the router and configure the router's network addresses and area information (see Figure 8–11).

Figure 8–11
You can define either a network or an interface address in the OSPF configuration.

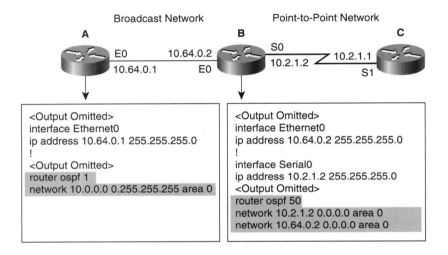

To configure OSPF, perform the following steps:

1. Enable OSPF on the router using the following configuration:

   ```
   router(config)#router ospf process-id
   ```

   process-id is an internally used number to identify when you have multiple OSPF processes running within a single router. The process-id need not match process-ids on other routers. Running multiple OSPF processes on the same router is not recommended because it creates multiple database instances that add extra overhead.

2. Identify IP networks on the router.

   For each network, you must identify the area to which the network belongs. The network value can vary in that it can be the network address supported by the router, or the specific interface addresses configured. The router knows how to interpret the address by comparing the address to the wildcard mask. Use the following configuration:

```
router(config-router)#network address wildcard-mask area area-id
```

network area Command	Description
address	Can be the network address, subnet, or the address of the interface. Instructs router to know which links to advertise, which links to listen to advertisements on, and what networks to advertise.
wildcard-mask	An inverse mask used to determine how to read the *address*. The mask has wildcard bits where 0 is a match and 1 is "don't care"; for example, 0.0.255.255 indicates a match in the first two bytes. If specifying the interface address, use mask 0.0.0.0.
area-id	Specifies the area to be associated with the address. Can be a number or can be similar to an IP address A.B.C.D. For a single area, the ID should equal 0.

Optional Configuration Commands

The following commands can be used to modify OSPF behavior.

• *Modifying the OSPF router ID to a loopback address*:

```
router(config-if)#interface loopback number
```

The highest IP address used as the router ID can be overridden by configuring an IP address on a loopback interface. OSPF is more reliable if a loopback interface is configured because it is always active and cannot go "down" like a real interface. So it is recommended that you use the loopback address on all key routers, at least. If you plan to publish your loopback address with the **network area** command, make sure you use a private IP address. Note that a loopback address requires a different subnet for each router.

Pros and cons exist in using a "made-up" or bogus address as opposed to using real subnet addresses. In addition to reliability, a bogus address saves on real IP addresses, but the address does not appear in the OSPF table, so it cannot be pinged. This decision represents a trade-off between the ease of debugging the network and conservation of address space.

Figure 8–12 shows a router that could be configured using the bogus loopback address of 1.1.1.1 or the real subnet address of 131.108.17.5.

To determine the router ID of a router, type **show ip ospf interface**.

Figure 8–12
The router ID is the number by which the router is known to the OSPF environment.

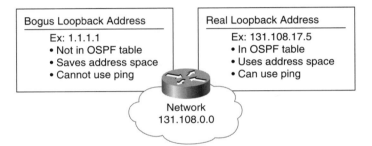

- *Modifying router priority*—Changing the OSPF priority on an interface is accomplished using the following interface command:

```
router(config-if)#ip ospf priority number (from 0 to 255)
```

The default is 1. A priority value of 0 indicates an interface cannot be elected as DR or BDR.

- *Modifying the link cost*—Override the default cost value assigned to an OSPF interface, as follows:

```
router(config-if)#ip ospf cost cost
```

cost—A number from 1 to 65535 that indicates the metric assigned to the interface. Path cost is the total of the costs assigned to all interfaces that forward traffic along the path to the destination.

Cisco's OSPF default cost assignment is based on the bandwidth of the link. Other vendors might use a different mechanism to assign OSPF cost to a link, so you may have to change the default cost because all interfaces connected to the same link must agree on the link's cost.

In general, the path cost in Cisco routers is calculated using the formula $10^8/Bandwidth$. Using this formula, the following are some example default costs:

- 56-kbps serial link. Default cost is 1785.

- T1 (1.544-Mbps serial link). Default cost is 128.

- Ethernet. Default cost is 10.

- 16-Mbps Token Ring. Default cost is 6.

TIPS

On serial lines, the default bandwidth is 1.544 Mbps. If the line is a slower speed, use the **bandwidth** command to specify the real link speed. The cost of the link will then change to correspond to the bandwidth you configured.

VERIFYING OSPF OPERATION

This section discusses common commands used to verify that OSPF operation and router connectivity to other routers is working. You should become familiar with these commands to ensure your routers are configured and performing properly.

You can use the following commands in Table 8–1 to verify OSPF operation and statistics.

Command	Description
show ip protocol	Displays parameters about timers, filters, metrics, networks, and other information for the entire router.
show ip route	Displays the routes known to the router and how they were learned. This is one of the best ways to determine connectivity between the local router and the rest of the internetwork.
show ip ospf interface	Verifies that interfaces have been configured in the intended areas. If no loopback address is specified, the interface with the highest address is taken as the router ID. It also gives the timer intervals including the hello interval and shows the neighbor adjacencies.
show ip ospf	Displays the number of times the shortest path first (SPF) algorithm has been executed. It also shows the link-state update interval, assuming no topological changes have occurred.
show ip ospf neighbor detail	Displays details list of neighbors, their priorities, and their state (for example: init, exstart, or full).
show ip ospf database	Displays the contents of the topological database maintained by the router. The command also shows the router ID and the OSPF process ID. A number of database types can be shown with this command using keywords. Refer to www.cisco.com for details about the keywords.

Table 8–1
OSPF operation and statistics commands.

The following commands and their associated options can be used when trouble-shooting OSPF:

- To reset the IP routing table using the following options:

```
p2r2#clear ip route ?
  *       Delete all routes
  A.B.C.D Destination network route to delete
```

- To debug a variety of OSPF operations using the following debug options:

```
p2r2#debug ip ospf ?
    adj                OSPF adjacency events
    events             OSPF events
    flood              OSPF flooding
    lsa-generation     OSPF lsa generation
    packet             OSPF packets
    retransmission     OSPF retransmission events
    spf                OSPF spf
    tree               OSPF database tree
```

SUMMARY

As you have learned in this chapter, OSPF is a scaleable, standards-based link-state routing protocol. OSPF's benefits include no hop count limitation, the capability to multicast routing updates, faster convergence rates, and better path selection. You learned the basic steps to configuring OSPF in a single area: 1) establish router adjacencies, 2) select a designated router and a backup designated router, 3) discover routes, 4) select appropriate routes to use, and 5) maintain routing information.

In Chapter 9, you will learn how to connect multiple OSPF areas in order to support a larger hierarchical routing environment. It discusses additional OSPF capabilities that you can configure, depending on the size of your network.

Chapter Eight Test
Configuring OSPF in a Single Area

Estimated Time: 15 minutes

Complete all the exercises to test your knowledge of the materials contained in this chapter. Answers are listed in Appendix A, "Chapter Test Answer Key."

Use the information contained in this chapter to answer the following questions.

Question 8.1

List four reasons why OSPF operates better than RIP in a large internetwork.

A. _____

B. _____

C. _____

D. _____

Question 8.2

What does a router do when it receives an LSU?

A. If the entry already exists and the received LSU has the same information:

_____

B. If the entry already exists but the LSU includes new information:

_____

C. If the entry already exists but the LSU includes older information:

_____

Question 8.3

Identify when the exchange protocol and the flooding protocol are used, and describe how each operates.

A. _____

_____

B. _____

_____

Question 8.4

Write a brief description of each of the following:

A. Internal router

_____

B. LSU

_____

C. DDP

_____

D. Hello packet

_____

Question 8.5

Match the term with the statement most closely describing it. Write the letter of the description next to the term.

_____ Area

_____ Full state

_____ DR

_____ Exchange state

A. The router responsible for route synchronization

B. Indicates routers can route information

C. Indicates routers can discover link-state information

D. A collection of routers and networks

Interconnecting Multiple OSPF Areas

This chapter describes OSPF multi-area capabilities, when to use the capabilities, and how to configure the capabilities on a Cisco router. In this chapter, you also learn the issues involved in interconnecting multiple areas and how OSPF addresses each issue, as well as the differences between the possible types of areas, routers, and link state advertisements (LSAs).

CREATING MULTIPLE OSPF AREAS

Thus far, you have seen how OSPF operates within a single area. What issues would arise if this single area ballooned into 400 networks? The issues shown in Figure 9–1, at a minimum, would need to be addressed.

The issues shown in Figure 9–1 are described as follows:

- *Frequent SPF calculations*—With such a large network, network changes are inevitable, so the routers spend many more CPU cycles recalculating the routing table.

- *Large routing table*—Each router needs to maintain at least one entry for every network; that is, at least 400 networks. Assuming also that there are multiple paths to 25 percent of the networks, that adds another 100 entries.

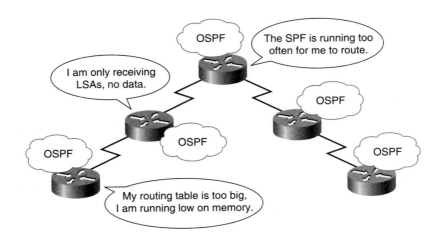

- *Large link-state table*—Because the link-state table includes the complete topology of the network, each router needs to maintain an entry for every network in the area, even routes that are not used, because better routes exist.

It is because of these kinds of issues that OSPF was written. OSPF allows large areas to be separated into smaller, more manageable areas that can still exchange routing information.

OSPF Hierarchical Routing

OSPF's capability to separate a large internetwork into multiple areas is referred to as *hierarchical routing*. Hierarchical routing enables you to separate large internetworks (autonomous system) into smaller internetworks that are called *areas*. With this technique, routing still occurs between the areas (called *inter-area routing*), but many of the minute internal routing operations, such as recalculating the database, are kept within an area. For example, if area 1 shown in Figure 9–2 is having problems with a link going up and down, routers in other areas need not continually run their SPF calculation because they are isolated from the area 1 problem.

The hierarchical topology possibilities of OSPF have several important advantages:

- *Reduced frequency of SPF calculations*—Because detailed route information is kept within each area, it is not necessary to flood all link-state changes to all other areas. Thus, not all routers need to run the SPF calculation, only those affected by the change.

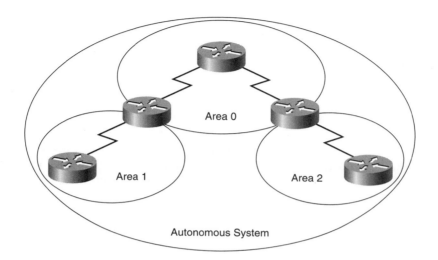

- *Smaller routing tables*—When using multiple areas, detailed route entries for specific networks within an area are kept in the area. Rather than advertising these explicit routes outside the area, you can have the routes summarized into one or more summary addresses. Advertising these summaries reduces the amount of LSAs propagated between areas, but keeps all networks reachable.

- *Reduced LSU overhead*—LSUs can contain a variety of LSA types, including link-state information and summary information. Rather than send an LSU about each network within an area, you can advertise a single or fewer summarized routes between areas to reduce the overhead associated with link-state updates when they are crossing areas.

OSPF Multi-Area Components

Hierarchical routing enables routing efficiency because it allows you to control the types of routing information that you allow in and out of an area. The way OSPF enables different types of routing updates is to assign characteristics to each area and the routers connecting the areas.

The characteristics an area and router have govern how they process routing information, including what types of LSUs a router can create, receive, and send. This subsection provides an overview of the following OSPF multi-area components (details about their usage and configuration appear in the following section):

- Types of areas

- Types of routers

- Types of LSAs

Key Concept The hierarchical topology possibilities of OSPF have three important advantages: reduced frequency of SPF calculations, smaller routing tables, and reduced LSU overhead.

Types of OSPF Routers

To control the traffic types that go in and out of the various types of areas, you need certain types of OSPF routers, as shown in Figure 9–3.

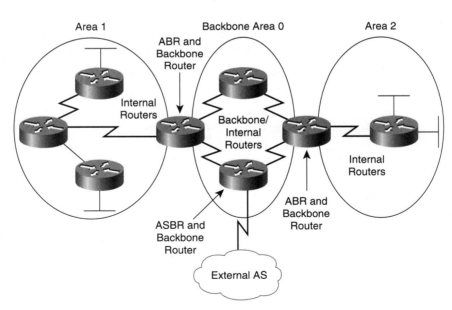

Figure 9–3
Routers can be multiple types.

The router types are as follows:

- *Internal router*—As discussed previously, routers that have all interfaces in the same area are called internal routers. Internal routers within the same area have identical link-state databases and run a single copy of the routing algorithm.

- *Backbone router*—Routers that sit on the perimeter of the backbone area are called backbone routers. They have at least one interface connected to area 0 (the backbone area). These routers maintain OSPF routing information using the same procedures and algorithms as internal routers.

- *Area Border Router (ABR)*—Routers that have interfaces attached to multiple areas. These routers maintain separate link-state databases for each area to which they are connected, and route traffic destined for or arriving from other areas. ABRs are exit points for the area, which means routing information destined for another area can only get there via the local area's ABR. ABRs summarize information from their link-state databases of their attached areas and distribute the information into the backbone. The backbone ABRs then forward the information to all other connected areas. An area can have one or more ABR.

- *Autonomous System Boundary Router (ASBR)*—Routers that have at least one interface into an external internetwork (another autonomous system), such as a non-OSPF network. These routers can import (referred to as redistribution) non-OSPF network information to the OSPF network, and vice-versa.

A router can be more than one router type. For example, if a router interconnects to area 0 and area 1, as well as to a non-OSPF network, it would be both an ABR and ASBR.

Types of Link-State Advertisements (LSAs)

The link-state database can include multiple types of LSAs, as shown in Figure 9–4.

Figure 9–4
*The OSPF
link-state data-
base can
contain multi-
ple entry
types.*

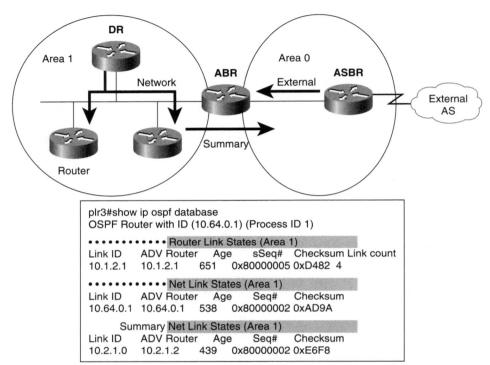

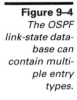

```
plr3#show ip ospf database
OSPF Router with ID (10.64.0.1) (Process ID 1)

• • • • • • • • • • • • Router Link States (Area 1)
Link ID     ADV Router   Age    sSeq#      Checksum Link count
10.1.2.1    10.1.2.1     651    0x80000005 0xD482  4

• • • • • • • • • • • • Net Link States (Area 1)
Link ID     ADV Router   Age    Seq#       Checksum
10.64.0.1   10.64.0.1    538    0x80000002 0xAD9A

         Summary Net Link States (Area 1)
Link ID     ADV Router   Age    Seq#       Checksum
10.2.1.0    10.2.1.2     439    0x80000002 0xE6F8
```

Table 9–1 shows the types of LSAs that can be included in an LSU.

Table 9–1
*Types of
link-state
advertisemen
ts.*

LSA Type	Name	Description
1	Router link entry (record) (O-OSPF)	Generated by each router for each area to which it belongs. It describes the states of the router's link to the area. These are only flooded within a particular area. The link status and cost are two of the descriptors provided.
2	Network link entry (O-OSPF)	Generated by the designated driver in multiaccess networks. They describe the set of routers attached to a particular network. Flooded within the area that contains the network only.

LSA Type	Name	Description
3 or 4	Summary link entry (IA-OSPF Inter area)	Originated by ABRs. Describes the links between the ABR and the internal routers of a local area. These entries are flooded throughout the backbone area to the other ABRs. Type-3 describes routes to networks within the local area and are sent to the backbone area. Type-4 describes reachability to ASBRs. These link entries are not flooded through totally stubby areas.
5	Autonomous system external link entry (E1-OSPF external Type-1) (E2-OSPF external Type-2)	Originated by the ASBR. Describes routes to destinations external to the autonomous system. Flooded throughout an OSPF autonomous system except for stub and totally stubby areas.

Table 9–1
Types of link-state advertisements

Types of Areas

The characteristics you assign to an area control the type of route information it can receive. The area types possible are shown in Figure 9–5 and are described as follows:

- *Standard area*—An area that operates as discussed in Chapter 8, "Configuring OSPF in a Single Area." This area can accept link updates and route summaries.

- *Backbone area*—When interconnecting multiple areas, the backbone area is the central entity to which all other area must connect. The backbone area is always labeled "Area 0." All other areas must connect to this area to exchange and route information. The OSPF backbone area has all the properties of a standard OSPF area.

NOTES

If an area is not directly connected to Area 0 in OSPF, then a virutal link must be established. The "in-between" area used for the virutal link is called a Transit Area.

- *Stub area*—Refers to an area that does not accept information about routes external to the autonomous system (that is, the OSPF internetwork), such as routes from non-OSPF sources. If routers need to route to networks outside the autonomous system, they use a default route. A default route is noted as 0.0.0.0.

- *Totally stubby area*—An area that does not accept external autonomous system (AS) routes and summary routes from other areas internal to the autonomous system. Instead, if the router needs to send a packet to a network external to the area, it sends it using a default route.

Figure 9–5
Each area type has unique characteristics.

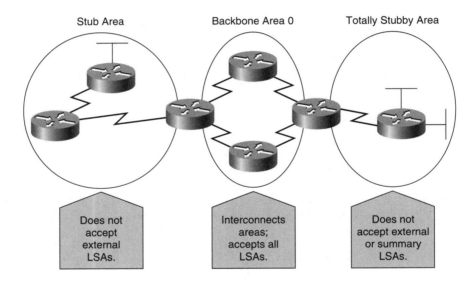

Stub Area   Backbone Area 0   Totally Stubby Area

Does not accept external LSAs.

Interconnects areas; accepts all LSAs.

Does not accept external or summary LSAs.

Configuring OSPF Operation Across Multiple Areas

This section summarizes how routers generate link and flood information, and how they build their routing tables when operating within a multi-area environment.

There are some differences when flooding is used across multiple areas versus its use within an area.

Costs are defined as metric values associated with a link. The cost of a path is determined by adding up the cost to cross each link in a path. Forwarding decisions are based on the cost of each path. Calculation of the cost for summary and external routes is as follows:

Calculating Costs for Summary and External Routes

- Calculating the cost for summary routes

  The cost of a summary route is the smallest cost of a given inter-area route that appears in the summary plus the cost of the ABR link to the backbone. So if the ABR link to the backbone was 50, and the summary router had two inter-area routes, one at cost 49 and the other at cost 50, the total cost associated with the summary route would be 99. This calculation is done automatically for each summary route.

- Calculating the cost for external routes

  The cost of an external route differs depending on the external type configured on the ASBR. You configure the router to generate one of the following external packet types:

  o Type-1 (E1)—If a packet is an E1, then the metric is calculated by adding the external cost to the internal cost of each link the packet crosses. Use this packet type when you have multiple ASBRs advertising a route to the same autonomous system.

  o Type-2 (E2)—If a packet is an E2, then the packet will always have the external cost assigned, no matter where in the area it crosses (this is the default). Use this packet type if only one router is advertising a route to the autonomous system. Type-2 routes are preferred over Type-1 routes unless two same-cost routes exist to the destination.

Figure 9–6 shows the costs calculated by two OSPF networks on the internetwork.

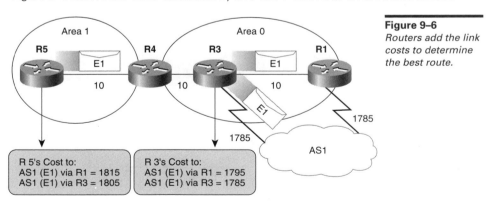

Figure 9–6
Routers add the link costs to determine the best route.

When different routing protocols exchange routing information, it is referred to as *redistribution*. Redistribution is discussed in Chapter 11, "Optimizing Routing Update Operation."

Forwarding Packets in a Multi-Area Network

Before reviewing how ABRs and other router types process route information, you should know how a packet makes its way across multiple areas. In general, the path a packet must take is as follows:

- If the packet is destined for a network within an area, it is forwarded from the internal router through the area to the destination internal router.

- If the packet is destined for a network outside the area, as shown in Figure 9–7, it must go through the following path:

  - The packet goes from the source network to an ABR.

  - The ABR sends the packet through the backbone area to the ABR of the destination network. All packets must cross the backbone when being forwarded from one area to another.

  - The destination ABR then forwards the packet through the area to the destination network.

Figure 9–7
*Inter-area
routing.*

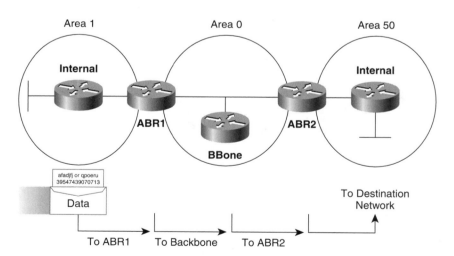

Flooding LSUs to Multiple Areas

ABRs are responsible for generating routing information about each area to which they are connected and flooding the information through the backbone area to the other areas to which they are connected. The general process for flooding is as follows:

1. The intra-area routing processes, as discussed in the previous chapter, occur. Note that the entire intra-area must be synchronized before the ABR can begin sending summary LSAs.

2. The ABR reviews the resulting link-state database and generates summary LSAs.

    By default, the ABR sends summary LSAs for each network that it knows about. To reduce the number of summary LSA entries, you can configure route summarization so a single IP address can represent multiple networks. To use route summarization, your areas need to use contiguous IP addressing, as discussed in Chapter 7, "Extending IP Addresses Using VLSMs." The better your IP address plan, the lower the number of summary LSAs entries an ABR sends to advertise.

3. The summary LSAs (Type-3 and Type-4) are placed in an LSU and distributed through all ABR interfaces, with the following exceptions:

    • If the interface is connected to a neighboring router that is in a state below the exchange state, then the summary LSA is not forwarded.

    • If the interface is connected to a totally stubby area, then the summary LSA is not forwarded.

    • If the summary LSA includes a Type-5 (external) route and the interface is connected to a stub or totally stubby area, then the LSA is not sent to that area (see Figure 9–8).

4. After an ABR or ASBR receives summary LSAs, they add them to their link-state databases, and flood them to their local area. The internal routers then assimilate the information into their databases.

    To reduce the number of route entries internal routers maintain, you can define the area as stub, totally stubby, or not so stubby.

Figure 9–8
*ABRs gener-
ate summary
LSAs for each
network they
know about.*

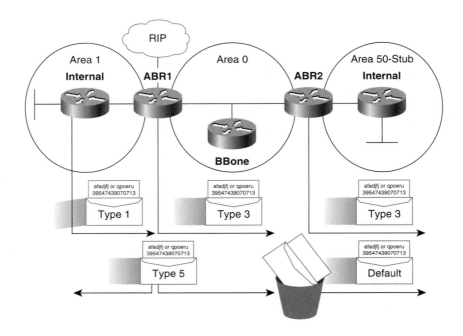

Updating the Routing Table

After all router types receive the routing updates, they must add them to their link-state databases and recalculate their routing tables. The order in which paths are calculated is as follows:

1. All routers first calculate the paths to destinations within their area and add these entries into the routing table. These are the Type-1 and Type-2 LSAs.

2. All routers then calculate the paths to the other areas within the internetwork. These paths are the inter-area route entries, or Type-3 and Type-4 LSAs. If a router has an inter-area route to a destination and an intra-area route to the same destination, the intra-area route is kept.

3. All routers, except those that are in a form of stub area, then calculate the paths to the AS external (Type-5) destinations.

At this point, a router can get to any network within or outside the OSPF autonomous system.

USING AND CONFIGURING OSPF MULTI-AREA COMPONENTS

This section covers some of the OSPF capabilities and associated configurations in more detail. You learn how to configure an ABR, how to configure route summarization, how to use and configure stub/totally stubby areas, and how to use and configure virtual links.

Configuring OSPF ABRs

There are no special commands to make a router an ABR or ASBR. The router takes on this role by virtue of the areas to which it is connected. As a reminder, the basic OSPF configuration steps are as follows:

1. Enable OSPF on the router.

   ```
   router(config)#router ospf process-id
   ```

2. Identify which IP networks on the router are part of the OSPF network. For each network, you must identify to which area the network belongs. When configuring multiple OSPF areas, make sure to associate the correct network addresses with the desired area ID.

   ```
   router(config-router)#network address wildcard-mask area area-id
   ```

3. (Optional) If the router has at least one interface connected into a non-OSPF network, perform the proper configuration steps. At this point the router will be acting as an ASBR. How the router exchanges (redistributes) non-OSPF route information with the other OSPF routers is discussed in Chapter 11.

Refer to Chapter 8 for details about basic OSPF configuration commands. Figure 9–9 shows the configuration commands used to make a regular and an ABR router.

Figure 9–9
By defining separate areas, you can configure an ABR.

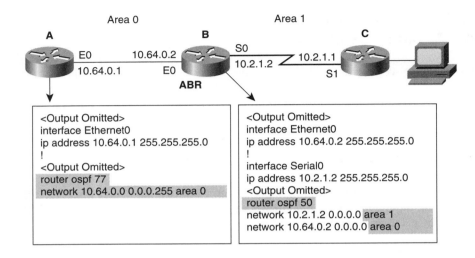

The most common OSPF configuration error is to assign the network(s) to the wrong area.

Using Route Summarization

Summarizing is the consolidation of multiple routes into one single advertisement. Proper summarization requires contiguous (sequential) addressing, such as 200.10.10.0, 200.10.11.0, 200.10.12.0, and so on. Route summarization is different than an LSA summary route.

Route summarization directly affects the amount of bandwidth, CPU, and memory resources consumed by the OSPF process. With summarization, if a network link fails, the topology change will not be propagated into the backbone (and other areas by way of the backbone). As such, flooding outside the area will not occur, so routers outside the area with the topology change will not have to run the SPF algorithm (also called the Dijkstra algorithm after the computer scientist who invented it). Running the SPF algorithm is a CPU-intensive activity.

Following are the two types of summarization:

- *Inter-area route summarization*—Inter-area route summarization is done on ABRs and applies to routes from within each area. It does not apply to external routes injected into OSPF via redistribution. In order to take advantage of summarization, network numbers within areas should be assigned in a contiguous way so as to be able to consolidate these addresses into one range. Figure 9–10 illustrates where inter-area summarization occurs.

- *External route summarization*—External route summarization is specific to external routes that are injected into OSPF via redistribution. Here again, it is important to ensure that external address ranges that are being summarized are contiguous. Summarization overlapping ranges from two different routers could cause packets to be sent to the wrong destination. Only ASBRs can summarize external routes. These types of routes cannot be summarized by any other router type.

In order to take advantage of summarization, as discussed in Chapter 7, network numbers in areas should be assigned in a contiguous way to be able to group these addresses into one range.

In Figure 9–10, for example, the list of six networks in router B's routing table can be summarized into two summary address advertisements.

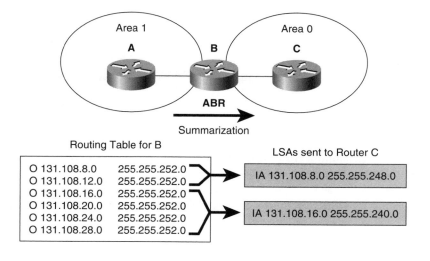

Figure 9–10
One entry can represent several subnets.

To illustrate which addresses can be summarized, the third octet of each address is shown in binary:

```
00001000
00001100
Summarized as '8'
00010000
00010100
00011000
00011100
Summarized as '16'
```

Configuring Route Summarization

Summarization is off by default. To configure route summarization on the ABR, perform the following steps:

1. Configure OSPF as discussed in the "Configuring OSPF ABRs" section.

2. Instruct the ABR to summarize routes for a specific area before injecting them into a different area, as follows:

```
router(config-router)#area area-id range address mask
```

area range Command	Description
area-id	Identifier of the area about which routes are to be summarized. The *area-id* requested is *not* the ID of the area into which the routes are going.
address	Summary address designated for a range of addresses
mask	IP subnet mask used for the summary route

To configure route summarization on an ASBR to summarize external routes, perform the following steps:

1. Configure OSPF, as discussed in the "Configuring OSPF ABRs" section.

2. Instruct the ASBR to summarize external routes before injecting them into the OSPF domain, as follows:

```
router(config-router)#summary-address address mask
```

summary-address Command	Description
address	Summary address designated for a range of addresses
mask	IP subnet mask used for the summary route

Figure 9–11 shows that route summarization can occur in both directions.

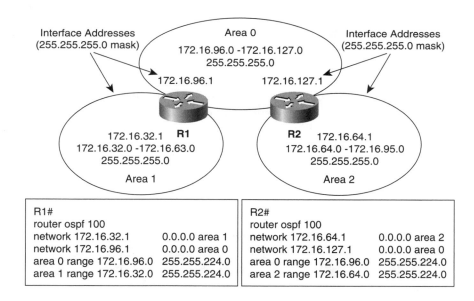

Interface Addresses (255.255.255.0 mask)

Area 0
172.16.96.0 -172.16.127.0
255.255.255.0

Interface Addresses (255.255.255.0 mask)

172.16.96.1   172.16.127.1

172.16.32.1 **R1**
172.16.32.0 -172.16.63.0
255.255.255.0
Area 1

R2 172.16.64.1
172.16.64.0 -172.16.95.0
255.255.255.0
Area 2

```
R1#
router ospf 100
network 172.16.32.1      0.0.0.0 area 1
network 172.16.96.1      0.0.0.0 area 0
area 0 range 172.16.96.0  255.255.224.0
area 1 range 172.16.32.0  255.255.224.0
```
```
R2#
router ospf 100
network 172.16.64.1      0.0.0.0 area 2
network 172.16.127.1     0.0.0.0 area 0
area 0 range 172.16.96.0  255.255.224.0
area 2 range 172.16.64.0  255.255.224.0
```

Figure 9–11
Route summarization configuration example.

In Router 2's configuration shown in Figure 9–11, the following commands are used:

- **area 0 range 172.16.96.0 255.255.224.0**—Identifies area 0 as the area containing the range of networks to be summarized into area 1. The ABR R1 is summarizing the range of subnets from 172.16.96.0 to 172.16.127.0 into one range: 172.16.96.0 255.255.224.0. This summarization is achieved by masking the first three left-most bits of subnet 96 using the mask 255.255.224.0.

- This summarization was successful because you are summarizing two distinct subnet ranges into the backbone: 32 to 63 and 64 to 95.

- **area 1 range 172.16.32.0 255.255.224.0**—Identifies area 1 as the area containing the range of networks to be summarized into area 0. The ABR R1 is summarizing the range of subnets from 172.16.32.0 to 172.16.63.0 into one range: 172.16.32.0 255.255.224.0.

The configuration on the right works exactly the same way. Note that, depending on your network topology, you may not want to summarize area 0 networks. If you have more than one ABR between an area and the backbone area, for example, sending a summary LSA with the explicit network information will ensure that the shortest path is selected. If you summarize the addresses, a suboptimal path selection may occur.

Using Stub and Totally Stubby Areas

Recall that a *stub area* is an area that does not accept information about routes external to the autonomous system (that is, the OSPF internetwork), such as routes from non-OSPF sources. A *totally stubby area* is an area that does not accept external autonomous system (AS) routes and summary routes from other areas internal to the autonomous system. OSPF allows areas to be configured as stub and totally stubby areas, as shown in Figure 9–12.

Figure 9–12
Totally stubby area creation is a Cisco-specific feature.

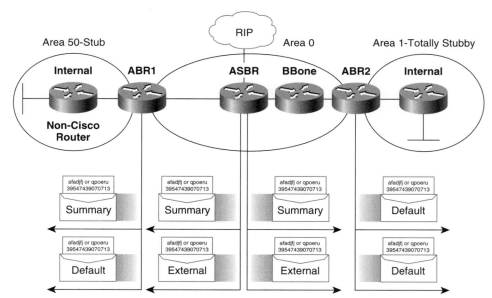

Their differences are as follows:

- Configuring a stub area reduces the size of the link-state database inside an area and, as a result, reduces the memory requirements of routers inside that area. External networks (Type-5 LSAs), such as those redistributed from other protocols into OSPF, are not allowed to be flooded into a stub area.

- Routing from these areas to the outside world is based on a *default* route (0.0.0.0). A default route means that if a packet is addressed to a network that is *not* in an internal router's route table, the router automatically forwards the packet to the ABR that sent a 0.0.0.0 LSA, which allows routers within the stub to reduce the size of their routing tables because a single default route replaces the many external routes.

- A stub area is typically created when you have a hub and spoke topology, with the spoke being the stub area, such as a branch office. In this case, the branch office does not need to know about every network at the headquarters site. It can instead use a default route to get there.

- To further reduce the number of routes in a table, you can create a totally stubby area, which is a Cisco-specific feature. A totally stubby area is a stub area that blocks external Type-5 LSAs *and* summary (Type-3 and Type-4) LSAs (inter-area routes) from going into the area. This way, intra-area routes and the default of 0.0.0.0 are the only routes known to the stub area. ABRs inject the default summary link 0.0.0.0 into the totally stubby area. Each router picks the closest ABR as a gateway to everything outside the area.

- Totally stubby areas further minimize routing information (as compared to stub areas) and increase stability and scalability of OSPF internetworks. This is typically a better solution than creating stub areas, unless the target area uses a mix of Cisco and non-Cisco routers.

Stub and Totally Stubby Area Restrictions

An area can be qualified as a stub or totally stubby when it meets the following criteria:

- There is a single exit point from that area, as shown in Figure 9–13, or if there are multiple exits (ABRs), routing to outside of the area does not have to take an optimal path. If the area has multiple exits, one or more ABRs will inject a default into the stub area. In this situation, routing to other areas or autonomous systems could take a suboptimal path in reaching the destination by going out of the area via an exit point that is farther from the destination than other exit points.

- All OSPF routers inside the stub area (ABRs and internal routers) are configured as stub routers so they will become neighbors and exchange routing information. The configuration commands for creating stub networks are covered later in this chapter.

- The area is not needed as a transit area for virtual links. (Virtual links are discussed at the end of this chapter.)

- No ASBR is internal to the stub area.

- The area is not the backbone area (area 0).

Figure 9–13
Stub and totally stubby areas typically have only a single exit point.

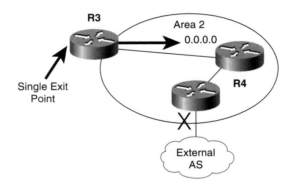

These restrictions are made because a stub/totally stubby area is mainly configured not to carry external routes, and any of the situations described cause external links to be injected in that area.

Configuring Stub and Totally Stubby Areas

To configure an area as stub or totally stubby, perform the following steps:

1. Configure OSPF, as described in the "Configuring OSPF ABRs" section.

2. Define an area as stub/totally stubby by adding the following command to *all* routers within the area:

```
router(config-router)#area area-id stub [no-summary]
```

area stub Command	Description
area-id	Identifier for the stub/totally stubby area. The identifier can be either a decimal value or an IP address.
no-summary	(Only for ABRs connected to totally stubby areas.) Prevents an ABR from sending summary link advertisements into the stub area. Use this option for creating a totally stubby area.

The **area stub** command is configured on each router in the stub, which is essential for the routers to become neighbors and exchange routing information. When this command is configured, the stub routers exchange hello packets with the E bit set to 0. The state of this bit must be agreed upon or the routers will not become neighbors.

3. (Optional for ABRs only) Define the cost of the default route that is injected in the stub/totally stubby area, as follows:

```
router(config-router)#area area-id default-cost cost
```

area default-cost Command	Description
area-id	Identifier for the stub area. The identifier can be either a decimal value or an IP address.
cost	Cost for the default summary route used for a stub/totally stubby area. The acceptable value is a 24-bit number. The default cost is 1.

TIPS

To reduce the number of route entries that internal routers maintain, you can define the area as stub, totally stubby, or not so stubby.

OSPF Stub Area Configuration Example

In Figure 9–14, area 2 is defined as the stub area. No external routes from the external autonomous system will be forwarded into the stub.

Figure 9–14
*The **area 2** stub command defines the stub area.*

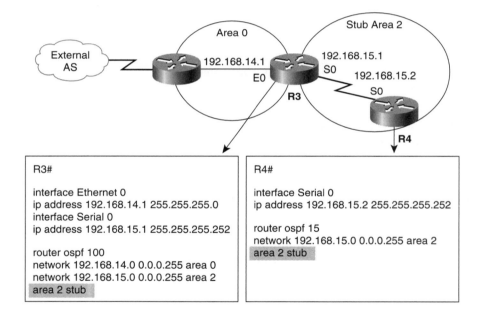

The last line in each configuration, **area 2 stub,** defines the stub area. The **area stub default-cost** has not been configured on R3, so this router will advertise 0.0.0.0 (the default route) with a default cost metric of 1 plus any internal costs.

Each router in the stub must be configured with the **area stub** command.	**Key Concept**

The only routes that will appear in R4's routing table are intra-area routes (designated with an O in the routing table), the default route, and inter-area routes (both designated with an IA in the routing table; the default route will also be denoted with an asterisk).

TIPS

The **area stub** command determines whether the routers in the stub become neighbors. This command must be included in all routers in the stub if they are to exchange routing information.

OSPF Totally Stubby Configuration Example

In Figure 9–15, the keyword **no-summary** has been added to the **area stub** command on R3. This keyword causes summary routes (inter-area) to also be blocked from the stub. Each router in the stub picks the closest ABR as a gateway to everything outside the area.

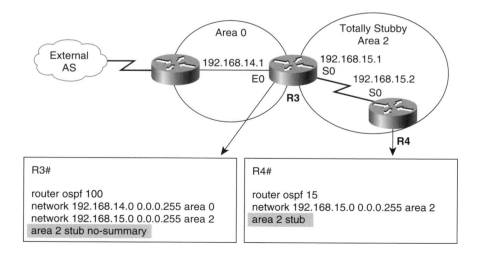

Figure 9–15
*Use the **no-summary** keyword to block routing summaries from going to area 2.*

The only routes that will appear in R4's routing table are intra-area routes (designated with an O in the routing table) and the default route. No inter-area routes (designated with an IA in the routing table) will be included.

TIPS

It is necessary to configure the **no-summary** keyword only on the totally stubby border routers because the area is already configured as stub.

MEETING THE BACKBONE AREA REQUIREMENTS

OSPF has certain restrictions when multiple areas are configured. One area must be defined as area 0, the backbone area. It is called the *backbone* because all communication must go through it. That is, all areas should be physically connected to area 0 so the routing information injected into area 0 can be disseminated to other areas.

Key Concept   **The backbone area must always be configured as Area 0.**

Creating a Virtual Link

There are situations, however, when a new area is added after the OSPF internetwork has been designed and configured and it is not possible to provide that new area with direct access to the backbone.

In these cases, a *virtual link* can be defined to provide the needed connectivity to the backbone area, as shown in Figure 9–16. The virtual link provides the disconnected area a logical path to the backbone.

All areas must connect directly to the backbone area or through a transit area.

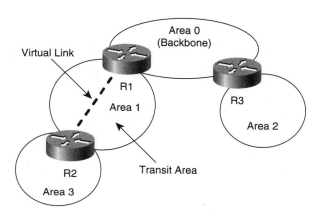

Figure 9–16
A virtual link connects remote areas to the back-bone area.

The virtual link has the following two requirements:

- It must be established between two routers that share a common area.

- One of these two routers must be connected to the backbone.

When virtual links are used, they require special processing during the SPF calculation. That is, the "real" next hop router must be determined so the true cost to get to a destination across the backbone can be calculated.

Virtual links serve the following purposes:

- Linking an area that does not have a physical connection to the backbone. This linking could occur, for example, when two organizations merge.

- Patching the backbone in case discontinuity of area 0 occurs.

Figure 9–17 illustrates the second purpose. Discontinuity of the backbone might occur if, for example, two companies, each running OSPF, are trying to merge the two separate networks into one with a common area 0. The alternative is to redesign the entire OSPF network and create a unified backbone.

Another reason for creating a virtual link is to add redundancy in cases when a router failure causes the backbone to be split into two.

Figure 9–17
*A transit area
can be used to
connect two
separate net-
works.*

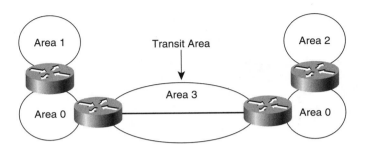

In Figure 9–17, the disconnected area 0s are linked via a virtual link through the common area 3. If a common area does not already exist, one can be created to become the transit area.

TIPS

Area 0 could become partitioned, for example, if two OSPF networks become merged.

Configuring Virtual Links

To configure a virtual link, perform the following steps:

1. Configure OSPF, as described in the "Configuring OSPF ABRs" section.

2. On each router that will make the virtual link, create the virtual link. The routers that make the links are the ABR that connects the remote area to the transit area and the ABR that connects the transit area to the backbone area.

```
router(config-router)#area area-id virtual-link router-id
```

area virtual-link Command	Description
area-id	Area ID assigned to the transit area for the virtual link (decimal or dotted-decimal format). There is no default.
router-id	Router ID of the virtual link neighbor.

If you do not know the neighbor's router ID, you can Telnet to it and type the **show ip ospf** command. The results are shown here:

```
remoterouter#show ip ospf interface ethernet 0
Ethernet0 is up, line protocol is up
    Internet Address 10.64.0.2/24, Area 0
    Process ID 1, Router ID 10.64.0.2, Network Type BROADCAST, Cost: 10
    Transmit Delay is 1 sec, State DR, Priority 1
    Designated Router (ID) 10.64.0.2, Interface address 10.64.0.2
    Backup Designated router (ID) 10.64.0.1, Interface address 10.64.0.1
```

OSPF Virtual Link Configuration Example

In Figure 9–18, area 3 does not have a direct physical connection to the backbone (area 0), which is an OSPF requirement because the backbone is a collection point for LSAs. ABRs forward summary LSAs to the backbone, which in turn forwards the traffic to all areas. All interarea traffic transits the backbone.

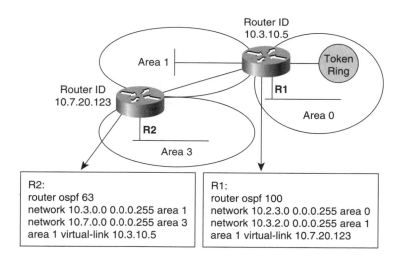

Figure 9–18
A virtual link between R1 and R2.

NOTES

The example shows an established virtual-link pointing to the actual Router ID (RID) of the other router. This is not necessary. The important part is that whichever IP on the other router your choose for the virtual link address is the one reachable through an entry in the routing table.

To provide connectivity to the backbone, a virtual link must be configured between R2 and R1. Area 1 will be the transit area and R1 will be the entry point into area 0. R2 will have a logical connection to the backbone through the transit area.

Both sides of the virtual link must be configured, as follows:

- R2: **area 1 virtual-link 10.3.10.5**—With this command, area 1 is defined to be the transit area and the router ID of the other side of the virtual link is configured.

- R1: **area 1 virtual-link 10.7.20.123**—With this command, area 1 is defined to be the transit area and the router ID of the other side of the virtual link is configured.

VERIFYING OSPF OPERATION

This section discusses the OSPF commands that can be used to verify operation of the OSPF features covered in this chapter. Note that the commands covered in the previous chapter also apply, but the ones listed in this section are more specific to the capabilities discussed so far.

You can use the same **show** commands listed in Chapter 8 to verify OSPF operation in multiple areas. Some additional commands include the following:

- **show ip ospf border-routers**—Displays the internal OSPF routing table entries to an ABR.

- **show ip ospf virtual-links**—Displays parameters about the current state of OSPF virtual links.

- **show ip ospf** *process-id*—Displays information about each area to which the router is connected, and indicates whether the router is an ABR, ASBR, or both. The process ID is an internally used identification parameter. It is locally assigned and can be any positive integer number. The number used here is the number assigned administratively when enabling the OSPF routing process.

- **show ip ospf database**—Displays the contents of the topological database maintained by the router. Several keywords can be used with this command to get specific information about the following links:

○ **show ip ospf** [*process-id area-id*] **database** [**network**]—Displays network link-state information. The area ID is the area number associated with the OSPF address range defined in the network router configuration command when defining a particular area.

○ **show ip ospf** [*process-id area-id*] **database** [**summary**]—Displays summary information about router link states.

○ **show ip ospf** [*process-id area-id*] **database** [**asbr-summary**]—Displays information about ASBR link-states.

○ **show ip ospf** [*process-id area-id*] **database** [**external**]—Displays information about autonomous system external link states.

○ **show ip ospf** [*process-id area-id*] **database** [**database-summary**]—Displays database summary information and totals.

SUMMARY

In this chapter, you learned the advantage of multiple area OSPF configurations and the OSPF components used in a large multiple area OSPF internetwork, which include reduced frequency of SPF calculations, smaller routing tables, and reduced LSU overhead. You learned about the types of areas, including stub, totally stubby, and transit areas, as well as the various types of routers and link-state advertisements. Recall that totally stubby areas are a Cisco-specific feature.

In the next chapter, you learn how to configure Enhanced IGRP.

Chapter Nine Test
Interconnecting Multiple OSPF Areas

Estimated Time: 15 minutes

Complete all the exercises to test your knowledge of the materials contained in this chapter. Answers are listed in Appendix A, "Chapter Test Answer Key."

Use the information contained in this chapter to answer the following questions.

Question 9.1

Define hierarchical routing and explain what internetwork problems it solves.

_____

_____

_____

Question 9.2

An internal router will receive Type-5 LSAs if it is what type of area?

_____

Question 9.3

What area types are connected to the backbone area?

_____

Question 9.4

The backbone must be configured as what area?

_____

Question 9.5

Write a brief description of the following:

LSA Type	Name	Description
1	Router link entry (record)	
2	Network link entry	
3 or 4	Summary link entry	
5	Autonomous system external link entry	

Question 9.6

Describe the path a packet must take to get from one area to another.

_____

Question 9.7

When is a default route injected into an area?

_____

Configuring Enhanced IGRP

EIGRP (Enhanced Interior Gateway Routing Protocol) is a Cisco-specific routing protocol. This chapter focuses on EIGRP features and operation, as well as the steps required to configure EIGRP routing and test your setups. Understanding EIGRP helps you determine whether it is the appropriate routing protocol for your environment.

ENHANCED IGRP OVERVIEW

Enhanced IGRP (EIGRP) is a Cisco proprietary protocol that combines the advantages of link-state and distance vector routing protocols. As a hybrid protocol, EIGRP includes the following features:

- *Rapid convergence*—EIGRP uses an algorithm called the *Diffusing Update Algorithm (DUAL)* to achieve rapid convergence. A router running Enhanced IGRP stores backup routes, when available, for destinations so that it can quickly adapt to alternative routes. If no appropriate route or backup route exists in the local routing table, EIGRP queries its neighbors to discover an alternative route. These queries are propagated until an alternative route is found. The DUAL algorithm guarantees loop-free operation at every instant throughout a route computation and allows all routers involved in a topology change to synchronize at the same time. Routers that are not affected by topology changes are not involved in recomputations. The convergence time with DUAL rivals that of any other existing routing protocol.

- *Reduced bandwidth usage*—EIGRP does not make periodic updates. Instead, it sends partial updates about a route when the path changes or when the metric for that route changes. When path information changes, the DUAL algorithm sends an update about that link only, rather than about the entire table. In addition, the information is sent only to the routers that need it, in contrast to link-state protocol operation, which sends a change update to all routers in an area.

- *Multiple network-layer support*—EIGRP supports AppleTalk, IP, and Novell NetWare through the use of protocol dependent modules (PDMs). These modules are responsible for network-layer-specific protocol requirements.

Key Concept   **Enhanced IGRP supports automatic route summarization and VLSM addressing.**

EIGRP Support for Novell IPX RIP and SAP

Novell IPX RIP routers send out RIP and SAP updates every 60 seconds, regardless of whether a network topology change has occurred. These regular updates can consume a substantial amount of bandwidth, especially on serial interfaces. You can take advantage of EIGRP's fast convergence and bandwidth-saving partial updates to redistribute IPX route and services information. EIGRP has several capabilities that are designed to facilitate the building of robust Novell IPX networks, as follows:

- EIGRP supports incremental RIP and SAP updates. EIGRP sends out RIP and SAP updates only when changes occur, and only sends out the changed information.

  - Ethernet, Token Ring, or FDDI, use periodic SAP updates, by default. You can reduce SAP update traffic by configuring EIGRP to send incremental SAP updates.

  - Point-to-point interfaces use incremental SAP updates by default, as shown in Figure 10–1.

- EIGRP IPX networks have a diameter of 224 hops, instead of IPX RIP's 15-hop diameter. This enables connectivity between more distant devices and allows discovery products (such as management products) to "see" devices that are further away.

- EIGRP for Novell IPX provides optimal path selection. Unlike Novell IPX, which uses ticks and hop count to determine the best route, EIGRP for IPX uses bandwidth and delay to determine the best route to a destination.

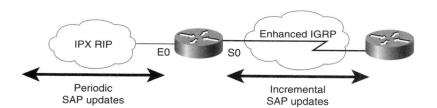

Figure 10–1
Point-to-point interfaces default to incremental updates.

In addition, redistribution of NetWare Link Services Protocol (NLSP) is automatic starting with Cisco IOS Release 11.1. NLSP is Novell's link state routing protocol for IPX-based networks. It is quite similar to OSPF.

EIGRP Support for AppleTalk

You can take advantage of EIGRP's advanced features to distribute route information in AppleTalk networks. The use of event-driven updates saves bandwidth on all links because it is more efficient than the periodic announcements used by AppleTalk Routing Table Maintenance Protocol (RTMP).

EIGRP for AppleTalk routers uses a configurable combination metric to determine the best route to a destination. AppleTalk's RTMP uses hop count. EIGRP routes are automatically preferred to RTMP routes.

EIGRP for AppleTalk can only be run in a clientless environment because AppleTalk clients expect RTMP information from a local source.

EIGRP Terminology

This section introduces you to a variety of terms related to EIGRP and used throughout this chapter:

- *Neighbor table*—Each EIGRP router maintains a neighbor table that lists adjacent routers. This table is comparable to the adjacencies database used by OSPF. It serves the same purpose, which is to ensure bidirectional communication between each of the directly connected neighbors. There is a neighbor table for each protocol that EIGRP supports.

- *Topology table*—Each EIGRP router maintains a topology table for each configured routing protocol. This table includes route entries for all destinations that the router has learned. All learned routes to a destination are maintained in the topology table.

- *Routing table*—EIGRP chooses the best (successor) routes to a destination from the topology table and places these routes in the routing table. The router maintains one routing table for each network protocol.

- *Successor*—A route selected as the primary route to use to reach a destination. Successors are the entries kept in the routing table.

- *Feasible successor*—A backup route. These routes are selected at the same time the successors are identified, but they are kept in a *topology* table. Multiple feasible successors for a destination can be retained.

ENHANCED IGRP OPERATION

In this section, you learn how EIGRP discovers neighbors, discovers routes, chooses routes, and maintain routes when there is a change in the network. This section focuses on the following elements of EIGRP router performance:

- Building the neighbor table

- Discovering routes

- Choosing routes

- Maintaining routes

Building the Neighbor Table

Recall that a *neighbor table* is a table that is maintained by the EIGRP router and that lists adjacent routers. Its purpose is to ensure bidirectional communication between each of the directly connected neighbors.

Like OSPF, EIGRP routers multicast hello packets to discover neighbor routers and to exchange route updates. If you recall, adjacent routers are the only ones that can exchange routing information. Each router builds a neighbor table from hello packets that it receives from adjacent EIGRP routers running the same network-layer protocol.

Hello packets are sent out periodically to verify an EIGRP neighbor's availability. On a multiaccess or point-to-point connection, hellos are sent every five seconds, by default. On an NBMA network, hellos are sent every 60 seconds, by default.

EIGRP maintains a neighbor table for each configured network-layer protocol. Use the **show ip eigrp neighbors** command to read the table, as shown in Figure 10–2.

p2r2

```
p2r2#show ip eigrp neighbors
IP-EIGRP neighbors for process 400
H Address      Interface  Hold  Uptime   SRTT  RTO  Q  Seq
                          (sec)  (ms)     Cnt Num
1 172.68.2.2   To0        13 02:15:30   8    200  0  9
0 172.68.16.2  Se1        10 02:38:29   29   200  0  6
```

Figure 10–2
Displaying the neighbor table.

The neighbor table includes the following key elements:

- *Neighbor address*—The network-layer address of the neighbor router.

- *Queue*—Indicates the number of packets waiting in queue to be sent. If this value is constantly higher than zero, then there may be a congestion problem at the router. A zero means that there are no EIGRP packets in the queue.

- *Smooth Round Trip Timer (SRTT)*—Indicates the average time it takes to send and receive packets from a neighbor. This timer is used to determine the retransmit interval (RTO).

- *Hold Time*—The interval to wait without receiving anything from a neighbor before considering the link unavailable. Originally, the expected packet was a hello packet, but in current Cisco IOS software releases, any EIGRP packets received after the first hello will reset the timer.

Discovering Routes

The neighbor establishment and discovering routes processes occur at the same time in EIGRP. A high-level description of the process is shown in Figure 10–3 and defined here:

1. A new router (router A) comes up on the link and sends out a hello through all interfaces.

2. Routers receiving the hello reply with update packets that contain all the routes they have in their topology tables, except those learned through that interface (the *split horizon* process requires that information not be sent back in the direction it was received). In addition, these update packets have the Init bit set, indicating that this is the initialization process.

   An update packet includes information about the routes a neighbor is aware of, including the metric that the neighbor is advertising for each destination.

3. Router A replies to each neighbor with an Ack (acknowledgment) packet, indicating that it received the update information.

4. Router A puts all update packets in its topology table.

   The topology table includes all destinations advertised by neighboring (adjacent) routers. It is organized such that each destination is listed, along with all the neighbors that can get to the destination, and their associated metrics.

5. Router A then exchanges update packets with each of its neighbors.

6. Upon receiving the update packets, each router sends an Ack packet to router A.

When all updates are received, the router is ready to choose the primary and backup routes to keep in the topology table.

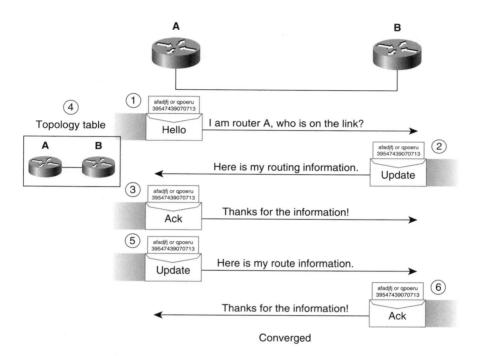

Figure 10–3
Neighbor routers exchange their routing tables.

Choosing Routes

EIGRP route selection is perhaps what distinguishes it most from other routing protocols. Following are its key characteristics:

- EIGRP selects primary and backup routes that are kept in the topology table (up to six per destination). The primary routes are then moved to a routing table.

  - Like OSPF, EIGRP supports several types of routes: internal, external (that is, non-EIGRP), and summary routes.

- EIGRP uses the same composite metric as IGRP to determine the best path. The metric can be based on five criteria. The *default* criteria used are as follows:

  ○ *Bandwidth*—The smallest bandwidth between source and destination

  ○ *Delay*—Cumulative interface delay along the path

  Following is additional criteria that can be used. These criteria are not recommended for use because they typically result in frequent recalculation of the topology table.

  ○ *Reliability*—Worst reliability between source and destination based on keepalives

  ○ *Loading*—Worst load on a link between source and destination based on bits per second

  ○ *MTU*—Smallest MTU in path

- EIGRP uses the DUAL algorithm to calculate the best route to a destination. DUAL selects routes based on the composite metric and ensures that the selected routes are loop-free.

In Figure 10–4, Enhanced IGRP's metric determines that the three-hop path using the T1 lines is a better route that the single 19.2-kbps link. RIP would select the single 19.2-kbps link by selecting the path based on hop count.

EIGRP uses the following process to determine which routes to keep in the topology and route tables:

1. DUAL is run on the topology table to determine the best and loop-free primary and backup routes to each destination.

   - "Best" is the lowest cost route that is calculated by adding the cost between the next-hop router and the destination (referred to as *advertised distance*) to the cost between the local router and the next-hop router (referred to as *feasible distance*). In Figure 10–5, for example, from router A, the advertised distance to network 7 using router B is 21, and the feasible distance is 31 because of the additional link cost between routers A and B, which is 10.

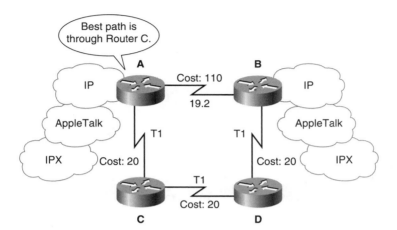

Figure 10–4
EIGRP uses a composite metric to pick the best path.

- The next-hop router(s) selected as the best path is referred to as the successor. Multiple successors can exist if they have the same feasible distance and use different next-hop routers. All successors are added to the route table. In Figure 10–5, router B is the successor for network 7.

- The next-hop router(s) for the backup path is referred to as the feasible successor. If the successor's route is no longer valid and a suitable feasible successor exists, this feasible successor replaces an invalid successor in the routing table without a recomputation. More than one feasible successor can be kept at one time. These routes need not have the same feasible distance, but their advertised distance must be less than the feasible distance of the successor route.

2. The successors and feasible successors are kept in the topology table, along with all other routes, and referred to as possible successors. The only routes removed are those that have a metric of infinity (unreachable).

EIGRP uses the same composite metric as IGRP to determine the best path. The default criteria used for that metric are *bandwidth* (the smallest bandwidth between source and destination) and *delay* (cumulative interface delay along the path).

Key Concept

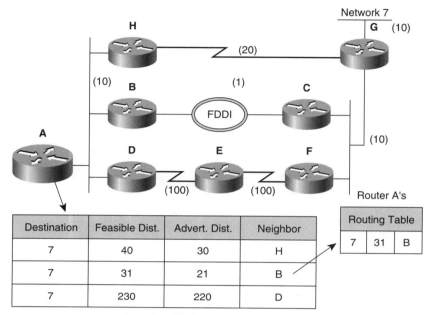

Figure 10–5
Router B is current successor and router H is the feasible successor.

Destination	Feasible Dist.	Advert. Dist.	Neighbor
7	40	30	H
7	31	21	B
7	230	220	D

Topology Table

Router A's Routing Table

7	31	B

Maintaining Routes

When there is a change in the network, the router that learned about the change advertises it to its neighbors by multicasting an update packet with the change. If the update packets are to notify the neighbors that a router was added to the network, then the process described in the previous "Discovering Neighbors" and "Discovering Routes" sections occurs. If the update packet says that a link has a worse metric, or is no longer available, however, the router must find an alternative path.

To obtain an alternative path, the router that lost the link looks for a new feasible successor in its topology table. If a feasible successor exists, it is promoted to a successor and added to the routing table, and then used. The topology table is then recalculated to determine whether there are any new feasible successors, based on the new successor's feasible distance.

If a feasible successor is not available, the following process is performed (see Figure 10–6).

1. The router (router A) flags the failed route as in an "active" state in the topology table. When routes are operating well, they are in "passive" state.

2. Router A looks for an alternative path by sending out a query packet to all its neighbors to learn whether they have a path to the given destination. The query packet is multicast out every interface except the one from which the dead link was learned about, thus following the split horizon rule.

Because the router expects a reply to the query from each neighbor, it tracks the sending and receiving of these packets from each neighbor from the topology table.

In Figure 10–6, for example, no feasible successor exists because no router's advertised distance is less than router B's feasible distance. As a result, the router must query its neighbors to find new successors and feasible successors. The route to network 7 changes from passive to active state.

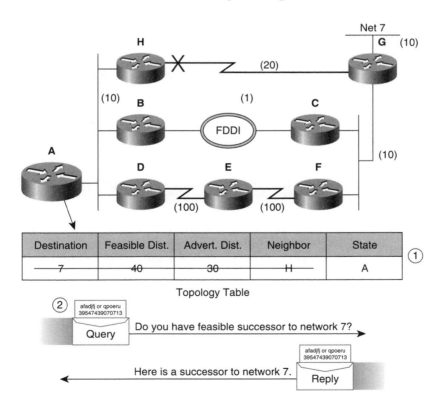

Figure 10–6
Router A will send a multicast request for a feasible successor to network 7.

Destination	Feasible Dist.	Advert. Dist.	Neighbor	State
7	40	30	H	A

Topology Table

3. If a neighbor has a feasible successor that does not use the querying router, or no route at all to the destination, it unicasts a Reply packet to the requestor indicating the appropriate information.

If a neighbor that receives the query is using the querying router as its feasible successor, then it sends its own Query packet to its neighbors, which creates a query ripple effect through the network until a major network boundary is met with, or until the router is on the autonomous system boundary (the end of EIGRP routers). In Figure 10–7, for example, you see router B send a query to its next network.

Figure 10–7
The feasible successor request ripples through the network.

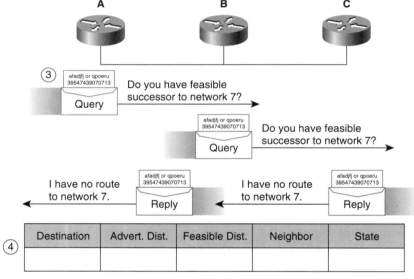

Topology Table

4. When the query router receives replies, it reacts, based on the answer in the reply:

- If the reply included a successor or feasible successor, the information is put into its topology table and the querying router waits until all replies are received. It then recalculates the topology table and adds the successor(s) to the routing table. The route returns to a passive state in the topology table and routing can continue.

- If none of the replies includes a successor or feasible successor, the querying router removes the active route from its topology and routing tables. In addition, the router console receives a message indicating that no route was found.

If one or more routers to which a query is sent do not respond with a reply within the active time of 180 seconds, EIGRP tears down the neighbor relationship with this rogue router and puts routes that used the rogue router into an active state. The querying router then generates queries for the route(s) it lost through the rogue router.

CONFIGURING EIGRP

This section discusses how to configure EIGRP for IP, IPX, and IPX SAP updates by defining the configuration steps and commands available in each of these cases.

Configuring EIGRP for IP

Perform the following steps to configure EIGRP for IP:

1. Use the following to enable EIGRP and define the autonomous system.

```
router(config)#router eigrp autonomous-system-number
```

autonomous-system-number is the number that identifies the autonomous system. It is used to indicate all routers that belong within the internetwork. This value must match all routers within the internetwork.

2. Indicate which networks are part of the EIGRP autonomous system.

```
router(config-router)#network network-number
```

network-number is the network number that determines which interfaces of the router are participating in EIGRP and which networks are advertised by the router.

The **network** command configures only connected networks. Network 3.1.0.0 (on the far left of Figure 10–8) is not connected, and, therefore, is not part of the configuration.

Figure 10–8
*Network
3.0.0.0 is not
configured on
router A
because it is
not directly
connected to
router A.*

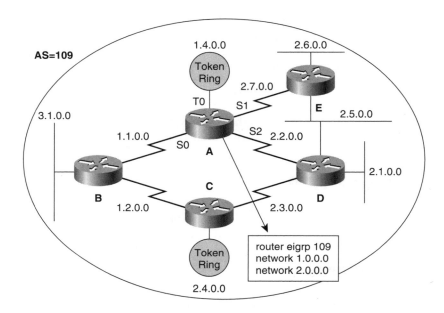

3. When using serial links, it is important to use the bandwidth on the interface to change the bandwidth used for calculating routing metrics. If you do not change the bandwidth for these interfaces, EIGRP assumes that the bandwidth on the link is of T1 speed. If the link is slower, the router may not be able to converge, routing updates might become lost, or suboptimal path selection may result.

```
router(config-if)#bandwidth kilobits
```

kilobits indicates the intended bandwidth in kilobits per second. For generic serial interfaces (PPP or HDLC), set the bandwidth to the line speed. For Frame Relay or point-to-point, set it to the CIR, or for multipoint connections set it to the sum of all CIRs.

You can change Enhanced IGRP's default percentage of bandwidth it uses to exchange route updates with the following commands:

ip bandwidth-percent eigrp

ipx bandwidth-percent eigrp

appletalk eigrp-bandwidth-percent

Note that the configured bandwidth affects load statistics that appear in some of the **show** commands.

Configuring EIGRP Support for IPX

To enable EIGRP for IPX, perform the following steps:

1. Enable IPX routing.

```
router(config)#ipx routing
```

2. Define EIGRP as the IPX routing protocol.

```
router(config-ipx-router)#ipx router {eigrp autonomous-system-number |
    rip}
```

If IPX EIGRP is selected, an autonomous system number must be specified. This number must be the same for all IPX EIGRP routers in the network.

ipx router Command	Description
eigrp autonomous-system-number	Specifies IPX EIGRP as the routing protocol. Integer from 1 to 65535. For IPX networks, the autonomous system number must be the same on all EIGRP routers.
rip	If you want to run RIP instead of EIGRP, select this keyword, as shown in Figure 10–9. RIP is on by default. In Figure 10–9, the **ipx router rip** command enables IPX RIP updates. The **no network 20** command disables IPX RIP updates on network 20. Enhanced IGRP incremental updates are enabled on interface serial 0, but IPX RIP updates are not enabled. As a result, updates are transmitted over the serial link only when network changes occur. IPX RIP periodic broadcasts are not sent over the serial link.

3. Indicate which networks are part of the EIGRP autonomous system.

```
router(config-router)#network network-number
```

Figure 10–9
*RIP is on by
default—dis-
able it if you
want to run
EIGRP.*

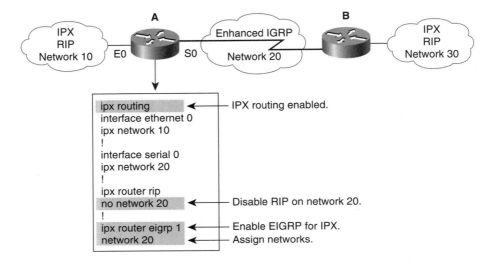

4. (Optional) If IPX RIP is also operating on the router, remove RIP from the networks using EIGRP by going to the **router rip** configuration entry and doing the following:

```
router(config-router)#no network network-number
```

Redistribution of RIP information between the RIP and EIGRP networks follows several very specific guidelines:

- When redistributing from RIP, the external hop count in the Enhanced IGRP update is the RIP hop count incremented by one. The external delay is the RIP delay.

- When sending an Enhanced IGRP learned route out in a RIP update (redistributing Enhanced IGRP into RIP), the Enhanced IGRP external hop count is incremented by one and used as the RIP hop count.

- The RIP delay is calculated by adding the Enhanced IGRP external delay, the delay of the outgoing interface, and the delay of the Enhanced IGRP cloud.

- The Enhanced IGRP metric is calculated by converting the RIP delay into an Enhanced IGRP style delay, in this case (5500 × delay), left-shifted 8 bits. This value is used with a static value of 9600-bps bandwidth in the Enhanced IGRP metric computation.

Configuring EIGRP for IPX SAP Updates

To reduce the frequency of SAP updates in a network that uses Cisco routers, perform the following steps:

1. Enable EIGRP for IPX, as discussed earlier.

2. Select the interface on which you want the SAP updates to be sent incrementally.

3. Instruct the router to issue SAP updates only when a change occurs in the network, instead of the periodic update interval:

```
router(config-if)#ipx sap-incremental eigrp autonomous-system-number
     [rsup-only]
```

ipx sap-incremental eigrp Command	Description
autonomous-system-number	An integer from 1 to 65535
rsup-only	(Optional) Use this keyword if you are using RIP instead of EIGRP to carry routing updates. Indicates that the system uses EIGRP to only carry reliable SAP updates. With this keyword and command, SAPs will be sent only when there is a change in the network.

LAN interfaces, such as Ethernet, Token Ring, and FDDI, have the **rsup-only** feature turned off by default. WAN links have the **rsup-only** feature turned on by default. When incremental updates are enabled on a LAN interface, another peer IPX EIGRP router should be present on that media. If an incremental update is enabled and no peer router is available, periodic SAP updates will be sent. If a peer router becomes available, incremental updates will then be sent.

EIGRP for IPX SAP Configuration Example

Figure 10–10 provides an example of a SAP incremental configuration.

Figure 10–10
*This config-
uration
enables incre-
mental-only
SAP updates
on an
Enhanced
IGRP FDDI
backbone to
conserve
bandwidth.*

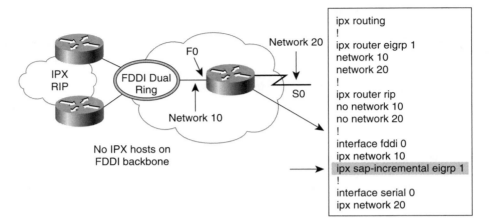

```
ipx routing
!
ipx router eigrp 1
network 10
network 20
!
ipx router rip
no network 10
no network 20
!
interface fddi 0
ipx network 10
ipx sap-incremental eigrp 1
!
interface serial 0
ipx network 20
```

The following definitions explain the setups used.

Command	Description
ipx router eigrp 1	Starts an EIGRP for IPX routing process as autonomous system 1
network 10	Assigns EIGRP for IPX updates to network 10
ipx router rip	Defines IPX RIP updates to be used
no network 10	Turns off IPX RIP updates on network 10
ipx sap-incremental eigrp 1	Enables incremental SAPs on networks configured on the interface

The router's FDDI interface (F0) carries IPX backbone traffic between the two IPX RIP networks. The **ipx sap-incremental eigrp 1** command configures incremental-only SAP updates on the FDDI interface for EIGRP autonomous system 1. As a result, the router sends only SAP changes from another EIGRP router on interfaces F0 and S0.

Summarizing EIGRP Routes for IP

EIGRP automatically summarizes routes at the *classful boundary* (the boundary where the network address ends as defined by class-based addressing). In some cases, how-ever, you may not want automatic summarization to occur. If you have discontiguous networks, for example, you need to turn off summarization to minimize router confusion. To turn off automatic summarization, initiate the following command:

```
router(config-router)#no auto-summary
```

If you want to summarize networks in an address that you define, perform the following steps:

1. Select the interface that will propagate the route summary.

2. Specify the format of the route summary and the autonomous system into which it needs to be injected by using the following:

```
router(config-if)#ip summary-address eigrp as-number address mask
```

ip summary-address eigrp Command	Description
as-number	Autonomous system number of the network being summarized.
address	The IP address being advertised as the summary address. This address does not need to be aligned on Class A, B, or C boundaries.
mask	The IP mask being used to create the summary address.

Enhanced IGRP does not summarize received routes. If a network was not summarized at the major network boundary, for example, routers A and B of Figure 10–11, then all of the subnet routes will be carried into the routing table of router C and other routers in the rest of the world. You are forcing a summary route out to the rest of the world, to keep that route advertisement small.

VERIFYING ENHANCED IGRP OPERATION

The **show** commands listed in Table 10–1 can be used to verify EIGRP for IP operation.

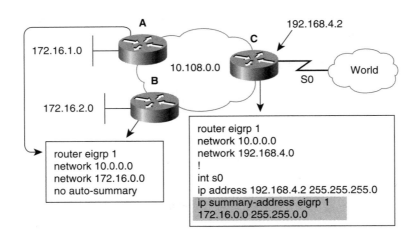

Figure 10–11
*Router C has
been config-
ured
for manual
summariza-
tion
of network
172.16.0.0's
networks.*

	Command	Description
Table 10–1 *The **show** commands used for EIGRP IP operations.*	**Command**	**Description**
	show ip eigrp neighbors	Displays neighbors discovered by EIGRP.
	show ip eigrp topology	Displays the EIGRP topology table. This command shows the topology table, the active/passive state of routes, the number of successors, and the feasible distance to the destination.
	show ip route eigrp	Displays the current EIGRP entries in the routing table.
	show ip protocols	Displays the parameters and current state of the active routing protocol process. This command shows the EIGRP autonomous system number. It also displays filtering and redistribution numbers as well as neighbors and distance information.
	show ip eigrp traffic	Displays the number of EIGRP packets sent and received. This command displays statistics on hello, updates, queries, replies, and acknowledgments.

Use the following **show** commands to verify EIGRP for IPX operation:

Command	Description
show ipx route	Displays the contents of the IPX routing table. You can use the **detailed** keyword to display detailed route information.
show ipx eigrp neighbors	Displays the IPX neighbors discovered by EIGRP.
show ipx eigrp topology	Displays the EIGRP topology table. This command shows the topology table, the active/passive state of routes, the number of successors, and the feasible distance to the destination.

SUMMARY

In this chapter, you learned that Enhanced IGRP (Interior Gateway Routing Protocol), a Cisco-specific routing protocol, is an advanced routing protocol that uses the DUAL algorithm. It combines the advantages of link-state and distance vector routing protocols, and, as such, includes features such as rapid convergence, reduced bandwidth usage, and multiple network-layer support.

You also learned that Enhanced IGRP converges rapidly, performs incremental updates, routes IP, IPX, and AppleTalk traffic, and summarizes routes. You learned how to configure and verify EIGRP configuration for various protocols.

In Chapter 11, "Optimizing Routing Update Operation," you learn how to optimize routing operations using static routes, default routes, and route filtering.

Chapter Ten Test
Configuring Enhanced IGRP

Estimated Time: 15 minutes

Complete all the exercises to test your knowledge of the materials contained in this chapter. Answers are listed in Appendix A, "Chapter Test Answer Key."

Use the information contained in this chapter to answer the following question.

Question 10.1

Place the letter of the description in front of the term that the statement describes. A statement may describe several terms.

Term	Statement
____ 1. Successor	A. A network protocol that EIGRP supports
____ 2. Feasible successor	B. A table that contains feasible successor information
____ 3. Hello	C. A table that contains current successor information
____ 4. Topology table	D. A neighbor router that has the best path to a destination
____ 5. IP	E. A neighbor router that has the best alternative path to a destination
____ 6. Update	F. An algorithm used by EIGRP that ensures fast convergence
____ 7. AppleTalk	G. A multicast packet used to discover neighbors
____ 8. Routing table	H. A packet sent by EIGRP routers when a new neighbor is discovered and when a change occurs
____ 9. DUAL	
____ 10. IPX	

Optimizing Routing Update Operation

This chapter discusses some of the more commonly used capabilities for controlling when and how routers receive and send routing updates. The capabilities covered include passive interfaces, default routes, static routes, route filtering, and redistributing routes between different routing protocols.

Understanding these capabilities and configurations enables you to design and configure the most efficient routing environment.

CONTROLLING ROUTING UPDATE TRAFFIC

Thus far, you have learned a variety of routing protocols and how they propagate routing information throughout an internetwork. There are times, however, when you do not want routing information propagated, as in the following examples:

- *When using an on-demand WAN link*—You may want to minimize, or stop entirely, the exchange of routing update information across this type of link; otherwise, the link will remain up constantly.

- *When you want to prevent routing loops*—Many companies have large enough networks where redundant paths are prominent. In some cases, for example, when a path is learned to the same destination by two different routing protocols, you may want to filter the propagation of one of the paths.

- *When you want to preserve bandwidth*—Available bandwidth becomes a precious resource as networks grow. You can ensure maximum bandwidth availability for data traffic by reducing unnecessary routing update traffic.

This section discusses the following ways you can control or prevent routing update exchange and propagation:

- *Passive interface*—Prevents all routing updates from being sent through an interface. For EIGRP and OSPF, this method includes hello protocol packets.

- *Default routes*—Instructs the router that if it does not have a route for a given destination, to send the packet to the default route.

- *Static routes*—A route to a destination that you configured in the router. In contrast, dynamic routes are those learned via routing protocol such as RIP or EIGRP.

- *Route update filtering*—Use access lists to filter route update traffic about specific networks.

In order to make these capabilities effective, you must know your network traffic patterns and know what the intended goal is when applying the capabilities. If you do not know the problem you want to resolve when using these capabilities, you will not know how to verify that they are being effective.

TIPS

You can use an analyzer, such as Network Associates' Sniffer, to monitor and document network traffic patterns.

Using and Configuring the passive-interface Command

The **passive-interface** command prevents all routing updates for a given routing protocol from being sent to or received from a network via a specific interface.

Remember that when using the **passive-interface** command in a network using a link-state routing protocol, the command prevents the router from establishing a neighbor adjacency with other routers connected to the same link as the one specified in the command. An adjacency cannot be established because the hello protocol is used to verify bidirectional communication between routers. If a router is configured to not send updates, then it cannot participate in bidirectional communication.

To configure a passive interface, regardless of the routing protocol, perform the following steps:

1. Select the router that requires the passive interface.

2. Determine which interface(s) you do not want routing update traffic to be sent through.

3. Configure the passive interface as follows:

```
router(config-router)#passive-interface type number
```

type refers to the type of interface, such as serial or Ethernet.

number refers to the interface number.

The **passive-interface** command is typically used in conjunction with other capabilities, as you will see in this chapter.

Use this command to prevent all route updates from being sent. If you want to be selective about which route updates not to send, you must use one of the other capabilities, such as route filtering and distribution filtering.

Using and Configuring Default Routes

Cisco enables you to configure default routes for other protocols. When you create a default route on a router, the router advertises an address of 0.0.0.0, in addition to the default network, unless it is IGRP or EIGRP. IGRP and EIGRP advertise only the network you configured. When a router receives the default route, it will forward any packets destined to a destination that does not appear in its routing table to the default route you configured. To specify a default route, perform the following steps:

1. Determine which network(s) you want as the default network.

2. Select the router(s) that need to have a default route defined. That is, identify the router(s) directly connected to the network for which a default route must be propagated, as shown in Figure 11–1.

Figure 11–1
*Router p2r2
advertises the
default route.*

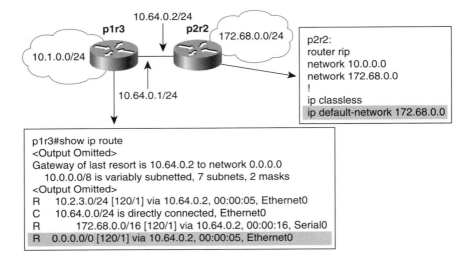

3. Configure the selected network as default.

   • For IP, use the following command:

   `router(config)#`**`ip default-network`** *`network-number`*

   network-number is the number of the destination network.

   • For IPX, use the following command:

   `router(config)#`**`ipx advertised-default-route-only`** *`network`*

4. For IGRP or RIP, enable these protocols to allow classless forwarding behavior.

```
router(config)#ip classless
```

This command allows the default path to be used for non-connected subnets of the same major classful network. If not enabled, the router drops the packet.

Using and Configuring Static Routes

Static routes are routes that you can manually configure on the router. Static routes are used most often to perform the following tasks:

- Define specific routes to use when two autonomous systems must exchange routing information, rather than having entire routing tables exchanged.

- Define static routes in stub environments where there is and will always be only one point of connection between two remote locations.

- Define routes to destinations over a WAN link to eliminate the need for a dynamic routing protocol. That is, when you do not want routing updates to enable or cross the link (this situation is discussed in Chapter 14, "Configuring Dial-on-Demand Routing").

When configuring static routes, keep in mind the following considerations:

- When using static routes, be aware that they have a lower administrative distance value than any routing protocol, so a static route will always be selected above an OSPF route, an IGRP route, and so on.

- To advertise a static route, you must use the redistribution capability. This capability is discussed later in this chapter.

- If you use only static routes (for example, no routing protocol), static route entries must be defined for all routes for which a router is responsible. To reduce the number of static route entries, you can define a default static route. Default static routes are advertised (redistributed) automatically.

In Figure 11–2, for example, router p1r2 has a static route entry for network 172.68.0.0.

Figure 11–2
Router p1r2
has one static
route entry.

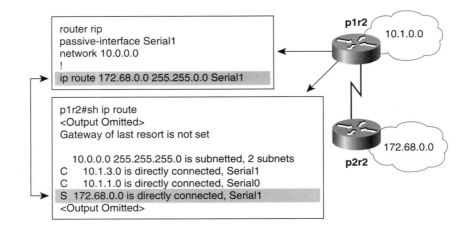

TIPS

Only a *default* static route is automatically advertised.

To configure a static route, the commands vary by protocol. Although the following tasks apply to all protocols that support static routes, only the commands for IP and IPX are shown. For more command information, refer to www.cisco.com.

1. Determine which networks you want defined as static. For example, if you are configuring static routes on a WAN router that is connecting to a branch office, you probably want to select the networks at the branch office.

2. Determine the next-hop router to the destination networks or local router's interface that will call the remote router.

3. Configure the static route on each router.

    • For IP, use the following command:

    ```
    router(config)#ip route prefix mask {address | interface}
            [distance] [permanent]
    ```

prefix is the network address (in classful format) for the destination.

mask is the prefix mask for the network address.

address is the IP address of the next-hop router that can be used to reach that network.

interface is the network interface to use to get to the destination network.

distance is the administrative distance to assign to this route. (Administrative distance refers to how believable the routing protocol is. It is discussed later in this chapter.)

permanent ensures that if the interface associated with the route goes down, the route will still remain in the routing table.

- Static routes for IPX use the following commands:

```
router(config)#ipx route {network | default}
    {network.node | interface} [floating-static]
```

network is the network address of the destination.

default specifies the destination as a static entry for the default route.

network.node is the network address and node ID of the next-hop router.

interface is the network interface to use to get to the destination network. Typical use is when using IPXWAN unnumbered interfaces.

floating static enables you to make IPX static routes floating (they are permanent by default). A floating static route is a static route that can be overridden by a dynamically learned route.

- If you configure IPX static routes, you must also consider configuring static SAPs. A static SAP is a server entry that is manually entered into the router's server information tables instead of being dynamically learned through a SAP broadcast.

Using and Configuring Route Filters

In the traffic management module, you learned how to filter different types of data and protocol traffic. This section discusses how access lists can be used to filter route (and IPX SAP) updates.

The Cisco IOS software can filter incoming and outgoing routing updates. In general, the process the router uses, shown in Figure 11–3, is as follows:

1. The router receives a routing update or is getting ready to send an update about one or more networks.

2. The router looks at the interface involved with the action.

    If it is an incoming update, for example, then the interface on which it arrived is checked. If it is an update that must be advertised, the interface out of which it should be advertised is checked.

3. The router determines whether a filter is associated with the interface or with the routing protocol. Filters can be associated with all interfaces running a specific routing protocol.

    If a filter is associated with the interface, the router views the access list to learn if there is a match for the given routing update.

    If a filter is not associated with the interface, the packet is processed as normal.

4. If there is a match, the route entry is processed as configured.

    If no match is found, the update is dropped due to the **implicit deny all** at the end of the access list.

Use route filters when you want to advertise selected routes only, such as only a default route and no other routes that are usually advertised by the router.

If you want to filter all updates advertised by an interface, use the **passive-interface** command instead.

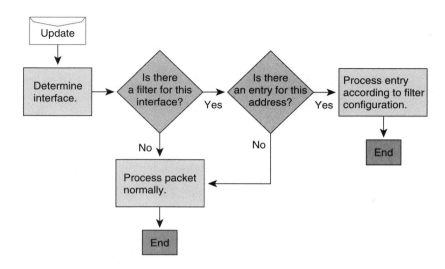

Figure 11–3
Filtering decision process.

You can filter routing update traffic for any protocol by defining an access list and applying it to specific routing protocol. To configure a filter, perform the following steps:

1. Identify the network addresses you want to filter and create an access list.

2. Determine whether you want to filter them on an incoming or outgoing interface.

3. Assign the access list to filter outgoing routing updates:

```
router(config-router)# distribute-list access-list-number | name out
       [interface-name | routing-process | autonomous-system-number]
```

distribute-list Command	Description
access-list-number	Standard access list number.
out	Define the filtering on outgoing routing updates.
interface-name	(Optional) Interface name.
routing-process	(Optional) Name of the routing process or the keyword **static** or **connected**.

Or, to assign the access list to filter incoming routing updates, use the following:

```
router(config-router)# distribute-list {access-list-number | name} in
    [type number]
```

type indicates the interface type.

number indicates the interface number of where the access list should be applied on incoming updates.

Note that the **distribute-list** syntax is different, depending on whether it is an inbound or outbound filter.

distribute-list Command	Description
access-list-number	Standard access list number
in	Defines the filtering on incoming routing updates
interface-name	(Optional) Interface name

The **distribute-list** command uses standard access lists and can be applied to inbound or outbound routing updates. It can be used with IP and IPX.

IPX Route Filtering Configuration Example

In Figure 11–4, networks 4a and 9e have been filtered from interface s0.

The **distribute-list** command applies access list 800 to outbound packets. The access list does not allow routing information from networks 4a and 9e to be distributed out the s0 interface. As a result, networks 4a and 9e are hidden.

When you filter RIP information, consider filtering SAPs as well.

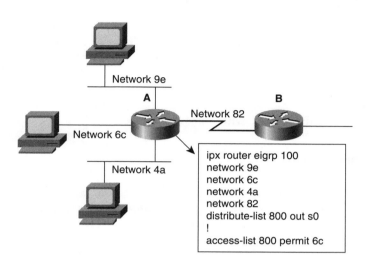

Figure 11–4
Only network 6c is advertised in routing updates.

Command	Description
distribute-list 800 out s0	Applies access list 800 as a route redistribution filter on routing updates sent on serial 0
access-list 800 permit 6c	
800	Access list number
permit	Traffic matching the parameters can be forwarded
6c	Network number

USING MULTIPLE ROUTING PROTOCOLS

Thus far, this chapter has looked at networks that use a single routing protocol. There are times, however, when you will need to use multiple routing protocols. The following are a few reasons why you might need multiple protocols:

- When you are migrating from an older IGP to a new IGP, multiple redistribution boundaries may exist until the new protocol has displaced the old protocol completely. Dual existence of protocols is effectively the same as a long-term coexistence design.

- When you want to use another protocol but need to keep the old protocol due to the needs of host systems.

- Different departments might not want to upgrade their routers or they might not implement a sufficiently strict filtering policy so you can protect yourself by terminating the interior route protocol.

- If you have a mixed router vendor environment, you can use a Cisco-specific protocol in the Cisco portion of the network and then use a common protocol to communicate with non-Cisco devices.

What Is Redistribution?

When any of the aforementioned situations arises, Cisco routers allow internetworks using different routing protocols (referred to as *autonomous systems*) to exchange routing information through a feature called route *redistribution*. Redistribution is defined as the capability for boundary routers connecting different autonomous systems to exchange and advertise routing information received from one autonomous system to the other autonomous system.

Within each autonomous system, the internal routers (in the case of Figure 11–5, the internal IGRP and EIGRP routers) have complete knowledge about all subnets that make up each network. The router interconnecting both autonomous systems is called an *autonomous system boundary router* (ASBR) and has both IGRP and Enhanced IGRP processes active. The ASBR is responsible for advertising routes learned from one autonomous system into the other autonomous system.

Figure 11–5
Redistribution enables routes to be learned from another routing protocol.

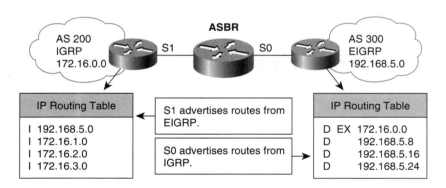

In Figure 11–5, network 192.168.5.0 is known via the S0 interface. The routing table for the router in AS 300 contains routes, such as 192.168.5.0 and 172.16.0.0, that are summarized at network boundaries. These routes are indicated by the "D" for Enhanced IGRP and "EX" for an external route that was learned from redistribution.

Redistribution Implementation Considerations

Redistribution, although powerful, increases the complexity and potential for routing confusion, so it should be used only when absolutely necessary. The key issues that arise when using redistribution are as follows:

- *Routing feedback (loops)*—Depending on how you employ redistribution, routers can send routing information received from one autonomous system back into the autonomous system, as shown in Figure 11–6. The feedback is similar to the split horizon problem that occurs in distance vector technologies.

  In Figure 11–6, information about network 172.16 crosses ASBR A to the EIGRP net. Because this internetwork has a loop, the same information propagates back to the RIP network through ASBR B.

- *Incompatible routing information*—Because each routing protocol uses different metrics to determine the best path, for example, RIP uses hops and OSPF uses cost, path selection using the redistributed route information may not be optimal. Because the metric information about a route cannot be translated exactly into a different protocol, the path a router chooses may not be the best.

- *Inconsistent convergence time*—Different routing protocols converge at different rates. For example, RIP converges slower than EIGRP, so if a link goes down, the EIGRP network will learn about it before the RIP network.

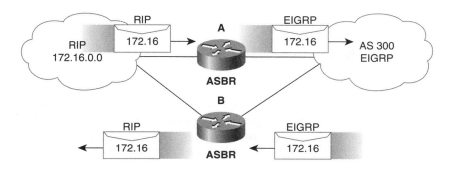

Figure 11–6
Problems may arise due to the loops and inconsistent convergence times.

To understand why some of these problems occur, you must understand how the Cisco routers convert the metrics used when importing routes from one autonomous system into another: this conversion is discussed on subsequent pages.

Key Concept   *Redistribution* **is the capability for boundary routers connecting different autonomous systems to exchange and advertise routing information received from one autonomous system to the other autonomous system.**

The next series of pages discusses how a router can select a path when it learns routes to a given destination from different routing protocols. Understanding how path selection occurs in this environment is important to prevent and troubleshoot routing feedback and poor path selection.

Selecting the Best Path

Most routing protocols have metric structures and algorithms that are not compatible with other protocols. In a network where multiple routing protocols are present, the exchange of route information and the capability to select the best path across the multiple protocols is critical.

In order for routers to select the best path when they learn two or more different routes to the same destination from two different routing protocols, Cisco uses *administrative distance*, which defines the believability of a routing protocol. Each routing protocol is prioritized in order of most to least (believable) reliable using a value called *administrative distance*.

This criterion is the first a router uses to determine which routing protocol to believe if two protocols provide route information for the same destination. The more believable protocol is selected, even when it advertises a suboptimal route.

What Protocol to Believe?

Table 11–1 lists the believability (administrative distance) of the protocols that Cisco supports. Note that the smaller the administrative distance, the more reliable the protocol. For example, if the router received a route to network 10.2.2.0 from IGRP and then received a route to the same network from OSPF, IGRP is more believable, so the IGRP version of the route would be added to the routing table.

Route Source	Default Distance
Connected Interface	0
Static Route	1
Enhanced IGRP Summary Route	5
External BGP	20
Internal Enhanced IGRP	90
IGRP	100
OSPF	110
IS-IS	115
RIP	120
EGP	140
External Enhanced IGRP	170
Internal BGP	200
Unknown	255

Table 11–1
Administrative Distances of Cisco-Supported Protocols.

When using route redistribution, occasionally there may be a need to modify the administrative distance of a protocol so that it has preference. If you want the router to select RIP-learned routers rather than IGRP-learned routes to the same destination, for example, then you must increase the administrative distance for IGRP. In the section "Using and Configuring Redistribution," later in this chapter, you learn how to modify the administrative distance.

After an ASBR selects the routing protocol to which to listen, it must be able to translate the metric of the received route from the source routing protocol into the other routing protocol. If an ASBR receives a RIP route, for example, it will have a hop count as a metric. To redistribute it into OSPF, however, the hop count must be translated into a cost value. The cost value you define during configuration is referred to as the *seed* or default metric.

After the seed metric is established, the metric will increment normally within the autonomous system. The exceptions are OSPF E2 routes, as discussed previously, which hold their default metric regardless of how far they are propagated across an autonomous system.

You should take some precautions when a loop exists between two autonomous systems, as shown earlier in Figure 11–6. Consider setting the default metric on the incoming redistributed route to something higher than what currently exists in the receiving protocol. This way, you get some degree of automatic protection from route loops.

Suppose a route loop exists where a routing protocol is getting preferred routes that it originally sourced. If those routes are in at a low metric, they can be preferred over the original route.

So, imagine a router Z in a RIP domain knows that network A, a route native to the RIP domain of which you are a member, is currently at a cost of three hops from my point of view. Now suppose that the route to A has been redistributed to some foreign protocol and is now coming back into the RIP domain from the outside and router Z is only one hop away from the point of redistribution.

If the redistributing router sets the metric for this new route to network A to one, router Z's cost to A is now only two hops and it now points toward the redistribution router. If the redistribution router sets the metric to four hops, for example, then all will be well even though technically a route loop is occurring. Setting the incoming default metric low may create a black hole for routes.

Redistribution Guidelines

Examples about how redistribution can be implemented are covered later in this chapter. At a high level, Cisco recommends that you consider employing the following guidelines when using redistribution:

- *Be familiar with your network*—This is the overriding recommendation. There are many ways to implement redistribution, so knowing your network will enable you to make the best decision. Use an analyzer to track your data flows.

- *Do not overlap routing protocols*—Do not run two different protocols in the same internetwork. Rather, have distinct boundaries between networks that use different protocols.

- *One-way redistribution*—To avoid routing loops and having problems with varying convergence time, only allow routes to be exchanged in one direction, not both directions. In the other direction, you should consider using a default route. This is important for cases when you have multiple points of redistribution. If you have only one ASBR, full two-way redistribution is recommended.

- *Two-way redistribution*—In case of only one point of redistribution(one ASBR only), there are no potential problems. If you have multiple ASBRs and if you must allow two-way redistribution, enable a mechanism to reduce the chances of routing loops. Examples of mechanisms already covered in this chapter are default routes, route filters, and modification of the metrics advertised. With these types of mechanisms, you can reduce the chances of routes imported from one autonomous system being reinjected into the same autonomous system as new route information.

Use the following **redistribute?** command to see a list of protocols that can be supported by redistribution:

```
p1r1(config-router)#redistribute?
    Bgp       Border Gateway Protocol (BGP)
    connected      Connected
    egp       Exterior Gateway Protocol (EGP)
    eigrp      Enhanced Interior Gateway Routing Protocol (EIGRP)
    igrp      Interior Gateway Routing Protocol (IGRP)
    isis       ISO IS-IS
    iso-igrp      IGRP for OSI networks
    mobile      Mobile routes
    odr       On Demand Stub Routes
    ospf       Open Shortest Path First (OSPF)
    rip       Routing Information Protocol (RIP)
    static      Static routes
```

As shown previously for IP, all protocols are supported by redistribution. Before implementing redistribution, consider the following points:

- You can only redistribute protocols that support the same protocol stack. For example, you can redistribute between IP RIP and OSPF because they both support the TCP/IP stack. But you cannot redistribute between IPX RIP and OSPF because IPX RIP supports the IPX/SPX stack and OSPF does not.

- How you configure redistribution varies among protocols and among combinations of protocols. For example, redistribution occurs automatically between IGRP and EIGRP when they have the same autonomous system number, but it must be configured between EIGRP and RIP.

Redistribution and EIGRP

EIGRP, because it supports multiple routing protocols, can be used to redistribute with IP, IPX, and AppleTalk as well. Consider the following when redistributing EIGRP with these protocols:

- In the IP environment, IGRP and EIGRP have a similar metric structure and therefore redistribution is straightforward. For migration purposes, when IGRP and Enhanced IGRP are both running in the same autonomous system and are using the same autonomous system numbers, redistribution is automatic. When redistributing between different autonomous systems, redistribution must be configured for Enhanced IGRP, just as it is required for IGRP.

- By design, EIGRP automatically redistributes route information with Novell RIP. Beginning with Cisco IOS Release 11.1, EIGRP can redistribute route information with NLSP, when configured.

- EIGRP for AppleTalk understands RTMP updates, and redistribution is enabled by default.

- All other IP routing protocols, both internal and external, require that redistribution be configured in order to communicate with EIGRP.

In the next section, you learn how to configure a Cisco router for redistribution.

USING AND CONFIGURING REDISTRIBUTION

This section covers how to configure redistribution, including modifying the administrative distance and defining the seed metric.

In addition, two redistribution examples that include before and after **show ip route** output are discussed.

Configuring route redistribution can be very simple or very complex, depending on the mix of protocols that you want to redistribute. The commands used to enable redistribution and assigned metrics vary slightly, depending on the protocols being redistributed. The following steps are generic enough to apply to virtually all protocol combinations; however, the commands used to implement the steps may vary. It is highly recommended that you review the Cisco IOS documentation for the configuration commands that apply to the specific protocols you want to redistribute.

1. Determine which routing protocol is the core or backbone protocol. Usually this is OSPF or EIGRP.

2. Locate the ASBR on which redistribution needs to be configured.

3. Determine which routing protocol is the edge or short-term (if you are migrating) protocol.

4. Access the routing process *into which* you want routes redistributed. Typically, you start with the backbone routing process. For example, to access OSPF, do the following:

```
router(config)#router ospf process-id
```

> The routing protocol on which you configure redistribution is the one *into* which you want to redistribute. Another way to look at it is you are preparing the *receiving* protocol, much like a house must be prepared to receive guests.
>
> The generic terms *core* and *edge* are used to simplify the discussion about redistribution. "Core" routing protocol refers to the routing protocol used on the backbone. "Edge" routing protocol refers to the other protocol that must perform redistribution with the core routing protocol.

5. Configure the router to redistribute routing updates from the short-term protocol into the backbone protocol. This command varies, depending on the protocol. The following command is for OSPF.

```
router(config-router)#redistribute protocol [process-id]
     [metric metric-value] [metric-type type-value] [subnets]
```

redistribute Command	Description
protocol	Source protocol from which routes are being redistributed. Keyword values are **bgp**, **egp**, **igrp**, **isis**, **ospf**, **static** [**ip**], **connected**, and **rip**.
process-id	OSPF process ID.
metric	(Optional) An OSPF optional parameter used to specify the metric used for the redistributed route. If this value is not specified, and no value is specified using the **default-metric** router configuration command, the default metric is 0. Use a value consistent with the destination protocol.
metric-type *type-value*	(Optional) An OSPF parameter that specifies the external link type associated with the default route advertised into the OSPF routing domain. This value can be **1** for type-1 external routes or **2** for type-2 external routes. The default is a type-2 external route.
subnets	A required OSPF parameter that specifies that subnetted routes should also be redistributed.

Key Concept You need to use the **redistribute** and **default-metric** commands to redistribute routes only between routing protocols that do not automatically perform route redistribution.

---

6. Define the seed metric that the receiving router uses to calculate the value of the route before redistributing the route.

   When redistributing IGRP or EIGRP, use the following:

   ```
   router(config-router)#default-metric bandwidth delay reliability
       loading mtu
   ```

default-metric Command	Description
bandwidth	Minimum bandwidth of the route in kilobits per second.
delay	Route delay in tens of microseconds.

default-metric Command	Description
reliability	Likelihood of successful packet transmission expressed in a number from 0 to 255.
loading	Effective bandwidth of the route expressed in a number from 0 to 255.
mtu	Maximum transmission unit (MTU) size on the route in bytes.

When redistributing OSPF, RIP, EGP, and BGP, use the following:

```
router(config-router)#default-metric number
```

default-metric Command	Description
number	The value of the metric, such as the number of hops for RIP.

7. Exit the routing process.

TIPS

To avoid routing loops, it is highly recommended that you set the default metric larger than the largest native metric, as discussed earlier in this chapter.

8. Enter configuration mode for the other routing process, usually the short-term process.

9. Depending on your network, this configuration will vary because you want to employ some techniques to reduce routing loops. For example, you may do any of the following:

- Redistribute a default route about the backbone autonomous system into the border autonomous system.

- Redistribute multiple static routes about the backbone autonomous system into the other autonomous system.

- Redistribute all routes from the backbone autonomous system into the border autonomous system, and then assign a distribution filter.

- Redistribute all routes from the backbone autonomous system into the border autonomous system, and then modify the distance associated with the received routes so they are not selected when multiple routes exist for the same destination. In some cases, the route learned by the native protocol is better, but may have a less believable administrative distance. Refer to the "Redistribution Example Using **distance**" for an example of this scenario.

The following sections illustrate two redistribution configuration examples. It is important to note, however, that every network is different and may require a different combination of commands to make redistribution operate properly.

Modifying Administrative Distance (Optional)

In some cases, you will find that a router will select a suboptimal path because it believes a routing protocol that, although it has a better administrative distance, has a poorer route. One way to make sure routes from the desired routing protocol are selected is to give the undesired routing protocol a larger administrative distance. Perform the following steps:

1. Create an access list of the networks to be redistributed.

2. Access the appropriate routing process.

3. Assign the access list to the **distance** command.

```
router(config-router)#distance weight [address mask
    [access-list-number | name]]
```

distance Command	Description
weight	Administrative distance
address	(Optional) IP address
mask	(Optional) Mask for IP address
*access-list-number	name*	Number of the name or standard access list to be applied to the incoming routing updates

Use this command only after routing loops are detected, or if you have done significant planning and really understand how packets are forwarded in the existing network.

IP Route Filtering Configuration Example

Figure 11–7 provides an example of how to hide a network using a route filter.

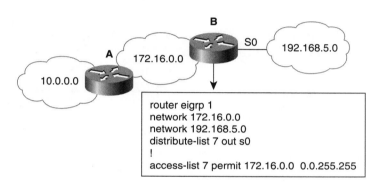

Figure 11–7
Router B's configuration hides network 10.0.0.0 using interface filtering.

Command	Description
distribute-list 7 out s0	Applies access list 7 as a route redistribution filter on routing updates sent on serial 0
access-list 7 permit 172.16.0.0 0.0.255.255	
7	Access list number
permit	Routes matching the parameters can be forwarded
172.16.0.0 0.0.255.255	Network number and wildcard mask used to qualify source addresses. The first two address octets must match and the rest are masked.

The **distribute-list** command applies access list 7 to outbound packets. The access list does not allow routing information from network 10.0.0.0 to be distributed out the S0 interface. As a result, network 10.0.0.0 is hidden.

IP network address 10.0.0.0 shown in Figure 11–7 is a private address that is not allowed onto the Internet.

IP Static Route Filtering Configuration Example

Figure 11–8 shows how to configure a static route, redistribute (exchange the static route with other routes), and filter the static route (redistribution is covered later in this chapter).

Figure 11–8
*Network
201.222.5.0 is
filtered.*

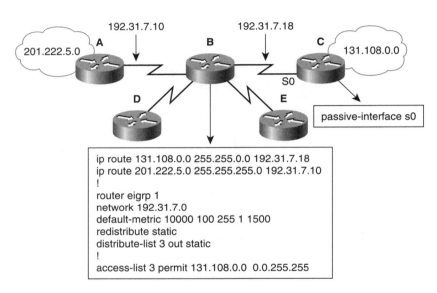

Command	Description
ip route 131.108.0.0 255.255.0.0 192.31.7.18	
131.108.0.0 255.255.0.0	Defines the IP address and subnet mask of the destination network.
192.31.7.18	Defines the next-hop address to use to reach the destination.
redistribute static	Assigns routes learned from static entries in the routing table to be redistributed into Enhanced IGRP.
distribute-list 3 out static	Filters routes, specified in distribute list 3, learned from static entries before those routes are passed to the Enhanced IGRP process.
access-list 3 permit 131.108.0.0 0.0.255.255	

Command	Description
3	The access list is list number 3.
permit	Routes that match the parameters will be advertised.
131.108.0.0 0.0.255.255	Packets from source IP addresses that match the first two octets of 131.108.0.0 will be forwarded.

Configure static route redistribution on one router only to eliminate the possibility of routing loops created by static route redistribution on routers with parallel routes between networks.

In Figure 11–8, the 131.108.0.0 route is passed to routers D and E. The 201.222.5.0 route is filtered by the access list.

This configuration might be used to route traffic from remote sites that connect using static routes. You might not want to make network 201.222.5.0 available to the remote users for security reasons or because the link to network 201.222.5.0 is slow or overused.

Redistribution Example Using ip default-network

This example demonstrates how you can redistribute in one direction and use a default route in the other direction, instead of redistributing in both directions.

Figure 11–9 illustrates an internetwork that uses three autonomous systems. In this case, OSPF is the core protocol and RIP is the "edge" protocol. The following pages illustrate how to configure a system:

- Allow the OSPF backbone to know all the routes in each autonomous system. This is done by configuring redistribution on the ASBRs so that RIP routes are redistributed into OSPF.

- Allow the RIP autonomous systems to know only about their internal routes, and use a default route to networks that are not in the autonomous system. This is done by configuring a default route on the ASBRs. The default route is advertised by the ASBRs into the RIP autonomous systems.

Figure 11–9
*OSPF pro-
vides the core
routingproto-
col.*

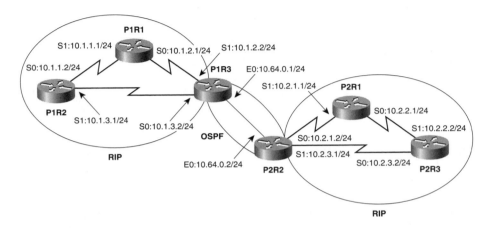

Note that many other ways to configure redistribution exist, so you must understand your network topology and requirements in order to choose the best solution.

The network shown in Figure 11–9 is the basis for the output shown on subsequent pages. The routers focused on are P1R3 (ASBR) and P1R1 (internal router).

Figure 11–10 shows the configurations for one of the ASBRs and a router in one of the RIP networks. Points about each configuration are as follows:

- Internal RIP router

  - No redistribution configuration is necessary because the intent is not to have this router learn about external routes.

  - The **ip classless** command is required on all RIP/IGRP routes that must use a default route. This command allows for classless forwarding, which means that the default paths can be used for unconnected subnets of the same major classful network rather than perform traditional classful behavior. Traditional classful behavior means the router drops packets when the target subnet is not present for the directly connected classful network.

- ASBR

  - When redistributing into OSPF, you need the subnets keyword for subnetted networks to be redistributed.

  - Define the default network to be advertised to the edge protocols.

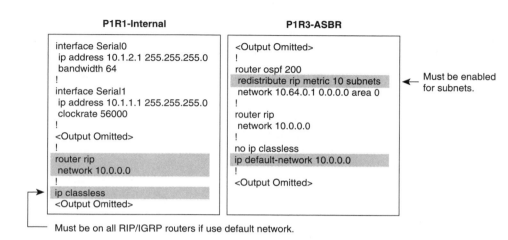

Figure 11–10
Router configuration output for P1R1 and P1R3.

The following illustrates the ASBR route tables of P1R3 after redistribution was enabled on both ASBRs:

```
P1R3#show ip route

   *        10.0.0.0/24 is subnetted, 6 subnets
C           10.1.3.0 is directly connected, Serial0
O E2        10.2.1.0 [110/10] via 172.6.31.6, 00:44:56, Ethernet0
C           10.1.2.0 is directly connected, Serial1
R           10.1.1.0 [120/1] via 10.1.3.1, 00:00:05, Serial0
                     [120/1] via 10.1.2.1, 00:00:17, Serial1
O E2        10.2.2.0 [110/10] via 172.6.31.6, 00:44:56, Ethernet0
O E2        10.2.3.0 [110/10] via 172.6.31.6, 00:44:56, Ethernet0
            172.6.0.0/24 is subnetted, 1 subnets
C           10.64.0.0 is directly connected, Ethernet0
```

For comparison, an example of the route table prior to redistribution is as follows:

```
P1R3#show ip route
<Output Omitted>

            10.0.0.0/24 is subnetted, 3 subnets
C           10.1.3.0 is directly connected, Serial0
C           10.1.2.0 is directly connected, Serial1
R           10.1.1.0 [120/1] via 10.1.3.1, 00:00:16, Serial0
```

```
                    [120/1] via 10.1.2.1, 00:00:28, Serial1
          172.6.0.0/24 is subnetted, 1 subnets
C         172.6.31.0 is directly connected, Ethernet0
```

Notice that in the "before" output, the 10.2.0.0/24 networks do not appear until redistribution is configured.

The following output shows one of the internal route tables of P1R1 after the default route was configured on the P1R3 ASBR.

```
P1R1#show ip route
<Output Omitted>

          10.0.0.0/24 is subnetted, 3 subnets
R         10.1.3.0 [120/1] via 10.1.1.2, 00:00:24, Serial1
              [120/1] via 10.1.2.2, 00:00:10, Serial0
C         10.1.2.0 is directly connected,  Serial0
C         10.1.1.0 is directly connected,  Serial1
R         0.0.0.0/0 [120/1] via 10.1.2.2, 00:00:10, Serial0
```

Using this route table, the P1R1 can successfully ping, for example, any network in the other RIP autonomous system, as follows:

```
P1R1#ping 10.2.2.1

Type escape sequence to abort.
Sending 5, 100-byte ICMP Echos to 10.2.2.1, timeout is 2 seconds:
!!!!!
Success rate is 100 percent (5/5), round-trip min/avg/max = 68/68/68 ms
P1R1#
```

Redistribution Example Using distance

This example uses RIP and IGRP to illustrate how a router can make a poor path selection due to the administrative distance values given to RIP and IGRP in a redundant network. The example also illustrates one possible way of correcting the problem.

Figure 11–11 illustrates the network prior to using multiple routing protocols. The R200 and Cen routers are the primary focus of this example, as are networks

172.16.6.0, 172.16.9.0, and 172.16.10.0. The configuration output and routing tables appear on the following pages.

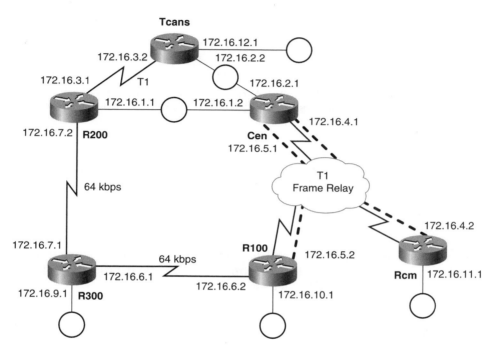

Figure 11–11
Redistribution using distance example.

There are a number of ways to correct path selection problems in a redistribution environment. The purpose of this example is to show how a problem can occur, where it appears, and one possible way of resolving it.

NOTES

The example solution that follows uses RIP and IGRP for simplicity. These and other protocol combinations can have the same problem occur, depending on the network topology, which is one reason why Cisco highly recommends that you study your network topology prior to implementing redistribution, and to monitor it after it is enabled.

The following is the complete IP route table for the Cen router:

```
Cen#show ip route
<Output Omitted>

      172.16.0.0/24 is subnetted, 11 subnets
I        172.16.12.0 [100/1188] via 172.16.2.2, 00:00:02, TokenRing0
I        172.16.9.0 [100/158813] via 172.16.1.1, 00:00:02, TokenRing1
I        172.16.10.0 [100/8976] via 172.16.5.2, 00:00:02, Serial0.1
I        172.16.11.0 [100/8976] via 172.16.4.2, 00:00:02, Serial0.2
C        172.16.4.0 is directly connected, Serial0.2
C        172.16.5.0 is directly connected, Serial0.1
I        172.16.6.0 [100/160250] via 172.16.5.2, 00:00:02, Serial0.1
I        172.16.7.0 [100/158313] via 172.16.1.1, 00:00:02, TokenRing1
C        172.16.1.0 is directly connected, TokenRing1
C        172.16.2.0 is directly connected, TokenRing0
I        172.16.3.0 [100/8539] via 172.16.2.2, 00:00:02, TokenRing0
                    [100/8539] via 172.16.1.1, 00:00:03, TokenRing1
```

Note the administrative distance and the composite metrics for each learned link. Recall that administrative distance refers to how believable the routing protocol is, and the composite metric is the value assigned to the link.

Now consider that you want to split the network into two autonomous systems—IGRP and RIP. Note that IGRP is more believable than RIP because it has an administrative distance of 100 and RIP has an administrative distance of 120.

Figure 11–12 shows the network with RIP and IGRP autonomous systems identified.

The configurations for two of the routers are as follows:

```
Router R200
router rip
redistribute igrp 1
passive-interface Serial0
passive-interface TokenRing0
network 172.16.0.0
default-metric 3
!
router igrp 1
redistribute rip
```

```
passive-interface Serial1
network 172.16.0.0
default-metric 10 100 255 1 1500
```

Router Cen
```
router rip
redistribute igrp 1
passive-interface Serial0.2
passive-interface TokenRing0
passive-interface TokenRing1
network 172.16.0.0
default-metric 3
!
router igrp 1
redistribute rip
passive-interface Serial0.1
network 172.16.0.90
default-metric 10 100 255 1 1500
```

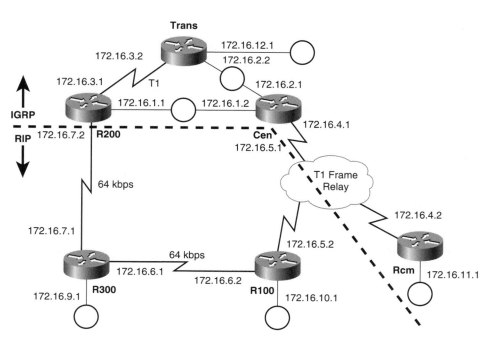

Figure 11–12
Splitting the network into two autonomous systems.

The **passive interface** command is used to prevent RIP routes from being forwarded needlessly on the links when the remote router cannot understand or is not using RIP, and similarly for IGRP.

Now, see what the route tables of the Cen router look like. The following shows the output from running the **show ip route** command on the Cen router:

```
Cen#show ip route
<Output Omitted>

      172.16.0.0/24 is subnetted, 11 subnets
R        172.16.9.0 [120/2] via 172.16.5.2, 00:00:01, Serial0.1
R        172.16.10.0 [120/1] via 172.16.5.2, 00:00:02, Serial0.1
I        172.16.11.0 [100/8976] via 172.16.4.2, 00:00:02, Serial0.2
C        172.16.4.0 is directly connected, Serial0.2
C        172.16.5.0 is directly connected, Serial0.1
R        172.16.6.0 [120/1] via 172.16.5.2, 00:00:02, Serial0.1
I        172.16.3.0 [100/8539] via 172.16.2.2, 00:00:02, TokenRing0
                    [100/8539] via 172.16.1.1, 00:00:02, TokenRing1
```

The Cen route table lists the routes that are relevant to the discussion in this section. Notice that the Cen router learned RIP and IGRP routes.

If you look at the network topology, there are several destinations whose paths are better when learned by RIP because they are in the RIP domain. These destinations are 172.16.9.0, 172.16.10.0, and 172.16.6.0. Regardless of the router, you want the RIP versions of these routes to be learned.

The following route table lists the routes that are relevant to the discussion in this section. The table shows the routes learned by R200. Notice that all the routes are learned from IGRP, even though R200 is also connected to a RIP network. Notice too that when you trace some of the routes, such as to network 172.16.9.0, the long way via router Cen rather than via router R300 appears in the following route table:

```
R200#show ip route
<Output Omitted>

Gateway of last resort is not set

      172.16.0.0/24 is subnetted, 11 subnets
I        172.16.9.0 [100/1000163] via 172.16.1.2, 00:00:37, TokenRing0
```

```
I       172.16.10.0 [100/1000163] via 172.16.1.2, 00:00:37, TokenRing0
I       172.16.11.0 [100/9039] via 172.16.1.2, 00:00:37, TokenRing0
I       172.16.4.0 [100/8539] via 172.16.1.2, 00:00:37, TokenRing0
I       172.16.5.0 [100/8539] via 172.16.1.2, 00:00:37, TokenRing0
I       172.16.6.0 [100/1000163] via 172.16.1.2, 00:00:37, TokenRing0
C       172.16.3.0 is directly connected, Serial0
```

Router R200 selected the poor paths because IGRP has a better administrative distance than RIP. To make sure that R200 selects the RIP routes, you can change the administrative distance, as shown in the Figure 11–13.

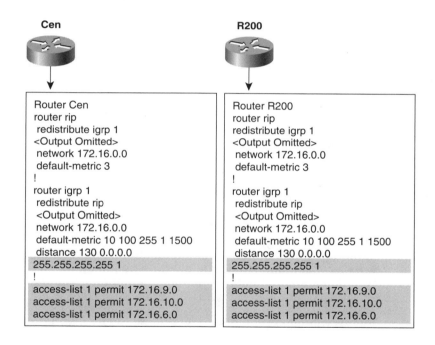

Cen   R200

Router Cen
 router rip
  redistribute igrp 1
  <Output Omitted>
  network 172.16.0.0
  default-metric 3
 !
 router igrp 1
  redistribute rip
  <Output Omitted>
  network 172.16.0.0
  default-metric 10 100 255 1 1500
  distance 130 0.0.0.0
  255.255.255.255 1
 !
 access-list 1 permit 172.16.9.0
 access-list 1 permit 172.16.10.0
 access-list 1 permit 172.16.6.0

Router R200
 router rip
  redistribute igrp 1
  <Output Omitted>
  network 172.16.0.0
  default-metric 3
 !
 router igrp 1
  redistribute rip
  <Output Omitted>
  network 172.16.0.0
  default-metric 10 100 255 1 1500
  distance 130 0.0.0.0
  255.255.255.255 1
 !
 access-list 1 permit 172.16.9.0
 access-list 1 permit 172.16.10.0
 access-list 1 permit 172.16.6.0

Figure 11–13
Router configurations.

On router R200, for example, it is configured to assign an administrative distance of 130 to IGRP routes to networks 172.16.9.0, 172.16.10.0, and 172.16.6.0. In this way, when the router learns about these networks from RIP, the RIP-learned routes will be selected and put in the routing table. Note that the **distance** command is for IGRP-learned routes because it is part of the IGRP routing process configuration.

Now consider the **show ip route** output from router R200, as follows:

```
R200#show ip route
<Output Omitted>

     172.16.0.0/24 is subnetted, 11 subnets
R       172.16.9.0 [120/1] via 172.16.7.1, 00:00:19, Serial1
R       172.16.10.0 [120/2] via 172.16.7.1, 00:00:19, Serial1
I       172.16.11.0 [100/9039] via 172.16.1.2, 00:00:49, TokenRing0
I       172.16.4.0 [100/8539] via 172.16.1.2, 00:00:49, TokenRing0
I       172.16.5.0 [100/8539] via 172.16.1.2, 00:00:49, TokenRing0
R       172.16.6.0 [120/1] via 172.16.7.1, 00:00:19, Serial1
C       172.16.3.0 is directly connected, Serial0
```

Router R200 now has retained the better route to some of the networks by learning them from RIP.

With this type of configuration, however, note the loss of routing information. That is, given the actual bandwidths involved, the IGRP path would have been better for the 172.16.10.0 network. But to select that route, you would need to retain the sub-optimal path for 172.16.9.0.

Key Concept

Important concepts of this example include the following:

- **Know your network traffic patterns before enabling redistribution.**
- **Verify redistribution operation after configuration.**
- **If suboptimal paths exist, determine the solution based on user requirements.**

This example illustrates that you should not only know your network prior to implementing redistribution, but also that you should view which routes the routers are selecting after redistribution is enabled. You should pay particular attention to routers that can select from a number of possible redundant paths to a network because they are more likely to select suboptimal paths.

VERIFYING REDISTRIBUTION OPERATION

Following is the best way to verify redistribution operation:

- Know your network topology, particularly where redundant routes exist.

- Show the routing table of the appropriate routing protocol on a variety of routers in the internetwork using the **show** command. For example, check the routing table on the ASBR as well as some of the internal routers in each autonomous system.

- Perform a **trace** on some of the routes that go across the autonomous systems to verify that the shortest path is being used for routing. Make sure that you especially run traces to networks for which redundant routes exist.

- If you do encounter routing problems, use **trace** and **debug** commands to observe the routing update traffic on the ASBRs and internal routers.

TIPS

Running **debug** requires extra processing by the router, so if the router is already over-loaded, initiating **debug** is not recommended.

SUMMARY

In this chapter, you learned that there are many ways to control routing update traffic, including passive interface, default routes, static routes, and route filtering. You also learned that *redistribution* (the capability for boundary routers connecting different autonomous systems to exchange and advertise routing information received from one autonomous system to the other autonomous system) enables you to exchange routing information between dissimilar routing protocols and requires some care when configuring.

In the next chapter, you learn how to connect an enterprise network to an Internet service provider (ISP).

Chapter Eleven Test
Optimizing Routing Update Operation

Estimated Time: 15 minutes

Complete all the exercises to test your knowledge of the materials contained in this chapter. Answers are listed in Appendix A, "Chapter Test Answer Key."

Use the information contained in this chapter to answer the following questions.

Question 11.1

Consider that you have a dial-up WAN connection between site A and site B. What can you do to prevent excess routing update traffic from crossing the list, but still have the boundary routers know the networks that are at the remote sites?

_____

_____

_____

Question 11.2

When configuring a default route for RIP, the default route 0.0.0.0 and the actual default network address will be advertised by the router. What can you do to prevent the router from advertising the actual default network address and advertise only the 0.0.0.0 network address?

_____

_____

_____

Question 11.3

List two reasons why you may not want routing information propagated.

A. _____

B. _____

Question 11.4

Match the term with the definition:

_____ Passive interface

_____ Default routes

_____ Static routes

A. Instructs the router that if it does not have a route for a given destination, it should send the packet to the default route.

B. A route to a destination that you configured in the router. In contrast, dynamic routes are those learned via routing protocol, such as RIP or EIGRP.

C. Prevents all routing updates from being sent through an interface. For EIGRP and OSPF, this method includes hello protocol packets.

Question 11.5

What are the three key issues to remember when implementing redistribution?

A. _____

B. _____

C. _____

Connecting Enterprises to an Internet Service Provider

This chapter focuses on connecting enterprises to an Internet service provider (ISP). It is the last in a series of discussions about scalable routing protocols. This discussion is unique because it includes information about the Border Gateway Protocol (BGP)—an IP exterior routing protocol.

Previous discussions have dealt with IP interior gateway protocols (IGPs) such as IGRP. This chapter focuses on BGP configuration tasks for local networks. BGP is used throughout the Internet by ISPs, but this chapter focuses on the use of BGP by enterprises to connect to an ISP, and on configuring static and default routes to connect to an ISP as alternatives to BGP.

BGP AND ISP CONNECTIVITY BASICS

BGP, an IP exterior routing protocol, was originally defined in RFCs 1163, 1267, 1654, and 1655. Further definition and modification was provided in RFCs 1771 and 1772.

BGP enables an interdomain routing system that guarantees loop-free exchange of routing information between autonomous systems. BGP differs from the IGPs mentioned earlier in this book in the following ways:

- BGP is a policy-based routing protocol. It does not use technical metrics, but rather makes routing decisions based on network policy decisions.

- BGP updates are carried in TCP segments. This means TCP connections must be negotiated between BGP neighbors before updates can be exchanged. This implies that prior to BGP, the neighbors have routes to reach each other.

These two key differences are the tip of the iceberg as to why BGP is very complicated to configure. Fortunately, ISPs deal with the brunt of this configuration. This is one reason why you pay ISPs to connect you to the Internet—they save you from having to deal with BGP and all its complexities.

This chapter focuses on configurations that have a primary goal of providing Internet connectivity for networks within a single autonomous system. In such a configuration, only minimal, if any, BGP is needed. Within the context of BGP, an *autonomous system* is a group of networks/routers sharing the same policies. The networks of an autonomous system are under a common administrative control.

When Not to Use BGP

In many cases, the routing policy that will be implemented in the autonomous system is consistent with the policy implemented in the ISP autonomous system. In these cases, it is not necessary or even desirable to configure BGP in the autonomous system. BGP technology and implementation is more complex than an Interior Gateway Protocol (IGP) such as IGRP or OSPF. Connectivity can be achieved through a combination of static routes and default networks.

When you connect to two different ISPs, it is frequently necessary to use BGP. Redundancy, load sharing, and lower tariffs at particular times of the day or night are reasons why some network administrators connect their enterprise to two different ISPs. If you have a backup link for redundancy, you can use a combination of static and default routes instead of BGP. If both of these connections are active at the same time, however, BGP is required. Also, any time your policy requirements differ from the policy of your ISP, BGP is again required.

In Figure 12–1, router A is advertising a default network backward into the autonomous system using a local IGP, such as RIP. A static route affords connectivity to router B and the ISP autonomous system. The ISP is running BGP and is recognized by other BGP routers in the Internet.

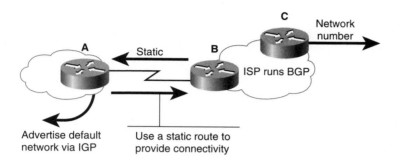

Figure 12–1
You can avoid BGP configuration by using default networks and static routes.

It is necessary to use BGP to connect to an ISP only when you have different policy requirements than the ISP.

Key Concept

For more information about the BGP protocol, refer to RFC 1654, *A Border Gateway Protocol 4* (BGP-4). To determine whether it is necessary to run BGP, refer to RFC 1930, *Guidelines for creation, selection, and registration of an Autonomous System (AS)*. For more information on the applicability of BGP, refer to RFC 1772, *Application of the Border Gateway Protocol in the Internet* (makes RFC 1655 obsolete).

Policy Drives BGP Requirements

In the example shown in Figure 12–2, autonomous system 400 is configured with a static route to router C. From the point of view of router A, the networks connected by router F have the same policy as the networks in the ISP autonomous system 200.

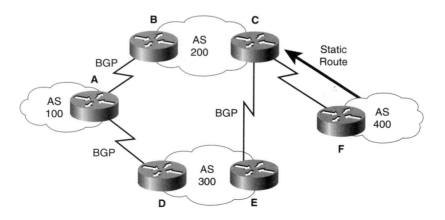

Figure 12–2
The policy for AS 100 is to always use AS 300 path to reach AS 400.

A new pathing policy that refers to autonomous system 400 cannot be implemented in autonomous system 100 because this requires being able to distinguish the networks in autonomous system 400 from other autonomous systems. In this case, for autonomous system 100 to know of the existence of autonomous system 400, autonomous system 400 will have to be connected via BGP.

In order to implement the policy discussed on the previous page, router F must be configured with BGP so that the autonomous system 400 is announced.

BGP Sessions

BGP sessions are carried by the Transmission Control Protocol (TCP), a reliable transport mechanism. BGP supports the following two types of sessions between a router and its neighbors:

- *External BGP (EBGP) session*—Occurs between routers in two different autonomous systems. These routers are usually adjacent to one another, sharing the same media and a subnet.

- *Internal BGP (IBPG) session*—Occurs between routers in the same autonomous system, as shown in Figure 12–3, and is used to coordinate and synchronize routing policy within the autonomous system. Neighbors may be located anywhere in the autonomous system, even several hops away from one another.

Figure 12–3
There are two types of BGP sessions: external and internal.

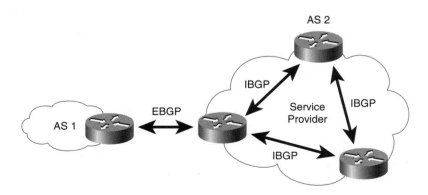

An IBGP session occurs between routers in the same autonomous system in an ISP. The IBGP session coordinates BGP routing policy within an autonomous system.

BGP Operation

BGP deals primarily with autonomous system pathing rather than routing decisions. For this reason, BGP must work with an IGP such as RIP, OSPF, or Enhanced IGRP in order to advertise routes into an autonomous system.

If you want the IGP to advertise BGP-learned routes into the autonomous system, you must use the **redistribute** command.

You must be careful when doing this, however. BGP tables can be quite large, so it is usually best to perform filtering with BGP redistribution (as discussed in Chapter 11, "Optimizing Routing Update Operation").

The BGP **network** command operates differently from an IGP network command. BGP uses the **network** command to determine which routes to advertise to other Autonomous Systems. In a sense, the **network** command for BGP redistributes the IGP routes into the BGP network.

CONNECTING TO AN ISP USING BGP AND ALTERNATIVES

This section covers connecting to an ISP using static routes, default routes, and BGP. First static routes will be presented, followed by a default route example, and then BGP itself.

Connecting an enterprise network to an ISP can involve using a combination of static and default routes, or if a different policy needs to be implemented, using BGP.

Static Route Command Review

Recall that a *static route* is a route to a destination that you configured in the router. In contrast, dynamic routes are those learned via routing protocol, such as RIP or EIGRP.

Use the **ip route** command to define a static route entry in the IP routing table. The source of a route is defined in the routing table by an *administrative distance* (the believability of a routing protocol). By default, the administrative distance of a static route specified with the *ip-address* parameter is set to 1. The default administrative distance of a static route specified with the interface parameter is set to 0. Floating static routes are available to establish another connection using an alternative Internet service provider.

ip route Command	Description
network mask	Describes remote network to be entered into the IP routing table.
interface	Identifies the local router outbound interface that must be traversed to reach the remote network.
ip-address	IP address of an adjacent interface of a peer router.
distance	Overrides the default values by assigning an administrative distance.

RIP Static Route Example

Figure 12–4 shows an RIP static route example. The route 0.0.0.0 is a default route in the IP routing table. If there is no matching route for the destination IP address in the routing table, the 0.0.0.0 will match the address and cause the packet to be routed out interface serial 0.

Figure 12–4
Place the static default route entry on serial 0 interface.

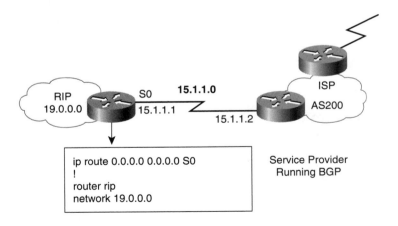

OSPF Example

The **default-information originate always** command in OSPF propagates a default route into the OSPF autonomous system. This has a similar effect as the previous RIP example. The **always** keyword causes the default route to always be advertised, whether or not the router has a default route. This ensures that the default route will get advertised.

Figure 12–5 shows an OSPF configuration that uses the default route.

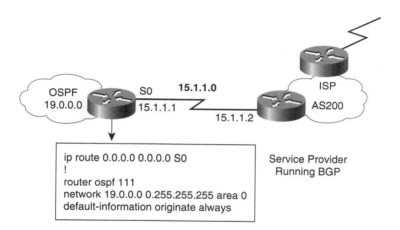

Figure 12–5
OSPF default configuration using a static route.

BGP Configuration Commands

The syntax of the BGP commands is similar to the syntax for configuring internal routing protocols; however, there are significant differences in the way that an external protocol functions.

Use the **router bgp** command to activate the BGP protocol and identify the local autonomous system. The autonomous system number will be assigned to you by the InterNIC. This is different than the AS numbers of IGRP, in which case any number could be used.

router bgp Command	Description
autonomous-system	Identifies the local autonomous system

Use the **network** command to permit BGP to advertise a network when it is present in the IP routing table.

network Command	Description
network-number	Identifies an IP network to be advertised by BGP

The **network** command must include all networks that you want to advertise from within your autonomous system, not just those locally connected.

The value placed in the autonomous system field of the **neighbor** command determines whether the communication with the neighbor is an EBGP or an IBGP session. If the autonomous system field configured in the **router bgp** command is identical, BGP will initiate an internal session. If the field values are different, BGP will have an external session.

Use the **neighbor remote-as** command to identify a peer router with which the local router will establish a session.

neighbor remote-as Command	Description
ip address	Identifies the peer router.
autonomous-system	Identifies the autonomous system of the peer router. If this is the same as the local autonomous system, the session will be internal. If the autonomous systems are different, the session will be external.

Use the **clear ip bgp** command to remove entries from the BGP routing table and reset BGP sessions. Use this command after every configuration change to ensure that the change is activated and that peer routers are informed.

clear ip bgp Command	Description
*	Clear all.
address	Identifies a specific network to be removed from the BGP table.

TIPS

Use the **clear** command with the asterisk option (clear all) whenever you make changes to a configuration in order for those changes to take effect.

The **clear** command really forces propagation of characteristics along EBGP sessions. Technically, it is not always required to make a configuration change take effect in the network. However, rather than attempt to teach the complicated conditions under which the **clear** command is required, it is simply safer to do it each time a configuration change is made, as a matter of habit. This practice ensures that changes will always be implemented correctly.

The alternative can be a lengthy problem analysis when the expected configuration change does not occur in the network.

BGP Configuration Example

It is likely that the simple configuration shown in Figure 12–6 will be the only BGP commands that you will need.

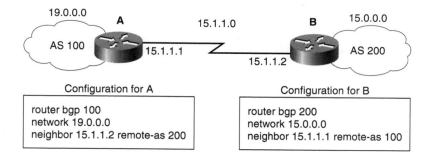

Figure 12–6
This configuration is representative of most common BGP configurations.

This configuration shows only the most basic BGP configuration. No policy has been configured. Configuring BGP policy is very complicated. Before attempting BGP policy configuration, further study on this topic is recommended.

VERIFYING BGP OPERATION WITH THE SHOW COMMANDS

Verifying BGP operation can be accomplished using the following **show** commands:

- **show ip bgp**—Displays entries in the BGP routing table. Specify a network number to get more specific information about a particular network, or use the **subnets** keyword.

- **show ip bgp paths**—Displays all the BGP paths in the database.

- **show ip bgp summary**—Displays the status on all BGP connections.

- **show ip bgp neighbors**—Displays the status of all BGP connections.

Other BGP **show** commands can be found in the user documentation.

SUMMARY

BGP is a protocol used to connect autonomous systems. BGP enables an interdomain routing system that guarantees loop-free exchange of routing information between autonomous systems. When the routing policy that will be implemented in the autonomous system is consistent with the policy implemented in the ISP autonomous system, it is not necessary or even desirable to configure BGP in the autonomous system.

You learned that static routes or default routes can be used if the autonomous system policy is consistent with ISP policy. In the next chapter, you review WAN connectivity.

Chapter Twelve Test
Connecting Enterprises to an Internet Service Provider

Estimated Time: 5 minutes

Complete all the exercises to test your knowledge of the materials contained in this chapter. Answers are listed in Appendix A, "Chapter Test Answer Key."

Use the information contained in this chapter to indicate whether the following statements are true or false.

Question 12.1

T F   Static and default routes are inferior alternatives to BGP for connecting to an ISP.

Question 12.2

T F   BGP is simpler to implement than a static or default route to connect to an ISP.

Question 12.3

T F   It is necessary to use BGP to connect to an ISP if you have different policy requirements than the ISP.

Question 12.4

T F   The Internet uses BGP extensively.

PART 4

Configuring Dialup Connectivity

WAN Connectivity Overview

The purpose of this chapter is to provide an overview of the different types of WAN connections, encapsulation types, and compression methods that Cisco supports.

In this chapter, you compare the differences between WAN connection types: dedicated, asynchronous dial-in, dial-on-demand, and packet-switched services. You then determine when to use PPP, HDLC, LAPB, and IETF encapsulation types.

WAN CONNECTIVITY OPTIONS

This chapter discusses several ways you can interconnect your remote sites using WAN technology. Although Cisco routers support a wide variety of WAN technologies, the other chapters in this book focus on configuring dial-up services over ISDN BRIs.

The variety of WAN connection types offered by telcos and service providers can be grouped into the following categories:

- Dedicated connectivity

- Asynchronous dial-in connectivity

- Dial-on-demand routing (DDR)

- Packet-switched networks (PSNs) and circuit-switched networks

The following section further details each of these connectivity options.

Dedicated Connectivity

Dedicated connectivity, also referred to as a leased line, provides full-time synchronous connections and is available in many Cisco products. Note that some Cisco routers require that a CSU/DSU (channel service unit/data service unit) is attached to the synchronous serial port, whereas other Cisco routers have built in CSU/DSUs, as shown in Figure 13–1.

Figure 13–1
Dedicated links are continuously available.

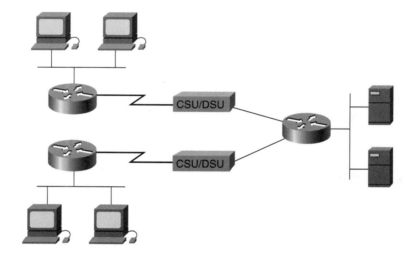

Dedicated, full-time connectivity is provided by point-to-point serial links. Connections are made using the router's synchronous serial ports with typical bandwidth use of up to 2 Mbps (E1) available through the use of a channel service unit/data service unit (CSU/DSU). Different encapsulation methods, such as PPP and HDLC at the data link layer provide flexibility and reliability for user traffic. These encapsulation methods are covered in more detail later in this chapter and in the Cisco Press book *Introduction to Cisco Router Configuration*.

Leased lines of this type are ideal for high-volume environments with a steady-rate traffic pattern or when other WAN connectivity options are not available. Use of available bandwidth is a concern because tariffs are paid even when the connection is idle.

Dedicated links are established using the synchronous serial ports of the routers. The router ports connect to the carrier service through CSU/DSUs operating at speeds from 56/64 kbps (DS-0) up to 115 Mbps (OC-3).

Asynchronous Dial-In Connectivity

Users with asynchronous modems can make temporary connections using the *Public Switched Telephone Network* (PSTN). Multiple dial-in clients connected to an access server can retrieve email or data from the LAN-based servers, as shown in Figure 13–2.

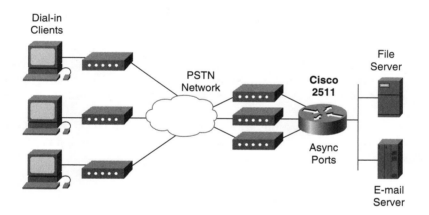

Figure 13–2
Asynchronous dial-up connections allow remote users access to shared data.

Cisco access servers provide the following services:

- *Remote-node services*—Connects a single user to the home office LAN.

- *Terminal services*—Supports several widely used terminal services, such as the following:

  o Telnet/rlogin—Telnet provides virtual terminal connections to a host computer. It is one of the most popular tools on the Internet. rlogin is similar to Telnet, but it works only in UNIX environments (such as those based on Berkeley UNIX).

o X.25 PAD—A character-based terminal in an X.25 environment does not normally contain the resources to implement the three levels of X.25, so it connects to a public switched network via a translation device called a packet assembler/disassembler (PAD).

o TN3270—TCP/IP Telnet 3270 (TN3270) is a virtual terminal protocol that can be used to access IBM 3270 applications.

- *Protocol translation services*—Translates between a specific set of terminal service protocols. Protocol translation services are provided between telnet, LAT, X.25 PAD, and TN3270.

- *vty-Async*—Translates an incoming X.25 call to PPP. Useful for remote node PPP users who want to call a local X.25 access point, such as CompuServe.

- *Asynchronous routing services*—Provides DDR for multiple protocols.

- *Security*—Call authentication can be done by PPP, or by such applications as TACACS+.

The connections shown in Figure 13–2 are asynchronous and data transfer rates depend on modem, line, and server characteristics. Current Cisco products support line speeds up to 115 kbps, except the AUX port, which only does 38.4 kbps.

Asynchronous connections are excellent for users reading e-mail and other temporary operations, but may not be well suited for the full-time, high-speed data transfers needed to support today's internetworks.

Dial-on-Demand Routing

Dial-on-demand routing (DDR) means that the connection is enabled only when a specific type of traffic initiates the call, or when you need a backup link. These circuit-switched calls are placed using PSTN or ISDN networks, as shown in Figure 13–3. DDR is available on Cisco products having asynchronous auxiliary ports, synchronous serial ports, or ISDN ports.

DDR is a substitute for leased lines when full-time circuit availability is not required, such as the following:

- When traffic patterns are low-volume or periodic.

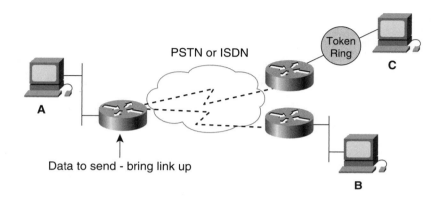

Figure 13–3
Connections are made only when traffic dictates a need.

- Calls are placed and connections are established only when traffic marked as "interesting" is detected by the router. Periodic broadcasts, such as routing protocol updates, should be prevented from triggering a call.

- When you need a backup connection for redundancy or load sharing.

- DDR can be used to provide backup load sharing and interface backup. For example, you might have several serial lines, but you want the second serial line to be used only when the first line is very busy so load sharing can occur.

- When your WAN lines are used for critical applications, you may want a DDR line configured in case the primary lines go down. At this point, the secondary line will enable itself so traffic can still get across.

TIPS

DDR provides a low-cost and infrequent connectivity solution for many internetworks. Some applications, however, cannot tolerate the call setup delay associated with circuit-switched services. What is required is a service that combines rapid connection setup with the flexibility to reach different destinations. Such a service is available using a packet-switched network.

ISDN provides WAN transport for all major routing protocols. ISDN also works with other WAN services such as X.25 and Frame Relay.

Cisco offers a broad range of ISDN products, including several router models that contain native ISDN interfaces. Administrators can use an SNMP-based network management application to control the ISDN interfaces. Routers use an ISDN Management Information Base (MIB) and can act as managed objects by maintaining performance statistics and supplying them to an authenticated SNMP management console.

The multiple, independent B channels on router ISDN configurations transmit data at the standard 64-kbps (DS0) rate, or you can configure for 56-kbps facilities. The bandwidth-on-demand option allows a pre-established load threshold setting to add available B-channel resources to an ISDN call. This DDR dialer load condition could, for example, add a DS0 on demand.

Another option on Cisco routers is to pre-establish table entries on a destination router to provide incoming ISDN call screening. The destination (or *called router*) acts on entries that specify which calls from a source router (or *calling router*) the destination will accept.

MultiLink PPP encapsulation offers improved capabilities for standards-based access to the Internet. Among these improvements are access control and compression methods. Multilink PPP (MP) is a methodology that combines several incoming connections from a single device to look like a single stream of traffic. This allows the user to get bandwidth as needed.

DDR improves the cost-effective use of ISDN by setting conditions that make the ISDN call, and then dropping the call once the link is no longer needed.

Packet-Switched Services

Packet-switched WAN services use virtual circuits that provide end-to-end connectivity. Physical connections are accomplished by statically programmed switching devices and are useful for connecting multiple sites, as shown in Figure 13–4. The client router, in this case, the router in Milpitas, California, is connected through a local loop to a packet switch point-of-presence. From there, it is packet switched until it reaches the final switch, where it goes through another local loop to the remote CPE. PSNs can be either privately or publicly maintained. The underlying switching fabric is transparent to the user, and the switches are responsible only for the internal delivery of data.

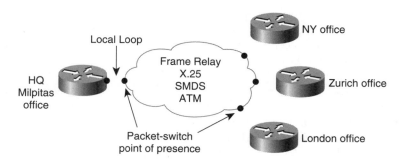

Figure 13–4
*Packet-switch
ed networks
are multi-
access, and
data is carried
within frames,
packets, or
cells.*

Packet-switched and cell-switched technologies used today include the following:

- Frame Relay

- Switched Multimegabit Data Service (SMDS)

- X.25

- ATM

A number of Cisco devices (such as the 2600, 3600, 4000 and 7000 series products and the LightStream 1010 ATM Switch) support ATM, whereas Frame Relay and SMDS are supported on all products containing synchronous serial interfaces. Some switched services require specialized equipment to connect the router to the switching device.

Frame Relay Networks

As an interface between user and network equipment, Frame Relay provides a means for *statistically multiplexing* (dynamically combining or multiplexing data from many logical channels into a single physical channel) many virtual circuits over a single physical transmission link. Frame Relay takes advantage of recent advances in digital transmission technology where error rates are extremely low. Over links with relatively high reliability, data-link-level protocols can forgo time-consuming error-correction algorithms, leaving them to be performed at higher protocol layers when required. Greater performance and efficiency, therefore, is possible without sacrificing data integrity.

Frame Relay is designed with this approach in mind. It includes a cyclic redundancy check (CRC) for detecting corrupted bits (so the data can be discarded), but it does not include any protocol mechanisms for correcting bad data (for example, by retransmitting it at this level of protocol).

The Frame Relay protocol does not include explicit flow control procedures that are redundant with those in higher layers. Rather, very simple congestion notification mechanisms are provided to allow a network to inform the Frame Relay data terminal equipment (DTE) when the network resources are nearly congested. Where the higher-layer protocol provides the necessary interfaces, this congestion notification can be used to alert the end systems that they should invoke flow control mechanisms.

TIPS

For a good overview of Frame Relay, X.25, and SMDS, see "Packet Services," available on Cisco Connection Online at www.cisco.com/warp/customer/732/Tech/pksrv_tc.htm.

X.25 Networks

X.25 provides end-to-end communication between DTEs through a bidirectional association called a *virtual circuit*. Virtual circuits permit communication between distinct network elements through any number of intermediate nodes on a switched network without the dedication of portions of the physical medium that characterizes physical circuits. Virtual circuits can either be permanent or switched (temporary).

Permanent virtual circuits are commonly called PVCs; switched virtual circuits are commonly called SVCs. PVCs are typically used for the most-often-used data transfers, whereas SVCs are used for sporadic data transfers.

Once a virtual circuit is established, the DTE sends a packet to the other end of the connection by sending it to the DCE using the proper virtual circuit. The DCE looks at the virtual circuit number to determine how to route the packet through the X.25 network. The Layer 3 X.25 protocol multiplexes between all the DTEs served by the DCE on the destination side of the network and the packet is delivered to the destination DTE.

X.25 uses three virtual circuit operational procedures:

- Call setup

- Data transfer

- Call clearing

Execution of these procedures depends on the virtual circuit type being used. For a PVC, X.25 is always in data transfer mode because the circuit has been permanently established. If an SVC is used, all three procedures are used.

Packets are used to transfer data. X.25 segments and reassembles user messages if they are too long for the maximum packet size of the circuit. Each data packet is given a sequence number, so error and flow control can occur across the DTE/DCE interface.

SMDS Networks

Switched Multimegabit Data Service (SMDS) is a high-speed, packet-switched, datagram service used for very high-speed WAN communication. SMDS is described in a series of specifications produced by Bellcore. With the advent of ATM, the future of SMDS is in question.

SMDS is a connectionless packet service. Connectionless services do not require the establishment of a logical connection or circuit between two end devices before transferring data. In such an environment, each transfer of data between source and destination is considered an independent, autonomous transaction. Because of this fact, addressing information must be included in every packet. The addressing information is evaluated at each switching device. Switching tables within these devices associate destination addresses with the next switching device along the path to the destination.

SMDS can use fiber- or copper-based media. It supports speeds of 64 kbps over digital signal level 1 (DS1) transmission facilities, or 44.736 Mbps over digital signal level 3 (DS3) transmission facilities.

The SMDS Interface Protocol (SIP) defines the SMDS DTE/DCE interface. The SIP is based on an IEEE standard protocol for metropolitan-area networks (MANs): the IEEE 802.6 Distributed Queue Dual Bus (DQDB) standard. Using this protocol, DTE such as routers can attach to an SMDS network and use the service for high-speed internetworking.

ATM Networks

ATM is a cell-switching and multiplexing technology designed to combine the benefits of circuit switching (constant transmission delay, guaranteed capacity) with those of packet switching (flexibility, efficiency for intermittent traffic). Like X.25, Frame Relay, and SMDS, ATM defines the DTE/DCE interface, which ATM refers to as the User-Network Interface (UNI).

ATM is connection-oriented and primarily uses PVCs to establish connections. Specialized switches forward the traffic within the ATM cloud. ATM technology is blossoming and, as a result, the standards are still evolving. New technologies will allow ATM to operate at transmission rates in excess of 600 Mbps.

Because those who created SMDS anticipated cell relay techniques, it is not a coincidence that ATM and SMDS share some features. For example, both ATM and SIP level 1 use 53-byte cells. Even the fields within these cells are similar or, in some cases, the same. SMDS/ATM similarities allow companies to easily replace SMDS DSUs with ATM DSUs or to upgrade the software within the DSUs to migrate from SMDS to ATM. Further, ATM-based access to SMDS networks is an industry trend.

Key Concept   **Each of these different connection types can be used in a modern network. In fact, most state-of-the-art internetworks employ some dial-in lines, some point-to-point connections, some circuit-switched periodic connections, and some carrier-provided packet-switched connections.**

WAN Encapsulation Protocols

Each WAN connection type uses a Layer 2 protocol to encapsulate traffic while it is crossing the WAN link, as shown in Figure 13–5. To ensure that the correct encapsulation protocol is used, you will need to configure the Layer 2 encapsulation type to use. The choice of encapsulation protocol depends on the WAN technology and the communicating equipment.

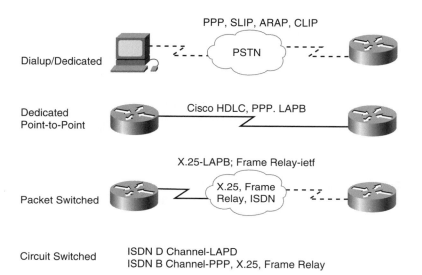

Figure 13-5
*WAN encap-
sulation proto-
cols.*

Dialup/Dedicated

PPP, SLIP, ARAP, CLIP

PSTN

Dedicated
Point-to-Point

Cisco HDLC, PPP. LAPB

X.25-LAPB; Frame Relay-ietf

Packet Switched

X.25, Frame
Relay, ISDN

Circuit Switched

ISDN D Channel-LAPD
ISDN B Channel-PPP, X.25, Frame Relay

Encapsulation protocols that can be used with the WAN connection types covered in this chapter are as follows:

- *PPP*—Common for dial-up single-user-to-LAN or LAN-to-LAN (router-to-router) access. PPP is standardized, so it supports vendor interoperability. It also supports the encapsulation of multiple upper-layer protocols including IP and IPX, and user authentication. SLIP is also available for dial-up users running IP.

- *HDLC*—The Cisco default encapsulation type on point-to-point links. It is used typically when communicating with another Cisco device. If communicating with a non-Cisco device, synchronous PPP is a viable option.

- *LAPB (layer 2 of the X.25 protocol stack)*—For packet-switched networks, the LAPB protocol is used to encapsulate X.25 packets. It can also be used over point-to-point links, if the link is unreliable or there is an inherent delay associated with the link, such as in a satellite link. LAPB provides reliability and flow control on a point-to-point basis.

- *Cisco/IETF*—Used to encapsulate Frame Relay traffic. The Cisco option is proprietary and can be used only between Cisco routers. It has a 4-byte header, with 2 bytes to identify the DLCI and 2 bytes to identify the packet type. *ietf* is defined in RFC 1490 and uses 2-octet addressing (with a 10-bit DLCI) and a 1-octet control field. Use *ietf* when connecting to another vendor's equipment.

CONNECTION CONSIDERATIONS

It is estimated that WAN usage costs are typically 80 percent of the entire IS budget. For this reason, selecting a WAN service that meet the desired needs but does not cost any more than necessary is an important process. To determine which WAN services meet the required needs, consider the following:

- *Availability of services*—Not all WAN services are available in all areas of the world, nor does every service provider offer each service. For example, ATM is not available in all geographic locations. Determine which services are available in your target areas.

- *Application traffic*—Categorize the type of application traffic that will cross the link. For example, traffic may consist of many small packets, such as a terminal session, or very large packets, such as large file transfers.

- *Bandwidth*—WAN bandwidth is expensive, and most organizations cannot afford to pay for more bandwidth than they need, so determining the amount of traffic that will cross the link, as well as how often during the day a WAN connection is required, is necessary.

- *Ease of management*—Network designers are often concerned about the degree of difficulty associated with managing connections. Connection management includes both the configuration at initial startup and the ongoing configuration tasks of normal operation. Traffic management is the connection's capability to adjust to different rates of traffic regardless of whether the traffic is steady-state or bursty (sporadically busy) in nature.

- *Routing protocol characteristics*—Routing protocols have overhead traffic in the form of broadcasts and routing updates. This traffic can cause degradation of performance across low-bandwidth serial lines. You can use a WAN analyzer or figure out the overhead of these protocols by multiplying routing update frequency by the packet size.

SUMMARY

This chapter covered the available WAN services, including dedicated links, asynchronous dial-in, dial-on-demand routing, and packet-switched.

Recall that most state-of-the-art internetworks employ some dial-in lines, some point-to-point connections, some circuit-switched periodic connections, and some carrier-provided packet-switched connections. Your solution will also most likely lead to a combination of services.

You also learned about the WAN encapsulation options of Cisco HDLC, PPP, and ietf. Finally, you learned about some connection guidelines for picking the most efficient service to meet your networking needs.

In the next chapter, you learn how to configure dial-on-demand routing to ensure the best performance with a minimum of connection time.

Chapter Thirteen Test
WAN Connectivity Overview

Estimated Time: 15 minutes

Complete all the exercises to test your knowledge of the materials contained in this chapter. Answers are listed in Appendix A, "Chapter Test Answer Key."

Use the information contained in this chapter to answer the following questions.

Question 13.1

List four issues that need to be considered when evaluating a WAN service.

A. _____

B. _____

C. _____

D. _____

Question 13.2

When full-time connectivity is required, which one of the following is a viable option?

A. PPP

B. Point-to-point over serial links

C. DDR

Question 13.3

DDR routing is useful for which one of the following environments?

A. Full-time connectivity between routers

B. When packets should be prioritized through an interface

C. When the number of packets crossing the link should be controlled

D. When only certain types of information contained in incoming packets should trigger a call

Question 13.4

Which WAN encapsulation type would you configure for a point-to-point link between Cisco routers?

A. SLIP

B. LAPB

C. Frame Relay

D. HDLC

Question 13.5

Which WAN encapsulation types can be used for point-to-point links between routers? (Mark all that apply.)

A. PPP

B. SLIP

C. LAPB

D. HDLC

Configuring Dial-on-Demand Routing

This chapter covers ISDN (Integrated Services Digital Network) and dial-on-demand routing (DDR) operation and configuration. It briefly summarizes ISDN BRI (Basic Rate Interface) and its associated components, and then discusses Legacy DDR and dialer profiles.

INTEGRATED SERVICES DIGITAL NETWORK (ISDN) BRI

ISDN stands for Integrated Services Digital Network. It refers to a collection of standards that define a digital architecture that provides an integrated voice/data capability to the customer premises facility, utilizing the public switched network. The ISDN standards define the hardware and call setup schemes for end-to-end digital connectivity. Prior to ISDN, many telephone companies had been using digital networks within their clouds, but using analog lines for the local access loop between the cloud and the actual customer site.

Bringing digital connectivity via ISDN to the local site has many benefits, including the following:

- The capability to carry a variety of user-traffic feeds. ISDN provides access to all-digital facilities for video, telex, packet-switched data, and enriched telephone network services.

- Much faster call setup than modem connections. For example, a duration of less than one second can be sufficient to make some ISDN calls. This out-of-band channel is called the *delta (D) channel* and is primarily used for call initiation and call tear down.

- Much faster data transfer rate at 64 kbps per channel as opposed to modem alternatives of 28.8 kbps. This data channel is called a *bearer (B) channel*. With multiple B channels, ISDN offers users more bandwidth on WANs (for example, two B channels equals 128 kbps) than they receive with a leased line at 56 kbps in North America or 64 kbps in much of the rest of the world.

In general, ISDN is fast becoming the transport of choice for applications using remote connectivity, access to the Internet, and the World Wide Web. Before the tremendous growth in these applications, many in the United States believed ISDN was a solution looking for a problem.

ISDN Standards

Work on standards for ISDN began in the late 1960s. A comprehensive set of ISDN recommendations was published in 1984 and was continuously updated by the then CCITT—now the International Telecommunication Union Telecommunication Standardization Sector (ITU-T). ITU-T groups and organizes the ISDN protocols into three topic areas: E-Series, I-Series, and Q-Series.

- *E-Series protocols*—Protocols that begin with "E" recommend telephone network standards for ISDN. For example, the E.164 protocol describes international addressing for ISDN.

- *I-Series protocols*—Protocols that begin with "I" deal with concepts, terminology, and general methods. The I.100 series includes general ISDN concepts and the structure of other I-series recommendations; I.200 deals with service aspects of ISDN; I.300 describes network aspects; I.400 describes how the User-Network Interface (UNI) is provided.

- *Q-Series protocols*—Protocols beginning with "Q" cover how switching and signaling should operate. The term *signaling* in this context means the process of call set used. Q.921 describes the ISDN data-link processes of LAPD, which functions like Layer 2 processes in the ISO/OSI reference model. Q.931 specifies ISO/OSI reference model Layer 3 functions.

  Q.931 recommends a network layer between the terminal endpoint and the local ISDN switch. This protocol does not impose an end-to-end recommendation. The various ISDN providers and switch types can and do use various implementations of Q.931. Other switches were developed before the standards groups finalized this standard.

  Because switch types are not standard, when configuring the router, you will need to specify the ISDN switch you are connecting to. In addition, Cisco routers have debug commands to monitor Q.931 and Q.921 processes when an ISDN call is initiated or being terminated.

ISDN Access Options

ISDN specifies two standard access methods, as follows:

- *Primary Rate Interface (PRI)*—In North America and Japan, 23 bearer (B) channels and one 64-kbps D channel (a T1/DS1 facility).

  In Europe and much of the rest of the world, PRI offers 30 B channels and a D channel (an E1 facility). PRI uses a data service unit/channel service unit (DSU/CSU) for T1/E1 connection.

- *Basic Rate Interface (BRI)*—Two 64-kbps bearer channels (2B) plus one 16-kbps data channel (+D) service. BRI operates with Cisco 1000, 2500, 3000, and 4000 series routers. BRI connects to an NT1 for 4-wire connection. NT1 is discussed later in this chapter.

As shown in Figure 14–1, Cisco offers many ISDN solutions. The Cisco 7000 router does not have a BRI connection.

The B channels can be used for digitized speech transmission or for relatively high-speed data transport. Narrowband ISDN is circuit-switching oriented. The B channel is the elemental circuit switching unit.

Figure 14-1
*ISDN equip-
ment control
varies
depending on
whether the
ISDN service
is offered in or
outside North
America.*

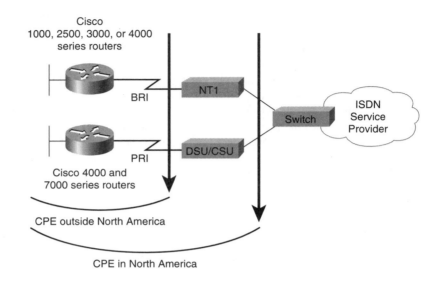

**Key
Concept** **BRI is sometimes written as 2B+D. This interface provides two B channels at
64 kbps and an additional 16-kbps D signaling channel.**

The ISDN D channel carries signaling information (call setup) to control calls on B
channels at the UNI. In addition to carrying signaling information, the D channel is
used to carry subscriber low-rate packet data, such as alarm systems. Cisco routers
do not currently use this facility. Traffic over the D channel employs the LAPD data
link-level protocol. LAPD is based on High-Level Data Link Control (HDLC).

In Figure 14-2, you see a typical BRI ISDN connection that supports two B channels
to carry data and one D channel for call signaling.

ISDN Encapsulation Options

As its configured encapsulation, ISDN defaults to High-Level Data Link Control
(HDLC). Alternatively, Point-to-Point Protocol (PPP) can also be used. With PPP, you
can enable the Challenge Handshake Authentication Protocol (CHAP), a popular,
authentication protocol for call screening. Among the other encapsulations for
end-to-end ISDN is Link Access Procedure: D Channel (LAPD).

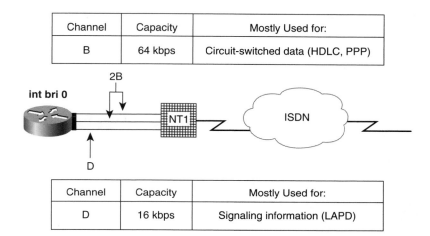

Channel	Capacity	Mostly Used for:
B	64 kbps	Circuit-switched data (HDLC, PPP)

Channel	Capacity	Mostly Used for:
D	16 kbps	Signaling information (LAPD)

Figure 14–2
The B channels carry data and the D channel carries control signals.

Although the ISDN call can statistically multiplex (or combine) packets from several higher-layer protocols, ISDN interfaces allow only a single encapsulation type.

If the end-to-end path for user traffic interconnects with an X.25 or Frame Relay service, the administrator specifies the WAN encapsulation choices for these two services that will use the ISDN interface. This selection facilitates internetworking between the traffic passed from the ISDN cloud to these other WAN services.

After an ISDN call has been established, the router can use an ISDN cloud to carry any of the network-layer protocols supported by the Cisco IOS software to multiple destinations.

ISDN Functions

To access the ISDN network, you must use customer premise equipment (CPE) that performs specific functions in order for proper connection to the ISDN network. In an ISDN network, the CPE is the local terminating equipment, such as the ISDN modem that is installed at the customer site and connects to the telephone company.

Because the ISDN standards define functions as a device type or hardware function that represents a transition point between the reference-point interfaces, vendors can create hardware that supports one or more functions. To select the correct CPE, you must be aware of what functions are available and how the functions relate to each other. Table 14–1 defines the customer premises ISDN device types, which are shown in Figure 14–3.

Figure 14–3
ISDN func-
tions.

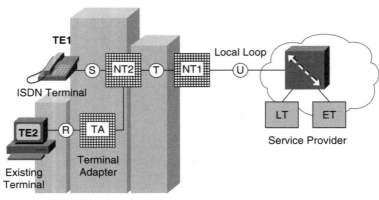

Table 14–1

Customer
premises
ISDN device
types.

Acronym	Device Type	Device Function
TE1	Terminal Endpoint 1	Designates a router as a device having a native ISDN interface
NT2	Network Termination 2	The point at which all ISDN lines at the customer site are aggregated and switched using a customer switching device
NT1	Network Termination 1	Converts BRI signals into a form used by the ISDN digital line
TE2	Terminal Endpoint 2	Designates a router as a device requiring a TA for its BRI signals
TA	Terminal Adapter	Converts EIA/TIA-232, V.35, and other signals into BRI signals

Table 14–2 defines the basic ISDN device types and their functions that apply to equipment at the service provider location.

Acronym	Device Name	Device Function
LT	Local Termination	Portion of the local exchange that terminates the local loop
ET	Exchange Termination	Portion of the exchange that communicates with other ISDN components in the ISDN cloud

Table 14–2
Basic ISDN device types for the service provider.

In order to connect devices that perform specific functions, the devices need to support specific interfaces. Because CPEs can include one or more functions, the interfaces they use to connect to other devices that support other functions can vary. As a result, the standards do not define interfaces in terms of hardware, but refer to them as reference points.

A *reference point* defines a connection type between two functions. In other words, reference points are a series of specifications that define the connection between specific devices, depending on their function in the end-to-end connection. It is important to know about these interface types because a CPE device such as a router can support different reference types, which could result in the need for additional equipment.

The reference points that affect the customer side of the ISDN connection, as shown in Figure 14–3, are as follows:

- *R*—References the point (connection) that is between a non-ISDN compatible device and a terminal adapter.

- *S*—References the points that connect into the NT2, or customer switching device. It is the interface that enables calls between the various customer premises equipment.

- *T*—Electrically identical to the S interface, it references the outbound connection from the NT2 to the ISDN network.

The electrical similarities between the S and T references is why some interfaces are labeled S/T interface, because although they perform totally different functions, the port is electrically the same and can be used for either function.

- *U*—References the connection between the NT1 and the ISDN network owned by the phone company.

Selecting a Cisco Router: Considerations

Not all Cisco routers include a native ISDN terminal, nor do all of them include interfaces for the same reference point. Therefore, you must evaluate each router carefully. To select a Cisco router, perform the following steps:

1. Determine whether the router supports ISDN BRI. Look on the back of your router for one of the following:

   - If you see a connector labeled "BRI," you already have a basic rate interface. With a native ISDN interface already built-in, your router is a TE1. Your router already contains the ISDN TA function.

   - If you do not see a connector labeled "BRI," your router has a nonnative ISDN interface and is a TE2. This usually is a serial interface. You need to obtain an external TA device and attach it to the serial interface to provide a BRI.

2. Determine whether you or the service provider provides the NT1. An NT1 terminates the local loop of wires to the central office (CO) of your ISDN provider. In the United States, for example, the NT1 is the responsibility of you, the customer, but in Europe, it is typically provided by the service provider.

   - If you need to provide the NT1, you can order a router, for example a Cisco 1004, that includes a U interface. The U interface indicates that the router has the NT1 interface built in.

   - If you do not need to provide the NT1, you can order a router, such as a Cisco 1003, that includes an S/T interface. It will connect to the NT1 provided by the service provider.

CAUTION _____

Never connect a router with a U interface into an NT1. It will most likely ruin the interface.

_____

ISDN Switch Types

ISDN service providers use a variety of switch types for their ISDN services. Services offered by the national Post, Telephone, and Telegraphs (PTTs) or other carriers vary considerably from nation to nation or region to region. Just like modems, each switch type operates slightly differently, and has a specific set of call setup requirements. As a result, before you can connect your router to an ISDN service, you must be aware of the switch types used at the CO.

You specify this information during router configuration so that the router can place ISDN network-level calls and send data. Following is a sample of countries and the ISDN switch types you are likely to encounter in your provider's ISDN cloud:

Country	Switch Type
United States and Canada	AT&T 5ess and 4ess; Northern Telecom DMS-100
France	VN2, VN3
Japan	NTT
United Kingdom	Net3 and Net5

In addition to learning about the switch type your service provider is using, you will also need to know what service profile identifiers (SPIDs) are assigned to your connection. In many cases, such as when configuring the router to connect to a DMS-100, you will need to input the SPIDs.

SPIDs are a series of characters that can look like phone numbers and that identify your connection to the switch at the central office. Once identified, the switch links the services you ordered to the connection. Remember, ISDN is typically used for dial-up connectivity. The SPIDs are processed during each call setup operation.

Configuring ISDN BRI

To enable ISDN BRI to operate, you must perform the following two tasks:

- *Configure ISDN-specific commands*—This section outlines the key ISDN-specific commands for enabling an ISDN BRI interface by performing the following two steps:

  Step 1: Define the switch type.

  Step 2: Set the Service Profile Identifier (SPID).

- *Configure an encapsulation to use over ISDN*—The next section (after configuring ISDN) discusses using PPP encapsulation with dial-on-demand routing (DDR) over ISDN BRI.

Step 1: Selecting the ISDN Switch Type

Before using ISDN BRI, you must define the **isdn switch-type** global configuration command to specify the CO switch to which the router connects. For BRI ISDN service example switch types include the following:

Switch Type	Description
basic-5ess	AT&T basic rate switches (USA)
basic-dms100	NT DMS-100 (North America)
basic-ni1	National ISDN-1 (North America)
basic-1tr6	German 1TR6 ISDN switches
basic-ts013	Australian TS013 switches
basic-net3	Switch type for Net3 in United Kingdom and Europe
ntt	NTT ISDN switch (Japan)
none	No specific switch specified

Step 2 (Optional): Setting SPIDs

When your ISDN service is installed, the service provider will give you information about your connection. Depending on the switch type used, you will be given two numbers, referred to as the SPIDs. Depending on the switch type, you will need to add these to your configuration. For example, the National ISDN-1 and DMS-100 ISDN switches require SPIDs to be configured, but the AT&T 5ess switch does not.

Use the **isdn spid1** and **isdn spid2** commands to access the ISDN network when your router makes its call to the local ISDN exchange.

```
isdn spid1 spid-number [ldn]
isdn spid2 spid-number [ldn]
```

isdn spid1 and isdn spid2 Command	Description
spid-number	Number identifying the service to which you have subscribed. This value is assigned by the ISDN service provider.
ldn	(Optional) Local dial number. This number must match the called-party information coming in from the ISDN switch in order to use both B channels on most switches.

Once you have configured the ISDN connection, you must configure an encapsulation to use over ISDN. The next section discusses using PPP encapsulation with dial-on-demand routing (DDR) over ISDN BRI.

DIAL-ON-DEMAND ROUTING

This section covers what DDR is, when and why to use DDR, DDR operation, basic DDR configuration, DDR configuration using access lists for greater control, and DDR operation verification.

Dial-on-demand (DDR) refers to a collection of Cisco features that allows two or more Cisco routers to establish a dynamic connection over simple dial-up facilities to route packets and exchange routing updates on an as-needed basis. DDR is used for low-volume, periodic network connections over the Public Switched Telephone Network (PSTN) or an ISDN.

Traditionally, networks have been interconnected by dedicated WAN lines. DDR addresses the need for periodic network connections over a circuit-switched WAN service. By using WAN connections only on an as-needed basis, DDR can reduce WAN usage costs.

The DDR features discussed in this chapter that can be used over ISDN, or other dial-up media, such as asynchronous lines, include the following:

- *Legacy DDR*—The capability to enable a PSTN connection only when there is traffic to send

- *Dialer profiles*—The capability to configure DDR such that the physical interface configurations are separate from the logical configurations required for making a DDR call

In the next chapter, you learn about some more advanced DDR configurations. DDR is the process of having the router connect to a public telephone network when there is traffic to send and hang up when the data transfer is complete. DDR is typically used when the following situations are present:

- There are telecommuters who need to connect to the company network periodically during the day.

- You have satellite offices that need to send sales transactions or order entry requests to the main computer at the central office.

- As a customer, you want to order products through the automated order system that your vendor has in place.

- Your customers prefer that you send them reports, for example, via email.

Figure 14–4 shows a DDR design that allows telecommuters and remote vendors access through dial-up links.

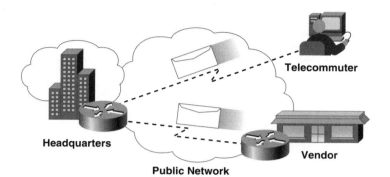

Figure 14–4
*The DDR links
are brought
up only when
data needs to
be sent.*

Generic DDR Operation

The following list provides a basic description of how DDR is implemented in Cisco routers:

1. The router receives traffic and does a route table lookup to determine whether there is a route to the destination. If so, the outbound interface is identified. If the outbound interface is configured for DDR, the router does a lookup to determine whether the traffic is *interesting*.

Interesting traffic is defined by you, the administrator. It is any traffic that you want to trigger a link so that the traffic can be transferred.

2. The router then identifies the next hop router and locates the dialing instructions in what is called the *dialer map*.

3. The router then checks to see whether the dialer map is in use; that is, if the interface is currently connected to the remote destination.

If the interface is currently connected to the desired remote destination, the traffic is sent and the idle timer is reset, based on the packet being interesting.

If the interface is not currently connected to the remote destination, the router, which is attached to a DCE such as ISDN TAs or modems that support V.25*bis* dialing, sends call setup information to the DCE device on the specified serial line. V.25*bis* is an ITU-T Standardization Sector standard for in-band signaling to bit synchronous DCE devices.

4. After the link is enabled, the router transmits both interesting and uninteresting traffic. Uninteresting traffic can include data and routing updates.

5. When no more interesting traffic is transmitted over the link, an idle timer starts. The call is disconnected after no interesting traffic is seen for the duration of the idle timeout period.

Figure 14–5 illustrates the basic DDR operation described in the previous steps.

Figure 14–5
Basic DDR
operation.

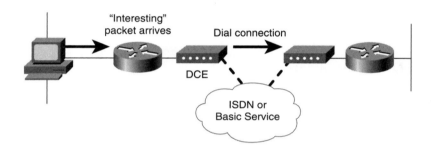

Selecting a DDR Implementation

Because DDR has a broad set of capabilities, you should determine your networking needs before selecting a DDR feature. The flowchart in Figure 14–6 summarizes how to select DDR solutions for your network.

The numbers shown in Figure 14–6 refer to the numbers of the steps as follows:

1. Select the connection type that you need. Note that selection will be partly based on the interfaces available on your router.

2. Select one or more encapsulation types, based on such items as cost, traffic needs, and geographical availability.

3. Determine whether you have bridging requirements.

4. Determine whether you have routing requirements.

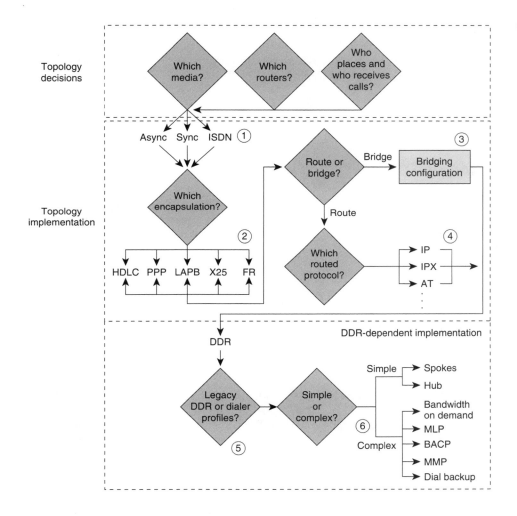

Figure 14–6
Selecting a DDR implementation.

5. You will most likely use Legacy DDR if you have enough physical interfaces for your DDR connection needs or if you want to use the same properties, such as timers, per call. Use dialer profiles if you have to dial out to more sites than you have physical interfaces, or if you want o use different call properties for each location. With dialer profiles, the connection information is applied to a physical interface only when a call needs to be made.

6. If you are a non-ISP organization, you will most likely use a simple topology of hub and spoke. If you are an ISP, you will most likely require additional, complex features such as Bandwidth Allocation Control Protocol (BACP) and Multichassis MultiLink PPP (MMP).

Note that, in this book, the complex features discussed are bandwidth-on-demand and dial backup.

LEGACY DDR

Legacy DDR is a term used to define a very basic DDR configuration in which a single set of dialer parameters is applied to an interface. If you need multiple unique dialer configurations on one interface, consider using dialer profiles (covered later in this chapter).

CONFIGURING LEGACY DDR

To configure Legacy DDR, you must perform the following tasks:

1. Specify interesting traffic. What traffic type should enable the link?

2. Define static routes. What route do you take to get to the destination?

3. Configure the dialer information. What number do you call to get to the next hop router and what service parameters do you use for the call?

Each of these tasks is discussed in the following sections.

Task 1: Specifying Interesting Traffic (What Enables the Connection?)

The first task required to set up a Legacy DDR link is to identify the protocol packets designated as *interesting* that will trigger a DDR call. Interesting packets are designated by you and can be defined on the basis of a variety of criteria, such as protocol type or addresses for source or destination hosts.

```
router(config)#dialer-list dialer-group protocol protocol-name [permit | deny
   | list] access-list-number
```

dialer-list protocol Command	Description
dialer-group	Used to define the interesting traffic for a specific interface. This same value is entered into the **dialer-group** command to instruct the router which interface to enable when interesting traffic is received.
protocol-name	Specifies the protocol for interesting packets to be considered for DDR. Choices include IP, IPX, AppleTalk, DECnet, and VINES.
**permit	deny**	Specifically permits or denies a protocol for DDR or specifies an access list. If field is not entered, all traffic is permitted by default.
list	The **list** keyword along with an access list number assigns an access list to the dialer group. The access list contains the interesting traffic definition. Use an access list to create the interesting traffic definition if you want finer granularity of protocol choices.

Figure 14–7 shows a network that consists of two remote offices connected by a DDR link. The IPX client's IPX-based traffic will bring up the WAN link.

TIPS

It is important to understand the operation of the protocols used to transfer the selected traffic because some protocols exchange periodic updates, in which case the DDR connection would remain up indefinitely. Use an analyzer to document your communications.

Figure 14–7
*Only "interest-
ing" traffic
should bring
up the link.*

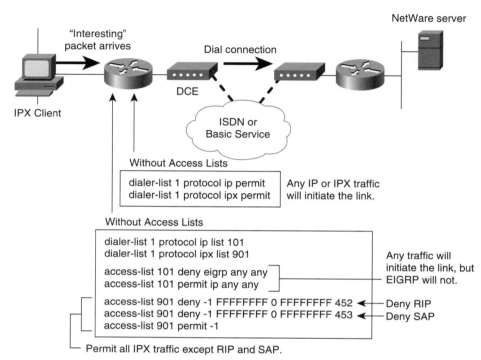

NetWare server

"Interesting"
packet arrives

Dial connection

DCE

IPX Client

ISDN or
Basic Service

Without Access Lists

dialer-list 1 protocol ip permit   Any IP or IPX traffic
dialer-list 1 protocol ipx permit   will initiate the link.

Without Access Lists

dialer-list 1 protocol ip list 101
dialer-list 1 protocol ipx list 901

access-list 101 deny eigrp any any   Any traffic will
access-list 101 permit ip any any   initiate the link, but
                                          EIGRP will not.

access-list 901 deny -1 FFFFFFFF 0 FFFFFFFF 452 ◄── Deny RIP
access-list 901 deny -1 FFFFFFFF 0 FFFFFFFF 453 ◄── Deny SAP
access-list 901 permit -1

Permit all IPX traffic except RIP and SAP.

Task 2: Defining Static Routes (Route to Destination)

To forward traffic, routers need to know what route to use for a destination. Because you do not want dynamic routing protocols running across the link, you manually configure the routes using static routes. (Refer to Chapter 11, "Optimizing Routing Update Operation," for command details.) When a dynamic routing protocol is used across a DDR connection, it causes the DDR interface to dial the remote sites for every routing update. The command for IP, for example, is as follows:

```
router(config)#ip route prefix mask {address | interface} [distance]
    [permanent]
```

As already discussed in this book, when configuring static routes, keep in mind the following considerations:

- When using static routes, all participating routers must have static routes defined so that they can advertise the remote networks. This requirement is necessary because static routes replace routing updates.

  If you want a router to advertise a static route, you must use the **redistribute** command.

- Static route entries must be defined for all routes for which a router is responsible. To reduce the number of static route entries, you can define a default static route. Default static routes are advertised (redistributed) automatically.

Figure 14–8 shows a configuration used to define the static routes on each side of the DDR link.

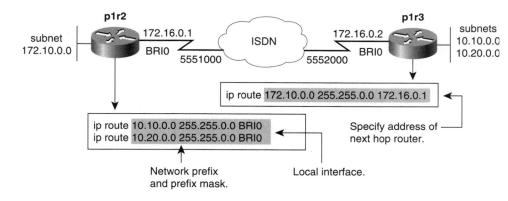

Figure 14–8
Static route entries list all routes/networks for which a router is responsible.

If a router must connect to a site that has numerous networks, to make sure that all routes are defined using the **static route** command, consider enabling a dynamic routing protocol to capture the list of all routes.

After all routes (and services for IPX) are known, turn off the dynamic routing protocol and use the captured information to define the necessary static routes.

Task 3: Configuring the Dialer Information

Perform the following steps to configure the dialer information on a given physical interface:

1. Select the physical interface that you want to be your dial-up line.

2. Configure the network address for the interface, as in the following example:

   ```
   router(config-if)#ip address ip-address mask
   ```

3. Configure the encapsulation type. If configuring PPP, for example:

   ```
   router(config-if)#encapsulation ppp
   ```

   For information on PPP authentication configurations, refer to www.cisco.com.

4. Depending on the interface, enable DDR when using an external dialing device.

   ```
   router(config-if)#dialer in-band [no parity | odd parity]
   ```

   This command (in-band) says that the same interface that is used to send the data must also perform call setup and teardown operation between the router and an external dialing device such as a modem. If using asynchronous interfaces or V.25*bis* on synchronous interfaces, you need to enable the router to perform dialing on the interface. V.25*bis* is an ITU-T standard for in-band signaling to bit-synchronous DCE devices. A variety of devices support V.25*bis*, ranging from analog V.32 modems to ISDN terminal adapters.

CAUTION

Do *not* use this command if using BRI because out-of-band means that another channel, in this case the D channel, performs call setup and teardown.

---

5. Bind the traffic definition to an interface by linking the interesting traffic definition you created in step 1 to the interface you specified in step 3.

```
router(config-if)#dialer-group group-number
```

group-number specifies the number of the dialer group to which the interface belongs. The group number can be an integer from 1 to 10. This number must match the **dialer-list** *group-number.*

Each interface can have only one dialer-group, but the same dialer-list (using the **dialer-group** command) can be assigned to multiple interfaces.

Figure 14–9 shows an example of using the **dialer-group** command.

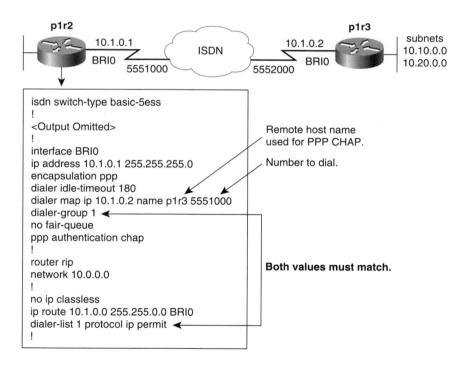

Figure 14–9
The **dialer-group** command applies rules defined by the **dialer-list** command to individual interfaces.

6. Define destination(s). Define one or more dial-on-demand numbers to reach one or more destinations for a particular interface.

```
router(config-if)#dialer map protocol next-hop-address [name
        hostname] [speed 56 | 64] [broadcast] dialer-string
```

dialer map Command	Description
protocol	IP, IPX, AppleTalk, DECnet, VINES, and others.
next-hop-address	The address of the next hop router.
name *hostname*	The host name of the remote device. This name is used for PPP authentication or ISDN calls supporting caller ID.
**speed 56	64**	Used for ISDN, this indicates the link speed in kbps to use. The default is 64.
broadcast	Indicates that broadcasts are to be forwarded to this destination only when the link is enabled by interesting traffic. DDR is nonbroadcast by default, so no update traffic will cross the link unless this is set.
dialer-string	The telephone number sent to the DCE device when packets with the specified next hop address are received.

The **dialer map** command must be used with the **dialer-group** command and its associated access list to initiate dialing. In Figure 14–9, router p1r2 has been configured to dial router p1r3.

Legacy DDR Configuration Tasks Summarized

The following output shows the results when all tasks are performed for Legacy DDR:

```
isdn switch-type basic-5ess
!
<output omitted>
!
interface BRI0
ip address 10.1.0.1 255.255.255.0
encapsulation ppp
dialer idle-timeout 180
```

```
dialer map ip 10.1.0.2 name p1r3 5551000      (3)
dialer-group 1
no fair-queue
ppp authentication chap
!
router rip
network 10.0.0.0
!
no ip classless
ip route 10.1.0.0 255.255.0.0 BRI0            (2)
dialer-list 1 protocol ip permit             (1)
!
```

Each task shown in the output is as follows:

1. *Specify interesting traffic*—What traffic type should enable the link?

2. *Define static routes*—What route do you take to get to the destination?

3. *Configure the dialer information*—What number do you call to get to the next hop router and what service parameters do you use for the call?

Note that the required configuration tasks are reviewed again here because there is another way of configuring DDR that is discussed later in the chapter. Understanding what commands affect each task will help you better determine the differences between configuring legacy DDR and dialer profiles.

Legacy DDR Optional Commands

The following optional commands can be used with Legacy DDR:

- Use the **dialer load-threshold** command to configure (Cisco proprietary) bandwidth on demand by setting the maximum load before the dialer places another call to a destination.

  If you had too much traffic trying to squeeze over one phone line, then, based on this parameter, you might want to place another simultaneous call to increase your bandwidth.

As of Cisco IOS Release 11.1 code, this command's format is as follows:

```
dialer load-threshold load [outbound | inbound | either]
```

In earlier releases, load was only monitored in the outgoing direction (transmitting). As a result, receiving large quantities of data did not trigger the second channel.

dialer load-threshold Command	Description
load	Interface load (from 1 to 255) beyond which the dialer will initiate another call to the destination. The bandwidth is defined as a ratio of 255, where 255 would be 100 percent of the available bandwidth.
outbound	inbound	either	(Optional) Outbound calculates the actual load using outbound traffic only. Inbound calculates the actual load using inbound traffic only. Either calculates the actual load using combined outbound and inbound loads.

- Use the **dialer idle-timeout** command to specify the number of idle seconds before a call is disconnected.

  The **dialer idle-timeout** command is like a stopwatch. When the last interesting packet leaves the router, the router sets a timer to measure how long the interface is idle (defined as the absence of interesting packets, not the absence of all traffic). If interesting packets arrive, then this timer is reset. If no interesting packets arrive at the interface before the timer expires, the call is hung up. This feature is important because many times there are expensive connection charges, but connection costs less after the first minute. So you do not want to hang up the line permanently because of a pause and have to incur the added expense of placing another call.

  Only interesting traffic can reset the idle timer. After an interesting packet is sent, the idle timer starts. If the link is up, any traffic can use the line, interesting or not. For this reason, an access list is often applied to a DDR interface to prevent unwanted traffic (such as partial or old routing information) from sneaking across a WAN link when the link is active. If uninteresting traffic is on the link when the idle timer expires, those packets will be lost when the line disconnects.

seconds (default is 120) is the amount of time to wait, in seconds, before an idle link is disconnected.

Legacy DDR Using ACLs Configuration Example

In Figure 14–10, Telnet and SMTP packets are defined as interesting traffic. After the link comes up, both interesting and uninteresting traffic can cross the enabled link.

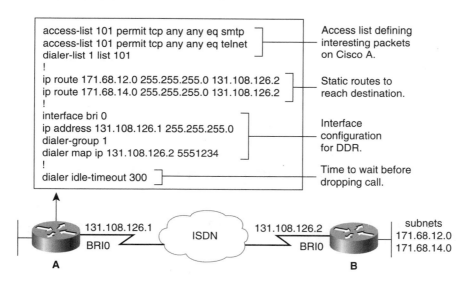

Access list defining interesting packets on Cisco A.

Static routes to reach destination.

Interface configuration for DDR.

Time to wait before dropping call.

Figure 14–10
Using ACLs for DDR set-ups.

An explanation of Figure 14–10 is as follows:

Command	Description
access-list 101 permit tcp any any eq smtp	Includes any host's email packets in the interesting traffic definition.
access-list 101 permit tcp any any eq telnet	Includes any host's telnet packets in the interesting traffic definition.

Command	Description
dialer-list 1 list 101	The first portion of the command (**dialer-list 1**) associates this dialer list with the dialer access group identified in the **dialer-group 1** command. The second portion (**list 101**) specifies access list 101 to define interesting traffic.
dialer-group 1	Associates BR0 interface with dialing access group 1. This access group was specified with the **dialer-list** command.

The DDR session occurs for interesting traffic. When the line is idle for 5 minutes (300 seconds), the call is dropped.

TIPS

Without the **broadcast** keyword in the **dialer map** command, broadcast routing updates are not exchanged.

Verifying and Troubleshooting Legacy DDR Operation

It is always important to recheck your dialer configuration to ensure correctness. The following commands can be used to verify that Legacy DDR is operating:

Command	Description
ping/telnet	When you ping or Telnet a remote site (assuming these are not filtered), or when interesting traffic triggers a link, the router will send a change in link status message to the console.
show dialer	Use this command to obtain general diagnostic information about an interface configured for DDR, such as the number of times the dialer string has been successfully reached, and the idle timer and the fast idle timer values for each B channel. Current call-specific information is also provided, such as the length of the call, and the number and name of the device to which the interface is currently connected.

Command	Description
show isdn active	Use this command when using ISDN. It shows that a call is in progress and lists the numbered called.
show isdn status	Use this command to show the statistics of the ISDN connection.
show ip route	(Use appropriate command for IPX, AppleTalk.) Displays the routes known to the router, including static and dynamically learned routes.

The following commands can be used to troubleshoot Legacy DDR operation:

Command	Description
debug q921	Verifies that you have a connection to the ISDN switch.
debug dialer	Shows information such as what number the interface is dialing.
clear interface	Used to clear a call that is in progress. In a troubleshooting situation, it is sometimes useful to clear historical statistics to track the current number of successful calls relative to failures. Use this command with care. It sometimes requires that you clear both the local and remote routers.

In the next section, you learn how to build more flexible DDR configurations using dialer profiles.

DIALER PROFILES OVERVIEW

With Legacy DDR, the dial-on-demand configuration, which includes the network-layer address, encapsulation type, and dial-timeout information, must be the same for all calls made via the physical interface. The same set of configuration parameters on a single dialer interface is applied to all users to which calls are made. To allow the creation of unique configuration profiles for users, Cisco created *dialer profiles*.

The Dialer profiles feature is available in Cisco IOS Release 11.2 and later. It is a feature that enables you to configure the dial-on-demand capabilities (in a dialer interface) separate from the physical interface. With dialer profiles, the physical interfaces become members of a *dialer pool*. A dialer pool is a readily available supply of interfaces that can be used on an on-demand basis. When a call must be made, based on a dialer interface configuration, a physical interface is borrowed from the dialer pool for the duration of the call. When the call is complete, the physical interface is returned to the dialer pool.

Dialer profiles consists of the following three elements (see Figure 14–11):

- *Dialer interface*—The dial-on-demand configuration for a given call destination, which includes interface configuration elements, such as network-layer address, call destination information, and encapsulation type, including authentication. In Figure 14–11, the dialer interface lists the call destinations Remote1, Home1 and Home2.

- *Dialer map class (Optional)*—The service details of a call, such as line speed and idle timeouts, can be configured under the interface or in a map class that is then applied to an interface. Because it can be tedious to type the same service details repeatedly for multiple interfaces, map classes were created so that you type them only once. After the map class is created, you assign dialer interfaces to the desired map class. Without this feature, you would need to configure the service options in each dialer interface, even if they were identical across multiple dialer interfaces.

- *Dialer pool*—One or more groups of available physical interfaces to be used when a dialer interface needs to make a call. A physical interface can be assigned to more than one pool, and can be prioritized within each pool, to avoid contention. For example, in Figure 14–11, if interface BRI0 belonged to two pools, it could be the primary interface to use in pool 1 and the secondary interface to use in pool 2.

Dialer profiles follow the process shown in Figure 14–12 to make dial-on-demand calls.

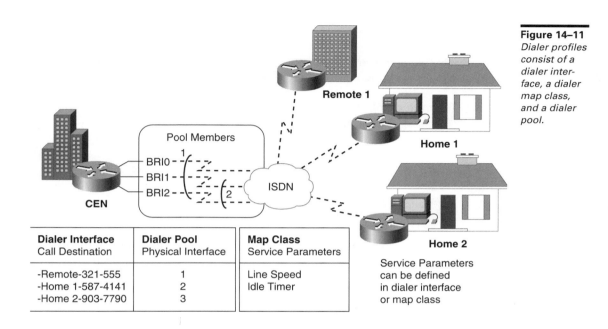

Figure 14–11
Dialer profiles consist of a dialer interface, a dialer map class, and a dialer pool.

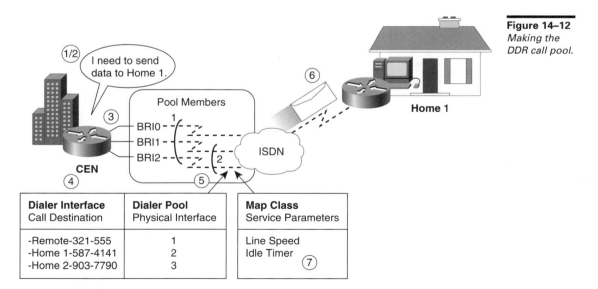

Figure 14–12
Making the DDR call pool.

The numbers shown in Figure 14–12 correspond to the following steps:

1. The router receives traffic and does a route table lookup for a route and the associated outbound interface. The outbound interface is dialer interface 1.

2. The router looks for a configured dialer list to determine whether the traffic is deemed interesting.

3. If the traffic is interesting, the router checks the dialer table to see whether dialer interface 1 is currently connected to the remote destination.

   If the dialer interface is currently connected to the remote destination, the traffic is sent and the idle timer is reset, based on the packet being interesting.

   If the dialer interface is not currently connected to the remote destination, it determines which physical interfaces are in its dialer pool. In this example, BRI1 and BRI2 are part of the pool. Assume that dialer interface 1 uses BRI1.

4. Dialer interface 1 then determines the dial string to call, as well as what service parameters to apply to BRI1. The services parameters are configured for the interface or by referring to a map class that is associated with the dial string.

5. Dialer interface 1 initiates BRI1, applying the map class and dialer interface 1 configuration.

6. After the link is up, the interesting and uninteresting traffic is transmitted to the call destination configured in dialer interface 1.

7. The call terminates when the idle timer that appears in the map class configuration has been met.

Configuring Dialer Profiles

To configure dialer profiles, perform the following major tasks:

Task 1 *Specify interesting traffic*—This task is the same as is done with Legacy DDR. Refer to the "Configuring Legacy DDR" section earlier in this chapter for details about this task.

Task 2 *Define static routes*—This task is the same as is done with LegacyDDR. Refer to the "Configuring Legacy DDR" earlier in this chapter section for details about this task.

Task 3 *Create the dialer interface*—This replaces the "Configuring Dialer Information" task performed when setting up Legacy DDR connections.

Task 4 *Make a physical interface a dialer pool member*—This is a new task required so the dialer interface created in task 3 can be assigned to a group of physical interfaces.

Task 5 (Optional) *Define the map class*—This is an efficient way of configuring service parameters once, and then applying them to the desired interfaces.

You can skip to Task 3 because Tasks 1 and 2 are the same as when configuring Legacy DDR, as discussed earlier in this chapter.

Task 3: Creating the Dialer Interface

To configure a dialer interface, perform the following steps:

1. Create a dialer interface and enter dialer interface configuration mode. This interface includes all the configuration parameters that will be applied to a physical interface when a call needs to be made.

   ```
   router(config)#interface dialer number
   ```

   number is the value that creates a dialer interface. You will assign physical interfaces to this group using the interface configuration command, **dialer pool-member.**

   This step puts you into interface configuration mode for the interface.

2. Configure a network address, as discussed in the section "Configuring Legacy DDR." When a physical interface is used to make a call, this network address will be applied to the interface.

3. Configure the encapsulation type for PPP.

   ```
   router(config-if)#encapsulation type
   ```

   The type should be defined as ppp.

4. Configure PPP authentication.

```
router(config-if)#ppp authentication type
```

5. Specify the remote router CHAP authentication. (This is the host name on the remote router.)

```
router(config-if)#dialer remote-name name
```

The name in the **dialer remote-name** command is case sensitive and should map the host name on the remote router.

6. Specify the dialing information to use to call the destination using one of the following:

```
router(config-if)#dialer-string string class class-name
```

string is the phone number to be dialed.

class-name is the map class that should be applied to the call.

7. Specify the dialer pool to associate with this dialer interface.

```
router(config-if)#dialer pool number
```

number specifies the pool to associate with the dialer interface. This number must also be configured for each physical interface that you want to add to the pool using the **dialer pool-member** command.

8. Assign the interesting traffic definition to the dialer interface.

```
router(config-if)#dialer-group number
```

number is the value that must match the dialer-group parameter that was specified using the dialer-list command configured as part of Task 1, "Specify Interesting Traffic."

9. Specify the service parameters for the interface, or define them in the map class (Task 5).

10. Exit interface configuration mode.

Figure 14–13 shows the configuration of a DDR using dialer profiles.

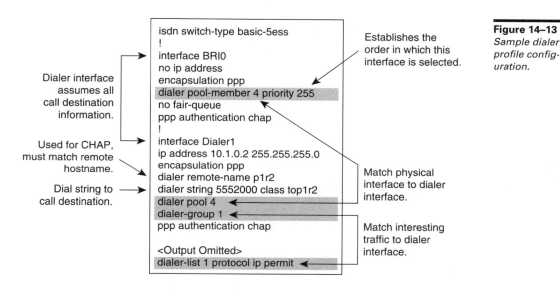

Dialer interface assumes all call destination information.

Used for CHAP, must match remote hostname.

Dial string to call destination.

```
isdn switch-type basic-5ess
!
interface BRI0
no ip address
encapsulation ppp
dialer pool-member 4 priority 255
no fair-queue
ppp authentication chap
!
interface Dialer1
ip address 10.1.0.2 255.255.255.0
encapsulation ppp
dialer remote-name p1r2
dialer string 5552000 class top1r2
dialer pool 4
dialer-group 1
ppp authentication chap

<Output Omitted>
dialer-list 1 protocol ip permit
```

Establishes the order in which this interface is selected.

Match physical interface to dialer interface.

Match interesting traffic to dialer interface.

Figure 14–13
Sample dialer profile config-uration.

Task 4: Making the Physical Interface a Dialer Pool Member

Perform the following to configure the physical interface as a dialer pool member:

1. Select the physical interface that you want to be part of the dialer profile, as in the following example:

   ```
   router(config)#interface bri0
   ```

2. Enable PPP encapsulation on this interface, as in the following.

   ```
   router(config-if)#encapsulation ppp
   ```

3. If this interface can also receive DDR calls, configure PPP authentication.

   PPP authentication needs to be configured because you need a way of knowing who is calling in so that you know to which dialer the incoming call needs to be bound.

4. Assign the interface to one or more dialer pools.

```
router(config-if)#dialer pool-member number [priority priority]
```

number (1-255) is the number of the dialer pool that you defined in the dialer interface to which you want this interface to be available.

priority (0-255) is the order in which you want this interface selected for use by a dialer interface. For example, if you want the dialer interface to always try selecting this interface first, make this number high; 0, the lowest priority, is the default, 255 is the highest priority.

Input this command for each dialer pool for which you want this interface to be a member.

Task 5: (Optional) Defining the Map Class

Perform the following steps to create map classes that will be used by dialer interfaces:

1. Create a map class and enter map class configuration mode, as follows:

```
router(config)#map-class dialer class-name
```

class-name is the name used to associate the given map class with the **dialer-string** command that is discussed under Task 3, "Creating the Dialer Interface."

2. Specify the desired timeout parameters.

- Define the time to wait before terminating the link when another call must be made.

```
router(config-map-class)#dialer fast-idle seconds
```

- Define the amount of time to wait, after there is no interesting traffic to send, before terminating the link.

```
router(config-map-class)#dialer idle-timeout seconds
```

- Define the amount of time to wait for a carrier to pick up the call after dialing the dial string. (Do not assign this command to ISDN BRI interfaces.)

```
router(config-map-class)#dialer wait-for-carrier-time seconds
```

3. If using ISDN, specify the desired speed of the ISDN line. The speed value is obtained from your service provider when you order the service.

```
router(config-map-class)#dialer isdn [speed speed]
```

4. Exit map class configuration mode.

Figure 14–14 provides an example of using a map class.

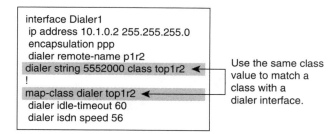

```
interface Dialer1
  ip address 10.1.0.2 255.255.255.0
  encapsulation ppp
  dialer remote-name p1r2
  dialer string 5552000 class top1r2
  !
  map-class dialer top1r2
  dialer idle-timeout 60
  dialer isdn speed 56
```

Use the same class value to match a class with a dialer interface.

Figure 14–14
Use a map class to simplify configuration when you have multiple interfaces with the same specifications.

Dialer Profiles Configuration Tasks Summarized

Figure 14–15 shows the results when all tasks are performed for dialer profiles.

The numbers shown in Figure 14–15 correspond to the following steps:

1. *Specify interesting traffic*—This task is the same as is performed with Legacy DDR. Specifies what traffic will enable the link.

2. *Define static routes*—This task is the same as is performed with Legacy DDR. Specifies the route to use for a specific destination.

Figure 14–15
*Dialer profile
configuration
example.*

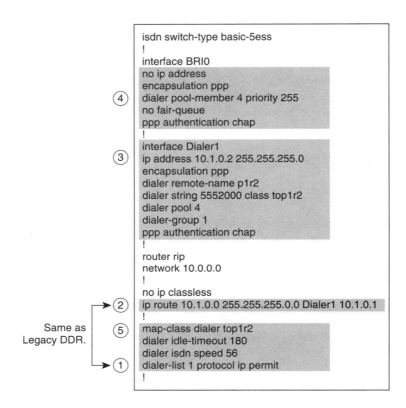

3. *Create the dialer interface*—This task replaces the "Configuring Dialer Information" task in the "Configuring Legacy DDR" section and defines the dialer information to use for a given destination.

4. *Make an physical interface a dialer pool member*—A new task is required so that the dialer interface created in Task 3 can be assigned to a group of physical interfaces. This step binds the logical dialer interface to a physical interface, but only for the duration of a call.

5. *(Optional) Define the map class*—This is an efficient way of configuring service parameters once, and then applying them to the desired interfaces. Map classes are useful only when you have a number of dialer interfaces that will have the same service parameters. Otherwise, define the service parameters when creating the dialer interface in task 3.

Dialer Profiles Configuration Example

Figure 14–16 illustrates a branch office router with a Legacy DDR configuration and a central office router using dialer profiles.

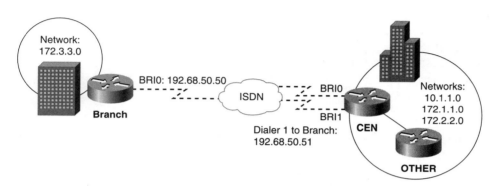

Figure 14–16
*Branch office
configuration
example.*

The complete configuration for both routers is shown on the subsequent page for comparison.

Branch Office Router—Legacy DDR Configuration

```
BRANCH#show run
Building configuration...

Current configuration:
!
version 11.2
no service udp-small-servers
no service tcp-small-servers
!
hostname BRANCH
!
enable secret 5 $1$vAef$oQsAbx.BbJWnkvmci5e/2/
enable password san-fran
!
username CEN password 7 02050D480809
isdn switch-type basic-5ess
!
```

```
interface Loopback3
 ip address 172.3.3.3 255.255.255.0
!
<Output Omitted>
!
interface BRI0
 ip address 192.68.50.50 255.255.255.0
 encapsulation ppp
 dialer idle-timeout 180
 dialer map ip 192.68.50.51 name CEN broadcast 2001
 dialer-group 1
 ppp authentication chap
!
router rip
 network 172.3.0.0
 network 192.68.0.0
!
no ip classless
ip route 10.1.1.0 255.255.255.0 192.68.50.51
ip route 172.1.1.0 255.255.255.0 192.68.50.51
ip route 172.2.2.0 255.255.255.0 192.68.50.51
!
dialer-list 1 protocol ip permit
!
<Output Omitted>
```

Central Office Router—Dialer Profile Configuration

```
CEN#show run
Building configuration...

Current configuration:
!
version 11.2
no service udp-small-servers
no service tcp-small-servers
!
hostname CEN
!
!
```

```
username BRANCH password 7 13061E010803
isdn switch-type basic-5ess
!
interface Loopback2
 ip address 172.1.1.1 255.255.255.0
!
<Output Omitted>
!
interface BRI0
 no ip address
 encapsulation ppp
 dialer pool-member 4
 ppp authentication chap
!
interface Dialer1
 ip address 192.68.50.51 255.255.255.0
 encapsulation ppp
 dialer remote-name BRANCH
 dialer idle-timeout 180
 dialer string 2003
 dialer pool 4
 dialer-group 1
 no cdp enable
 ppp authentication chap
!
router rip
 redistribute static metric 2
 network 192.68.0.0
 network 172.1.0.0
 network 10.0.0.0
!
no ip classless
ip route 172.3.3.0 255.255.255.0 Dialer1
!
dialer-list 1 protocol ip permit
!
<Output Omitted>
```

Verifying Dialer Profiles Operation

After configuring dialer profiles, you can verify that the connections are active using the same commands you used for Legacy DDR. They are as follows:

Command	Description
ping/telnet	When you ping or Telnet a remote site, or when interesting traffic triggers a link, the router will send a change in link status message to the console.
show dialer	Use this command to obtain general diagnostic information about an interface configured for DDR, such as the number of times the dialer string has been successfully reached, and the idle timer and the fast idle timer values for each B channel. Current call-specific information is also provided such as the length of the call and the number and name of the device to which the interface is currently connected.
show isdn active	Use this command when using ISDN. It shows that a call is in progress and lists the number called.
show ip route	(Use appropriate command for IPX, AppleTalk.) Displays the routes known to the router, including static and dynamically learned routes.
clear [dialer | interface]	Use this command to clear a call that is in progress. In a troubleshooting situation, it is sometimes useful to clear historical statistics to track the current number of successful calls relative to failures.

DDR USING ROTARY GROUP OVERVIEW

A dialer rotary group allows you to apply a single interface configuration to a set of physical interfaces, as shown in Figure 14–17, which allows a group of physical interfaces to be used for calling many destinations.

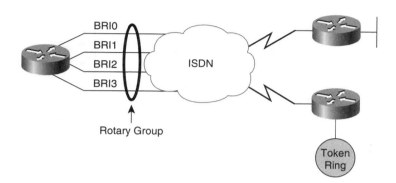

Figure 14–17
Several physical interfaces make up a single dialer interface example.

Dialer rotary groups simplify configuration efforts in environments that have multiple callers and calling destinations because they allow you to create a single configuration that is then bound to multiple interfaces. After a physical interface is configured into a rotary group, the interface assumes the parameters configured for the rotary group. A special, software-only *dialer interface* (also known as a *virtual dialer interface*) is used to apply the same configuration parameters to a rotary group of multiple physical interfaces.

When using dialer rotary groups, the IP address, definition for interesting traffic, and call parameters are associated with the dialer interface instead of the physical interfaces because when traffic triggers a call, the dialer interface must select a physical interface from the pool of physical interfaces.

The two ISDN B channels in a single BRI are, by definition, a rotary group. The dialer rotary groups discussed in this section are specific to Cisco routers and are not the same as the rotary groups used by telephone companies.

Configuring Dialer Rotary Groups

To configure dialer rotary groups, you must first define interesting traffic, as shown in Figure 14–18, and defined in the tasks that follow.

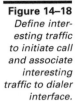

Figure 14–18
*Define inter-
esting traffic
to initiate call
and associate
interesting
traffic to dialer
interface.*

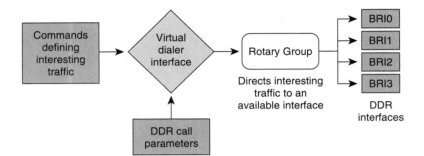

Task 1: Defining Interesting Traffic

Define interesting traffic, as discussed in the "Configuring Legacy DDR" section.

```
router(config)#dialer-list dialer-group protocol protocol-name [permit |
    deny | list] access-list-number
```

Task 2: Creating Dialer Interface for Dialer Rotary Groups

Perform the following steps to create a dialer interface for dialer rotary groups.

1. Create a dialer interface, as discussed in the "Configuring Dialer Profiles" section. This interface includes all the configuration parameters that will be applied to a physical interface when a call needs to be made.

```
router(config)#interface dialer number
```

number is a value that creates a dialer rotary group. You will assign physical interfaces to this group using the interface configuration **dialer rotary-group** command.

This step puts you into interface configuration mode for the interface.

2. Configure a network address, as discussed in the "Configuring Legacy DDR" section. When a physical interface is used to make a call, this network address will be applied to the interface.

3. Configure the encapsulation type, for example, PPP.

4. (Optional) If using PPP, configure PPP authentication, as discussed in the "PPP Authentication" section, later in this chapter.

5. Enable DDR, as discussed in the "Configuring Legacy DDR" section earlier in this chapter. Remember, this command is not necessary for ISDN interfaces because they use out-of-band dialing on the D channel.

   ```
   router(config-if)#dialer in-band [no parity | odd parity]
   ```

6. Bind traffic definition to an interface, as discussed in the "Configuring Legacy DDR" section earlier in this chapter.

   ```
   router(config-if)# dialer-group group-number
   ```

7. Define the destinations to call, as discussed in the "Configuring Legacy DDR" section earlier in this chapter.

   ```
   router(config-if)#dialer map protocol next-hop-address hostname
        broadcast dialer-string
   ```

8. Exit interface configuration mode and continue to the next task.

Task 3: Configuring the Physical Interfaces as a Rotary Group

Following are the steps to bind the physical interfaces to the dialer interface:

1. Select the physical interface that you want to be part of the dialer rotary group, as in the following example:

   ```
   router(config)#interface async 0
   ```

2. While in interface configuration mode, assign the interface to the dialer rotary group for the dialer interface you configured.

   ```
   router(config-if)#dialer rotary-group number
   ```

number is the number of the dialer interface in whose rotary group you want this interface included. This number must match the value configured in the **interface dialer** command for the desired dialer interface.

3. Continue to the next task.

Task 4: Configuring Static Routes

Configure static routes to each destination that the router will make a DDR call to, as discussed in the "Configuring Legacy DDR" section earlier in this chapter.

```
router(config)#ip route prefix mask {address | interface} [distance]
    [permanent]
```

Task 5: Disabling Routing Updates

Disable routing updates, as discussed in the "Configuring Legacy DDR" section earlier in this chapter.

Dialer Rotary Group Configuration Example

The example shown in Figure 14–19 creates a rotary group that includes interfaces BR0 through 3 on the router named 4000. A virtual dialer interface will be created including certain characteristics such as the encapsulation type. These characteristics will be passed to the physical interfaces that comprise the rotary group.

Figure 14–19
This rotary group consists of BRI0, BRI1, BRI2, and BRI3.

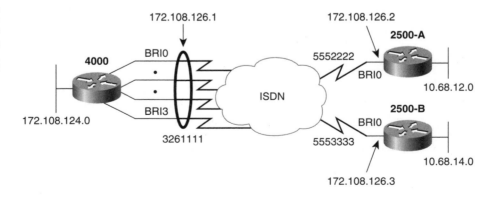

As before, static routes have been configured to reach subnets 12 and 14. Note the phone numbers to reach the routers connected to 2500-A (5552222) and 2500-B (5553333). These numbers must be included in the **dialer map** statement. If this interface is to be used for outgoing calls, add the phone number. If this interface is to be used only for incoming calls, there is no need for a telephone number.

The advantage of configuring a rotary group is that additional calls can be placed as needed to meet bandwidth demands. Because the virtual dialer interface passes configuration parameters to the physical interfaces, configuration is simplified.

Figure 14–20 shows the full configuration of the Cisco 4000.

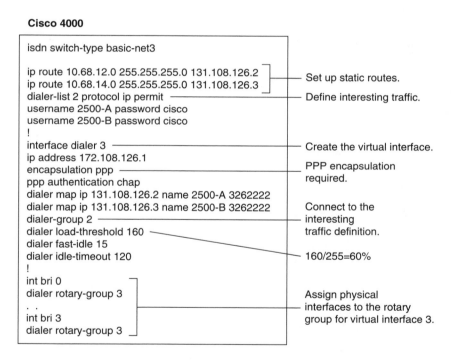

Cisco 4000

```
isdn switch-type basic-net3

ip route 10.68.12.0 255.255.255.0 131.108.126.2        Set up static routes.
ip route 10.68.14.0 255.255.255.0 131.108.126.3
dialer-list 2 protocol ip permit                        Define interesting traffic.
username 2500-A password cisco
username 2500-B password cisco
!
interface dialer 3                                      Create the virtual interface.
ip address 172.108.126.1
encapsulation ppp                                       PPP encapsulation
ppp authentication chap                                 required.
dialer map ip 131.108.126.2 name 2500-A 3262222
dialer map ip 131.108.126.3 name 2500-B 3262222         Connect to the
dialer-group 2                                          interesting
dialer load-threshold 160                               traffic definition.
dialer fast-idle 15
dialer idle-timeout 120                                 160/255=60%
!
int bri 0
dialer rotary-group 3                                   Assign physical
. .                                                     interfaces to the rotary
int bri 3                                               group for virtual interface 3.
dialer rotary-group 3
```

Figure 14–20
Cisco 4000 configuration example

The relevant rotary group commands are as follows:

Command	Description
interface dialer 3	Creates dialer interface 3.
ppp authentication chap	Specifies that password authentication for remote access will use the CHAP protocol.

Command	Description
dialer-group 2	Places the interface into dialer group 2 and links to a previously defined access list.
dialer load-threshold 160	Specifies additional calls will be placed by the rotary group when the load on one line reaches approximately 60 percent. The bandwidth is defined as a ratio of 255, where 255 would be 100 percent of the available bandwidth; the number 160 shown is about 60 percent of the available bandwidth.
dialer rotary-group 3	Places physical interface BR0 into a rotary group 3.

TIPS

Remember to disable routing updates using such techniques as passive interfaces or router update filtering.

Figure 14–21 shows the full configuration of the Cisco 2500-B.

Figure 14–21
Cisco 2500-Bconfig-uration.

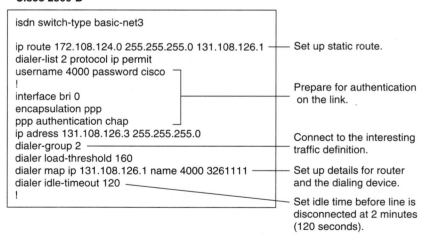

Cisco 2500-B

```
isdn switch-type basic-net3

ip route 172.108.124.0 255.255.255.0 131.108.126.1      — Set up static route.
dialer-list 2 protocol ip permit
username 4000 password cisco ⌐
!                                                         Prepare for authentication
interface bri 0                                           on the link.
encapsulation ppp
ppp authentication chap    ⌐
ip adress 131.108.126.3 255.255.255.0
dialer-group 2                                            Connect to the interesting
dialer load-threshold 160                                 traffic definition.
dialer map ip 131.108.126.1 name 4000 3261111         — Set up details for router
dialer idle-timeout 120                                    and the dialing device.
!
                                                        — Set idle time before line is
                                                          disconnected at 2 minutes
                                                          (120 seconds).
```

The relevant rotary group commands are as follows:

Command	Description
ip route 131.108.124.0 255.255.255.0 131.108.126.1	Establishes a static route to subnet 131.108.124.0 using the router at IP address 131.108.126.1 as the next hop device.
dialer-list 2 protocol ip permit	Defines IP as interesting traffic linked to interfaces that are part of dialer group 2.
dialer load-threshold 160	Specifies additional calls will be placed by the rotary group when the load on one line reaches approximately 60 percent. The bandwidth is defined as a ratio of 255, where 255 would be 100 percent of the available bandwidth; the number 160 shown is about 60 percent of the available bandwidth.
	Because the thresholds in the example are equal for both routers (160), if either side has the output threshold exceeded it will trigger secondary calls. The number of secondary calls made can be up to the maximum data channels you have.
dialer map ip 131.108.126.1 username 4000 3261111	Defines 3261111 as the number to be dialed when attempting to reach the router at IP address 131.108.126.1.
dialer idle-timeout 120	Disconnects the call after 120 seconds of idle time.

PPP AUTHENTICATION OVERVIEW

PPP authentication occurs during session establishment where the two PPP devices dynamically decide on the authentication protocol they will use followed by the authentication process. Two authentication protocols are supported: PAP and CHAP. PAP is not recommended because it is not secure, although it does provide a rudimentary way to authenticate the caller.

A PPP session establishment has the following three phases:

1. *Link establishment phase*—In this phase, each Point-to-Point Protocol (PPP) device sends Link Control Protocol (LCP) packets to configure and test the data link. LCP packets contain a Configuration Option field that allows devices to negotiate on the use of options, such as the maximum receive unit, compression of certain PPP fields, and the link authentication protocol. If a Configuration Option is not included in an LCP packet, the default value for that Configuration Option is assumed.

2. *Authentication phase (Optional)*—After the link has been established and the authentication protocol decided on, the peer may be authenticated. Authentication, if used, takes place before entering the network-layer protocol phase.

   PPP supports two authentication protocols: Password Authentication Protocol (PAP) and Challenge Handshake Authentication Protocol (CHAP). These protocols are detailed in RFC 1334, *PPP Authentication Protocols* and RFC 1994, *PPP Challenge Handshake Authentication Protocol*.

3. *Network-layer protocol phase*—In this phase, the PPP devices send Network Control Program (NCP) packets to choose and configure one or more network-layer protocol (such as IP). After each of the chosen network-layer protocols has been configured, datagrams from each network-layer protocol can be sent over the link.

Selecting a PPP Authentication Protocol

When configuring PPP authentication, you can select PAP or CHAP. In general, CHAP is the preferred protocol. A brief description of each follows.

PAP

PAP provides a simple method for a remote node to establish its identity using a two-way handshake, as shown in Figure 14–22. PAP is done only upon initial link establishment.

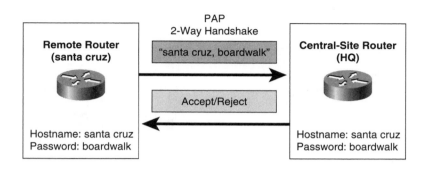

Figure 14–22
PPP passwords are sent in cleartext.

After the PPP link establishment phase is complete, a username/password pair is repeatedly sent by the remote node to the router until authentication is acknowledged or the connection is terminated.

PAP is not a strong authentication protocol. Passwords are sent across the link in cleartext and there is no protection from playback or repeated trial-and-error attacks. The remote node is in control of the frequency and timing of the login attempts.

Following is an example of a PAP exchange sequence that was obtained using the **debug ppp authentication** command:

```
PPP BRI0:1: PAP receive authenticate request p1r3

PPP BRI0:1: PAP authenticating peer p1r3

PPP BRI0:1: Remote passed PAP authentication sending Auth-Ack.

PPP BRI0:1: PAP ACK

Remote message is: PPP BRI0:1: Passed PAP authentication with remote.
```

CHAP

CHAP is used at the startup of a link, and periodically, to verify the identity of the remote node using a three-way handshake, as shown in Figure 14–23. CHAP is done upon initial link establishment and can be repeated any time after the link has been established.

Figure 14–23
The three-way handshake is used to verify the identity of a remote node.

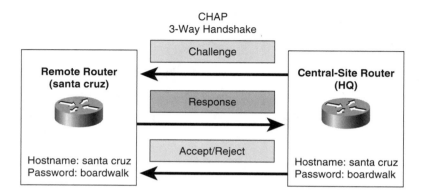

After the PPP link establishment phase is complete, the local router sends a "challenge" message to the remote node. The remote node responds with a value calculated using a one-way hash function (typically MD5). The local router checks the response against its own calculation of the expected hash value. If the values match, the authentication is acknowledged. Otherwise, the connection is terminated immediately.

CHAP provides protection against playback attack through the use of a variable challenge value that is unique and unpredictable. The use of repeated challenges is intended to limit the time of exposure to any single attack. The local router (or a third-party authentication server such as TACACS) is in control of the frequency and timing of the challenges.

Following is an example of a CHAP exchange sequence that was obtained using the **debug ppp authentication** command:

```
PPP BRI0:1: Send CHAP challenge id=55 to remote

PPP BRI0:1: CHAP challenge from p1r2

PPP BRI0:1: CHAP response received from p1r2

PPP BRI0:1: CHAP response id=55 received from p1r2

PPP BRI0:1: Send CHAP success id=55 to remote

PPP BRI0:1: remote passed CHAP authentication.

PPP BRI0:1: Passed CHAP authentication with remote.
```

Configuring PPP Authentication

Perform the steps shown in Figure 14–24 and as follows to configure PPP authentication.

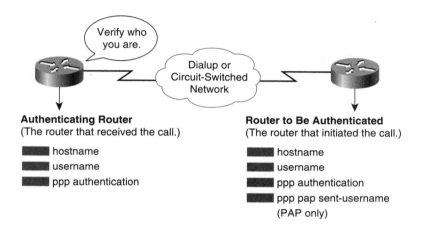

Figure 14–24
The PPP authentication elements.

1. On each router, define the username and password to expect from the remote router.

   ```
   router(config)#username name password secret
   ```

   name is the host name of the remote router. Note that this is case sensitive.

   secret is, on Cisco routers, the secret password that must be the same for both routers.

   Add a username for each remote system that the local router requires authentication from. The remote device must also have a username for the local router.

2. Enter interface configuration mode for the desired interface and configure the interface for PPP encapsulation.

   ```
   router(config-if)#encapsulation ppp
   ```

3. Configure PPP authentication.

    ```
    router(config-if)#ppp authentication {chap | chap pap | pap chap | pap}
    ```

    If both methods are enabled, the first method specified is requested during link negotiation. If the peer suggests using the second method or refuses the first, the second method is tried.

4. In Cisco IOS Release 11.1 or later, if you choose PAP and are configuring the router that will send the PAP information (that is, the router responding to a PAP request), you must enable PAP on the interface because PAP is disabled by default.

    ```
    router(config-if)#ppp pap sent-username username password password
    ```

Optional PPP Authentication Commands

You can use the following commands to simplify CHAP configuration tasks on the router:

* *Using the same host name on multiple routers*—When you want remote users to think they are connecting to the same router when authenticating, configure the same host name on each router.

  ```
  router(config-if)#ppp chap hostname hostname
  ```

* *Use a password to authenticate to an unknown host*—To limit username/password entries in the router, configure a password that will be sent to hosts that want to authenticate the router.

  ```
  router(config-if)#ppp chap password secret
  ```

  This password is not used when the router authenticates a remote device.

SUMMARY

In this chapter, you learned about the components that make ISDN operate and how to configure DDR features over ISDN. You learned that Legacy DDR configurations enable a connection only when there is traffic to send. You also learned that dialer profile configurations enable you to configure dial-on-demand routing such that the physical interface configurations are separate from the logical configurations required for making a the DDR call. Finally, you learned how to configure a rotary group and select an authentication method.

In the next chapter, you learn more advanced DDR configuration options.

Chapter Fourteen Test
Configuring Dial-on-Demand Routing

Estimated Time: 15 minutes

Complete all the exercises to test your knowledge of the materials contained in this chapter. Answers are listed in Appendix A, "Chapter Test Answer Key."

Use the information contained in this chapter to indicate whether the following statements are true or false.

Question 14.1

T   F   Because switch types are not standard, when configuring the router, you will need to specify the ISDN switch you are connecting to.

Question 14.2

T   F   BRI offers 23 bearer (B) channels and one 64-kbps D channel.

Question 14.3

T   F   BRI is sometimes written as 2B+D.

Question 14.4

T   F   The ISDN D channel carries signaling information.

Question 14.5

T   F   Although the ISDN call can statistically multiplex (or combine) packets from several higher-layer protocols, ISDN interfaces allow only a single encapsulation type.

Question 14.6

T   F   The TE1 is a required external device that converts the 4-wire connection on the T interface to a 2-wire.

Question 14.7

T   F   SPIDs are a series of characters that can look like phone numbers and that identify your connection to the switch at the central office.

Question 14.8

Given the list of ISDN functions and reference points, identify where the ISDN functions and reference points appear in Figure 14–25.

- TA

- NT2

- S/T

- NT1

- R

- U

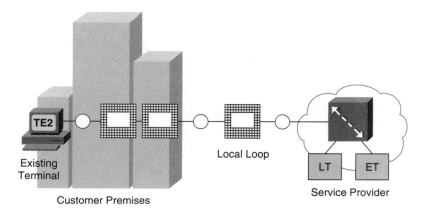

Figure 14–25
Identify the ISDN components.

TE2

Existing
Terminal

Customer Premises

Local Loop

LT   ET

Service Provider

Customizing
DDR Operation

This chapter focuses on how to configure some of the more advanced DDR (dial-on-demand routing) configurations. The topics covered include dial backup, MultiLink PPP, snapshot routing, and IPX spoofing.

DIAL BACKUP FOR DEDICATED CONNECTIONS

Cisco's dial backup feature enables you to back up your primary links in one of the two following situations:

- When a dedicated WAN link goes down, a dial backup configuration will raise the data terminal ready (DTR) signal on the router's backup serial port. A preconfigured autodial modem, DSU, or ISDN terminal adapter will then make a circuit-switched connection to the remote site. In this way, you do not lose connectivity to the remote site.

- When the bandwidth utilization on a dedicated WAN link reaches its traffic load threshold, a dial backup configuration will raise the secondary link for the duration that the load meets the load threshold value. Note that the load refers to traffic being transmitted and received.

The most significant difference between DDR and dial backup is the reason for placing the call. DDR is used to create periodic low-volume connections to a network to pass traffic over. There could be many reasons to want dial backup. Business reliability is a primary reason for having dial backup. For example:

- The first reason is when the primary line fails, which is communicated both by software and by hardware. The hardware signal to dial a backup is the loss of the Carrier Detect signal on the primary line. The software signal is the absence of three keepalive messages.

- The second reason for using dial backup is to augment the bandwidth of the primary, so that if the primary becomes overloaded, you can use the secondary line to provide load balancing during busy periods.

A backup interface can back up only one primary interface. The primary interface must be a dedicated leased line. If the primary interface is already dynamically demand-driven (such as an asynchronous or ISDN BRI), there is no need for a backup interface.

Configuring Dial Backup for Primary Links

To configure a backup line, as shown in Figure 15–1, perform the following steps:

Figure 15–1
Configuring dial backup for primary links.

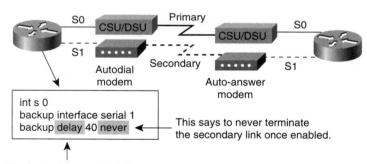

1. Select the primary interface and go into interface configuration mode.

2. Indicate the backup interface to use in case of a primary link failure or in case a load threshold is exceeded.

```
router(config-if)#backup interface interface-name
```

interface-name specifies the interface or dialer interface to use for backup.

3. Define the number of seconds to wait before enabling the backup link when the primary link fails.

```
router(config-if)#backup delay {enable-delay | never}
    {disable-delay | never}
```

backup delay Command	Description
enable-delay	Number of seconds to wait after the primary link has failed that must be reached before the backup line is brought up
disable-delay	Number of seconds to wait after the primary link is available that must be reached before the backup line is torn down
never	Prevents the secondary line from being activated or deactivated

The **backup delay** command sets timers. When the primary goes down, you may not want to dial the expensive backup line immediately. You might want to wait a minute to see whether the primary will recover service. That is what is set in seconds by the enable-delay parameter. One option is **never**, which causes the backup line to never be dialed (a rather inexplicable feature).

TIPS

As a rule of thumb, wait at least 20 seconds before initiating the backup line just in case it was a glitch and the link bounced.

After service on the primary line is restored, you might want to wait for a minute to see whether the primary is back in service before dropping the backup line. The time to wait after primary service has been restored is set with *disable-delay*. While both lines are up, load balancing is occurring. You could set this parameter to **never**, which causes the backup line to never drop out. If the connection is not expensive, you could keep the backup line up as a way of finding out whether the backup line was used overnight.

TIPS

As a rule of thumb, wait five seconds to ensure the link stays up.

If the modem lights are on when you arrive in the morning, the primary was lost during the night, and you will have to turn off the backup manually.

You can define how much time should elapse before a secondary line status changes and after a primary line status has changed with the **backup delay** interface configuration command.

The **backup delay** is specified at 40 seconds in Figure 15–1 and refers to the duration of the primary line being down. This delay prevents accidental secondary connection because of rapid "down-up-down-up" transitions on the communication facility. These transitions occur when a link is rapidly brought up and down due to some type of intermittent line failure. The disconnect delay of never means that the router will not automatically disconnect the secondary line once the primary line is back up.

Configuring Dial Backup for Excessive Traffic Load

If you periodically have peak traffic times where the traffic load is too much for the primary link, you can configure dial backup to enable the secondary link to assist in transmitting the excess traffic. Perform the following steps to configure dial backup for excess traffic:

1. Perform steps 1 and 2 in the "Configuring Dial Backup for Primary Links" section, earlier in this chapter.

2. Set the traffic load thresholds for dial backup service.

```
router(config-if)#backup load {enable-threshold | never}
    {disable-load | never}
```

backup load Command	Description
enable-threshold	Percentage of the primary line's available bandwidth that must be reached before the backup line is brought up
disable-load	Percentage of the primary line's available bandwidth that must be reached before the backup line is torn down
never	Sets the secondary line never to be activated due to traffic load

The software monitors the traffic load on the primary link and computes a five-minute moving average. If this average exceeds the value you set for the line, the secondary line is activated.

In Figure 15–2, the secondary link is established when the primary load reaches 60 percent capacity. It will remain active until the combined total traffic load on both lines drops to five (5) percent of the capacity of the primary link.

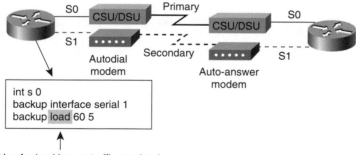

Use for backing up traffic overloads.

Figure 15–2
Use the **backup load** *command to configure a router to handle excessive loads.*

MultiLink PPP Overview

MultiLink PPP is a mechanism for increasing bandwidth between two sites by grouping or bundling interfaces and then splitting and recombining packets to run over the bundled interfaces. By splitting and recombining packets over a bundle, you can reduce latency and potentially increase the effective *maximum receive unit* (MRU), which is the maximum size of the information transported, in bytes, in the PPP packet received by the local equipment. Prior to this feature, there was no standardized way to group interfaces, such as two ISDN B channels, and ensure proper sequencing of packets.

MultiLink PPP is defined in RFC 1990 and is based on an LCP option negotiation that permits a router to indicate to its peer that it is capable of combining multiple physical links into a bundle. Only under exceptional conditions would a given pair of systems require the operation of more than one bundle connecting them.

Cisco IOS release 11.1 is the first IOS release to support MultiLink PPP. It is designed to work with both analog and digital technologies that allow hosts to originate multiple links to the destination device.

Typical uses for this feature are between telecommuters and central offices using ISDN, for example, or between office sites that have multiple ISDN, synchronous, or asynchronous connections.

TIPS

In Cisco IOS Release 11.3, a feature referred to as *Bandwidth Allocation Control Protocol (BACP)* is used to enable two routers configured for MultiLink PPP to negotiate which peer will add or remove links during a session. Without this feature, both routers can potentially attempt the adding or removing of a link simultaneously.

MultiLink PPP Operation

MultiLink PPP works over any interface that supports dialer profiles or dialer rotary groups including ISDN, synchronous, and asynchronous interfaces. With MultiLink

PPP, datagrams are split, sequenced, and transmitted across a bundle, and then recombined at the destination. The bundler is responsible for taking the streams of data from the multilink device and combining them into a single packet/stream going to the destination. On the return trip, it will take the single stream/packet and divide it into multiple streams to be sent to the other multilink device where that device takes the streams and builds a packet or data stream.

During MultiLink PPP's LCP option negotiation, a system indicates to its peer that it is willing to multilink by sending the maximum received reconstructed unit (MRRU) option as part of the initial LCP option negotiation (see Figure 15–3).

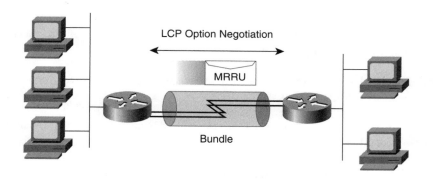

Figure 15–3
The MRRU option indicates a Multi-Link PPP connection is desired.

Multilink systems must be able to do the following:

- Combine multiple physical links into one logical bundle

- Receive and reassemble upper-layer protocol data units (PDUs)

- Receive PDUs of a negotiated size

After the LCP negotiation has completed, the remote destination must be authenticated and a dialer map with the remote system name must be configured. The authenticated username or caller ID is used to determine to which bundle to add the link.

Configuring MultiLink PPP

Configure MultiLink PPP using the following steps:

1. Configure either dialer profiles or dialer rotary groups on selected interfaces, or select a single BRI.

2. Configure the dialer interface, if using dialer profiles, with the following command:

    ```
    router(config-if)#ppp multilink
    ```

    The maximum number of links in a bundle is the number of interfaces in the dialer/rotary group interface.

3. Specify the load threshold that the interface should reach before enabling one or more additional links.

    ```
    router(config-if)#dialer load-threshold load [outbound | inbound |
        either]
    ```

    This command can be used on either end of the link (except for an access server that is not responsible for initiating additional links) and has been extended to allow the threshold determination to be decided by any of the following:

    - Outbound traffic only (default)
    - Inbound traffic only
    - The maximum of either inbound or outbound traffic

MultiLink PPP Configuration Example

The network topology in Figure 15–4 represents the configuration on the following pages.

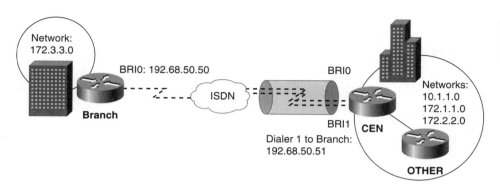

Figure 15–4
MultiLink PPP configuration.

Note the following when reviewing the configurations:

- On the branch office router, no dialer rotary group was configured. MultiLink PPP was configured on the BRI because the two B channels in a BRI are, by default, a rotary group, so no group definition was required. The B channels are candidates for being added to a bundle.

- If there were multiple BRIs that needed to be part of the MultiLink PPP bundle, a rotary group would need to be configured and the BRIs would then need to be assigned to it.

- On the central office router, MultiLink PPP is configured on the dialer interface. In this case, all physical interfaces that are members of the specified dialer interface could be added to a MultiLink PPP bundle, when traffic load requires it.

The following output shows the branch office router—legacy DDR/MLP configuration:

```
BRANCH#show run
<Output Omitted>
!
hostname BRANCH
!
enable secret 5 $1$vAef$oQsAbx.BbJWnkvmci5e/2/
enable password san-fran
!
username CEN password 7 104D000A0618
isdn switch-type basic-5ess
```

```
!
interface Loopback3
 ip address 172.3.3.3 255.255.255.0
!
<Output Omitted>
!
interface Serial1
 no ip address
 shutdown
!
<Output Omitted>
!
interface BRI0
 ip address 192.68.50.50 255.255.255.0
 encapsulation ppp
 dialer idle-timeout 180
 dialer map ip 192.68.50.51 name CEN broadcast 2001
 dialer load-threshold 50 either
 dialer-group 1
 no fair-queue
 ppp authentication chap
 ppp multilink
!
router rip
 network 172.3.0.0
 network 192.68.0.0
!
no ip classless
ip route 10.1.1.0 255.255.255.0 192.68.50.51
ip route 172.1.1.0 255.255.255.0 192.68.50.51
ip route 172.2.2.0 255.255.255.0 192.68.50.51
!
dialer-list 1 protocol ip permit
!
line con 0
line aux 0
line vty 0 4
 password cisco
 login
!
end
```

The following output shows the central office router—dialer profiles/MLP configuration:

```
CEN#show run
<Output Omitted>
!
hostname CEN
!
!
username BRANCH password 7 14141B180F0B
isdn switch-type basic-5ess
!
interface Loopback2
 ip address 172.1.1.1 255.255.255.0
!
<Output Omitted>
!
interface Serial1
 ip address 10.1.1.1 255.255.255.0
 bandwidth 64
 clockrate 64000
 no cdp enable
!
<Output Omitted>
!
interface BRI0
 ip address 10.32.0.1 255.255.255.0
 encapsulation ppp
 dialer pool-member 4
 ppp authentication chap
!
interface Dialer1
 ip address 192.68.50.51 255.255.255.0
 encapsulation ppp
 dialer remote-name BRANCH
 dialer idle-timeout 180
 dialer string 2003
 dialer load-threshold 5 either
 dialer pool 4
 dialer-group 1
 no fair-queue
```

```
 no cdp enable
 ppp authentication chap
 ppp multilink
!
router rip
 redistribute static metric 2
 network 172.1.0.0
 network 10.0.0.0
!
no ip classless
ip route 172.3.3.0 255.255.255.0 Dialer1
!
dialer-list 1 protocol ip permit
!
line con 0
line aux 0
line vty 0 4
 login
!
end
```

Verifying MultiLink PPP Operation

The following are the two primary commands used for verifying MultiLink PPP operation:

- The **show dialer** command displays information about existing bundles, as follows:

  ```
  router#show dialer
  ```

- The **debug ppp multilink** command is used to display ppp multilink event information, as follows:

  ```
  router#debug ppp multilink
  ```

Other commands include those already reviewed in Chapter 14, "Configuring Dial-on-Demand Routing," as in the following:

- Those related to the interface type, for example, the **show isdn** command for ISDN

- Others related to the dialer, such as the **show dialer interface** command

So far, this chapter has examined the basic steps required to configure multilink PPP and has used the **show** and **debug** commands to verify operation. In the next section, you learn about controlling the traffic by cutting down on overhead, which is defined as unnecessary traffic that would otherwise bring up a DDR link.

DISABLING OVERHEAD TRAFFIC

There are several types of traffic that can bring up the DDR link unnecessarily. These include, but are not limited to, routing updates, keepalives, and watchdog traffic. Keepalives and watchdogs maintain a connection between two processes across a link.

There are several ways to disable routing updates so that they will not bring up a DDR connection. In Chapter 3, "Managing IP Traffic," you learned about using access lists to filter routing updates. In Chapter 14, passive interfaces were discussed. In this section, the following two additional techniques are covered:

- *Snapshot routing*—The process of snapshot routing involves building a routing table based on a snapshot of routing information exchanged during an active time on the network. The snapshot version of the routing table is used until another active time occurs, at which time the router obtains a new picture of the network. No routing information is exchanged during the quiet time on the network. Snapshot routing can be applied to distance vector protocols, including IP RIP, IGRP, IPX RIP, and AppleTalk RTMP.

- *IPX spoofing*—In the NetWare environment, two connections are maintained through a periodic polling process: client connections to the server and SPX-based connections. IPX spoofing is applied to both IPX keepalives and SPX watchdog spoofing.

Snapshot Routing

Snapshot routing is a routing update mechanism that provides the following two key benefits:

- It eliminates the need for configuring and maintaining large static tables by allowing dynamic routing protocols to be used on DDR lines.

- It enables the exchange of routing updates across the DDR link only when you specify it to.

Snapshot routing controls WAN costs because you can specify the time of the connection used for exchanging routing updates. Snapshot routing controls the routing update traffic by defining active/inactive periods and should be used in conjunction with access control lists to control normal DDR traffic.

Key Concept   *Snapshot routing* **refers to the process of obtaining a list of network routes during an active period and taking a snapshot of the entries in the routing table. These entries remain frozen during a quiet period. At the end of the quiet period, another active period starts during which routing information is again exchanged. For example, a router on one end of a DDR link would gather routing information from the router on the other end of the link during an active time. The local router would then take a snapshot of the information learned and use this information for a preconfigured length of time (the quiet time).**

ISDN is a primary target for snapshot routing, but other media, such as dedicated leased lines, can also benefit from its reduction of the number of periodic updates. Snapshot routing can be used with all distance vector (periodic update) routing protocols for all supported protocols on DDR lines.

Snapshot routing is designed for hub-and-spoke environments where remote sites dial into the same central router. It is not recommended for use in meshed networks, where static routes are more efficient.

TIPS

Link-state routing protocols cannot be used with snapshot routing because they send periodic hellos that would trigger the link every five or ten seconds. Enhanced IGRP also sends hellos and therefore cannot be used with snapshot routing.

Snapshot routing is an effective alternative to using static routing, depending on your network needs. Before implementing snapshot routing, verify that your network meets the following criteria:

- *Network size and rate of growth*—If the network is large or quickly evolves and requires scalability without static routing lists maintenance, snapshot is a solution. However, if the network is small with basic management tools, it is recommended that you use static routes only.

- *The network topology is client/server*—Snapshot requires a hub-and-spoke topology to be used efficiently. The snapshot mechanism is based on the client/server principle.

Snapshot Routing Operation and Configuration

Figure 15–5 shows how snapshot routing operates.

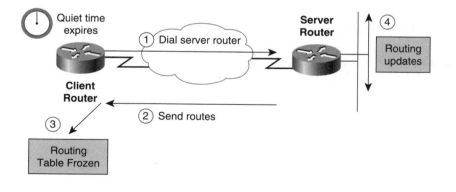

Figure 15–5
Snapshot routing's four-step operation.

The following steps correspond with the callout numbers in Figure 15–5:

1. A "client" router (the spoke router) is configured for the interval at which routing updates need to be exchanged. When the interval for exchanging routing updates is reached, the client router establishes an "active period" and enables the DDR link to all routers that it has configured in the snapshot dialer map. The routers in the map are called the "server" routers and are the hub routers.

By default, the client router makes router requests during an active period and when the DDR link is transmitting interesting traffic.

2. When the client router establishes a connection with a server router, the server router exchanges routing information with the client. The server router exchanges routing updates with any client router that calls in.

If the dial-out line is busy when an active period should begin, you can configure a retry interval. The retry interval instructs the router to retry making the call at an administrator-defined interval.

3. After routing updates are exchanged and the active period is complete, the client router takes a snapshot of the entries in the routing table and goes into a *quiet period*. During the quiet period, no updates go through the link (up or down) and the routing information previously collected is kept unchanged (frozen) in the routing tables.

4. While snapshot is asleep, the server router sends routing updates out of the local LAN interfaces as per the routing-protocol update timer. This is so that local routers are spoofed and believe that they have a fully active connection.

Snapshot routing requires the configuring of the client (spoke) routers and the configuring of the server (hub) routers, as shown in Figure 15–6.

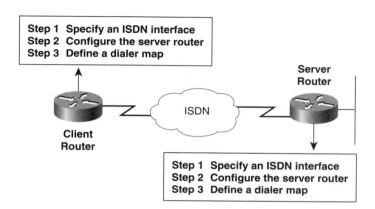

Figure 15-6
*Use the same
configuration
steps on both
sides of the
link.*

Configuring the Client (Spoke) Routers

To configure the client routers for snapshot routing, follow these steps:

1. Enter the interface configuration mode for the physical or dialer interface you want to perform snapshot routing on.

2. Enable snapshot routing on the client router.

```
router(config-if)#snapshot client active-time quiet-time
    [suppress-statechange-updates] dialer
```

snapshot client Command	Description
active-time	(No default) Amount of time that routing updates are exchanged between client and server routers. Range is 5 to 100 minutes. A typical value is 5 minutes.
quiet-time	(No default) Amount of time that the client freezes routing entries. Range is 8 to 100000 minutes. The minimum quiet time is the active time plus 3 minutes.

snapshot client Command	Description
suppress-statechange-updates	(Optional) Disables the exchange of routing updates each time the link state goes from "down" to "up."
dialer	(Optional) Used when the client router must dial the remote router in the absence of regular traffic. It is used to point to the appropriate dialer map to use in case the snapshot must initiate a call to a server router.

Use the **suppress-statechange-updates** keyword when the network is stable or when the normal call duration is shorter than the time required to exchange updates.

To decide whether to allow routing updates to be exchanged when the DDR link is activated for interesting traffic, use the following guidelines:

- *Network stability*—In case of instability (new applications popping up), it is useful to offer updates at each data connection. In other cases, you can control the frequency of active periods (set to several hours or every day, for instance) during which routing information is exchanged.

- Determine which overhead cost is acceptable—When usual data connections last more than five minutes, snapshot offers free dynamic updates at each data connection.

- If data connections are short (fewer than five minutes) and calls frequent, the "send-update-every-time" state will affect the bill.

- Opening active periods independently of data connections offers a stable update cost. For example, you can define active periods that occur during the evening when telephone rates are low.

3. Define a dialer map that includes the server router(s) to call for routing updates.

```
router(config-if)#dialer map snapshot sequence-number name name
    dial-string
```

dialer map snapshot Command	Description
sequence-number	A number (1 to 254, inclusive) that uniquely identifies a dialer map and prioritizes the sequence in which the client router calls the server routers, if multiple server routers are configured
name *name*	Name of remote host
dial-string	Snapshot server's telephone number to be called during active period

Configuring the Server (Hub) Router

Perform the following steps to configure the server routers for snapshot routing:

1. Select the physical or dialer interface and get into interface configuration mode.

2. Enable snapshot routing.

   ```
   router(config-if)#snapshot server active-timer [dialer]
   ```

   This time must match the active time configured on the client router. The quiet period is configured only on the client router because the client controls the quiet period.

3. Define a dialer map that includes the client router(s) that will call for routing updates.

   ```
   router(config-if)#dialer map snapshot sequence-number name name
       dial-string
   ```

Snapshot Routing Configuration Example

In Figure 15–7, the client router is configured as follows:

- **interface BRI 0**—Selects BRI 0 as the interface over which snapshot routing will be run.

- **snapshot client 5 720 dialer**—Configures this device to be a client router and sets the active and quiet periods at 5 and 720 minutes (12 hours), respectively. The dialer option is enabled, allowing the client to call the server in the absence of regular traffic at the end of a quiet period.

- **dialer map snapshot 1 name server-router 14155551212**—Defines the dialer map for the snapshot routing protocol to call the server router. The number 1 uniquely identifies this dialer map, and 1-415-555-1212 is the number to call to get to the device.

Figure 15–7
Snapshot routing con-figuration example.

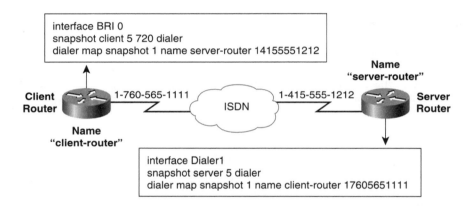

In Figure 15–7, the router on the right is configured as the server router. Notice that it has the same active period value and also has a dialer map to the client.

Verifying and Troubleshooting Snapshot Routing Operation

The following commands can be used to verify that snapshot routing is operating:

Command	Description
show snapshot	Verifies that the snapshot interface is operable. The statements "line protocol is up" and "snapshot client up" shown in Figure 15–8 indicate that the snapshot interface has been properly configured. You can also verify the active, quiet, and retry period values, the current state (active or quiet) of the snapshot interface; and the time remaining before the interfaces change state.

Command	Description
clear snapshot quiet-time	Use to end the quiet period (within two minutes) and begin an active period. Use this command when you suspect that the routing information the client is holding needs an instant refresher, for example, in the case where some planned network adds or changes have occurred at the central site.

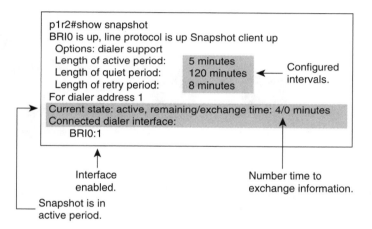

Figure 15–8
Verifying snapshot routing.

In addition to these specific commands, you can use the DDR **show** commands discussed in Chapter 14 to verify the status of the DDR connections.

The following commands can be used to troubleshoot snapshot routing:

Command	Description
debug snapshot	Used to debug snapshot operation. It tracks the progression of active and quiet periods.
debug ip rip	To verify that routing updates are being transmitted, you can enable the appropriate **debug** command for the given protocol and observe the exchange of routing updates.

IPX Spoofing

IPX spoofing is the process of pretending that the WAN link is up and keepalive traffic is being answered across it on a regular basis. NetWare maintains connections between clients and their servers and between SPX-based peers on behalf of connection-oriented applications. In Figure 15–9, for example, the NetWare server will periodically send a watchdog packet toward the clients. Rather than bringing up the WAN link, the Cisco router responds on behalf of the clients.

Figure 15–9
Spoofing allows the router to respond while the DDR interface is idle.

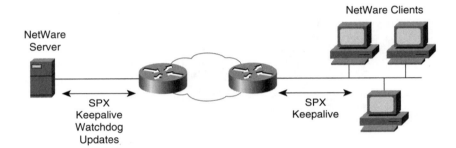

In addition to routing updates, IPX uses the following "network monitoring" protocols to monitor the state of the following network components:

- NetWare uses a watchdog protocol to periodically query for inactive workstation connections.

- NetWare applications such as RCONSOLE and RPRINTER use SPX for guaranteed, sequenced delivery of packets. When an SPX connection is established, both ends of the connection exchange keepalive requests to track periods when no data is transmitted.

On DDR WAN links, the watchdog and SPX keepalives can consume a large portion of bandwidth and cause a DDR line to remain connected even when no actual data is being transmitted. Cisco routers provide the following solutions to minimize the number of these packets over DDR:

- Cisco routers can respond to a server's watchdog requests on behalf of remote clients so that the server does not time out the client's connection across a silent DDR link. Instead of bringing up the link to the client's network, the Cisco router answers the watchdog update query on behalf of the client. This feature is called *watchdog spoofing.*

- Cisco routers can respond to SPX keepalive packets. This feature is known as *SPX spoofing.*

Note that in this chapter, IPX spoofing refers to both watchdog and SPX spoofing.

IPX spoofing refers to the process of replying on behalf of another device that is being polled in order to avoid bringing up a DDR link for overhead traffic. This includes both watchdog and SPX spoofing.   **Key Concept**

Configuring IPX Spoofing for DDR

To configure IPX spoofing in order to reduce the number of SPX and watchdog packets crossing a silent DDR link, perform the following tasks:

1. Turn off route caching on the interface that is spoofing. This is a requirement because the router needs to look inside the packet to determine its contents (in order to know whether it needs to spoof).

```
router(config)#no ipx route-cache
```

2. Enable SPX spoofing of the idle DDR link.

```
router(config)#ipx spx-spoof
```

3. Enable IPX watchdog spoofing.

```
router(config)#ipx watchdog-spoof
```

4. Set the time in seconds that must elapse before SPX spoofing of keepalive packets can occur.

```
router(config)#ipx spx-idle-time
```

By default, SPX keepalive packets are sent every 15 seconds. You should always set this command to at least three times the SPX keepalive interval to ensure that the router's SPX connection table is updated with the current SPX keepalive sequence number.

DDR for IPX Configuration Example

In Figure 15–10, a static route has been configured to reach IPX network 20.

Figure 15–10
IPX spoofing example.

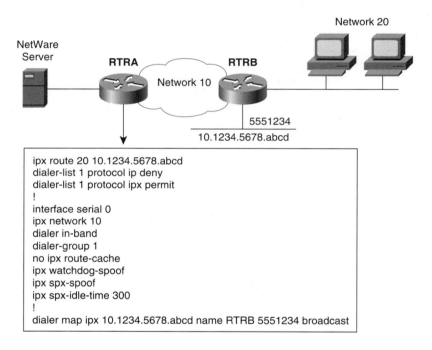

```
ipx route 20 10.1234.5678.abcd
dialer-list 1 protocol ip deny
dialer-list 1 protocol ipx permit
!
interface serial 0
ipx network 10
dialer in-band
dialer-group 1
no ipx route-cache
ipx watchdog-spoof
ipx spx-spoof
ipx spx-idle-time 300
!
dialer map ipx 10.1234.5678.abcd name RTRB 5551234 broadcast
```

IPX fast switching is turned off by the **no ipx route-cache** command. Watchdog spoofing and SPX spoofing are enabled on serial 0. The **ipx spx-idle-time 300** command sets the SPX idle time to 300 seconds (five minutes).

If the dialer idle time is three minutes, the DDR connection will time out three minutes after the last packet has been received on the interface. The SPX idle time completes five minutes later, and the line drops.

SAP updates can also keep the DDR connection active if NetWare servers are on both sides of the routers. In this case, the servers would exchange SAP updates every 60 seconds, by default. You can block SAP updates using one of two following solutions:

- *IPX access lists*—Filter SAP by filtering RIP (socket 452), SAP (453), and the SEQ-CHK (457).

- *Static SAPs*—When using static SAPs for each peer router, you will need to define static SAP entries. On the client router, list the static SAPs with a hop count that allows all desired clients to be able to access the local servers. If there is a client server that local and remote clients needed to access, the server router would add a static SAP entry with a hop count of 1 or 2 (for reachability) pointing that server at the client site.

  Also, remember that when doing dynamic SAPs, you must put the **broadcast** keyword in the dialer map statement so that SAPs can be exchanged when the link is enabled.

SUMMARY

As you learned in this chapter, Cisco routers support many DDR enhancements including dial backup, snapshot routing, and IPX spoofing. Recall that Cisco's dial backup feature enables you to back up your primary links in one of two situations: when a dedicated WAN link goes down or when the bandwidth utilization on a dedicated WAN link reaches its traffic load threshold.

Snapshot routing refers to the process of taking a quick look at the routes available and using that information for a configured time instead of bringing up the DDR to periodically exchange routing information. *IPX spoofing* is the process of pretending to be a NetWare client by answering polling packets in order to leave a DDR link in the down state.

In the next chapter, you learn the differences between routing and bridging and how to set up a bridged network.

Chapter Fifteen Test
Customizing DDR Operation

Estimated Time: 15 minutes

Complete all the exercises to test your knowledge of the materials contained in this chapter. Answers are listed in Appendix A, "Chapter Test Answer Key."

Use the information contained in this chapter to answer the following questions.

Question 15.1

Refer to Figure 15–11 and configure both routers for snapshot routing so that the branch office calls headquarters every 24 hours and exchanges routing updates for eight minutes. Write your configuration in the space provided.

Figure 15–11
Configure snapshot routing for these routers.

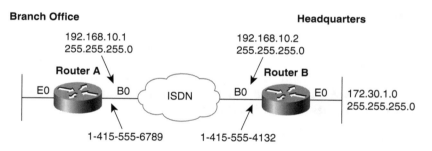

Branch Office   Headquarters

192.168.10.1   192.168.10.2
255.255.255.0   255.255.255.0

Router A   Router B

E0   B0   ISDN   B0   E0   172.30.1.0
                                                 255.255.255.0

1-415-555-6789   1-415-555-4132

Router A   **Router B**

Question 15.2

T   F   During MultiLink PPP's LCP option negotiation, MMRU is used to indicate that a device is willing to multilink.

Question 15.3

T   F   Use the **backup delay** command to specify that you don't want to dial an expensive backup line immediately when the primary goes down.

Question 15.4

T   F   You should set the **backup delay** to wait at least 20 seconds before initiating the backup line just in case it was a glitch and the link bounced.

Question 15.5

T   F   With MultiLink PPP, datagrams are split, sequenced, and transmitted across separate virtual circuits.

Question 15.6

T   F   Snapshot routing can be used to reduce the overall number of route entries maintained by a WAN router.

PART 5

Integrating Nonrouted Services

CHAPTER 16

Bridging Overview

The purpose of this chapter is to describe some of the router configuration options available to handle nonroutable traffic. Nonroutable traffic has no Layer 3 addressing and must, therefore, be bridged. Bridging is discussed from the standpoint of how routers, acting as bridges, handle traffic.

INTRODUCTION TO BRIDGING

A *bridge* is an internetworking device designed to interconnect LANs to form the appearance of a single larger data link. Bridges have the following functionality:

- They isolate intersegment traffic, which results in a reduction in traffic on a given segment. On an Ethernet segment, this traffic reduction results in reduced contention, and consequently, a reduced number of collisions.

- They are used to meet the size limitations in Ethernet. The maximum Ethernet cable length is specified such that a station transmitting the smallest legal-sized frame can detect a collision with any other station on that segment. To comply with these length restrictions, a bridge is frequently deployed to divide a segment into two. For Token Ring, each station on the ring introduces an increased delay because each Token Ring station repeats each frame to its downstream neighbor. A bridge reduces the number of stations per ring and consequently reduces the delay.

- With bridges, connectivity occurs at Layer 2 (data link layer) of the OSI model, as shown in Figure 16–1, so that forwarding decisions are based on the Media Access Control (MAC) address (for transparent bridges). Routers make forwarding decisions based on the Layer 3 protocol/network-layer address.

- Bridges are less sophisticated devices and therefore require less configuration than routers. In environments that do not require a complex routing feature, bridging is a simpler alternative.

- Bridged networks are inherently flat because all devices on bridged segments are part of the same network address space. For this reason, bridges forward all broadcast frames to all connected segments (except the originating segment). In contrast, routing allows for networks to be divided into smaller units so that broadcasts are kept only on the local network.

Figure 16–1
Bridging forwards traffic based on the data link layer (Layer 2) address.

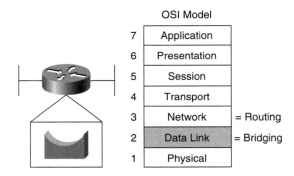

- Transparent bridging

NONROUTED PROTOCOL SUPPORT

Some protocols, such as Local Area Transport (LAT), a network virtual terminal protocol developed by Digital Equipment Corporation, cannot be routed because it doesn't contain routing layer functionality. This protocol must be bridged. Cisco routers support many bridging types, as shown in the following list:

- Transparent bridging

- Encapsulated bridging

- Integrated routing and bridging (IRB)

- Source-route bridging (SRB)

- Source-route transparent bridging (SRT)

- Source-route translational bridging (SR/TLB)

Other bridging technologies (not covered in this book) are *Data-link switching (DLSw)* and *DLSw+*. DLSw provides a means to transport SNA and NetBIOS traffic over a multiprotocol backbone. Cisco's extension to DLSw is called DLSw+. DLSw+ provides many enhancements to DLSw, including simplified configuration and enhanced control over network operation, increased security, and increased availability through the use of a backup router. *Remote source-route bridging (RSRB)*, a subset of DLSW, can also be used to transport SNA traffic over IP.

ROUTING VERSUS BRIDGING

Routing is based on the logical addresses contained in the network layer of the OSI reference model. Bridging, on the other hand, is based on the MAC-layer address contained in the data link layer of the OSI reference model.

Using the Cisco IOS bridging capability, all routable protocols can be bridged. With a few exceptions that will be noted later when discussing integrated routing and bridging (IRB), enabling routing of a given protocol means that it is no longer a candidate for bridging.

Some protocols such as local-area transport (LAT), Maintenance Operation Protocol (MOP), and NetBIOS have no network-layer addressing and therefore cannot be routed. These and all nonroutable protocols must be bridged.

Native (nonroutable) NetBIOS is used in many IBM networks to transport Logical Link Control (LLC) 2. Some NetBIOS implementations run on top of either IPX or IP to make them routable. NetBIOS is not routable because it is a session layer protocol. It was originally designed to work on a source route bridged network (which is a routed network at the data link layer). When it is removed from its native token ring, it required either IPX or IP to replace the missing routing function. NetBIOS over IPX is used by a number of third-party packages. One such example is a software package that allows a Novell PC to gain connectivity to an IBM gateway. NetBIOS over IP is found in Windows NT installations.

BASIC ROUTER/BRIDGE OPERATION

Notwithstanding newer Cisco bridging technologies such as IRB and concurrent routing and bridging, if the network-layer protocol was enabled within the router, the packet was passed to the routing software. If the protocol had no network layer or the network-layer protocol was not configured on the router, the frame was passed to the bridging software if the router was configured for bridging (see Figure 16–2).

Figure 16–2
*Basic router/
bridge opera-
tion.*

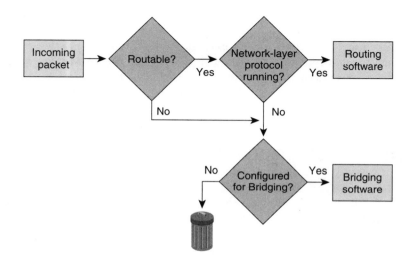

With IRB, certain routable protocols can be bridged across bridged groups and the same protocol can also be routed through a routed interface. IRB is discussed in Chapter 17, "Configuring Transparent Bridging and Integrated Routing and Bridging."

CISCO-SUPPORTED BRIDGING TYPES

There are several different types of bridging solutions. They each offer a different set of attributes and place the bridging information responsibility in different locations. In this next section, you learn about each of these bridging technologies and differentiate between them.

Transparent Bridging

Transparent bridging is used to connect two or more physical networks into one LAN. It is traditionally and most often found in Ethernet and Institute of Electrical and Electronic Engineers (IEEE) 802.3 networks in which bridges pass frames along one hop at a time based on tables associating end nodes with bridge ports. A *transparent bridge* is so named because it does not alter the data frame, is never a source or destination for frames (that is, the bridge's MAC address is never in the frame), and makes the attached segments look like one cable.

Transparent bridges were first developed at Digital Equipment Corporation (Digital) in the early 1980s. Digital submitted its work to the IEEE, and the IEEE incorporated Digital's work into the IEEE 802.1D standard.

Encapsulated Bridging

Encapsulated bridging is used to connect LANs via an independent transport connection, normally FDDI or serial. Encapsulated bridging consists of encapsulating the bridged frame inside another data link layer protocol (such as HDLC) and de-encapsulating it on the other side of the link. Encapsulated bridging provides for the encapsulation of transparently bridged frames over WAN and LAN links, such as FDDI).

Sometimes the bridges on either side of the WAN link are called half-bridges because, when taken together, they appear to be a single bridge between LANs.

With FDDI, sometimes encapsulated bridging is called *transit bridging*, which means that the sending and receiving stations cannot be on the FDDI medium itself. This approach makes the FDDI a very efficient backbone for a bridged network. Stations A and B in Figure 16–3 require encapsulated bridging to communicate.

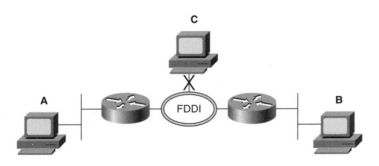

Figure 16–3
Bridge frames use serial or FDDI encapsulations.

In Figure 16–3, for example, stations A and C are on different media, so they require a bridge to translate frames into the appropriate format. Such a bridge is called a *translational bridge*.

Integrated Routing and Bridging

IRB, a Cisco IOS software Release 11.2 (and later) feature, allows combinations of routing and bridging functionality to be selectively provided. With IRB, you can route a given protocol between routed interfaces and bridged interfaces within a single router. Before IRB, you could bridge or route a given protocol within the same router, but you could not route and bridge the same protocol on the same interface, as shown in Figure 16–4. This feature was called *concurrent routing and bridging*. Concurrent routing and bridging could not switch a packet between a routed and bridged interface.

Figure 16–4
IRB provides integrated routing and bridging functions in a single device.

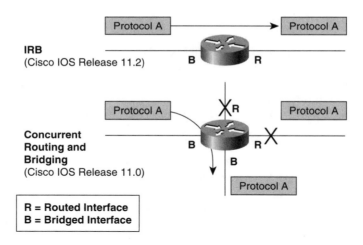

Before concurrent routing and bridging, the bridging or routing of a given protocol was done on a per-protocol basis: the protocol was either bridged or routed.

Source-Route Bridging

Source-route bridging (SRB) is a method of bridging developed by IBM for use in Token Ring networks. With SRB, the entire route to a destination is predetermined, in real-time, prior to the sending of data (contrast this with transparent bridging, where bridging occurs on a hop-by-hop basis).

With SRB, the source places the complete source-to-destination route in the frame header of all inter-LAN frames, as shown in Figure 16–5. To discover a route to the destination, end stations transmit an explorer frame to determine where the destination is located. The source host then includes the desired path information in the frame. Bridges along the path simply forward the frame according to the path contained therein.

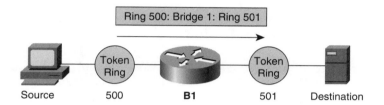

Ring 500: Bridge 1: Ring 501

Source   500   **B1**   501   Destination

Figure 16–5
In source-route bridging, the source is responsible for determining path to destination before sending data.

Source-Route Transparent Bridging

Source-route transparent bridging (SRT) bridges employ both SRB and transparent bridging technologies in one device, as shown in Figure 16–6. SRT bridges handle both SRB and transparent bridging at the same time, one packet per transfer. SRT is used for Token Ring networks where some stations are performing source routing and some are not.

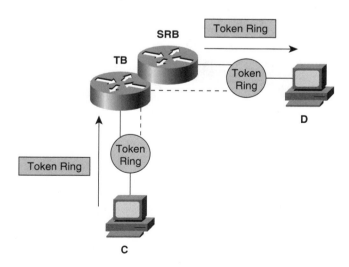

SRB

TB

Token Ring

D

Token Ring

C

Figure 16–6
Source-route transparent bridges perform SRB and transparent bridging.

An SRT bridge does not translate between the two bridging domains, nor does it convert frames from Ethernet to Token Ring networks. Traffic with routing information (in the SRB sense of the term) will be handled using SRB configuration, and traffic without routing information will be handled using the transparent bridging configuration.

IBM introduced SRT in 1990. SRT is specified in the IEEE 802.1D.

Source-Route Translational Bridging

Source-route translational bridging (SR/TLB) provides the functionality to connect the two hosts shown in Figure 16–7. Host A is on an Ethernet segment containing a transparent bridge. Host B is on a Token Ring segment containing an SRB. In order for these two devices to communicate, each frame must be converted from an Ethernet frame containing no routing information to a Token Ring frame containing routing information. In addition, many other issues are associated with the frame conversion including differences in maximum transmission unit (MTU) sizes and differences in bit ordering.

Figure 16–7
Source-route translational bridges translate between bridging domains.

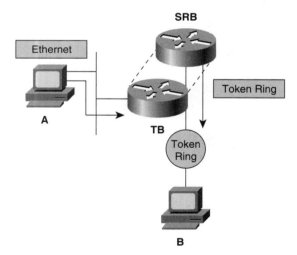

SUMMARY

In this chapter, you learned about several kinds of nonrouted protocol support that Cisco routers support. Recall that a *bridge* is an internetworking device designed to interconnect LANs to form the appearance of a single larger data link. The bridge technologies covered here include transparent bridging, integrated routing and bridging (IBR) for transparently bridged networks, source-route bridging (SRB), source-route transparent bridging (SRT), and source-route translational bridging (SR/TLB).

In the next chapter, you learn how to configure Cisco bridges to support various network situations.

Chapter Sixteen Test
Bridging Overview

Estimated Time: 15 minutes

Complete all the exercises to test your knowledge of the materials contained in this chapter. Answers are listed in Appendix A, "Chapter Test Answer Key."

Use the information contained in this chapter to answer the following questions. For each multiple choice question, circle the correct answer.

Question 16.1

A protocol is routable if it has which one of the following?

A. A MAC address

B. A network layer

C. A data link layer

D. A Layer 2 header

Question 16.2

Which one of the following is an example of a nonroutable protocol?

A. IP

B. IPX

C. DECnet

D. LAT

Question 16.3

Which one of the following is an example of a routable protocol?

A. AppleTalk

B. MOP

C. NetBIOS

D. SNA

Question 16.4

Source-route bridging (SRB) is a mechanism where SRB end nodes:

A. Send data and rely on the source-route bridge to determine the route to the destination.

B. Place ring number/bridge number combinations in all inter-ring frames.

C. Determine the entire route to the destination node before sending data.

D. Participate in the spanning-tree algorithm to eliminate network-wide loops.

Question 16.5

If a station on an Ethernet segment needed to communicate with a station on another Ethernet segment, which bridging scheme would most likely be chosen?

A. SR/TLB

B. SRT

C. SRB

D. Transparent bridging

Question 16.6

If a station on an Ethernet segment needed to communicate with a station on a Token Ring segment, which bridging scheme would most likely be chosen?

A. SR/TLB

B. SRB

C. Transparent bridging

D. None of the above

Question 16.7

Traditionally, Token Ring devices have used which bridging mechanism to communicate with other Token Ring devices?

A. SR/TLB

B. SRT

C. SRB

D. Transparent bridging

Question 16.8

In a Token Ring network consisting of some stations that do not support source routing, which bridging implementation would you use?

A. SR/TLB

B. SRT

C. SRB

D. Transparent bridging

Configuring Transparent Bridging and Integrated Routing and Bridging

This chapter describes two router configuration options available to handle non-routable traffic: transparent bridging and integrated routing and bridging (IRB). Upon completion of this chapter, you will be able to identify the need for transparent bridging and IRB, know the basic configuration steps, and be able to verify proper operation of these bridged configurations.

TRANSPARENT BRIDGING

Routers configured as *transparent bridges* forward packets based on the MAC address contained in the destination address field of the MAC-layer header. These types of bridges maintain a forwarding database that is built dynamically based on traffic seen on the network. Transparent bridges do not require that end devices support any additional bridging software. The intelligence is in the bridge unit.

Transparent Bridging Operation

Transparent bridging is predominantly used in Ethernet environments. A transparent bridge has the following major functions:

- *Learning*—A transparent bridge learns which stations can be reached on each of its ports (or interfaces) by monitoring the source MAC addresses of all incoming frames.

- *Forwarding*—A transparent bridge forwards frames from an inbound interface to the correct outbound interface to reach the destination.

- *Filtering*—A bridge will not forward a frame if the source and destination addresses are in the bridging table and are located on the same segment.

- *Avoiding loops*—The *spanning-tree protocol* solves the problems associated with bridge loops by allowing redundant paths (loops), but ensuring a loop-free topology through a bridge-to-bridge protocol.

Each of these is explored on the next pages.

Learning

When a transparent bridge is first powered up, it knows nothing of the network topology. It learns which stations can be reached on each of its ports (or interfaces) by monitoring the source MAC addresses of all incoming frames. For this reason, a transparent bridge is sometimes also called a *learning bridge*.

A transparent bridge maintains a database of learned MAC addresses and their associated interfaces in a table. These table entries are cached. The bridge updates the table regularly when a station sends a frame, and flushes entries of stations not heard from within a specified (implementation-dependent) time period.

In Figure 17–1, for example, the bridge has learned about four devices based on their initial startup communication. The bridge associates each of these devices with the interface closest to the device.

During the startup phase, when station .1111 sends to .2222, the bridge does not yet know where .2222 is located. So, in order to provide connectivity, it sends or floods the frame out to all connected interfaces except the interface on which the packet was received. Then, when it sees .2222 reply, the bridge adds .2222 to its table. Because it already knew the port location of .1111, the bridge has no need to flood again.

Forwarding

If the bridging table contains an association between the destination address and any of the bridge's interfaces (aside from the one on which the frame was received), a

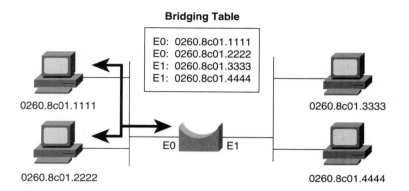

Bridging Table

EO: 0260.8c01.1111
EO: 0260.8c01.2222
E1: 0260.8c01.3333
E1: 0260.8c01.4444

0260.8c01.1111

0260.8c01.2222

EO   E1

0260.8c01.3333

0260.8c01.4444

Figure 17–1
The source MAC address is associated with the inter-face.

transparent bridge forwards frames from an inbound interface to the correct out-bound interface to reach the destination.

A transparent bridge forwards out all interfaces (except the one from which the frame was received), all broadcast and multicast frames, and frames from unknown sta-tions. (A station is unknown if it is not in the bridging table.) This action is also known as flooding.

How does a bridge learn addresses and forward traffic? If the source and destination address are located on different bridged segments, and if neither address is known to the bridge, the bridge does the following:

1. Notes the source address and updates its table.

2. Forwards the frame out to all interfaces (except the interface on which the frame was received).

3. If a reply comes back, the bridge examines the source address (which was the original target destination) and adds the entry to its table.

4. The bridge forwards subsequent communication between the devices.

Once again, refer to Figure 17–1. If a packet destined for .4444 was sent from .1111, the bridge would forward it based on its forwarding table.

Filtering

A bridge will not forward a frame if the source and destination addresses are in the bridging table and are located on the same segment. This behavior is known as *filtering*.

A bridge learns addresses and filters traffic as follows (assume that the source and destination stations are located on the same segment, and only the destination address is unknown), as in the following:

1. The source sends a frame to the destination.

2. The bridge sees the frame and floods the frame out to all interfaces (except the interface on which the frame was received).

3. When the reply comes back, the bridge reads the source address and updates its table.

4. The bridge discards, or filters, subsequent frames between the devices.

The effect of this filtering is that it conserves bandwidth. In Figure 17–1, for example, packets from .1111 that are destined to .2222 will not be forwarded.

Avoiding Bridging Loops with the Spanning-Tree Protocol

A *bridging loop* occurs when there is more than one path between any two bridged LANs in the network. A topology with loops can be useful as well as potentially harmful. Without loops, the topology has no redundancy. Without redundancy, if a bridge or LAN segment fails, connectivity is lost.

Without a bridge-to-bridge protocol, the transparent bridging algorithm fails when there are multiple paths of bridges and LANs between any two stations in the network. Recall that a bridge must flood all broadcast frames, by default. In a network containing a bridging loop, as shown in Figure 17–2, a single broadcast frame can cause a *broadcast storm*—an undesirable network event in which many broadcasts are sent simultaneously across all network segments, consuming all available network bandwidth and resources and ultimately leading to a disruption in network service to users.

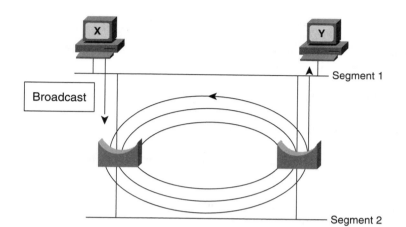

Figure 17–2
*Bridging loops
can consume
all available
network
resources.*

Loops occur in routed networks but are not as harmful. In routing, a packet is addressed to a specific router (and the MAC layer) and the router only forwards a packet out a single interface. As a result, routers do not procreate packets like bridges do. There also is generally a Time To Live (TTL) field in the routed packet so the router will eventually discard the looping packet. If such a field exists in the bridged packet, bridges do not see it or decrement it so a packet can loop indefinitely.

Figure 17–2 shows how a broadcast frame can disrupt network service when the network has a loop:

1. Station X sends a broadcast frame looking for station Y.

2. Each bridge (by default) must forward the broadcast frame onto all connected segments. Now there are two broadcast frames on segment 2.

3. Both bridges see the broadcast frames again, and again forward the frames.

4. A broadcast storm ensues.

The *spanning-tree protocol* solves the problems associated with bridge loops by allowing redundant paths (loops), but ensuring a loop-free topology through a bridge-to-bridge protocol. The spanning-tree protocol creates this loop-free topology by blocking one path where duplicate paths exist between network segments and automatically activating backup paths if a link segment or bridge fails.

The following two spanning-tree protocol versions exist for transparent bridging:

- DEC—Digital Equipment Corporation developed the first spanning tree protocol that was the basis for the IEEE 802.1D specification.

- IEEE 802.1D—The IEEE (Institute of Electrical and Electronic Engineers) approved spanning tree protocol to resolve bridging loops through bridge-to-bridge communications and path resolution.

Note that the DEC and IEEE 802.1D spanning tree versions differ enough that they cannot both run on the same network.

Cisco supports both protocol types. Although Digital's implementation served as the foundation for the IEEE implementation, the two are not compatible.

The basic operation of the spanning-tree algorithm is as follows:

1. The protocol elects a root bridge based on a unique bridge identifier. The bridge with the lowest identifier becomes the root. The first two bytes of the bridge identifier contain a user-configurable priority field, and the last six bytes contain one of the bridge's MAC addresses. The network administrator can configure the priority field to determine which bridge becomes the root (preferable) or allow the protocol to automatically determine it. If you configure a bridge to be root, select a bridge that is in the middle of the traffic flow, as defined by a protocol/network analyzer.

2. Each bridge selects the lowest-cost path to the root bridge based on a metric assigned to each link along the path to the root bridge.

3. Interfaces with alternate paths will block traffic to prevent loops. In Figure 17–3, bridge A's E1 interface is blocked to prevent looping.

In Figure 17–3, two bridges are in parallel, causing a loop. The spanning-tree algorithm will disable one of the bridge's interfaces to prevent the logical loop from affecting traffic. If something happened to bridge B, bridge A would act as a backup and would take over support of the network segment.

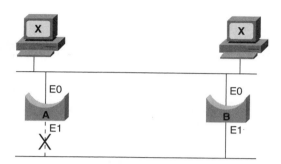

Figure 17–3
*The span-
ning-tree algo-
rithm disables
interfaces.*

Transparent Bridging Configuration Tasks

To configure transparent bridging, perform the following tasks in global configuration mode:

- Select a spanning-tree protocol in global configuration mode.

- Assign a priority to the bridge (optional) in global configuration mode.

- Assign the interface to a spanning-tree group in interface configuration mode.

- Assign a cost to the outgoing interface (optional) in interface configuration mode.

In this next section, you learn the available bridge configuration commands for each of the steps mentioned.

Step 1: Select a Spanning-Tree Protocol

Using the **bridge protocol** command, select either the DEC or IEEE spanning-tree implementation. Note that all routers must use the same implementation. The two implementations are not compatible, so the protocol must be set the same for all bridges that are to be part of the same spanning tree.

The **bridge protocol** command is run in global configuration mode and defines a specific spanning-tree algorithm for a bridge group:

```
router(config)#bridge bridge-group protocol {ieee | dec}
```

bridge protocol Command	Description
bridge-group	Identifies a particular set of bridged interfaces, a decimal number from 1 to 63. Sometimes referred to as a bridge number.
protocol	Either DEC or IEEE. Only DEC and IEEE spanning-tree protocols are used for transparent bridging.

Step 2: Assign a Priority to the Bridge (Optional)

To control which bridge becomes the root bridge, use the **bridge priority** command to set the priority on one bridge to be lower than all of the others. If you want to control which bridge takes over in case the root bridge fails, configure another bridge with the second-lowest priority field. Leave all other bridge priorities at their default value of 128 (for DEC), or if using IEEE, the value is 32768.

The **bridge-group** command assigns an interface to a particular bridge group:

```
router(config-if)#bridge-group bridge-group number
```

where *bridge-group number* is a decimal number from 1 to 63.

Some things to note about bridge groups are as follows:

- Interfaces not participating in a bridge group will not forward bridged traffic.

- There is no communication between bridge groups.

- An interface can be part of only one bridge group.

Step 3: Assign the Interface to a Spanning-Tree Group

Determine which interfaces you want to belong to the same group, and use the **bridge-group** command to assign those interfaces to that group. These interfaces will all be a part of the same spanning tree. Interfaces not participating in a bridge group will not forward bridged traffic.

The **bridge priority** command assigns a specific priority to the bridge, assisting in the spanning-tree root definition. The lower the priority, the more likely the bridge will be selected as the root:

```
router(config)#bridge bridge-group number priority number
```

bridge priority Command	Description
bridge-group number	A number from 1 to 63.
number	Assigns the priority level, value is 0 to 255 (DEC), or 0 to 64000 (IEEE). The default value for DEC (Digital) is 128, and 32768 for IEEE.

Step 4: Assign a Cost to the Outgoing Interface (Optional)

To control the path cost assigned to an interface, use the **bridge-group path-cost** command. Otherwise, the default values are used in calculating the best-cost path to reach the root bridge. The default is 1000Mbps divided by the data rate of the attached LAN. As a result, links supporting higher data rates have lower (preferred) costs.

The **bridge-group path-cost** command is used to assign a path cost to a particular interface. The cost is used in the spanning-tree algorithm to determine the best path to another area of the network. The default is 1000Mbps divided by the data rate of the attached LAN. Once the costs of all possible paths is determined, the spanning tree bridges consider the lowest-cost paths as the preferred path. Higher-cost paths are considered backup paths and are used should the preferred path become unavailable.

```
router(config-if)#bridge-group bridge-group path-cost cost
```

bridge-group path-cost Command	Description
bridge-group	A number from 1 to 63.
cost	A number from 0 to 65535. Higher values indicate higher costs. This same range applies regardless of which spanning-tree protocol is configured.

Transparent Bridging Example

Figure 17–4 depicts a transparent bridging example. In this example, Cisco A becomes the root bridge because it has a lower priority.

Figure 17–4
*Transparent
bridging
example.*

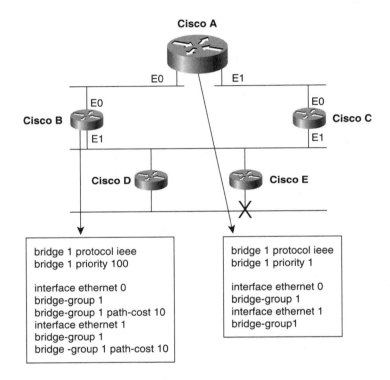

The default path cost for Ethernet is 100. Because Cisco B has a lower path cost than the default configured on Ethernet 0 and on Ethernet 1, the blocked interface will occur on the right side of the network, eliminating the loop.

On Cisco B, the priority has been changed to 100 from the default of 128. The path costs for both Ethernet interfaces have been changed to 10 from the default of 100. To the devices connected to the network on which Cisco D and Cisco E reside, the path through Cisco D and Cisco B to reach the root Cisco A is clearly lower and preferred. Therefore, Cisco E will block frames originating on segment 1 and Cisco D will forward them.

Verifying Transparent Bridging

The **show bridge** command, used in Figure 17–5, displays the following information.

```
Router#show bridge

Total ot 300 station blocks, 295 free
BG      Hash      Address           Action    Int    Age    RX count    TX count
1       00/0      FFFF.FFFF.FFFF    discard   -      P      0           0
1       09/0      0000. 0C00. 0009  forward   E 0    o      2           0
1       49/0      0000. 0C00. 4009  forward   E 0    0      1           0
1       CA/0      AA00.0400. 06CC   forward   E 0    0      25          0

Router#
```

Figure 17–5
*Use the **show bridge** command to verify bridge operation.*

Element	Description
Total of 300 station blocks	Total number of forwarding database elements in the system. The memory to hold bridge entries is allocated in blocks of memory sufficient to hold 300 individual entries. When the number of free entries falls to fewer than 25, another block of memory sufficient to hold another 300 entries is allocated. Therefore, the size of the bridge-forwarding database is limited to the amount of free memory in the router.
295 free	Number in the free list of forwarding database elements in the system. The total number of forwarding elements is expanded dynamically, as needed.
BG	Bridging group to which the address belongs.
Hash	Hash key/relative position in the keyed list.
Address	Canonical (Ethernet ordered) MAC address.
Action	Action to be taken when that address is looked up. Choices are to discard or forward the datagram.
Interface	Interface, if any, on which that address was seen.

Element	Description
Age	Number of minutes since a frame was received from or sent to that address. The letter P indicates a permanent entry. The letter S indicates the system as recorded by the router.
RX/TX count	Number of frames received from/transmitted on that address.

Verifying Spanning Tree Operation

Figure 17–6 shows the output of the **show span** command.

Figure 17–6
*Use the show
span com-
mand to verify
spanning tree
operation.*

```
Router# show span
Bridge Group 1 is executing the IEEE compatible spanning tree protocol
   IEEE bridge domains are not used for this bridge group
   Bridge Identifier has priority 32768, address 0000.0c00.ab40
   Configured hello time 2, max age 20, forward delay 15
   We are the root of the spanning tree
   Acquisition of new addresses is enabled
   Forwarding of multicast source addresses is disabled
   LAT service filtering is disabled
   Topology change flag not set, detected flag not set
   Times: hold 1, topology change 30, notification 30
    hello 2, max age 20, forward delay 15
   Timers: hello 2, topology change 0, notification 0
   Port 9 (Ethernet2) bridge group 1 forwarding, Path cost 100, priority 0
   Designated root has priority 32768, address 0000.0c00.ab40
   Designated bridge has priority 32768, address 0000.0c00.ab40
   Designated port is 1, path cost 0
   Timers; message age 0, forward delay 0, hold 0
```

The first line of output indicates which type of spanning-tree protocol (IEEE or DEC) the bridge group is executing. The next three lines show the current operating parameters of the spanning tree.

The remaining lines display related information that is useful when examining the spanning-tree parameters, as follows:

Element	Description
Port 9	Port number associated with the interface.
(Ethernet2)	Interfaces on which spanning tree has been configured.
bridge group 1	Bridge group to which the interface has been assigned.
forwarding	State of the interface. Other possible values include down, listening, learning, and blocking.
Path cost 100	Path cost associated with this interface.
priority 0	Port priority.

INTEGRATED ROUTING AND BRIDGING

There are times when you may want to bridge local traffic within several segments but also want hosts on the bridged segments to reach the hosts or routers on routed networks. If you are migrating bridged topologies into routed topologies, for example, you may want to start by connecting some of the bridged segments to the routed networks. Prior to Cisco IOS software Release 11.2, it was impossible to connect bridged segments to routed networks with a single router for a given protocol because the bridging and routing functions within the router were completely disjointed. IRB allows the routing and bridging of packets, for example, but not between the same protocol on the same interface.

The IRB feature enables you to route a given protocol between routed interfaces and bridge groups or between bridge groups within a single router. Specifically, local or unroutable traffic will be bridged among the bridged interfaces in the same bridge group, whereas routable traffic will be routed to other routed interfaces or bridge groups.

In Figure 17–7, for example, DEC traffic can be bridged within the bridge group, local IPX traffic can be bridged within the bridge group, and remote IPX traffic can be routed.

IRB is the next-generation solution beyond concurrent routing and bridging. Concurrent routing and bridging enables you to bridge or route given protocols within the same box, but you can only bridge the protocol among the bridged interfaces and route the protocol among the routed interfaces. Concurrent routing and bridging cannot switch a packet of the same protocol between a bridged interface and a routed interface.

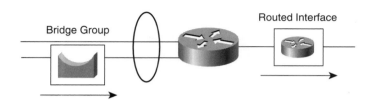

Figure 17–7
IRB permits bridging of nonroutable protocols and simultaneous routing of routable protocols.

In Cisco IOS Release 11.2 software, IRB supports the routing of IP, IPX, and Apple-Talk between routed interfaces and bridged interfaces in the same router, in both fast-switching and process-switching paths.

Some examples of when to use IRB follow:

- When you want to interconnect a bridged network with a routed network, the IRB feature enables the router to act as a true bridge/router (sometimes referred to as a *brouter*). For example, when you are migrating a bridged network to a routed network, or when the remote site does not have routing capabilities, you can use the router to interconnect the bridged and routed networks.

- When you want to conserve IP, IPX, and AppleTalk addresses by connecting network segments with bridges and assigning each bridge group one network address.

- When you want to break one big segment into several small segments to increase end stations' performance.

- When you want to add VLANs to your network topology.

Evaluate the following limitations before implementing IRB:

- It is not supported on cBus (CiscoBus) platforms (AGS+ and 7000 series).

- It is not supported on X.25 and ISDN bridged interfaces.

- It is supported for transparent bridging but not for source-route bridging.

- It cannot operate with concurrent routing and bridging at the same time on the same router.

IRB Operation

IRB provides the capability to route between a bridge group and a routed interface using a concept called *Bridge-Group Virtual Interface* (BVI). Because bridging is in the data link layer and routing is in the network layer, they have different protocol configuration models. With IP, for example, bridge group interfaces belong to the same network and have a collective IP network address, whereas each routed interface represents a distinct network and has its own IP network address. The concept of a BVI was created to enable these interfaces to exchange packets for a given protocol.

The BVI is a virtual interface within the router that acts like a normal routed interface that does not support bridging but represents the corresponding bridge group to routed interfaces within the router. The interface number of the BVI is the number of the bridge group that this virtual interface represents. That number is the link between this BVI and the bridge group.

When you configure the BVI and enable routing on it, packets entering on a routed interface that are destined for a host on a segment in a bridge group go through the following processes:

1. The packet is routed to the BVI.

2. From the BVI, the packet is forwarded to the bridging engine.

3. From the bridging engine, the packet exits through a bridged interface.

Similarly, packets that come in on a bridged interface but are destined for a host on a routed network first go to the BVI and the BVI forwards them to the routing engine before sending them out the routed interface.

BVI Addressing

To be able to receive routable packets from a bridged interface that are destined for a routed interface, the BVI must have the appropriate addresses and attributes, which are assigned to the BVI in the following ways:

- *MAC address*—The BVI uses the MAC address from one of the bridged interfaces in the corresponding bridge group.

- *Network-layer address and attributes*—The BVI has the same configuration requirements as any other routed interface, as shown in Figure 17–8. For each protocol that you want routed between routed interfaces and bridge groups, you must do the following:

  - Enable routing.

  - Configure network-layer addresses.

  - Assign additional attributes as necessary, such as access control lists and secondary addresses.

Figure 17–8
BVI addressing includes a MAC address and a network-layer address.

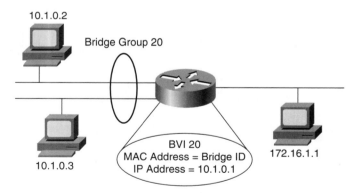

Making Bridging or Routing Decisions

In this section, you examine some network designs to determine whether the router will use bridging technology or routing technology to forward packets. Figure 17–9 shows an example of how IRB switches packets from a bridged to a routed interface.

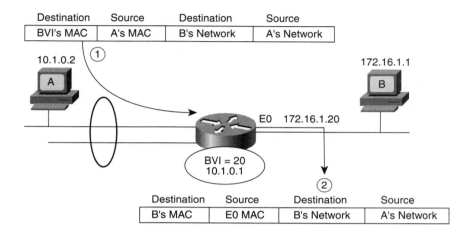

Figure 17–9
*Destination
MAC is BVI's
address.*

Assume that host A wants to send a packet to host B. Because host B is on a different subnet, host A determines that it needs to send the packet to the router so the router can route it. By configuring a default gateway of 10.1.0.1 (the BVI) on hosts to the left of the router, the hosts know how to reach the BVI. Now all they need to determine is the BVI's MAC address, which can be learned through the Address Resolution Protocol (ARP).

Host A then addresses the packet as follows and sends the packet:

Destination	Source	Destination	Source
10.1.0.1's MAC address	10.1.0.2's MAC Address	172.16.1.1	10.1.0.2

When the bridged interface receives the packet, it must determine whether to bridge or route the packet. If the destination MAC address is one of the router's interfaces and if the network-layer protocol is configured for routing, the packet will be routed. The bridging code will make the packet look like it is coming from the BVI (instead of the bridge group) and will forward it to the routing engine. As a result, the packet then will be routed through interface 172.16.1.20 to host B. From interface 172.16.1.20's perspective, it has received a packet from routed interface 10.1.0.1.

The IRB switches packets from a routed to a bridged interface similar to the process described. To switch packets within the same bridge group, the bridged interface determines that the destination is not to any router interface (indicating the host addressed the packet to a device on a local network segment), and so the packet is bridged to the appropriate bridge group if the MAC address is known, or it is flooded across all bridge group interfaces if the address is unknown.

IRB Configuration Tasks

Configure bridge groups and routed interfaces as you normally would. Following are the steps to configure IRB and the BVI:

1. Enable IRB. This provides for the *capability* to route routable traffic from the bridged interfaces. You must complete the rest of the steps for proper routing operations to occur.

    ```
    router(config)#bridge irb
    ```

2. Configure the BVI by assigning the corresponding bridge group's number to the BVI. Each bridge group can have only one corresponding BVI.

    ```
    router(config-if)#interface bvi bridge-group
    ```

3. Enable the BVI to accept and route routable packets received from its corresponding bridge group using the following command:

    ```
    router(config)#bridge bridge-group route protocol
    ```

    You must configure this command for each protocol that you want the BVI to route from its corresponding bridge group to other routed interfaces.

4. Enable routing on the BVI for those protocols that you want to route to and from the bridge group. For example, to enable IP routing on the BVI, use the following commands:

    ```
    router(config)#interface bvi 1
    ```

    ```
    router(config-if)#ip address ip-address mask
    ```

5. (Optional) Configure additional routing attributes to the BVI.

Configuration Example: IRB and the BVI

In Figure 17–10, IRB is enabled and the BVI configured as follows.

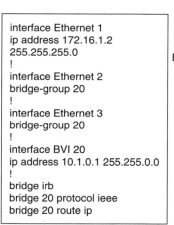

```
interface Ethernet 1
ip address 172.16.1.2
255.255.255.0
!
interface Ethernet 2
bridge-group 20
!
interface Ethernet 3
bridge-group 20
!
interface BVI 20
ip address 10.1.0.1 255.255.0.0
!
bridge irb
bridge 20 protocol ieee
bridge 20 route ip
```

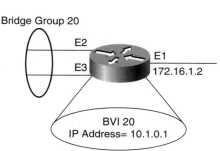

Figure 17–10
IRB configuration example.

Command	Description
interface Ethernet 1	Configures protocol addresses on routed interfaces
ip address 172.16.1.2 255.255.255.0	
interface Ethernet 2	Assigns Ethernet interfaces 2 and 3 to bridge group 20
bridge-group 20	
!	
interface Ethernet 3	
bridge-group 20	
interface BVI 20	Configures the BVI by assigning the corresponding bridge group number to the BVI, and enables routing on the BVI
ip address 10.1.0.1 255.255.0.0	
bridge irb	Enables the IRB
bridge 20 protocol ieee	Creates bridge group 20
bridge 20 route ip	Enables the BVI to accept and route IP packets from bridge group 20

Enabling Routing on a Bridge Group

IRB enables you to both bridge and route specific protocols, but you can still only bridge or only route other protocols, as shown in Figure 17–11.

Figure 17–11
*Enabling rout-
ing on a
bridge group.*

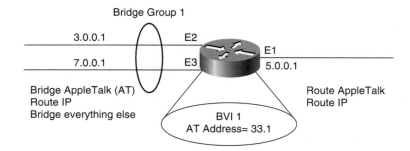

After you have IRB and the BVI configured for the desired protocols, perform the following additional steps to route other protocols over the bridge group interfaces:

1. Ensure that IRB and BVI are configured for desired protocols.

2. Disable bridging over a defined bridge group for those protocols that you want to route only over the bridge group interfaces.

   ```
   router(config)#no bridge bridge-group bridge protocol
   ```

   You must use the **no** form of the command because the default is to bridge every protocol. Note that you cannot disable bridging for nonroutable protocols, such as local-area transport (LAT).

3. Enable the routing of the protocols that you want to route over the defined bridge group.

   ```
   router(config)#bridge bridge-group route protocol
   ```

Figure 17–12 shows a configuration example for routing on the bridge group interfaces. You can see the configuration used to set up the router shown in Figure 17–11. Figure 17–12 shows the configuration for IRB routing and bridging of AppleTalk and the routing only of IP.

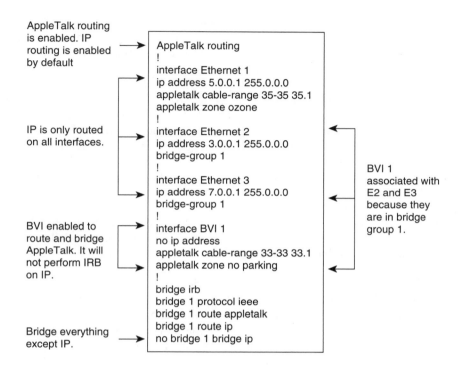

Figure 17–12
Routing and bridging example.

AppleTalk routing is enabled. IP routing is enabled by default →

IP is only routed on all interfaces. →

BVI enabled to route and bridge AppleTalk. It will not perform IRB on IP. →

Bridge everything except IP. →

```
AppleTalk routing
!
interface Ethernet 1
ip address 5.0.0.1 255.0.0.0
appletalk cable-range 35-35 35.1
appletalk zone ozone
!
interface Ethernet 2
ip address 3.0.0.1 255.0.0.0
bridge-group 1
!
interface Ethernet 3
ip address 7.0.0.1 255.0.0.0
bridge-group 1
!
interface BVI 1
no ip address
appletalk cable-range 33-33 33.1
appletalk zone no parking
!
bridge irb
bridge 1 protocol ieee
bridge 1 route appletalk
bridge 1 route ip
no bridge 1 bridge ip
```

BVI 1 associated with E2 and E3 because they are in bridge group 1.

IRB Configuration Considerations

Consider the following before configuring IRB:

- The default route/bridge behavior in a bridge group when IRB is enabled is to bridge all packets. Make sure you explicitly configure routing on the BVI for protocols that you want routed.

- Packets of nonroutable protocols, such as LAT, will always be bridged. You cannot disable bridging for the nonroutable traffic, but you can use access lists to filter traffic.

- When using IRB to bridge and route a given protocol, no protocol attributes should be configured on the bridged interfaces. Bridging attributes cannot be configured on the BVI.

- Because bridges link several segments into one big and flat network and you want to bridge the packet coming from a routed interface among bridged interfaces, the whole bridge group should be represented by one network-layer segment—in the router, an interface.

- The MTU of the BVI is the same as the largest MTU among those bridged interfaces in this bridge group. This MTU is adjusted dynamically when bridge group membership changes. The drawback of increasing the MTU is that fragmentation cannot be done on routed packets, which results in the dropping of big packets in the bridging path when the outputting interface has a smaller MTU than the BVI's MTU. To alleviate this problem, the BVI's MTU is user-configurable using the **mtu** command.

- The BVI has default data-link and network-layer encapsulations, which are the same as on the Ethernet except that you can configure the BVI with some encapsulations that are not supported on a normal Ethernet interface.

In some cases, the default encapsulations provide appropriate results; in other cases they do not. For example, with default encapsulation, ARPA packets from the BVI are translated to SNAP when bridging IP to a Token Ring or FDDI bridged interface. But for IPX, Novell-ether encapsulation from the BVI is translated to raw-token or raw-FDDI when bridging IPX to a Token Ring or FDDI bridged interface. Because this behavior is usually not what you want, you must configure IPX SNAP or SAP encapsulation on the BVI.

Verifying IRB Operation

You can use the **show interface** *interface-name* command to view information about the BVI or the other interfaces on the router, including the BVI MAC address and the processing statistics. Figure 17–13 depicts the output of the **show interface** command. The output indicates that BVI1 is up and the line protocol is up. You can also see the frame type used is ARPA.

By running the same command and defining the local network interface, as shown in Figure 17–14, you can view the local interface statistics and see the following type of information:

- Protocols that this bridged interface can route to the other routed interface (if this packet is routable), such as AppleTalk and IP.

```
router# show interface bvi1
BVI1 is up, line protocol is up
 Hardware is BVI, address is 0000.0c14.5733 (bia 0000.0000.0000)
 MTU 1500 bytes, BW 10000 Kbit, DLY 5000 usec, rely 255/255, load 1/255
 Encapsulation ARPA, loopback not set, keepalive set (10sec)
 ARP type: ARPA, ARP Timeout 04:00:00
 Last input 00:00:04, output 00:00:01, output hang never
 Last clearing of "show interface" counters never
 Output queue 0/40, 0 drops; input queue 0/75m, 0 drops
 5 minute input rate 0 bits/sec, 1 packets/sec
 5 minute output rate 0 bits/sec, 1 packets/sec
    345 packets input, 55088 bytes, 0 no buffer
    Received 151 broadcasts, 0 runts, 0 giants
    0 input errors, 0 CRC, 0 frame, 0 overrun, 0 ignored, 0 abort
    0 input packets with dribble condition detected
    578 packets output, 48223 bytes, 0 underruns
    1 output errors, 0 collisions, 1 interface resets
    0 babbles, 0 late collision, 0 deferred
    1 lost carrier, 0 no carrier
    0 output buffer failures, 0 output buffers swapped out
```

Figure 17–13
Verifying IRB operation.

- Protocols that this bridged interface bridges, such as Vines, IPX and XNS.

- Entries in the software MAC-address filter, such as ffff.ffff.ffff (broadcast).

```
router # show interfaces ethernet 2 irb

Ethernet2

Routed protocols on Ethernet2:
 appletalk ip

Bridged protocols on Ethernet2:
 appletalk clns decnet vines
 apollo ipx xns

Software MAC address filter on Ethernet2
 Hash   Len   Address          Matches   Act   Type
 0x00:  0     ffff.ffff.ffff   4886      RCV   Physical broadcast
 0x1F:  0     0060.3e2b.a221   7521      RCV   Interface MAC address
 0x1F:  1     0060.3e2b.a221   0         RCV   Bridge-group Virtual
Interface
 0x2a:  0     0900.2b01.0001   0         RCV   DEC spanning tree
 0xA5:  0     0900.0700.00a2   0         RCV   Appletalk zone
 0xC2:  0     0180.c200.0000   0         RCV   IEEE spanning tree
 0xF8:  0     0900.07ff.ffff   2110      RCV   Appletalk broadcast
```

Figure 17–14
*The **show interfaces irb** output.*

SUMMARY

In this chapter, you learned the differences between transparent bridging and IRB, which include the fact that a transparent bridge simply learns and forwards packets based on its MAC address, whereas IRB enables you to bridge local traffic within segments while also enabling these hosts to reach hosts or routers on routed networks. You learned how to configure and verify transparent and IRB configuration.

In the next chapter, you examine source route bridging.

Chapter Seventeen Test
Configuring Transparent Bridging and
Integrated Routing and Bridging

Estimated Time: 15 minutes

Complete all the exercises to test your knowledge of the materials contained in this chapter. Answers are listed in Appendix A, "Chapter Test Answer Key." Use the information contained in this chapter to answer the following questions.

Refer to Figure 17–15 to complete this exercise. You will use IRB to migrate a bridged IPX network to a routed network while maintaining IP routing throughout the network. The IPX network numbers are provided.

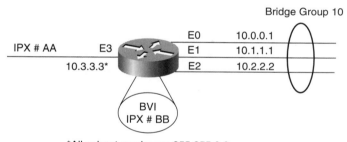

*All subnet masks are 255.255.0.0

Figure 17–15
*Configuring
IRB exercise.*

Question 17.1

Create a bridge group of 10 and assign interfaces E0, E1, and E2 to it. Configure the IEEE spanning-tree protocol to run over this bridge group. Write your configuration here:

_____

_____

_____

Question 17.2

Configure the BVI and assign it the IPX network number shown in Figure 17–15. You will not be assigning an IP address to the BVI because you are not performing IRB on IP over these bridge group interfaces. IP will be routed over these interfaces as it normally is, that is, without the help of the BVI. Be sure to specify the command to ensure that the BVI is not configured for IP routing. Write your configuration here:

_____

_____

Question 17.3

Enable IRB operation to route IPX over the bridge group interfaces. Because you want to route IP only over the bridge group interfaces, be sure to include the command to disable bridging over the bridge group interfaces. Write your configuration here:

_____

_____

_____

CHAPTER 18

Configuring Source-Route Bridging

In this chapter, you learn to configure source-route bridging (SRB) to bridge between LANs. Source-route transparent bridging (SRT), which combines the implementations of transparent bridging and SRB bridging, is also presented in this chapter. Source-route translational bridging (SR/TLB), a method of bridging between networks with dissimilar MAC sublayer protocols, is also taught in this chapter.

SOURCE-ROUTER BRIDGING (SRB) OVERVIEW

The source-route bridging (SRB) algorithm was developed by IBM and originally proposed to the 802.1 (MAC-layer bridging) committee as a standard bridging mechanism between LANs. The 802.1 committee, however, standardized on transparent bridging, compelling IBM to take the source routing proposal to the IEEE 802.5 committee. The IEEE 802.5 committee subsequently adopted SRB into the IEEE 802.5 Token Ring LAN specification. Source-route bridging (SRB) is a bridging method in which one end host locates another end host by discovering available source-to-destination paths. SRB determines the entire route to a destination, in real time, prior to the sending of data.

Explorer packets are special packets used to perform this discovery. There are three types of explorer frames:

- *Local-ring test frame*—Checks the local ring for the destination end station.

- *All-routes explorer*—Finds all routes to the destination host by checking all rings. The target destination will receive as many frames as there are routes from the source to the destination. This packet is also known as the *all-routes explore packet.*

- *Single-route explorer packet*—Allows the algorithm to find the best (spanning) route to the destination host after checking all rings. Only bridge ports that have been put in forwarding mode in the spanning tree forward the frame. These bridges add the bridge number and attached ring number to the packet as it is forwarded. The single-route explorer reduces the number of frames sent during the discovery process. This packet is also known as a spanning-tree explorer packet, limited-route explorer packet or spanning explorer.

In Figure 18–1, host X sends a local-ring explorer frame first. When no response is received, host X then sends an all-routes explorer frame.

Figure 18–1
Explorer pack-ets discover the route des-tination.

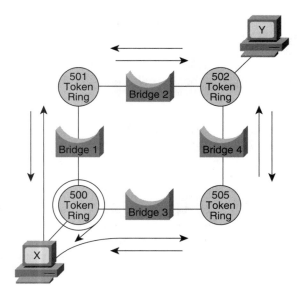

When a source end station wants to send a frame to an unknown destination, the following steps are performed:

1. For SNA, the source end station first sends a local test frame to determine whether the target destination is on the local Token Ring, as shown in Figure 18–1. If the test frame comes back without a positive indication that the target destination has seen it, the source end station resends the test frame as an all-routes explorer frame.

2. If the destination is not found on the local ring, depending on the protocol implementation, the source will send either an all-routes (if SNA) or a single-route (if NetBIOS) explorer broadcast frame. Each bridge adds route information as it forwards the frame to outbound ports.

3. The destination end station replies to each frame individually, reversing the direction of the frame and causing it to traverse back along the same path to the source end station. If using NetBIOS, the source end station sends a single-route broadcast frame to the destination device. The destination device responds with an all-routes broadcast.

Usually, the source end station selects the first route received and disregards the others. The assumption is that the first frame received contains the fastest path. Both stations use this route for the duration of their sessions.

Source-Route Bridging Operation

Figure 18–2 examines the source-route bridge operation once a destination device has been discovered.

Host X performs the following steps to locate host Y:

1. Host X transmits a local-ring explorer looking for host Y on the local ring. In this case, the local-ring test frame returns without finding host Y.

2. Because host Y is not on the local ring, host X transmits an all-routes explorer, which follows each path to the destination. Each bridge adds route information as it forwards the frame to all outbound ports. The path to the destination is a combination of Token Rings and source-route bridges. The target destination receives as many copies as there are routes. In this case, there are two routes from host X to Y:

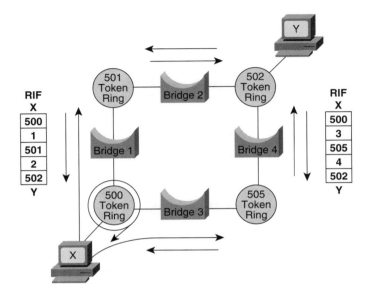

Figure 18–2
The source chooses a path to the destination based on the discovery replies.

- Ring 500 to bridge 1 to ring 501 to bridge 2 to ring 502

- Ring 500 to bridge 3 to ring 505 to bridge 4 to ring 502

3. Host Y returns the packet as an all-routes explorer.

4. Host X receives routing information fields (RIFs) identifying alternative routes to host Y.

5. Host X selects the path it will use. The source gets to choose the route.

The IEEE 802.5 does not mandate the criteria the source should use in choosing a route, but it makes several suggestions, including the first frame received. Other alternatives for choosing a route can be based on the response with the minimum number of hops, the response with the largest allowed frame size, or various combinations of these criteria.

Routing Information Indicator

Source-route bridges use information in the 802.5 MAC header to identify SRB traffic. The Routing Information Indicator (RII) is bit 0 of the first byte of the source address within an 802.5 MAC frame.

The RII is set by the source. Setting the RII bit equal to 1 indicates that the RIF contains routing information. If the RII bit is not set (equal to 0), it means that no routing information is present.

The RIF is part of the IEEE 802.5 MAC header and contains the route to a particular destination. RIF is included in frames destined for other LAN segments. RIF has the routing control (RC) field and the route descriptor (RD) fields.

The RII bit, by being set, cues source-route bridges to look further into the frame for routing and control information contained in the RIF.

The RIF contains the Routing Central (RC) field and the Route Descriptor (RD) fields, as shown in Figure 18–3.

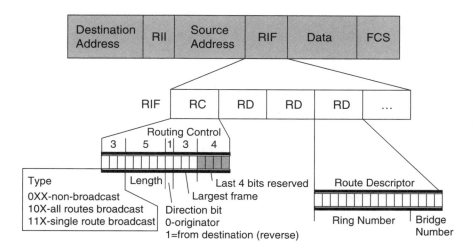

Figure 18–3
The RII bit indicates that routing information is contained in the frame.

The RC field consists of the following:

- *Type*—3 bits

    - 0XX = Specific route

    - 10X = All rings/all routes

    - 11X = Spanning route

- *Length of RIF, measured in bytes*—5 bits

- *Direction*—Which way to interpret RIF

- *Largest frame*—Code indicating largest frame accepted on route to the destination

The RD field consists of the following:

- *Ring number*—Unique ring number within the network

- *Bridge number*—Unique bridge number connecting two rings

Specifications for IBM Token Ring define a maximum of eight rings and seven bridges. Specifications for 802.5 Token Ring define a maximum of 14 rings and 13 bridges.

SOURCE-ROUTER BRIDGING CONFIGURATION

Use the **source-bridge** command to specify the ring and bridge number to which the interface is attached:

```
router(config-if)#source-bridge local-ring bridge-number target-ring
```

source-bridge Command	Description
local-ring	Number of this interface's ring. It must be a decimal number from 1 to 4095 that uniquely identifies a network segment or ring within the bridged Token Ring network.

source-bridge Command	Description
bridge-number	Number from 1 to 15 that uniquely identifies the bridge connecting the two rings.
target-ring	Number of the target ring. This target ring can also be a ring group.

To enable spanning-tree on specific interfaces (referred to as manual spanning tree) so that only specific interfaces participate in spanning tree—that is, send single-route explorer packets to each other—use the **source-bridge spanning** command.

```
router(config-if)#source-bridge spanning
```

The **source-bridge** command is used in simple SRB configurations. The local ring is the Token Ring connected to the interface to which the command is applied.

Cisco routers implement the automatic Spanning-Tree Protocol. The **source-bridge spanning** command is applied to any interface that will pass single-route explorers that are received on the interface. If spanning is disabled, the interface will drop single-route explorers. In either case, the interface propagates all-route explorers.

In the current release of Cisco IOS, an interface may only participate in a single spanning tree group. When a Token Ring interface is part of a transparent bridge group, such as in an SRT or SR/TLB configuration, the Token Ring interfaces must be statically configured to permit spanning explorers with the command **source-bridge spanning**.

Note that leaving off the group number in the **source-bridge spanning** command unconditionally permits spanning explorers to leave the interface.

The **source-bridge spanning** command configures the router to forward spanning explorers. The router always forwards all-routes explorer packets.

TIPS

The IBM implementation of spanning tree is not compatible with the IEEE 802.1D implementation, mainly because the IEEE specification was created for transparent bridges, not source-route bridges. These two types of bridges are totally incompatible. If you have a mixed environment of source-routing and transparent bridges, you cannot implement spanning tree across all bridges; however, you can use source-route transparent (SRT) bridges that contain both functions within one bridge device.

To enable spanning tree for automatic spanning tree, use the following commands:

```
router(config)#bridge bridge-group protocol ibm
```

bridge-group—Number from 1 to 9 that uniquely identifies all interfaces that participate in the automatic spanning-tree algorithm

```
router(config-if)#source-bridge spanning bridge-group [path-cost path-cost]
```

bridge-group—Matches the value put in the **bridge protocol ibm** command

SRB Manual Spanning-Tree Configuration Example

Figure 18–4 shows a dual-port bridge, in which the router connects two Token Ring LANs.

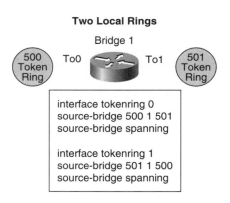

Figure 18–4
Manual spanning-tree configuration example.

Two Local Rings

Bridge 1

500 Token Ring   To0   To1   501 Token Ring

```
interface tokenring 0
source-bridge 500 1 501
source-bridge spanning

interface tokenring 1
source-bridge 501 1 500
source-bridge spanning
```

The **source-bridge 500 1 501** command enables SRB on Token Ring interface 0 using bridge number 1. This interface is part of Token Ring 500. The target ring is 501. It is also part of bridge 1 on the router.

The **source-bridging spanning** command enables the forwarding of spanning-tree explorers on all ring interfaces.

A spanning-tree explorer packet is an explorer packet sent to a defined group of end stations that have been configured as part of the spanning tree in the network. In contrast, an all-routes explorer packet is sent to every end station in the network on every path.

You can configure several separate dual-port bridges on the same router; however, only the routers connected to the dual-port bridge pairs can communicate with one another.   **Key Concept**

SRB Automatic Spanning-Tree Configuration Example

As shown in Figure 18–5, you can configure a single path for spanning explorers to traverse from a given node in the network to another.

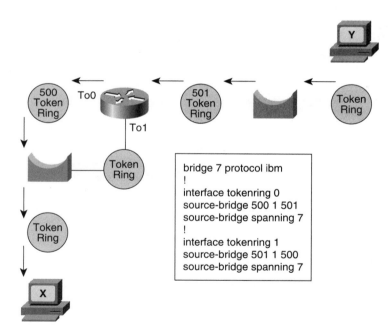

Figure 18–5
Automatic spanning-tree example.

```
bridge 7 protocol ibm
!
interface tokenring 0
source-bridge 500 1 501
source-bridge spanning 7
!
interface tokenring 1
source-bridge 501 1 500
source-bridge spanning 7
```

The **bridge 7 protocol ibm** command configures a bridge group that runs the automatic spanning-tree function.

In Figure 18–5, the **source-bridge spanning 7** command enables the automatic use of spanning-tree explorers for bridge group 7. The bridge group specified by the

source-bridge spanning command must be the same bridge group defined by the **bridge protocol ibm** command.

TIPS

SRB and transparent bridging use separate spanning trees.

Multiport Configuration

Cisco IOS software supports virtual rings, also known as *ring groups*. These ring groups are created using a multiport configuration, where the router is connected to multiple rings and the router itself acts as a virtual ring connecting the other token rings. This feature helps resolve the limitation that all IBM Token Ring chips can only process two ring numbers.

A ring group is a collection of Token Ring interfaces in one or more routers that share the same target ring number. As a result, each of the three rings can bridge traffic to the other two interfaces. To take advantage of this feature, each Token Ring interface on the router must be configured to belong to the same ring group.

The virtual ring number is used just like a true bridge number, as shown in Figure 18–6.

Figure 18–6
A multiport configuration creates a virtual ring.

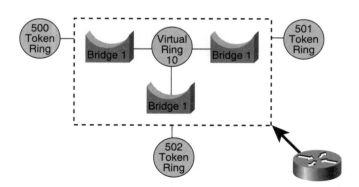

Use the **source-bridge ring-group** command to build a software-generated virtual ring inside the router. The *ring-group-number* is the number of the virtual ring, which replaces the target ring number. The valid range is 1 to 4095.

TIPS

A ring group must be assigned a ring number that is unique throughout the network because the other devices in the network see the ring group as a real ring.

In the second example shown in Figure 18–7, Token Ring interfaces 0, 1, and 2 are part of ring group 10.

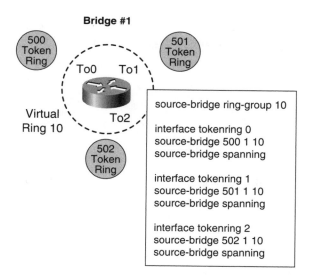

Figure 18–7
Multiport configuration example.

Token Rings 500, 501, and 502 are all source-route bridged to each other across ring group 10.

This configuration example adds a ring to the source route network. As a result, the traffic passes through an additional hop. Traffic that enters Token Ring 500 and exits

Token Ring 501 passes through three rings (500, 10, 501). These ring numbers will be added to the RIF.

This configuration can cause problems if the traffic must traverse any combination of more than eight virtual and real rings because the RIF can contain only seven bridges.

Proxy Explorer Configuration

The **source-bridge proxy-explorer** command enables an interface to convert explorer packets to specifically routed frames. The router sends these frames to the destination, if that destination is in the RIF cache.

Use proxy explorers to limit the amount of explorer traffic propagating through the source-bridge network, especially across low-bandwidth serial lines. The proxy explorer is most useful for multiple connections to a single node.

In Figure 18–8, host A sends an all-routes explorer frame for host Z. If bridge 1 has RIF information for host Z, bridge 1 changes the all-routes explorer frame to a specifically routed frame with the RIF and forwards the frame to host Z.

Figure 18–8
A proxy explorer configuration helps control explorer traffic.

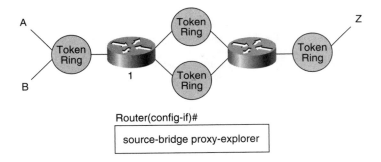

```
Router(config-if)#

source-bridge proxy-explorer
```

Proxy explorer is typically used on a WAN link to limit the amount of explorer traffic propagating through the source-bridge network.

Multiring Configuration

If you want the software to bridge routed protocols across a source-route bridged network, you must configure Cisco IOS software to collect and use RIF information. The router can use this information to bridge packets across a source-route bridged network.

The **multiring** command enables these routed frames to pass through the SRB bridge. This command enables collection and use of RIF information.

```
multiring {protocol-keyword [all-routes | spanning] | all | other}
```

multiring Command	Description
protocol-keyword	Specifies a routed protocol that will have RIF information inserted in its frame. Options include **apollo, appletalk, clns, decnet, ip, ipx, vines,** and **xns**
all-routes	Uses all-routes explorers
spanning	Uses spanning-tree explorers
all	Enables multiring for all frames
other	Enables multiring for any routed frame that is not among the supported protocols listed under keyword

In Figure 18–9, two routed domains are separated by a source-route bridged domain. In order for the routed frames to traverse the source-route bridged network, the routed frames must have RIFs inserted.

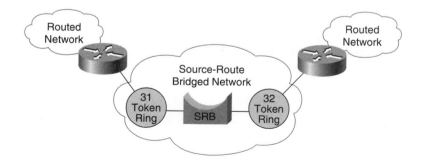

Figure 18–9
*The **multiring** command enables the collection and use of RIF information.*

Multiring Configuration Example

In Figure 18–10, the **multiring ip** command enables the collection of RIF information for IP RIFs. RIF information is not collected for IPX frames. As a result, the IP frames are bridged across the source-route bridged network. IPX frames are not bridged.

Figure 18–10
Multiring
configuration.

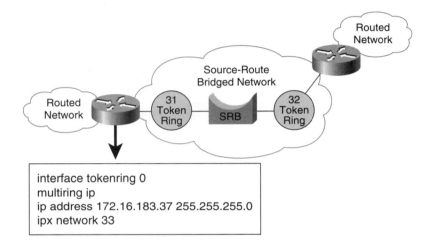

```
interface tokenring 0
multiring ip
ip address 172.16.183.37 255.255.255.0
ipx network 33
```

SOURCE-ROUTE TRANSPARENT BRIDGING (SRT) OVERVIEW

Source-route transparent bridging (SRT) combines implementations of the transparent bridging and SRB algorithms. SRT bridges employ both technologies in one device and do not translate between bridging protocols. They can forward traffic from both transparent and source-route end nodes, and they can form a common spanning tree with transparent bridges that allows end stations of each type to communicate with end stations of the same type in a network of arbitrary topology.

Key Concept   The fundamental difference between source-route bridging and transparent bridging technologies is that source-route bridging end nodes determine the entire route to the destination node before sending data.

IBM introduced SRT in 1990 to address some weaknesses of translational bridging. SRT is specified in the IEEE 802.1D.

Token Ring-to-Ethernet communication using mixed bridging mechanisms (source routing to transparent or transparent to source routing) is not provided by SRT.

SRT Operation

SRT bridges use the RII bit to distinguish between frames employing SRB and transparent bridging, as shown in Figure 18–11.

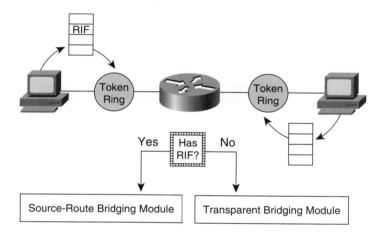

Figure 18–11
*SRT is a
hybrid bridge.*

If the RII bit is 1, indicating a RIF is present in the frame, the bridge performs source routing.

If the RII bit is 0, a RIF is not present in the frame, and the bridge performs transparent bridging.

SRT bridges do not add or remove RIFs to frames that they are bridging. Therefore, these bridges do not integrate source-route bridging with transparent bridging. In other words, a host connected to a source-route bridge that expects RIFs does not communicate with a device across a bridge that does not understand RIFs.

SRT Configuration Example

To configure SRT, enable transparent and SRB bridging on interfaces used for SRT bridging. Traffic without RIF information is transparently bridged, and traffic with RIF information is source-route bridged.

In Figure 18–12, the **bridge 4 protocol ieee** command configures the IEEE spanning-tree protocol to be used by members of bridge group 4.

Figure 18–12
*SRT configu-
ration exam-
ple.*

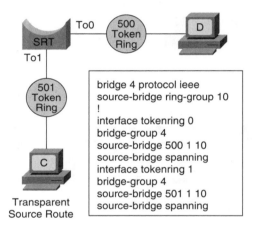

Token Ring interfaces 0 and 1 are configured as members of bridge group 4. These Token Ring interfaces use bridge number 1 to connect Token Rings 500 and 501.

Spanning explorers are enabled for use in these source-route interfaces.

SOURCE-ROUTE TRANSLATIONAL BRIDGING (SR/TLB) OVERVIEW

Source-route translational bridging (SR/TLB) is a Cisco IOS feature that allows you to combine SRB and transparent bridging networks without the need to convert all your existing source-route bridges to SRT nodes, as shown in Figure 18–13.

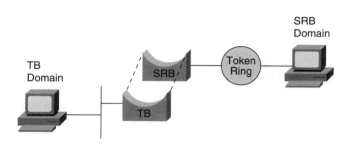

Figure 18–13
SR/TLB translates between transparent and SRB bridging.

Bridging between Ethernet and Token Ring provides a number of challenges, as follows:

- No RIFs can be passed into the Ethernet environment.

  The RIF does not exist in Ethernet. When bridging from the SRB domain to the transparent bridging domain, SRB information is removed. RIFs are usually cached for use by subsequent return traffic.

- The MTU sizes are different. Ethernet's MTU is approximately 1500 bytes.

  Token Ring frames can be much larger (about 4KB to 18KB). Translational bridges that send frames from the transparent bridging domain to the SRB domain usually set the MTU size field to 1500 bytes to limit the size of Token Ring frames entering the transparent bridging domain.

- The internal representation of MAC addresses differs between Ethernet and Token Ring.

  Ethernet transmits the least-significant bit first (called the *low endian* method) and Token Ring transmits the most-significant bit first (called the *big endian* method). Translational bridges reorder source and destination address bits when translating between Ethernet and Token Ring frame formats.

SR/TLB can help address the problem posed in Figure 18–14. Traffic from host B on a transparently bridged Ethernet segment cannot be bridged to host C on an SRT network. SR/TLB creates a software connection between a specified ring group and a transparent bridge group.

Figure 18-14
*TB sees SRT
as "virtual"
bridge group;
SRT sees TB
as pseudo
(false) ring.*

To the source-route station this software bridge looks like a standard source-route bridge. A ring number and bridge number are associated with a ring that represents the entire transparent bridging domain. When bridging from the SRB domain (Token Ring) to the transparent bridging domain (Ethernet), the source-route fields are removed. The RIFs are cached for use by subsequent return traffic.

To the transparent bridging station, the bridge represents just another port in the bridge group. When bridging from the transparent bridging domain to the SRB domain, RIF information is added to frames.

The SR/TLB software handles the transparent bridging to SRT bridging issues:

- Adding and removing RIF information

- Setting the MTU size for both environments

- MAC address representation

- Identifying MAC address information in the data portion of packets

SR/TLB Configuration Example

Before using the **source-bridge transparent** command, source-route bridging and transparent bridging must be configured, as shown in Figure 18–15.

Use the **source-bridge transparent** command to create two virtual environments that enable communication between the two different domains. The syntax of this command is as follows:

```
source-bridge transparent ring-group pseudo-ring bridge-number tb-group
    [oui]
```

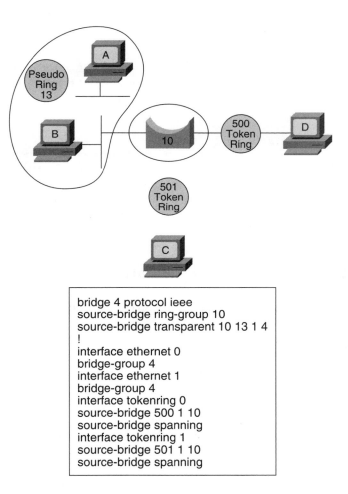

Figure 18–15
*SR/TLB
configuration
example.*

```
bridge 4 protocol ieee
source-bridge ring-group 10
source-bridge transparent 10 13 1 4
!
interface ethernet 0
bridge-group 4
interface ethernet 1
bridge-group 4
interface tokenring 0
source-bridge 500 1 10
source-bridge spanning
interface tokenring 1
source-bridge 501 1 10
source-bridge spanning
```

In Figure 18–15, the source-bridge transparent setting can be interpreted as follows:

source-bridge transparent 10 13 1 4 Command	Description
10	Defines ring group (SRB virtual ring) to be ring number 10
13	Establishes the transparent domain as a pseudo ring with the number 13

source-bridge transparent 10 13 1 4 Command	Description
1	Sets to 1 the bridge number of the bridge that belongs to the transparent bridging domain
4	The transparent bridge group that you want to tie into your SRB domain

Key Concept	Transparent bridging and SRB both use the spanning-tree algorithm to try to avoid loops, but the particular algorithms employed by the two bridging methods are incompatible. Because the two spanning-tree implementations are not compatible, multiple paths between the SRB and the transparent bridging domains are typically not allowed.

Verifying Source-Route Bridging Operation

There are two primary commands used to verify SRB operation:

- show source-bridge

- show rif

The show source-bridge Command

As displayed in Figure 18–16, the **show source-bridge** command displays the following:

Entries	Description
max hp	Maximum route descriptor length in hops
receive cnt:bytes	Number of frames and bytes received on interface for SRB
transmit cnt:bytes	Number of frames and bytes transmitted on interface for SRB
Srn	Ring number of this Token Ring
Bn	Bridge number of this router, for this ring

Entries	Description
Trn	Group in which the interface is configured (the target ring number or virtual ring group)
Rings	Describes the ring groups, including the bridge groups; ring groups; whether the group is local or remote; the MAC address; the network address or interface type; and the number of packets forwarded
Explorers	Describes the explorer packets that the router has transmitted and received
TR0	Interface on which explorers were received
Spanning	Number of spanning-tree explorers
All-rings	Number of all-routes explored
Total	Total number of spanning and all-routes explorers

```
Router# show source-bridge
Local Interfaces:max receive transmit
 srn bn trn r p s n hp  cnt:bytes cnt: bytes drops
TR0 5 1 10 * * 7 39: 1002 23:62923
Ring Group 10:
  This peer TCP: 172.16.92.92
  Maximum output TCP queue length, per peer: 100
  Peers:              state      lv  pkts_rx  pkts_tx   expl_gn      drops TCP
   TCP 172.16.92.92 -            2    0        0         0           0    0
   TCP 172.16.93.93 open         2*   18       18        3           0    0
Rings
   bn: 1 rn:5    local ms: 4000.3080.844b TokenRing0          fwd: 18
   bn: 1 rn: 2  remote ma: 4000.3080.8473 TCP 172.16.93.93  fwd: 36
Explorers: ------ input ------        ------ output ------
       spanning all-rings    total    spanning all-rings    total
TR0         0    3     3        3       5     8
Router#
```

Figure 18–16
The show source-bridge command.

In Figure 18–16, interface Token Ring 0 is on Token Ring number 5. This interface is part of target ring number (ring group) 10. In the top portion of the output, additional field definitions are as follows:

- r—ring group defined

- p—proxy enabled

- s—spanning tree enabled

- n—NetBIOS cache enabled

Refer to the **show source-bridge** entry in the *Bridging and IBM Networking Command Reference* for a complete listing of output fields.

The show rif Command

As shown in Figure 18–17, the **show rif** command displays the following:

Column Heading	Description
How	Means through which the RIF was learned. Possible values include a ring group (rg) or interface (TR)
Idle (min)	Number of minutes since the last response was received directly from this node
Routing Information Field	Lists the RIF

Figure 18–17
*The **show rif**
command.*

```
Router# show rif

Codes: * interface, - static, + remote
Hardware Addr How      Idle(min)   Routing Information Field
5C02.0001.4322 rg5     -           0630.0053.00B0
5A00.0000.2333 TR0     3           08B0.0101.2201.0FF0
5B01.0000.4444 -       -           -
0000.1403.4800 TR1     0           -
0000.2805.4C00 TR0     *           -
0000.2807.4C00 TR1     *           -
0000.28A8.4800 TR0     0           -
0077.2201.0001 rg5     10          0830.0052.2201.0FF0

Router#
```

You can use the **show interfaces tokenring** command to display information about the Token Ring interfaces and the state of source-route bridging on those interfaces as well.

SR/TLB Configuration

Use the **source-bridge transparent** command to establish communication between the transparent and the source-route configurations and to activate media translation features:

```
router(config)#source-bridge transparent ring-group pseudo-ring
    bridge-number tb-group [oui]
```

source-bridge transparent Command	Description
ring-group	The virtual ring group that was created by the **source-bridge ring-group** command. This is the source-bridge virtual ring to associate with the transparent bridge group. The valid range is 1 to 4095.
pseudo-ring	The ring number used to represent the transparent bridging domain to the source-route bridged domain. This number must be unique in the source-route bridged network.
bridge-number	The SRB number assigned to the router.
tb-group	The number of the transparent bridge group that you want to tie into your source-route bridged domain.
oui	Organizational Unique Identifier that holds the vendor code of the interface that sourced this frame. Possible values include **90-compatible, standard,** and **cisco.**
	Use the **90-compatible** OUI when communicating with Cisco routers. This OUI provides the most flexibility.
	Specify the **standard** OUI when communicating with IBM 8209 bridges and other vendors' equipment. Use of the **standard** keyword causes the OUI code in Token Ring frames to always be 0x000000, which identifies the frame as an Ethernet Type II frame.
	The **cisco** OUI is provided for compatibility with future equipment.

Use this command only after you have completely configured your router using multiport source bridging and transparent bridging in order to tie together the two configured environments.

SUMMARY

In this chapter, you learned how SRB uses special explorer packets to discover routing information in the network and return it to the host system. Recall that source-route bridging (SRB) is a bridging method in which one end host locates another end host by discovering available source-to-destination paths.

You also learned how SRT combines transparent and SRB bridging algorithms and how SR/TLB integrates transparent bridging and SRB. (Recall that source-route translational bridging (SR/TLB) is a Cisco IOS feature that allows you to combine SRB and transparent bridging networks without the need to convert all your existing source-route bridges to SRT nodes.) Finally, you learned to verify SRB with the **show source-bridge** and **show rif** commands.

Congratulations, you have now completed this book! The appendixes contain the answer key to the chapter exercises (you have been taking those exams, haven't you?), as well as some good information on managing AppleTalk traffic, configuring NetWare's link-state routing protocol, NLSP, configuring T1/E1 and ISDN PRI options, and even a short appendix on configuring SMDS.

Chapter Eighteen Test
Configuring Source-Route Bridging

Estimated Time: 15 minutes

Complete all the exercises to test your knowledge of the materials contained in this chapter. Answers are listed in Appendix A, "Chapter Test Answer Key."

Use the information contained in this chapter to answer the following questions. Respond to each multiple choice exercise by circling the letter (A through D) preceding the correct answer.

Question 18.1

The fundamental difference between source-route bridging and transparent bridging technologies is that source-route bridging end nodes:

A. Send data and rely on the source-route bridge to determine the route to the destination.

B. Place ring-number/bridge-number combinations in frames that travel from one ring to another ring.

C. Determine the entire route to the destination node before sending data.

D. Participate in the spanning-tree algorithm to eliminate network-wide loops.

Question 18.2

In an IEEE 802.5 MAC frame, the RIF route descriptor has information about these two source-route characteristics:

A. Ring numbers

B. Type

C. Direction

D. Bridge numbers

Question 18.3

The Routing Information Indicator (RII) is:

   A. Removed by source-route bridges when the bridged has already seen an all-rings (routes) explorer packet from the source.

   B. In the RIF's routing control field.

   C. The first bit in the source address of an 802.5 MAC frame.

   D. A one-octet value set by each bridge in the path.

Question 18.4

You are configuring a router that has interface Token Ring 0 connected to ring 102 and Token Ring interface 1 connected to ring 53. Use bridge number 1. In the space provided, write the **source-bridge** and **source-bridge spanning** command to enable source-route bridging of these interfaces.

_____

_____

_____

_____

_____

Question 18.5

What Token Ring limitation does the **source-bridge ring-group** command help overcome?

_____

Question 18.6

What is the purpose of the **source-bridge proxy-explorer** command?

_____

Question 18.7

Which command enables the router to bridge routed protocols across a source-route bridged network?

Question 18.8

T F   Source-route bridging normally provides bridging between SRB and transparent bridging networks.

Question 18.9

SRT bridges examine which bit to distinguish between SRB and transparent bridging frames?

Question 18.10

T F   The **source-route transparent** command is used to configure SRT on a Cisco router.

Appendixes

Chapter Test
Answer Key

CHAPTER 1: OVERVIEW OF SCALABLE INTERNETWORKS

1.1.

Network Problem	Key Requirement	Cisco IOS Feature(s)
Connectivity restrictions	Accessible, but secure	Dedicated and switched access technologies
Single paths available to all networks	Reliable and available	Scalable protocols Dial backup
Too much broadcast traffic	Efficient	Access lists Scalable protocols
Application sensitivity to traffic delays	Responsive	Weighted fair queuing Priority queuing Custom queuing
Convergence problems with metric limitations	Reliable and available	Scalable protocols

Network Problem	Key Requirement	Cisco IOS Feature(s)
Competition for bandwidth	Efficient, Responsive *(This is also a valid answer because you can reduce competition by defining routing policies using the queuing technologies.)*	Access lists Snapshot routing Compression over WANs Queuing mechanisms Generic Traffic Shaping
Illegal access to services on the internetwork	Accessible but secure	Access lists (not an end-all solution) Authentication protocols Lock and Key Security TACACS/RADIUS Logging
Single WAN links available to each remote site	Reliable and available	Dial backup
Expensive tariffs on WAN links that do not get much use	Efficient	Switched access technologies
Very large routing tables	Efficient	Route summarization Incremental updates
Integrate networks using legacy protocols	Adaptable	Bridging Mechanisms

CHAPTER 2: INTRODUCTION TO MANAGING TRAFFIC AND CONGESTION

2.1.   A. Bursts of user application traffic
        B. Multicast and broadcast traffic
        C. Too much traffic on low-bandwidth links
        D. Network design issues
        E. Other answers possible

2.2. A. Filtering unwanted traffic (ACL)

B. Reducing the amount of overhead and broadcast traffic (router-config)

C. Prioritizing traffic for each serial link (queuing)

CHAPTER 3: MANAGING IP TRAFFIC

3.1. The following configuration shows one solution that satisfies the exercise requirements:

```
Router B
access-list 1 permit 172.16.1.3
access-list 1 deny 172.16.3.3
access-list 1 deny 172.16.1.0 0.0.0.255
access-list 1 permit 172.16.0.0 0.0.255.255
!
interface Ethernet 2
ip access-group 1
! This is an outbound access list by default.
```

3.2. A. False

B. False

C. True

D. True

3.3. The show line command is used to view access lists applied to vty ports.

3.4. The access-list 103 permit tcp any 128.88.0.0 0.0.255.255 established command will ensure that new TCP connections are not allowed through this router.

3.5. The ACK bit is not set and the SYN bit is set on an incoming packet.

3.6. The show access-list command can verify access list commands for all protocols.

3.7. The ip route 192.168.2.0 255.255.255.0 null configuration sends all traffic bound for 192.168.2.0 to the null interface.

3.8. One possible configuration for the exercise is as follows:

```
Router R1:
interface ethernet 0
ip address 144.253.1.10 255.255.255.0
ip helper-address 144.253.6.3
ip helper-address 144.253.3.4
```

CHAPTER 4: MANAGING NOVELL IPX/SPX TRAFFIC

4.1.   A. True
            B. False
            C. True
            D. True
            E. True

4.2.
```
access-list 1004 deny -1 7
access-list 1004 permit -1
!
interface S 0
IPX network 2b
IPX output-sap-filter 1004
ipx sap-interval 5
```
Note that there are several different print services (7=print server, 47=advertising print server, and 112=HP print server).

4.3.
```
interface tunnel 0
ipx network 2b
tunnel source 131.108.99.1
tunnel destination 131.108.99.2
tunnel mode gre ip
no ip address
```

CHAPTER 5: CONFIGURING QUEUING TO MANAGE TRAFFIC

5.1.   False
5.2.   True
5.3.   False
5.4.   True
5.5.   False
5.6.   False
5.7.   True
5.8.   False
5.9.   True
5.10.   False
5.11.   True
5.12.   True
5.13.   False

CHAPTER 6: ROUTING PROTOCOL OVERVIEW

6.1. A router needs the following in order to route traffic:
A. Destination network address
B. Identify neighbors
C. Discover routes
D. Select routes
E. Maintain routing information

6.2. A. LS
B. DV
C. DV
D. LS
E. LS
F. DV
G. LS

CHAPTER 7: EXTENDING IP ADDRESSES USING VLSMS

7.1.

Router C Route Table Entries	Routes That Can Be Advertised to Router D from Router C
172.16.1.192/28	172.16.1.192/26 Summarizes: 172.16.1.192/28, 172.16.1.208/28
172.16.1.208/28	172.16.1.64/26 Summarizes: 172.16.1.64/28, 172.16.1.80/28, 172.16.1.96/28, 172.16.1.112/28
172.16.1.64/28	
172.16.1.80/28	
172.16.1.96/28	
172.16.1.112/28	

7.2. Before implementing private addressing, consider these points:
   A. Determine which hosts do not need to have network-layer connectivity to the outside. These hosts are considered private hosts. Private hosts can communicate with all other hosts within your network, both public and private, but they cannot have connectivity to external hosts.
   B. Routers that connect to external networks should be set up with the appropriate packet and routing filters at both ends of the link in order to prevent the leaking of the private IP addresses. You should also filter any private networks from inbound routing information in order to prevent ambiguous routing situations that can occur when routes to the private address space point outside the network.
   C. Changing a host from private to public will require changing its address, and, in most cases, its physical connectivity. In locations where such changes can be foreseen, you might want to configure separate physical media for public and private subnets to make these changes easier.

7.3. The private IP addresses are as follows:
   A. Class A—10.0.0.0 to 10.255.255.255
   B. Class B—172.16.0.0 to 172.31.255.255
   C. Class C—192.168.0.0 to 192.168.255.255

7.4. NAT can be used when you need hosts that use private addresses to be able to periodically access the Internet without having to redo their IP addresses.

CHAPTER 8: CONFIGURING OSPF IN A SINGLE AREA

8.1. Four reasons why OSPF operates better than RIP in a large internetwork include:
   A. faster convergence
   B. greater hop count
   C. better paths
   D. lower routing update overhead

8.2. When a router receives an LSU, it follows these steps:
A. If the entry already exists and the received LSU has the same information, it ignores the LSA entry.
B. If the entry already exists but the LSU includes new information, it sends an LSAck to the DR, adds the entry to its link-state database and updates its routing table.
C. If the entry already exists but the LSU includes older information, it sends an LSU with its information back to the DR.

8.3. A. The exchange process is used to get neighboring routers into a Full state.
To be initiated, two routers must agree on a master-slave relationship. The process enables them to synchronize their link-state databases using DDPs. Once in a Full state, the exchange process does not get done again unless the Full state is changed to a different state.
B. The flooding process is used anytime there is a change in a link-state, such as the link goes down or a new link is added to the network.
In this process, all link-state changes are sent in LSU packets to the DR/BDR of the area. The DR is then responsible for forwarding the LSUs to all other routers in the network.

8.4. A. An internal router is a router that resides within an area and routes traffic.
B. An LSU is a link-state update packet. This packet includes update information about link-state advertisements.
C. A DDP is a database description packet. This packet is used during the exchange protocol and includes summary information about link-state entries.
D. A hello packet is used during the hello process and includes information that enables routers to establish themselves as neighbors.

8.5. A. DR
B. Full state
C. Exchange state
D. Area

CHAPTER 9: INTERCONNECTING MULTIPLE OSPF AREAS

9.1. OSPF's capability to separate a large internetwork into multiple areas is also referred to as hierarchical routing. Hierarchical routing enables you to separate your large internetwork (autonomous system) into smaller internetworks that are called *areas*. The advantages include smaller routing tables, reduced frequency of SPF calculations, and reduced LSU overhead.

9.2. If it is an area that is *not* configured for stubby or totally stubby, an internal router will receive Type-5 LSAs.

9.3. All area types must be connected to the backbone area, either physically or through a virtual link.

9.4. The backbone area must always be area 0.

9.5.

LSA Type	Name	Description
1	Router link entry (record)	Generated by each router for each area it belongs to. It describes the states of the router's link to the area.
2	Network link entry	Generated by DRs in multiaccess networks. They describe the set of routers attached to a particular network.
3 or 4	Summary link entry	Originated by ABRs. Describes the links between the ABR and the internal routers of a local area.
5	Autonomous system external link entry	Originated by the ASBR. Describes routes to destinations external to the autonomous system.

9.6. The packet must go through the interarea, through the ABR, through the backbone area, through the next ABR, and then through the internal routers to its final destination.

9.7. When the area is configured for stub or totally stubby, a default route is injected into an area.

CHAPTER 10: CONFIGURING ENHANCED IGRP

10.1.

	Term	Statement
__D__	1. Successor	A. A network protocol that EIGRP supports.
__E__	2. Feasible successor	B. A table that contains feasible successor information.
__G__	3. Hello	C. Administrative distance determines routing information that is included in this table.
__B__	4. Topology table	D. A neighbor router that has the best path to a destination.
__A__	5. IP	E. A neighbor router that has the best alternative path to a destination.
__H__	6. Update	F. An algorithm used by EIGRP that ensures fast convergence.
__A__	7. AppleTalk	G. A multicast packet used to discover neighbors.
__C__	8. Routing table	H. A packet sent by EIGRP routers when a new neighbor is discovered and when a change occurs.
__F__	9. DUAL	
__A__	10. IPX	

CHAPTER 11: OPTIMIZING ROUTING UPDATE OPERATION

11.1. Configure static routes in combination with a passive interface.

11.2. Define a filter using the **distribute-list** command.

11.3. You may not want routing information propagated when:
  A. Using an on-demand WAN link
  B. You want to prevent routing loops
  C. Passive interface

11.4.
  A. Default routes
  B. Static routes

11.5. The three key issues to remember when implementing redistribution are as follows:

A. Know your network traffic patterns before enabling redistribution.

B. Verify redistribution operation after configuration.

C. If suboptimal paths exist, determine the solution based on user requirements.

CHAPTER 12: CONNECTING ENTERPRISES TO AN INTERNET SERVICE PROVIDER

12.1. False

12.2. False

12.3. True

12.4. True

CHAPTER 13: WAN CONNECTIVITY OVERVIEW

13.1. Any four of the following are correct:

A. Availability

B. Cost

C. Bandwidth

D. Ease of management

E. Application traffic

F. Routing protocol characteristics

13.2. B. Point-to-point over serial links

13.3. D. When only certain packets should trigger a call

13.4. D. HDLC

13.5. All types can be used for point-to-point links:

A. PPP

B. SLIP

C. LAPB (Applies in that it is used for flow control on the D channel of an ISDN BRI when the B channels use PPP, for example.)

D. HDLC

CHAPTER 14: CONFIGURING DIAL-ON-DEMAND ROUTING

14.1. True

14.2. False

14.3. True

14.4. True
14.5. True
14.6. False
14.7. True
14.8. The answers are shown in Figure A–1.

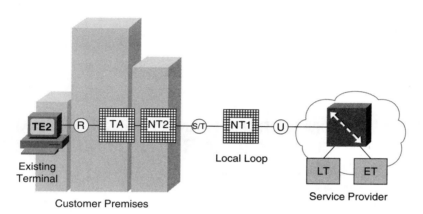

Figure A–1
The ISDN components identified.

Existing Terminal

Local Loop

Customer Premises

Service Provider

CHAPTER 15: CUSTOMIZING DDR OPERATION

15.1. Router A:

```
interface B 0
snapshot client 8 1440 dialer
dialer map snapshot 60 name RouterA 14155554132
```

Router B:

```
interface B 0
dialer map snapshot 1 name RouterB 14155556789
snapshot server 8 dialer
```

15.2. True
15.3. True
15.4. True
15.5. False
15.6. False

CHAPTER 16: BRIDGING OVERVIEW

16.1. B.   A network layer
16.2. D.   LAT
16.3. A.   AppleTalk
16.4. C.   Determine the entire route to the destination node before sending
               data.
16.5. D.   Transparent bridging
16.6. A.   SR/TLB
16.7. C.   SRB
16.8. B.   SRT

CHAPTER 17: CONFIGURING TRANSPARENT BRIDGING AND INTEGRATED ROUTING AND BRIDGING

17.1. `interface ethernet 0`
          `ip address 10.0.0.1`
          `bridge-group 10`

          `interface ethernet 1`
          `ip address 10.1.1.1`
          `bridge-group 10`

          `interface ethernet 2`
          `ip address 10.2.2.2`
          `bridge-group 10`

          `bridge 10 protocol ieee`
17.2. `interface BVI 10`
          `ipx network BB`
          `no ip address`
17.3. `bridge irb`
          `bridge 1 route IPX`
          `no bridge 1 bridge ip`

CHAPTER 18: CONFIGURING SOURCE-ROUTE BRIDGING

18.1. C. The fundamental difference between source-route bridging and transparent bridging technologies is that source-route bridging end nodes determine the entire route to the destination node before sending data.

18.2. A. Ring numbers, and d) Bridge numbers

18.3. C. The RII is the first bit in the source address of an 802.5 MAC frame.

18.4.
```
interface tokenring 0
source-bridge 102 1 53
source-bridge spanning
interface tokenring 1
source-bridge 53 1 102
source-bridge spanning
```

18.5. The **source-bridge ring-group** command helps overcome the limitation that IBM Token Ring chips can only process two ring numbers.

18.6. Using the **source-bridge proxy-explorer** command means that the router can convert an explorer packet to a specifically routed frame to reduce the overhead of the explorer process (especially on a WAN link).

18.7. The **multiring all** command enables the router to bridge routed protocols across a source-route bridged network.

18.8. False

18.9. SRT bridges examine the RII bit to distinguish between SRB and transparent bridging frames.

18.10. False

APPENDIX B

Managing AppleTalk Traffic

This chapter covers filtering techniques for controlling access to the AppleTalk network and for reducing unwanted traffic in an AppleTalk network. Understanding how to control your AppleTalk traffic will help ensure the best performance on your network. Covered Cisco IOS filtering options include: zone filters, RTMP filters, and NBP filters.

APPLETALK TRAFFIC OVERVIEW

AppleTalk was designed to be a "plug-and-play" network. This means that an AppleTalk user can plug a computing device into the network and use it immediately with little or no configuration. Locating network-wide services in an AppleTalk network is extremely easy. Several AppleTalk features account for this ease-of-use capability; for example, *dynamic address acquisition,* which is the capability of a client to learn an address when it boots up; and *automatic name lookup*, which locates devices on the network.

Apple's native routing protocol is the *Routing Table Maintenance Protocol (RTMP).* RTMP broadcasts its entire routing table every 10 seconds. RTMP broadcasts can cause congestion on the network.

As AppleTalk networks grow, so does the associated traffic that occurs when hosts attempt to locate servers and printers and when routers exchange routing updates.

Using Cisco IOS filters allows a network manager to preserve the easy-to-use nature of AppleTalk networks and at the same time create AppleTalk networks that scale.

Before you learn how to control AppleTalk traffic, you must understand AppleTalk functions and services. The next section gives a brief overview/review of AppleTalk technology.

AppleTalk Protocol Stack

At the hardware layers, most standard media types are supported. Many Apple products contain a LocalTalk interface that operates over twisted-pair cable at 230 kbps. There is no LocalTalk interface available on Cisco products. LocalTalk devices can be adapted to Ethernet, Token Ring, or FDDI where the physical media are referred to as EtherTalk, TokenTalk, and FDDITalk. As compared to the OSI network layer, the *Datagram Delivery Protocol* (DDP) provides a connectionless datagram service. Running on top of DDP are several protocols. The *Name Binding Protocol* (NBP) provides name-to-address association. The *Zone Information Protocol* (ZIP) provides a means of maintaining zone name mappings to network numbers.

This chapter focuses on the protocols RTMP, NBP, and ZIP. As AppleTalk networks grow, filtering these protocols may be necessary to control excessive broadcast and multicast traffic or to prohibit unwanted access. The Cisco IOS software offers extensive AppleTalk filtering capabilities for each of these protocols.

AppleTalk Services

Hosts and servers are assembled in logical groups called *zones*, as shown in Figure B–1.

When a Macintosh user requires a service, the Chooser provides a list of zones and types of services (including AppleShare file servers, printers, and fax services). After you select the zone and type of service, the device names of available matching services are presented. The user selects the preferred device, and a logical link for that service is retained in the Macintosh for future reference.

The underlying AppleTalk protocols provide user-selectable network services, as follows. When the Chooser is opened, a GetZoneList query goes to a router to populate the zone list at the lower left. The box at the upper left is populated with all the network drivers loaded on the Macintosh. The user selects a zone and a driver, and an

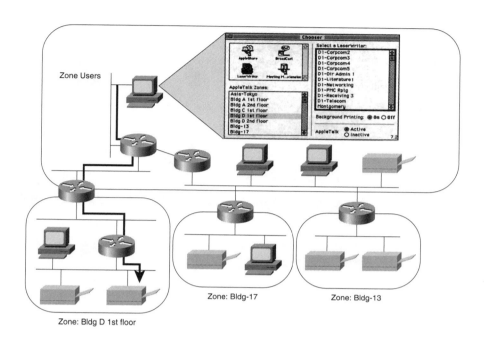

Figure B–1
Zones provide a logical grouping of hosts and servers.

NBP query goes out. The responses to the NBP query populate the window on the right with the names of the networked devices that offer the selected service in the selected zone.

In the past, the Chooser caused a considerable amount traffic because it generated an NBP broadcast every 10 seconds as long as the window was open and a zone and device driver were selected. In 1989, Apple released version System 7.0 of the Mac OS, which includes an exponential timing backoff algorithm so that NBP broadcasts go out far less frequently.

Nonextended/Extended Networks

AppleTalk supports two network types: Nonextended (Phase 1) and Extended (Phase 2), as shown in Figure B–2.

Figure B–2
Nonextended and extended networks.

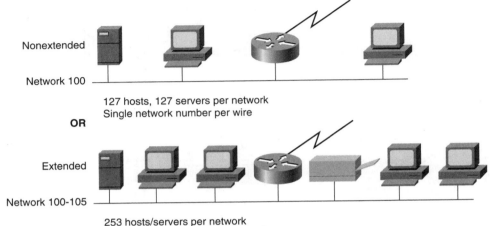

These two networks are distinguished as follows:

- Nonextended (AppleTalk Phase 1) networks allow 127 hosts and 127 servers per network. Only a single network number is allowed per wire, and only a single zone is allowed per wire. The data-link encapsulation type is Ethernet II. If this is too limiting, companies use extended networks.

- Extended (AppleTalk Phase 2) networks allow a total of 253 devices (in any combination of hosts and servers) per wire. A range of network numbers, called a *cable range*, is allowed per wire. The data-link encapsulation type is Ethernet Subnetwork Access Protocol (SNAP).

Extended AppleTalk Internetwork

An AppleTalk Phase 2 internetwork can have multiple zones per cable range. In Figure B–3, both zone A and zone B are located on cable range 101-101. Zone B is also located on cable range 110-110, illustrating the concept that zones can cross noncontiguous cable ranges.

An AppleTalk Phase 2 network can also have multiple cable ranges per zone. In Figure B–3, zone A includes some devices on cable range 101-101 and all devices on cable range 120-129.

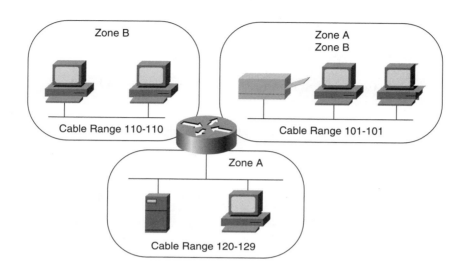

Figure B–3
Extended networks may have multiple zones per cable range and multiple cable ranges per zone.

AppleTalk Zones

AppleTalk zones provide a way to localize broadcast traffic and to create *communities of interest*. A community of interest in the context of an AppleTalk network is a group of users that is typically collocated and shares local resources, such as servers and printers.

As the network grows, more zones and more users per zone are added, and thus more traffic is generated to locate and track services. Therefore, filtering "unnecessary" traffic becomes an integral part of maintaining the overall health of the network. What constitutes unnecessary traffic is relative: what is considered unwanted traffic to users on one zone is essential for accessing services for users in another zone. Understanding these communities of interest is the basis of defining filtering systems for service-location traffic.

AppleTalk Filtering Options

There are four types of filters to isolate network, zone, and name information in an AppleTalk network, as follows:

- GetZoneList filter

  Filters ZIP information locally between a router and hosts.

Used to hide specific zones from users on specific networks.

- ZIP reply filter

Cisco IOS software Release 10.2 feature used to hide zone information between routers.

Does not prevent hosts from getting zones lists.

- Distribute list

Controls RTMP broadcasts between routers.

Used to block the advertisement of cable ranges/network numbers or the acceptance of cable ranges/network numbers into the routing table.

Recommended not to be used to hide zones because it can cause complex iterations.

- NBP filter

Cisco IOS software Release 11.0 (and later) feature used to filter NBP packets to hide services, reduce traffic, and control dial-on-demand routing (DDR).

AppleTalk filters, like other filters, have two fundamental tasks, as shown in Figure B–4.

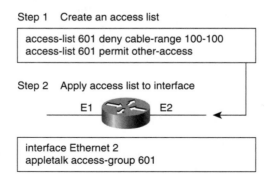

Figure B–4
Configuring AppleTalk filters.

Step 1　　Create an access list

```
access-list 601 deny cable-range 100-100
access-list 601 permit other-access
```

Step 2　　Apply access list to interface

E1　　　　　　E2

```
interface Ethernet 2
appletalk access-group 601
```

The two fundamental tasks of the AppleTalk filters are as follows:

1. Create an access list filter in global configuration mode. (All AppleTalk access lists are from 600–699.)

   Define which zones, networks, or names should be filtered (or denied access) if the access list conditions are matched.

   In Figure B–4, the access list 601 is created and cable range 100–100 denied with the following command:

   ```
   access-list 601 deny cable-range 100-100
   ```

   Define the default action to take for all zones, networks, or names not explicitly enumerated in the access list.

   In Figure B–4, the default action to permit access for all other networks and cable ranges besides 100–100 is established with the following command:

   ```
   access-list 601 permit other-access
   ```

2. Apply the access list you created to an interface in interface configuration mode.

   In Figure B–4, access list 601 is assigned to E2 with the following command:

   ```
   appletalk access-group 601
   ```

   The syntax of the command that assigns the access list to an interface varies from filter to filter.

GetZoneList Filtering

When the Chooser is opened, the Macintosh sends a GetZoneList (GZL) request to its router to obtain a list of all zones on the internetwork, as shown in Figure B–5. An AppleTalk device selects a router dynamically by listening to RTMP packets. In this way, an AppleTalk device also can dynamically find redundant routers.

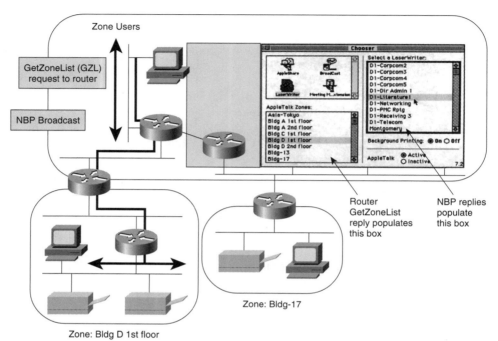

Figure B–5
*The Get-
ZoneList
request is sent
when Chooser
is opened.*

After a device has a session open with a remote device, it uses what Apple calls the
best routing algorithm, which means the device keeps track of the router through
which it is receiving packets from the remote device. It uses that router for sending
packets to the remote device for the duration of a session. If that router goes away,
the local device can try a different router.

The router's GZL reply contains a list of all of the (unfiltered) zones on the internetwork. This response populates the Chooser's lower-left window with zones.

When the user selects a device type (LaserWriter or AppleShare server) and zone
name, the user's Macintosh sends out an NBP request looking for the names of all
such devices in the specified zone. The router forwards this lookup into the requested
zone. Devices implementing the service respond to the originator, and their NBP
replies populate the right box of the user's Chooser with the device names.

If the requirement is to prevent users in one zone (such as the Operation zone in Figure B–5) from accessing users in another zone (such as the Accounting zone) through
the Chooser, a GZL filter can be used, as described next.

GZL Filter Hides Zones from User

A GZL filter filters ZIP information locally between a router and hosts, as shown in Figure B–6. It is used to hide specific zones from users.

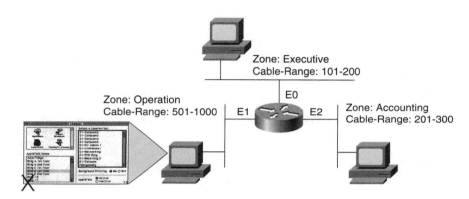

Zone: Executive
Cable-Range: 101-200

E0

Zone: Operation
Cable-Range: 501-1000

E1 · E2

Zone: Accounting
Cable-Range: 201-300

Figure B–6
Using a GZL filter, the router does not include Accounting in GZL reply.

A Macintosh's default router is chosen dynamically. If multiple routers exist on the same cable segment, the Macintosh's default router can be any one of them. Therefore, when you implement a GZL filter on a given cable segment, you must configure all routers on that segment with identical GZL filters. For this reason, a GZL filter is not a scalable solution for cable segments containing several routers.

A GZL filter is not completely secure. By using a device alias, users can still access a device even if it is not listed in the Chooser.

GetZoneList Filtering Commands

Use the **access-list zone** command to create an entry in the zone filter list:

```
router(config)#access-list access-list-number {deny | permit} zone zone-name
```

access-list zone Command	Description
access-list-number	The number of the access list; a number in the range of 600 to 699.
deny	**permit**	Denies or permits access if conditions are matched.
zone-name	The name assigned to the zone being filtered.

Use the **access-list additional-zones** command to specify the default action for all other zones not specified in the access list. If not specified, the implicit deny all is in effect, so a given router will not include any zones in the GZL reply. The syntax of this command is as follows:

```
router(config)#access-list access-list-number {deny | permit}
    additional-zones
```

Use the **appletalk getzonelist-filter** command to assign the access list to an interface. The access list should be placed on the interface on which the request arrives, but the filter controls what zones are sent out. The syntax of this command is as follows:

```
router(config-if)#appletalk getzonelist-filter access-list-number
```

where *access-list-number* is the number of the access list; a number in the range of 600 to 699.

GetZoneList Filtering Example

Figure B–7 illustrates a GetZoneList filtering example.

Figure B–7
*GetZoneList
filtering
example.*

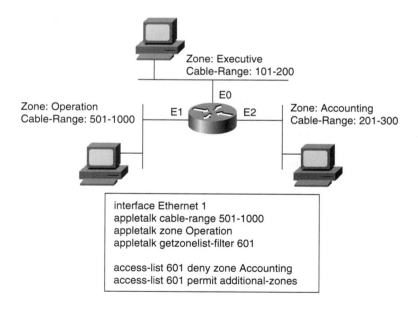

The requirement is to prevent users in the Operation zone from accessing the Accounting zone. To accomplish this requirement, you can create a GZL filter denying the Accounting zone.

Access list 601 is created and specifies the following:

- **access-list 601 deny zone Accounting**. The Accounting zone is not included in the router's GZL reply and is therefore invisible to the user.

- **access-list 601 permit additional-zones**. All other zones besides Accounting are accessible (in this example, the Executive zone).

Access list 601 is linked to Ethernet 1 with the **appletalk getzonelist-filter 601** command.

The result of this configuration is as follows. When users on cable range 501–1000 in the Operation zone open the Chooser and request a list of zones from the router, the router will not include the denied Accounting zone in its reply. The router will include all other zones it knows about (in this example, Executive and Operation). The Accounting zone will not be visible from the user's Chooser.

ZIP Reply Filtering

GZL filtering will satisfy ZIP GZL requests only from the Chooser to the router. In order to filter zone information exchange between routers, you should use ZIP reply filtering. When a router has a routing entry without any zone name associated with it (either because of a new route or the zone name has been aged out), the router will send a ZIP query to the next-hop router for that network to find out the zone names. (Typically this query is not a broadcast unless the router is first coming online and does not know its own network number and zones for its own cable.)

As a result, the other routers on the same cable segment will reply with a ZIP reply packet with the correct zone name. ZIP reply filtering can be done on the replying routers to hide zones. It is useful when connecting two AppleTalk administrative domains.

The ZIP reply filter allows RTMP details to propagate between RTMP peers, but blocks specific zones when the routers reach back for zone information. The filtered zones are invisible to all downstream routers and nodes.

In Figure B–8, the zone information is gained through the following steps:

1. R1 sends RTMP update with network numbers.

2. R2 sends a ZIP request asking for the associated zones.

3. R1 sends a Zone Information Table (ZIT).

Figure B–8
*Hiding
Paris_Acct
from R2.*

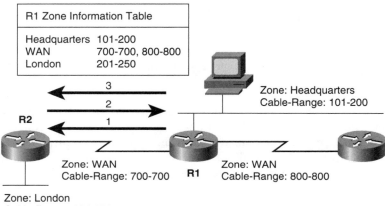

In Figure B–9, the requirement is to hide Paris_Acct zone from R2. A ZIP reply filter preventing R1 from including Paris_Acct zone in response to R2's ZIP request will accomplish this requirement.

Because of the complexity involved, adhere to the following rules when implementing a ZIP reply filter:

- If multiple routers exist on the cable segment, you should implement the ZIP reply filter on all routers on that segment.

- You should not filter a network segment's zone name if the segment only has one zone defined. Otherwise, connectivity problems may appear because the cable range of the filtered zone segment will be deleted from the routing table to prevent ZIP storms.

If you deny a zone, the adjacent routers may still have the zone name in their Zone Information Table (ZIT). Therefore, you should restart the AppleTalk routing process

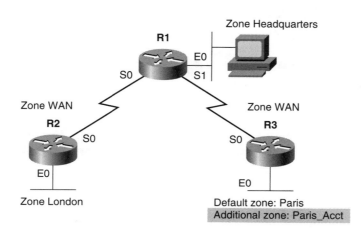

Figure B–9
*Use ZIP reply
filter on R1 so
R2 won't know
about
Paris_Acct
zone.*

on the adjacent routers. (Waiting for the zone name to age out may not work if there is a loop situation where a packet can be forwarded back and forth between parallel routers.)

The default zone is the first one configured on the router.   **Key Concept**

Use the **access-list zone** command to create an entry in the zone filter list. It must use an access list number in the range 600 to 699.

```
router(config)#access-list access-list-number {deny | permit} zone zone-name
```

access-list zone Command	Description
access-list-number	The number of the access list; a number in the range of 600 to 699.
zone-name	The name assigned to the zone being filtered.

Use the **access-list additional-zones** command to specify the default action for all other zones not specified in the access list. If not specified, the implicit deny all is in effect, so a given router will not include any zones in the ZIP reply. The syntax of this command is as follows:

```
router(config)#access-list access-list-number {deny | permit}
    additional-zones
```

Use the **appletalk zip-reply-filter** command to assign the access list to an interface. The syntax of this command is as follows:

```
router(config-if)#appletalk zip-reply-filter access-list-number
```

where *access-list-number* is the number of the access list; a number in the range of 600 to 699.

In Figure B–10, the requirement is to hide Paris_Acct zone from R2 and any downstream routers and users. To accomplish this requirement, you can use a ZIP reply filter.

Figure B–10
*ZIP reply filter-
ing example.*

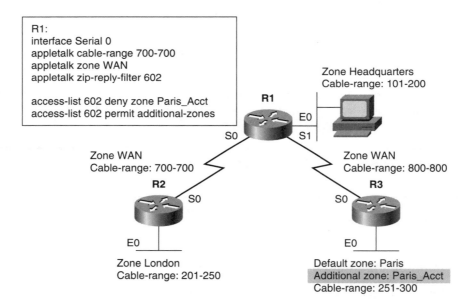

```
R1:
interface Serial 0
appletalk cable-range 700-700
appletalk zone WAN
appletalk zip-reply-filter 602

access-list 602 deny zone Paris_Acct
access-list 602 permit additional-zones
```

Zone Headquarters
Cable-range: 101-200

R1
E0
S0   S1

Zone WAN
Cable-range: 700-700
R2
S0

Zone WAN
Cable-range: 800-800
R3
S0

E0
Zone London
Cable-range: 201-250

E0
Default zone: Paris
Additional zone: Paris_Acct
Cable-range: 251-300

Access list 602 is created and specifies the following:

- **access-list 602 deny zone Paris_Acct**—The Paris_Acct zone is not included in R1's ZIP reply on serial 0 and is therefore invisible to R2 and users in the London zone.

- **access-list 602 permit additional-zones**—R1 includes all other zones besides Paris_Acct in its ZIP reply and they are therefore accessible (in this example, the Paris, WAN, and Headquarters zones).

Access list 602 is linked to R1's serial 0 interface with the **appletalk zip-reply-filter 602** command. Note that the filter was not placed on R3 because you want Head-quarters to see Paris_Acct.

The result of this configuration is as follows. When R1 advertises cable range 251–300 to R2, R2 will respond with a ZIP query requesting all zones associated with network 251–300. R1's ZIP reply will not include the denied Paris_Acct zone but will include the Paris zone because of the inclusion of the **permit additional-zones** command, which specifies the default action to take for zones not specified in the access list.

Use the **show appletalk zone** command to display the contents of the zone table and to verify the effect of a ZIP reply filter as shown here:

```
Tokyo#show appletalk zone
Name    Network(s)
Ozone   12810-12819
Azone   3210-3219 3230-3230 3220-3220
Fzone   11250-11259
Total of 3 zones
```

If you are performing this command on any router downstream from the router where you configured your ZIP reply filter denying one or more zones, you should not see the denied zone appearing in the ZIT.

Other useful commands are the **show appletalk access-lists** command, which checks access list statements, and the **show appletalk interface** command, which ensures that the access lists have been applied to the intended interface.

RTMP Filtering

AppleTalk's routing protocol is RTMP. RTMP, like RIP, is a distance-vector protocol. It has the following operation characteristics:

- Follows split horizon.

- The maximum hop count is 15.

- RTMP updates occur every 10 seconds.

- A routing packet contains routing tuples. A *tuple* consists of a cable range and a hop count. Zone names are not included in RTMP packets.

An RTMP filter can be used to reduce the number of AppleTalk routing table updates or prevent knowledge of routes. Alternatively, the Enhanced IGRP routing protocol can be used to reduce routing overhead. Enhanced IGRP is covered in Chapter 10, aptly named "Configuring Enhanced IGRP."

RTMP Filtering Examples

In Figure B–11, for example, R1 broadcasts its routing tables out all active interfaces every 10 seconds. If the requirement is to block the highlighted cable range 251-300 so that it does not appear in R2's routing table, you can configure an RTMP filter with the **distribute-list** command.

Figure B–11
*Use **distribute-list** filter so R1 does not advertise cable range 251-300.*

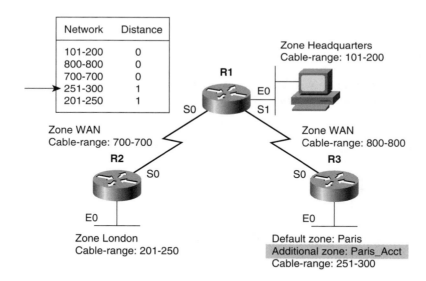

The **distribute-list** filter controls RTMP broadcasts between routers and can be used to reduce broadcasts or block cable ranges. Using the **distribute-list** command to hide zones is not recommended because this can cause complex iterations.

Use the **access-list network** command to define access for a single (nonextended) network number, as in the following:

```
router(config)#access-list access-list-number {deny | permit} network network
```

access-list network Command	Description
access-list-number	The number of the access list; a number in the range of 600 to 699.
network	AppleTalk network number.

Use the **access-list cable-range** command to define an access list for a cable range (for extended networks only), as in the following:

```
router(config)#access-list access-list-number {deny | permit} cable-range
    cable-range
```

access-list cable-range Command	Description
access-list-number	The number of the access list; a number in the range of 600 to 699.
cable-range	Start-end values of the cable range (from 1-65279) separated by a hyphen. Starting values must be less than or equal to ending values.

Use the **access-list other-access** command to specify the default action for network numbers or cable ranges not specified in the access list:

```
router(config)#access-list access-list-number {deny | permit} other-access
```

where *access-list-number* is the number of the access list; a number in the range of 600 to 699.

Use the **appletalk distribute-list in** command to control which routing updates the local routing table accepts. Filters for incoming routing updates use access lists that define conditions for networks and cable ranges only. The syntax for this command is as follows:

```
router(config-if)#appletalk distribute-list access-list-number in
```

Use the **appletalk distribute-list out** command to filter which routes the local router advertises in its routing updates. Filters for outgoing routing updates use access lists that define conditions for networks and cable ranges, and for zones. The syntax for this command is as follows:

```
router(config-if)#appletalk distribute-list access-list-number out
```

It is important to note that the access list referred to in **access-list-number** is applied to the contents of the update and not to the source or destination of the routing update packets. The router decides whether to include those contents in its routing table based on those access lists.

In Figure B–12, the requirement is to prevent cable range 251–300 from being advertised to R2.

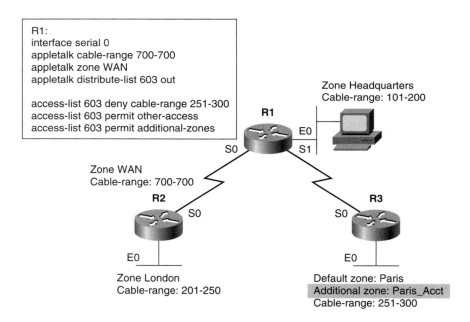

Figure B–12
RTMP filtering example.

R1:
interface serial 0
appletalk cable-range 700-700
appletalk zone WAN
appletalk distribute-list 603 out

access-list 603 deny cable-range 251-300
access-list 603 permit other-access
access-list 603 permit additional-zones

Zone Headquarters
Cable-range: 101-200

R1
E0
S0   S1

Zone WAN
Cable-range: 700-700

R2
S0

R3
S0

E0

E0

Zone London
Cable-range: 201-250

Default zone: Paris
Additional zone: Paris_Acct
Cable-range: 251-300

Access list 603 is created in Figure B–12 and specifies the following:

- **access-list 603 deny cable-range 251–300**—Cable range 251–300 is not included in the routing update R1 sends out the serial 0 interface (even though R1 has the route in its routing table).

- **access-list 603 permit other-access**—Other network numbers are included in R1's routing update (in this example, 800–800, and 101–200).

- **access-list 603 permit additional-zones**—All other zones not part of 251–300 are permitted.

Access list 603 is linked to R1's serial 0 interface with the **appletalk distribute-list 603 out** command.

The result of this configuration is as follows. When R1 sends its RTMP broadcast to R2, it sends all known network numbers except the denied 251–300. Users in the London zone will be unable to access users in either the Paris or Paris_Acct zones. In fact, users in the London zone will probably not see either of these zones in their Chooser. If R2 already has Paris and Paris_Acct in its ZIT and there are more routes in London, the zones may still be seen in London. These are called *phantom zones*. You must restart AppleTalk routing on R2 to clear the phantom zones.

Figure B–13, for example, shows a distribute-list filter denying R2 from including cable range 301–301 in its routing table. If access to any network in a zone is denied, access to that zone is also denied by default. Because cable range 301–301 is denied and is located in Operation zone, cable range 201–201 would also be denied because it is also located in Operation zone. By using the **appletalk permit-partial-zones** global configuration command, cable range 201–201 is still accepted into R2's routing table and would therefore be accessible to users in the Accounting zone.

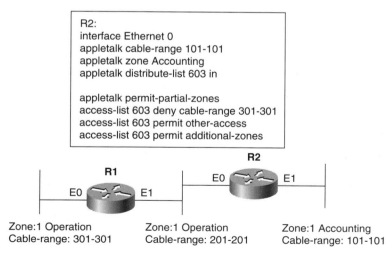

```
R2:
interface Ethernet 0
appletalk cable-range 101-101
appletalk zone Accounting
appletalk distribute-list 603 in

appletalk permit-partial-zones
access-list 603 deny cable-range 301-301
access-list 603 permit other-access
access-list 603 permit additional-zones
```

Figure B–13
If access to any network in a zone is denied, access to that zone is also denied by default.

R1   R2
E0   E1   E0   E1

Zone:1 Operation   Zone:1 Operation   Zone:1 Accounting
Cable-range: 301-301   Cable-range: 201-201   Cable-range: 101-101

RTMP Filtering Considerations

There are some considerations you should address before configuring RTMP filters.

Use the **show appletalk route** command to display the contents of the AppleTalk routing table. This command is useful for verifying that a **distribute-list in** filter has been correctly configured and that any denied routes are not in the routing table, as follows:

```
Tokyo#show appletalk route
Codes: R—RTMP derived, E—EIGRP derived, C—connected, A—AURP, S—static
    P—proxy
5 routes in internet
The first zone listed for each entry is its default (primary) zone.
C Net 3210-3219 directly connected, Ethernet0, zone Azone
C Net 3220-3220 directly connected, Serial0, zone Azone
C Net 3230-3230 directly connected, Serial1, zone Azone
R Net 11250-11259 [1/G] via 3211.4, 7 sec, Ethernet0, zone Fzone
C Net 12810-12819 directly connected, Ethernet1, zone Ozone
```

Use the **show appletalk access-lists** command to check access list statements, and use the **show appletalk interface** command to ensure that the access lists have been applied to the intended interface.

NBP Filtering

Users prefer to use the names of networked devices rather than their network numbers. In order to communicate with the named entity, the name must be converted into an address for use by the lower-layer protocols. In AppleTalk, the NBP handles this conversion.

The NBP process has four stages in AppleTalk. When the Chooser is activated to search for a service, the software sends a broadcast request packet to the local router because only routers know which networks are in which zones. The router looks in its ZIT and forwards the request to a router for each network listed in the table as being associated with the specified zone. Each router then sends a multicast frame on its network, specifying that a node is looking for a service. The nodes that implement the service respond to the originator.

The NBP lookup process can generate considerable overhead traffic in an AppleTalk network.

NBP filters can be used to manage traffic in an AppleTalk network, as shown in Figure B–14. They offer better network bandwidth utilization by filtering unwanted NBP traffic and improved security by hiding AppleTalk devices. The NBP filter can be applied to the AppleTalk access list to filter NBP packets. With NBP filters, access can be denied to a single device such as a Macintosh or laser printer or to all such devices within a zone.

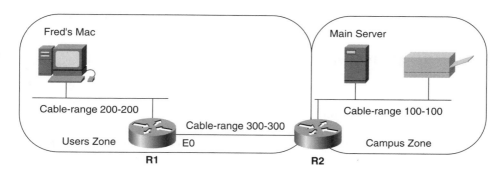

Fred's Mac

Main Server

Cable-range 200-200

Cable-range 100-100

Cable-range 300-300

Users Zone   E0

Campus Zone

R1

R2

Figure B–14
NBP filters can deny access to a single device or to all devices within a zone.

Identifying the Network Visible Entities (NVEs)

To configure an NBP filter, you must know how to identify an AppleTalk object. Apple refers to a node service accessible over an AppleTalk network as a *network-visible-entity* (NVE). The actual nodes are not considered NVEs, but the socket through which the node offers a service is an NVE.

NVEs can be referred to by an entity name. An entity name is an ASCII string with three fields: object, type, and zone. The form of the entity name is object:type@zone. The object field is the name of the device; for example, Fred's Mac. The type field is an attribute associated with the entity; for example, Workstation. The zone field is the location of the entity; for example, Users Zone. Taken together, the entity name is Fred's Mac:Workstation@Users Zone.

Special characters can be used as wildcards in place of defined character strings. An equal sign (=) in the object or type fields means "any." For example, =:AFP Server@Campus Zone means any AFPServer located in the Campus Zone. An asterisk (*) in the zone field means the local zone to the user requesting the name.

Following is a list of some common entity types:

Type	Description
AFPServer	AppleShare servers or System 7 file sharing enabled
LaserWriter	Any AppleTalk PostScript laser printer
Workstation	Any Mac with System 7 loaded
2.0Mail Server	Microsoft Mail Server
ciscoRouter	Cisco router with AppleTalk routing enabled

NBP Filtering Commands

Use the **access-list nbp** command in global configuration mode to define access for a class of NBP entities (*type*), a particular name (*object*), or location of the entity (*zone*). The syntax for this command is as follows:

```
router(config)#access-list access-list-number {deny | permit} nbp seq
    {type | object | zone} string
```

access-list nbp Command	Description
access-list-number	The number of the access list; a number in the range of 600 to 699.
seq	A number used to tie the object, type, and zone together. Each command entry must have a sequence number. Use the same sequence number for tuples that are part of the same named entity.
string	The character string of the object, type, or zone. Each string can be up to 32 characters in length. Wildcard characters, for example, would be the equal and asterisk signs (=,*)—are permitted.

Use the **access-list other-nbps** command in global configuration mode to define the default action to take for NBP named entities not specified in the list. The syntax for this command is as follows:

```
route(config)#access-list access-list-number {deny | permit} other-nbps
```

Use the **appletalk access-group** command in interface configuration mode to apply the NBP filter to an interface for any type of incoming NBP packet. The syntax for this command is as follows:

```
route(config-if)#appletalk access-group access-list-number
```

In Figure B–15, the requirement is to deny access to Color Laser from devices in Users Zone. To accomplish this requirement, you can create an NBP filter.

Denying a Single Device

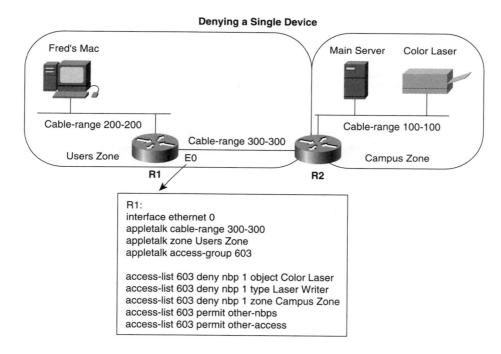

Figure B–15
NBP filtering example.

AppleTalk access list 603 is created for this purpose. Because NBP filters apply to incoming traffic, the access list is placed in R1's Ethernet 0 interface. The number 1 after the keyword "nbp" in the access list is a sequence number that ties together all three portions (object, type, and zone) of the named entity. Therefore, the entity that is inaccessible is Color Laser:LaserWriter@Campus Zone. Access list 603 also specifies the following:

- **access-list 603 permit other-nbps**—Allows users to access the Main Server.

- **access-list 603 permit other-access**—Must be included or no DDP traffic (data packets) will be allowed.

Access list 603 is linked to R1's Ethernet 0 interface with the **appletalk access-group 603** command specifying the number of the access list. An NBP filter is applied against the inbound traffic when the filter is used with the **appletalk access-group** command. When used with dialer lists, the NBP filter is applied against outbound traffic and controls what traffic type initiates a DDR call. Because the NBP filter works on all incoming NBP packets—broadcast request, forward request and lookup, and reply—carefully select the proper router and interface on which to place the NBP filter.

The effect of this filter is that when users on cable range 200–200 send NBP broadcasts to router R1 looking for LaserWriters, R1 forwards the request to R2, which sends an NBP lookup into the Campus Zone. The device Color Laser replies, R2 forwards the reply to R1, and the reply gets dropped at R1 Ethernet 0. As a result, users in the Users Zone do not see Color Laser in their Chooser nor are they able to access it through an alias.

Use the **show appletalk access-lists** and **show appletalk interface** commands to verify the settings on your NBP filter. Additionally, use the **show appletalk nbp** command to verify the named entities known to the router. This command shows information associated with the device including the network number, name, type, and zone. This information is useful when creating NBP filters and, once created, for verifying that the filter you created had the intended results on downstream routers.

SUMMARY

In this appendix, you learned that locating services and routing updates cause overhead in an AppleTalk network. Understanding groups of common interest is key to controlling service location traffic. You also learned that filtering strategies must ensure that routing information needed for service location is accessible to routers. Cisco's IOS software provides many features for reducing the volume of service location and routing traffic, and for controlling access.

Configuring NetWare Link Services Protocol

This appendix discusses Novell's NetWare Link Services Protocol (NLSP), a link-state routing protocol that provides fast convergence and reduces routing and service advertising update traffic in an IPX internetwork.

CONFIGURING NLSP

The Novell NetWare architecture consists of upper-layer applications support, midlevel transport and routing protocols, and lower-level media-access protocols. NLSP is a link-state routing protocol that is based on the ISO Intermediate System-to-Intermediate System (IS-IS) protocol. NLSP was created to perform the following tasks:

- Improve scalability of IPX networks.

- Route more effectively and efficiently.

- Reduce overhead and management demands.

Instead of using a distance vector routing protocol such as IPX RIP in your topology, you can use NLSP, a link-state routing protocol. NLSP provides the following several advantages over RIP:

- NLSP sends updates only when there is a change in the topology, or at least every two hours (default).

- Convergence is generally faster with NLSP than RIP because when a router floods new information, each router receiving the information copies the packet and then continues forwarding it. This is in contrast to RIP, where a router must recalculate its routing table with the new information first.

- Routing loops are virtually nonexistent because each router receives the new information firsthand.

- Like OSPF, NLSP uses a cost metric that can go up to 128. A greater hop count enables NetWare clients to communicate with NetWare servers that are further away than the RIP 15 hop limit.

- NLSP is backward-compatible with RIP and SAP.

Cisco IOS Release 11.1 software supports NLSP revision 1.1, which includes support for multiple areas and route aggregation. NLSP areas can exchange routing information. *Route* aggregation is the NLSP method for defining logical areas and performing route summarization.

NLSP Operation

Before NLSP routers can exchange information, they must learn about each other and the network topology. This is done using the following process:

1. Each router exchanges Hello packets with its immediate neighbors to establish an adjacency with each neighbor and to determine the designated router (DR) for the LAN.

   An adjacency needs to be established so that each router can determine the reachability of its neighbors. An adjacency entry is the record that a router keeps about the state of its connectivity with a neighboring router. Two routers must see each other before either creates an adjacency entry in the adjacency database. Figure C–1 shows this process.

2. Each router creates a link-state packet (LSP) that includes information from its adjacency database.

   An LSP includes route and services information for each link that the router knows about.

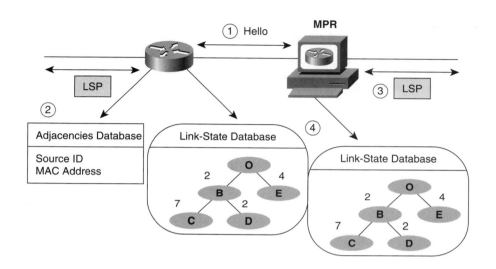

Figure C–1
NLSP routers share a common view of the network.

3. Each router floods its LSP to all routers in the network topology.

Flooding is the process whereby each router in the network topology receives the information directly. (This is in contrast to RIP/SAP, which sends updates only to immediate neighbors.) Flooding LSPs occurs as a directed broadcast on WANs; for LANs, LSPs multicast to other NLSP routers. Broadcast is used when a device on the LAN does not support multicast.

4. Each router receives the LSPs and puts them in its LSP database.

The link state database is the router's view of the network topology. All routers in the same area have identical LSP databases.

5. To make sure all routers in the same area have synchronized LSP databases, a DR on the LAN periodically floods a summary of its LSP database in a complete sequence number packet (CSNP) to all routers on the LAN it represents. Non-DR routers verify that they have the same information as the DR. If they do not, one of the following occurs:

- If a router has a missing or out-of-date LSP, it multicasts a partial sequence number packet (PSNP) requesting the complete LSP. The DR multicasts the complete LSP to all routers on the LAN.

- If a router has a more up-to-date or newer LSP than the DR, it floods the LSP on the LAN.

A PSNP is also used when a WAN-based router receives an LSP. The non-DR router on the WAN responds to an LSP with a PSNP to acknowledge receipt of the LSP. This is how each router synchronizes its LSP databases. No CSNPs are exchanged between routers on a WAN link.

6. Using the LSP database, the router must determine the best path to each network. Using cost as the metric, each router independently calculates the shortest path to each destination using SPF algorithm. The results of the calculation are placed in the forwarding database, as shown in Figure C–2.

Each router's forwarding database is unique because path calculation is from each router's perspective. When a router receives a new LSP, the router waits five seconds before recomputing its forwarding database. This allows the router to act on several accumulated changes it receives during the given time period. This can also stop the router from constantly running the forwarding database computation if a link is *flapping*: going up and down in quick succession.

Figure C–2
Building the forwarding database.

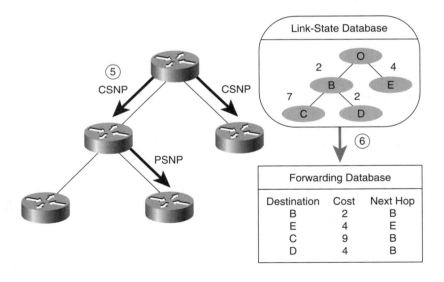

7. The router forwards packets using the paths listed in the forwarding database.

The DR is established to represent the routers on the LAN and to manage the database synchronization process. The DR represents the LAN by flooding the information about the segment not only for itself but also for its neighbors. It is not necessary, nor efficient, for each neighbor to flood essentially the same information about the segment. This is the primary reason for the existence of the DR.

Because the DR represents the LAN, LSP traffic is reduced. Without a DR, each router would need to send a similar LSP indicating that it can connect to each router on the same LAN. Instead, the DR represents the LAN by establishing a pseudonode. A *pseudonode* is a logical representation of the LAN. Each router floods an LSP with its internal network number and area-address information and circuit/adjacency information that it can connect to the pseudonode.

In addition, the DR sends a pseudonode LSP. A pseudonode LSP contains all the RIP and SAP information for the circuit. This one is potentially very large. Without the DR, each router would send its own, but they would all be more or less identical.

Refer to the *Novell NetWare Link Services Protocol (NLSP) Specification Revision 1.1* (available at www.novell.com) for more information on how the pseudonode is created and operates.

NLSP Configuration Commands

Global IPX routing must already be configured on your router before you enter statements to run NLSP. This means your configuration must have an IPX routing entry. For NLSP, LAN interfaces must already have an IPX network number and encapsulation-type entry. To configure NLSP, perform the following steps:

1. The command **ipx internal-network** *network-number* establishes the number you specify as a primary network number that refers to the router. The number is a hexadecimal value up to four bytes long. You do not need to type in leading zeros (for example, b0b is a legal address). You must select a number for this entry that is unique across your IPX internetwork. NLSP will advertise and accept packets for this internal network number at all the router interfaces.

   In the case of NLSP routers, this number is used as the seed for the router identification number and as a method of selecting a master router across a WAN link using Novell's IPXWAN protocol. Refer to the NLSP specifications at www.novell.com for more information on IPXWAN.

2. Enable NLSP on the router with the **ipx router nlsp** command. The *tag* parameter names the NLSP process. If you are running only one NLSP process, defining *tag* is optional.

3. The final mandatory router command **area-address** *address mask* sets the area for link-state network grouping.

    The command **area-address** *address mask* sets a 32-bit hexadecimal address and mask that define how many of the 32 bits are used as the network number prefix. If the *address* and *mask* arguments are both set to 0, all networks are included in the area. NLSP uses this area address to define which routers can be in the same area.

4. The interface command **ipx nlsp enable** starts NLSP routing on each interface or subinterface that you want to use NLSP. It uses the internal network number. NLSP does not support secondary networks. In addition, if you need to define multiple encapsulations, you must use subinterfaces.

To configure NLSP on a WAN interface, you must enable nlsp on the interface and enable a dependent protocol: IPXWAN. IPXWAN is used to establish a connection between NLSP routers across a WAN and to time the link.

To configure NLSP on a WAN interface, perform the following tasks starting in global configuration mode:

1. Specify a serial interface. For example, for serial interface 1, use the command **interface serial number1**.

2. Enable IPXWAN using the **ipx ipxwan** command. The full syntax for this command is:

    ```
    ipx ipxwan [local-node unnumbered local-server-name retry-interval
        retry-limit]
    ```

The components of the **ipx ipxwan** command are as follows:

ipx ipxwan Command	Description
local-node	(Optional) Primary network number of the router. This is an IPX network number that is unique across the entire internetwork. The device with the higher number is determined to be the link master. A value of 0 causes the Cisco IOS software to use the configured internal network number.
network-number	(Optional) IPX network number to be used for the link if this router is the one determined to be the link master. The number is an eight-digit hexadecimal number that uniquely identifies a network cable segment. It can be a number in the range 0 to FFFFFFFD. A value of 0 is equivalent to specifying the keyword **unnumbered**.
unnumbered	(Optional) Specifies that no IPX network number is defined for the link. This is equivalent to specifying a value of 0 for the network-number argument.
local-server-name	(Optional) Name of the local router. It can be up to 47 characters long, and can contain uppercase letters, digits, underscores (_), hyphens (-), and *at* signs (@). This is the name of the router as configured via the **hostname** command; that is, the name that precedes the standard prompt, which is an angle bracket (>) for EXEC mode, or a pound sign (#) for privileged EXEC mode.
retry-interval	(Optional) Retry interval, in seconds. This interval defines how often the software will retry the IPXWAN start-up negotiation if a start-up failure occurs. Retries will occur until the retry limit defined by the retry-limit argument is reached. It can be a value from 1 to 600. The default is 20 seconds.

ipx ipxwan Command	Description
retry-limit	(Optional) Maximum number of times the software retries the IPXWAN start-up negotiation before taking the action defined by the **ipx ipxwan error** command. It can be a value from 1 to 100. The default is 3. The ipx ipxwan error command reset supports three parameters: *reset* (resets the link when negotiations fail—the default action), *resume* (when negotiations fail, IPXWAN ignores the failure, takes no special action, and resumes the start-up negotiation attempt), and *shutdown* (shuts down the link when negotiations fail).

3. Enable NLSP on the interface using the **ipx nlsp** [*tag*] **enable** command, for which [tag] is an optional name for the NLSP process. The tag can be any combination of printable characters.

NLSP Configuration Example

This simple NLSP configuration example in Figure C–3 shows two networks that use NLSP.

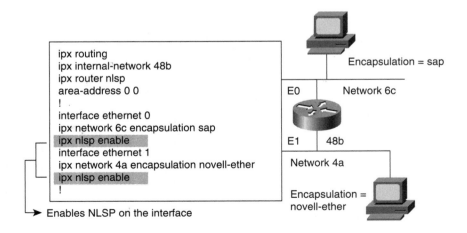

Figure C–3
Simple NLSP example.

```
ipx routing
ipx internal-network 48b
ipx router nlsp
area-address 0 0
!
interface ethernet 0
ipx network 6c encapsulation sap
ipx nlsp enable
interface ethernet 1
ipx network 4a encapsulation novell-ether
ipx nlsp enable
!
```

Enables NLSP on the interface

Encapsulation = sap

E0   Network 6c

E1   48b

Network 4a

Encapsulation = novell-ether

Consider the following when configuring NLSP:

- The routing protocol RIP is already running by default; it starts automatically when the router executes the global command for IPX routing. If you do not want to route using both protocols, you must explicitly disable IPX RIP with the **no ipx router rip** command.

- Many options allow changes to default settings. For example, you can override RIP/SAP automatic compatibility, hops, ticks, interface throughput cost, and other aspects of NLSP. Refer to the technical documentation and Novell specifications for more details.

CAUTION

You should not change optional parameters unless you are having a specific problem. Changing parameters without understanding your network topology may have unexpected results.

VERIFYING NLSP OPERATION

Use the **show ipx route** command to see a summarized routing table for a node, as shown in Figure C–4.

The NA indicator refers to an NLSP aggregate route. Following are the fields in Figure C–4:

The L indicator refers to the internal network number manually configured as an NLSP global entry.

An N entry refers to NLSP. The NLSP-derived routing entries provide information on target network, NLSP cost, delay/hop count, metric address of next hop port, age of entry in the table, and the outgoing interface.

[20]—Cost

Figure C–4
*Routes
learned by
NLSP.*

```
Router# show ipx route
Codes:        C - Connected primary network, c - Connected secondary network
       S- Static, F - Floating static, L - Local (Internal), W - IPXWAN
       R - RIP, E - EIGRP, N - NLSP, X - External, s- seconds, u - usecs

8 Total IPX routes, Up to 2 parallel paths and 16 hops allowed.

No default route known.

N A snn000 ITTI0000 [19][02/06] via 91,0000,3020, ccdb 163, E0
L          48b is the internal network
C          4a(SAP),         Et1
C          6c(NOVELL-ETHER),      Et0
W          C0(ppp),         Se0
N          1 [20] [02/01] via      6C.0000.0c02.8cf9,2s,Et0
N          3 [20] [02/01] via      4A.0000.0c02.8cfc,2s,Et1
N          E222 [40][03/02] via    4A.0000.0c02.8cfc,2s,Et1
N          E303 [40][03/02] via    6C.0000.0c02.8cf9,2s,Et0
N          E03E03 [40][03/02] via    4A.0000.0c02.8cfc,2s,Et1
NX         C0000000 [20][01/02] [00/01] via 4A.0000.0c02.8cfc,2s,Et1
```

[02/01]—Ticks/Area Count

6C.0000.0c02.8cf9—Next hop

2s—Age in seconds

Et0—Interface from which received

You can also verify an NLSP router's connection to the network and other NLSP routers. Figure C–5 shows two ways to verify NLSP operation.

The **show ipx nlsp neighbor detail** command displays the network address of connected nodes on each interface, the interface state (Up), and other information.

holdtime is the time in seconds that a router will keep a previously established adjacency. Without a hello from adjacent routers, the holdtime decreases to zero and that adjacency is deleted from the table. This causes a link change. Then other NLSP operations including SPF recalculation occur. Priority and circuit ID are used to elect an NLSP designated router on the LANs.

```
Router# show ipx nlsp neighbor detail

System Id              Interface  State  Holdtime  Priority  Circuit Id
0000.0C01.D879         Serial0    Up     42        0         03
  IPX Address: c0.0000.0000.0001
  IPX Areas: 00000000/00000000
0000.0C01.D879 Ethernet0  Up      51     44        0000.0C02.8CF9.02
  IPX Address: 6c.0000.0c01.d879
  IPX Areas: 00000000/00000000
0000.0C01.D879 Ethernet1  Up      48     44        0000.0C02.8CF9.04
  IPX Address: 4a.0000.0c01.f4c5
  IPX Areas: 00000000/00000000
```

```
Router# ping ipx c0.0000.0000.0001
Repeat count [5]:
Datagram size [100]:
Timeout in seconds [2]:
Verbose [n]:
Novell Standard Echo [n]: y
Sending 5 100-byte Novell echos to c0.0000.0000.0001, timeout is
2 seconds
!!!!!
Success rate is 100%, round trip min/avg/max = 1/24 ms.
```

Figure C–5
*Verifying
NLSP
connectivity.*

The **ping** command includes the Novell standard echo. This enhancement makes it possible for NLSP-compliant nodes, such as MPRs and third-party routers, to respond as ping targets.

You can use the **show ipx nlsp database** command to display the link-state database. Each router has its own adjacencies, link state, and forwarding databases. These databases operate collectively as a single process to discover, select, and maintain route information about the area.

SUMMARY

As you've learned in this appendix, NLSP is an IPX link-state routing protocol. You learned how to configure an NLSP router and use **show** commands to verify NLSP operation and connectivity.

APPENDIX D

Configuring T1/E1 and ISDN PRI Options

The purposes of this appendix are to discuss T1/E1, including channelized T1/E1 configuration commands and examples, and to discuss ISDN PRI, including controller options, configuration examples, and configuration commands.

CONFIGURING T1 AND E1

Wide-area connectivity has become an integral part of large corporate networking. Dedicated serial lines can connect to digital carrier facilities to transmit data through the telephone hierarchy. Several technologies include key features of this WAN connectivity. They include the following:

- *T1*—A digital WAN service that transfers data at 1.544 Mbps through a switching network. T1 service is provided in the United States and Japan, as shown in Figure D–1.

- *E1*—Wide-area digital transmission scheme used predominantly in Europe and Australia that carries data at a rate of 2.048 Mbps, as shown in Figure D–1.

- *Channelized T1*—Access link operating at 1.544 Mbps that is subdivided into 24 channels of 64 kbps each. The individual channels or groups of channels connect to different destinations. Channelized T1 supports PPP, HDLC, Frame Relay, and X.25. Also referred to as fractional T1.

- *Channelized E1*—Access link operating at 2.048 Mbps that is subdivided into 30 B channels and 1 D channel. Channelized E1 supports PPP, HDLC, Frame Relay, and X.25.

- *DS-0 (digital signal level 0)*—Framing specification used in transmitting digital signals over a single channel at 64 kbps on a T1/E1 facility. DS-0 is the data rate of each T1/E1 channel.

- *DS-1 (digital signal level 1)*—Framing specification used in transmitting digital signals at 1.544 Mbps.

- *Multiplexer/demultiplexer (MUX/DMUX)*—A method of combining multiple input ports to run over a trunk line and splitting them apart again at the other end. T1 multiplexers use time-dimension multiplexing (TDM) to combine multiple channels into a single byte stream.

Figure D–1
DS-1 framing for a single T1 offers 1.544-Mbps; E1 offers 2.108-Mbps.

Many organizations have based their WAN structures on dedicated lines using individual CSU/DSUs. Each of these lines is located on a multiple-port synchronous serial interface card. The port density of the interface card and the backplane capacity are limiting factors in how many WAN connections a router can support. T1 and E1 support increases the port density and overall throughput for WAN implementations.

The transmission rates are limited by the framing structure and number of channels available. The European T1 (E1) supports a different framing and synchronization method, which accounts for the difference in actual data transmission rates.

The Cisco 7000 models support the MultiChannel Interface Processor (MIP) that contains two full T1/E1 ports, as shown in Figure D–2. The Cisco 4000 models support a single-port interface for channelized T1/E1. Each port can be channelized to generate 24 DS-0 (64 kbps) lines for T1 or 30 DS-0 lines for E1. Multiple MIP cards can be configured into the Cisco 7000 chassis. Each line (subchannel) is individually configurable just as though it were a dedicated interface.

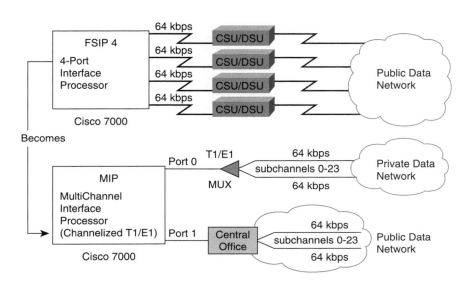

Figure D–2
Channelizing T1/E1 example.

The output of a port on the MIP card can be carried by a private data network. Alternatively, the MIP card can be connected directly to the service provider's facility, and the channel output can be carried by a private or public data network.

T1 and E1 support the following WAN protocols:

     X.25

     LAPB

     Frame Relay

     HDLC

     PPP

     SMDS

     ATM-DXI

Channelized T1/E1 Configuration Commands

Use the **controller** [t1 | e1] command to configure a T1 or E1 controller and to enter the controller configuration mode, as in the following:

```
router(config)#controller [t1 | e1] [slot/port | number]
```

The components of the **controller** [t1 | e1] command are as follows:

controller Command	Description
slot/port	Specifies MIP slot and port number
number	Specifies the network interface module (NIM) number

For example, to configure the MIP in slot 4, port 0 of a Cisco 7000 as a T1 controller, use the **controller t1 4/0** command. To configure NIM 0 of a Cisco 4000 as a T1 controller, use the **controller t1 0** command.

Use the **channel-group** command to define the time slots that belong to each T1/E1 circuit, as in the following:

```
router(config-controller)#channel-group number timeslots range speed
    {48 | 56 | 64}
```

The components of the **channel-group** command are as follows:

channel-group Command	Description
number	Channel-group number from 0 to 23 for T1 and 0 to 31 for E1.
timeslots *range*	Time slot or range of time slots belonging to the channel group. For a T1 controller, the time slot range is from 1 to 24. For an E1 controller, the time slot range is from 1 to 31.
speed {48|56|64}	Speed in kbps. The default line speed for a T1 controller is 56 kbps. For an E1 controller, the default is 64 kbps.

The channel-group number may be arbitrarily assigned and must be unique for the controller. The time slot range must match the time slots assigned to the channel group. The service provider defines the time slots that comprise a channel group. The timeslots assigned depend on the level of service and bandwidth that a company orders as well as the company's current bandwidth needs.

Use the **framing** command to select the frame type for the T1 line, as in the following:

```
router(config-controller)#framing {sf | esf}
```

The components of the **framing** command are as follows:

framing Command	Description
sf	This specifies Super Frame as the T1 frame type. Super Frame is the default.
esf	This specifies Extended Super Frame as the T1 frame type. AT&T proposed the Extended Superframe Format be implemented on its T1 circuits to provide in-service diagnostic capabilities.
crc4	This specifies CRC4 frame as the E1 frame type.
no-crc4	This specifies no CRC4 frame as the E1 frame type.
australia	(Optional) This specifies the E1 frame type used in Australia.

Use the **linecode** command to select the line-code type for the T1 line, as in the following:

```
router(config-controller)#linecode {ami | b8zs}
```

The components of the **linecode** command are as follows:

linecode Command	Description
ami	This specifies alternate mark inversion (AMI) as the line-code type. **ami** is the default.
b8zs	This specifies B8ZS as the line-code type. B8ZS (Binary Eight Zero Substitution) is an improvement to the **ami** line-code technique.

The service provider determines the framing type and the line code.

When you are connecting to a public network the clock source sources from the T1 line rather than the router interface. On a private network, however, clocking may need to be provided by the routers. Use the **clock source** command to set the T1 line clock source for the controller. Unless you are connecting to a private network where you control the clocking, this command is required only when connecting two devices back-to-back for testing purposes. The syntax of this command is as follows:

```
router(config-controller)#clock source {line | internal}
```

The components of the **clock source** command are as follows:

clock source Command	Description
internal	Specifies that the interface will clock its transmitted data from its internal clock.
line	Specifies the T1 line as the clock source. This is the default condition.

Channelized T1 Configuration Example

The MIP card allows up to 24 (T1) subchannels to be configured independently on one physical port. Subchannels have all the same configuration options and characteristics as ordinary serial ports. Channel groups are assigned from one or several DS-0s, which are assigned by the carrier and are usually numbered contiguously. Figure D–3 shows a channelized T1 example. The commands shown are defined as follows:

Command	Description
controller t1 4/1	This specifies the MIP card in slot 4, port 1 of a Cisco 7000.
framing esf	This specifies Extended Super Frame as the T1 frame type.
line code b8zs	This specifies B8ZS as the line-code type.
channel-group 0 timeslots 1	This specifies that circuit 0 is a single time slot.
channel-group 8 timeslots 6-11	This specifies that channel-group 8 will have six time slots (6 to 11). The line speed is the T1 default speed, 56 kbps.

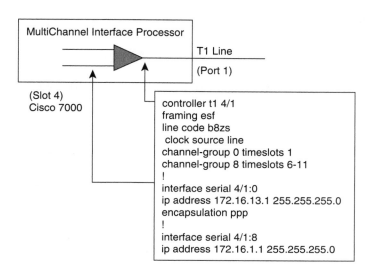

Figure D–3
Channelized T1 configuration example.

The controller card in slot 4 has port 1 configured for the appropriate frame and line-code types. Channel group 0 has a single time slot running at the default (56 kbps) speed. Channel group 8 has been assigned six time slots, all operating at the default 56 kbps. Subchannel 0 has been assigned an encapsulation type of PPP. Channel group 8 assumes the default encapsulation. Both subchannels are assigned to different subnets.

The line encoding and framing must be set to match the carrier equipment.

After you define T1 channel groups, you can configure each channel group as a serial interface. In this example, the **interface serial 4/1:0** command configures channel group 0 for PPP.

TIPS

Cisco MC3810 can also support a T1/E1 trunk interface with the multiflex trunk module (MFT). The MFT provides an RJ-48 connector for the network interface and a T1.403-compliant, onboard channel service unit/data service unit (CSU/DSU). The T1/E1 trunk interface to a Frame Relay network is capable of handling time-division multiplexing (TDM) trunk services.

Channelized E1 Configuration

Use the **framing** command to select the frame type for the E1 line, as in the following:

```
router(config-controller)#framing {crc4 | no-crc4} [australia]
```

The components of the **framing** command are as follows:

framing Command	Description
crc4	Specifies crc4 as the E1 frame type, the default.
no-crc4	Specifies that CRC checking is disabled in the E1 frame type.
australia	(Optional) Specifies the frame type for E1 lines in Australia.

Use the **linecode** command to select the line-code type for the E1 line, as in the following:

```
router(config-controller)#linecode {ami | hdb3}
```

linecode Command	Description
ami	Specifies AMI as the line-code type; the default.
hdb3	Specifies high-density bipolar 3 (HDB3) as the line-code type. Use hdb3 for E1 controllers only.

Channelized E1 Configuration Example

The MIP card allows up to 30 (E1) subchannels to be configured independently on one physical port. Subchannels have all the same configuration options and characteristics as ordinary serial ports. Channel groups are assigned from one or several 64-kbps DS-0s, which are assigned by the carrier and are usually numbered contiguously. Figure D–4 shows a channelized E1 example. The commands shown there are defined as follows:

Command	Description
controller e1 4/1	Specifies the MIP card in slot 4, port 1 of a Cisco 7000.
framing crc4	Specifies Extended Super Frame as the E1 frame type.
line code hdb3	Specifies HDB3 as the line-code type.
channel-group 0 timeslots 1	Specifies that circuit 0 is a single time slot.
channel-group 8 timeslots 5,7,12-15, 28	Specifies that channel-group 8 will have seven time slots (5, 7, 12-15, and 28). The line speed is the E1 default speed, 64 kbps.

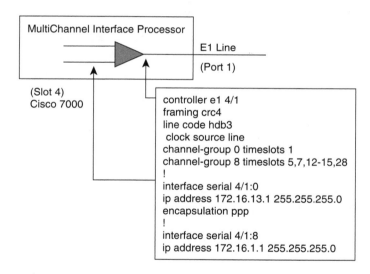

Figure D–4
Channelized E1 configuration example.

The controller card in slot 4 has port 1 configured for the appropriate frame and line-code types. Channel group 0 has a single time slot running at the default (64 kbps) speed. Channel group 8 has been assigned various time slot ranges, totaling 7, all operating at the default rate of 64 kbps. Subchannel 0 has been assigned an encapsulation type of PPP. Subchannel 8 assumes the default encapsulation. Both subchannels are assigned to different subnets.

The line encoding and framing must be set to match the carrier equipment. The channel group speed you choose must match the speed specified by your service provider.

The **interface serial 4/1:8** command configures channel group 8 as a serial interface.

CONFIGURING PRIMARY RATE INTERFACE

The Primary Rate Interface (PRI) is an ISDN interface that multiplexes multiple channels across a single transmission medium, as shown in Figure D–5.

Figure D–5
ISDN PRI multiplexes multiple channels across a single transmission medium.

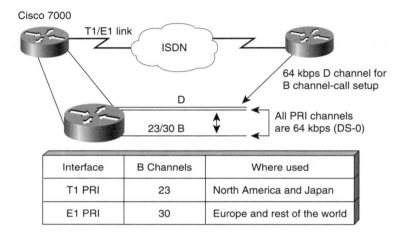

Interface	B Channels	Where used
T1 PRI	23	North America and Japan
E1 PRI	30	Europe and rest of the world

PRI is sometimes described as 23B+D, or as 30B+D, and has the following configurations:

- ISDN PRI in North America and Japan offers 23 B channels and 1 D channel, yielding a combined rate of 1.544 Mbps.

- ISDN PRI in Europe provides 30 B channels and 1 D channel with a combined rate of 2.048 Mbps.

Unlike ISDN BRI, PRI does not connect to an NT1 device. The physical interface is the same as for a T1 or an E1—that is, a CSU/DSU function bundled into the router. D-channel packet data is not available for PRI.

Use PRI configuration tasks in addition to the DDR-derived commands you saw earlier in BRI configurations. These PRI tasks are as follows:

1. Specify the correct PRI switch type that the router interfaces at the provider's central office.

2. Specify the T1/E1 controller, framing type, and line coding for the provider's facility.

3. Set a PRI group time slot for the T1/E1 facility and indicate the speed used.

4. Identify the interface that you will configure to act with DDR.

- On a Cisco 7000 series router, indicate the slot and port.

- On a Cisco 4000 series router, indicate the unit number.

- For both Cisco 7000 and Cisco 4000 routers, include a number that designates the PRI D channel.

ISDN PRI Configuration Commands

Use the **isdn switch-type** command to specify the central office PRI switch to which the router connects, as in the following:

```
router(config)#isdn switch-type primary-rate-switch-type
```

The components of the **isdn switch-type** command are as follows:

isdn switch-type Command	Description
pri-4ess	AT&T 4ESS-Primary switches (United States).
pri-5ess	AT&T 5ESS-Primary switches (United States).
pri-dms100	NT DSM-100 PRI switches (North America).
pri-ntt	NTT ISDN PRI switches (Japan).
pri-net5	European ISDN PRI switches.
none	No switch defined.

To configure a T1 or E1 controller and enter controller configuration mode, use the **controller** global configuration command.

```
controller {t1 | e1} slot/port (on the Cisco 7200 and Cisco 7500 series)
controller {t1 | e1} number (on the Cisco AS5200 and Cisco 4000 series)
```

controller Command	Description
t1	T1 controller.
e1	E1 controller.
slot/port	Backplane slot number and port number on the interface. See your hardware installation manual for the specific values and slot numbers.
number	Network processor module (NPM) number, in the range 0 through 2.

Default—No T1 or E1 controller is configured.

T1/E1 Controller Options for PRI

Use the **framing** controller configuration to specify the time slot frame type to use with the T1 or E1 facility, as in the following:

```
router(config-controller)#framing {esf | crc4}
```

The components of the **framing** controller configuration are as follows:

framing Command	Description
esf	Extended Super Frame. Use for T1 PRI configurations.
crc4	Cyclic redundancy check 4. Use for E1 PRI configurations.

Verify that the ISDN PRI circuits default to 64-kbps speed for each channel, which is why there are only two frame types.

Use the **linecode** controller configuration to specify the physical-layer line coding to use with the provider's T1 or E1 facility, as in the following:

```
router(config-controller)#linecode {b8zs | hdb3}
```

The components of the **linecode** controller configuration are as follows:

linecode Command	Description
b8zs	Binary 8-zero substitution. Use for T1 PRI configurations.
hdb3	High-density bipolar 3. Use for E1 PRI configurations.

ISDN PRI Configuration

The **pri-group** command configures the specified interface for PRI operation, as in the following:

```
router(config-controller)#pri-group [timeslots range]
```

timeslots *range* is the number of time slots allocated. For T1, use a value in the range of 1 to 23, and for E1 use a value from 1 to 31.

CAUTION

PRI is not available in every country.

The **interface serial** *slot/port | unit*:{**23** | **15**} command specifies an interface for PRI operation. The interface can be a serial interface to a T1/E1 on the Cisco 7000 or Cisco 4000 series router configured, as shown previously.

```
router(config)#interface serial slot/port :{23 | 15}
```

or

```
router(config)#interface serial unit :{23 | 15}
```

The components of the **interface serial** command are as follows:

interface serial Command	Description
slot/port	A slot/port designated on the Cisco 7000 series router served by the MIP controller.
unit	A unit number designated on the Cisco 4000 series router served by the NPM.
23	A T1 interface that designates channelized DS-0s 0 to 22 are B channels and DS-0 23 is the D channel.
15	An E1 interface that designates 30 DS-0s are B channels and DS-0 15 is the D channel.

Additional commands pertain to T1 and E1 operation. For T1, enter the commands **framing esf** and **linecode b8zs**. For E1, enter the commands **framing crc4** and **linecode hdb3**.

PRI Configuration Example

Figure D–6 shows a PRI configuration example. The commands shown there are defined as follows:

Command	Description
isdn switch-type primary-4ess	Selects a switch type of 4ESS to use on the Cisco 7000.
controller t1 2/0	Selects the T1 controller for slot 2.
pri-group timeslots 1-23	Establishes the interface port to function as PRI with 23 time slots designated to operate at a speed of 64 kbps.
framing esf	Selects Extended Super Frame, a T1 choice.
linecode b8zs	Selects line-code binary 8-zero substitution for T1.
interface serial 2/0:23	Use serial interface slot 2, port 0. Channel 23 has the D channel (T1).

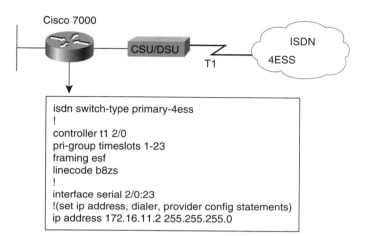

Figure D–6
PRI configura-
tion example.

```
isdn switch-type primary-4ess
!
controller t1 2/0
pri-group timeslots 1-23
framing esf
linecode b8zs
!
interface serial 2/0:23
!(set ip address, dialer, provider config statements)
ip address 172.16.11.2 255.255.255.0
```

TIPS

Static mapping and DDR commands are also used for configuring PRI. Although they are also required for ISDN operation, they are omitted from this example.

SUMMARY

This appendix presented channelized T1, channelized E1, and ISDN PRI configuration commands and examples. Channelized T1 contains an access link operating at 1.544 Mbps that is subdivided into 24 channels of 64 kbps each. The individual channels or groups of channels connect to different destinations. Channelized E1 contains an access link operating at 2.048 Mbps that is subdivided into 30 B channels and 1 D channel. Channelized E1 supports PPP, HDLC, Frame Relay, and X.25. ISDN PRI multiplexes multiple channels across a single transmission medium.

APPENDIX E

Configuring SMDS

This appendix defines SMDS (Switched Multimegabit Data Service), explains the configuration tasks involved in configuring SMDS, reviews the configurations commands for SMDS operation, and provides you with an example configuration of SMDS.

OVERVIEW OF SWITCHED MULTIMEGABIT DATA SERVICE (SMDS)

Switched Multimegabit Data Service (SMDS) is a packet-switched datagram service designed for very high-speed wide-area data communications. SMDS offers data throughputs in the 1- to 34-Mbps range, but has lost much momentum due to the acceptance of ATM and Frame Relay networks.

Some features of SMDS include the following:

- Provides a datagram, LAN-like service

- Data-link acknowledgments are not used

- No windowing capability is available

SMDS-specific CSU/DSU (channel service unit/data service unit) equipment (SDSU) is required to access the SMDS cloud, as shown in Figure E–1.

Figure E–1
*SMDS equip-
ment is
required to
access the
SMDS cloud.*

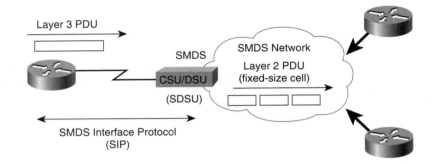

SIP level 3 functionality is provided in the router. As such, the router performs the following:

- Generates L3_PDUs

- Maps network protocol addresses to SMDS addresses

SIP level 2 and 1 functionality is provided in the SDSU; thus, it generates L2_PDUs (53-byte cells). Fixed-sized cells are propagated by the SMDS network, as shown in Figure E–2.

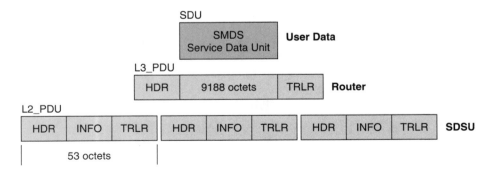

The L3_PDU information generated by the router is an encapsulated Data Exchange Interface (DXI) frame. Any serial interface can be used, but internal buffering capacities limit default MTU sizes to 1500 bytes on T1 interfaces and to 4470 bytes on T3

interfaces. Attempts to raise the MTU value on the interface with the **interface mtu** command will only raise the capacity to 2048 and 4500, respectively. Hardware connections between the router and the SDSU are specified to be EIA/TIA-449 or V.35-style cables.

SMDS addresses for the router are assigned by the service provider. SMDS uses 64-bit addresses specified in E.164 format, as shown in Figure E–3.

Figure E–3
SMDS addressing.

Individual or group addresses can be assigned. Individual addresses are unicast and are prefaced with the letter C. Group addresses are used for multicasting and are prefaced with the letter E, as in the following examples:

- Unicast C331691861245678

- Multicast E18008702535

The SMDS service provider can supply source and destination address screening.

SMDS CONFIGURATION TASKS

Preparing the router for operation in an SMDS environment requires configuration of interface parameters. Interface tasks include the following:

- Specifying the SMDS encapsulation type for the interface

- Establishing the SMDS address specified by the service provider

- Generating static-map statements that link upper-layer protocol addresses to SMDS addresses

- Linking a protocol broadcast to an SMDS multicast group address

- Turning on ARP to dynamically build the ARP cache

Routing tables are configured dynamically when DECnet, extended AppleTalk, IP, IPX, and ISO CLNS routing are configured.

SMDS CONFIGURATION COMMANDS

Use the **encapsulation smds** command to enable SMDS service on the desired interface. The syntax for this command is as follows:

```
router(config-if)#encapsulation smds
```

Use the **smds address** command to specify the SMDS individual address for a particular interface. The syntax for this command is as follows:

```
router(config-if)#smds address smds-address
```

where *smds-address* is the individual address provided by the SMDS service provider.

Use the **smds static-map** command to configure a static map between a higher-level protocol address and an individual SMDS address, as follows:

```
router(config-if)#smds static-map protocol-type protocol-address
    smds-address [broadcast]
```

smds static-map Command	Description
protocol-type	Can be appletalk, bridge, ip, decnet, xns, ipx, clns, or vines.
protocol-address	Address of the higher-level protocol.
smds-address	SMDS address used to complete the mapping.
broadcast	Indicates whether broadcast traffic will be carried.

Use the **smds multicast** command to map the protocol multicast address to an SMDS group address. The syntax for this command is as follows:

```
router(config-if)#smds multicast protocol-type smds-address
```

smds multicast Command	Description
protocol-type	Can be **appletalk, aarp, vines, bridge, decnet, decnet_router, decnet_node, ip, clns, clns_is, clns_es, ipx,** or **xns.**
smds-address	SMDS address; a group address must be defined to serve the broadcast function.

Use the **smds enable-arp** command to enable the Address Resolution Protocol (ARP). The multicast address for ARP must be set before this command is issued. The syntax for this command is as follows:

```
router(config-if)#smds enable-arp
```

SMDS CONFIGURATION EXAMPLE

In Figure E–4, for example, the command **smds address c141.5797.1313** specifies the individual address for interface serial 0. The address is represented as a 12-digit SMDS address in the dotted notation nnnn.nnnn.nnnn (48 bits long).

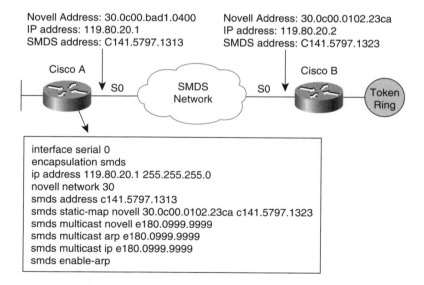

Novell Address: 30.0c00.bad1.0400
IP address: 119.80.20.1
SMDS address: C141.5797.1313

Novell Address: 30.0c00.0102.23ca
IP address: 119.80.20.2
SMDS address: C141.5797.1323

Cisco A

Cisco B

S0

SMDS
Network

S0

Token
Ring

```
interface serial 0
encapsulation smds
ip address 119.80.20.1 255.255.255.0
novell network 30
smds address c141.5797.1313
smds static-map novell 30.0c00.0102.23ca c141.5797.1323
smds multicast novell e180.0999.9999
smds multicast arp e180.0999.9999
smds multicast ip e180.0999.9999
smds enable-arp
```

Figure E–4
SMDS config-uration exam-ple.

SMDS has been enabled on interface serial 0, and an address of c141.5797.1313 has been assigned. Novell traffic for the next hop router 30.0c00.0102.23ca will use SMDS unicast address c141.5797.1323. Broadcasts for Novell, ARP, and IP protocols will use SMDS group address e180.0999.9999. Dynamic learning of addresses is allowed because ARP is enabled.

SUMMARY

In this appendix, you've learned that SMDS is a connectionless cell relay technology. You learned the addressing mechanism and configuration commands, including the **encapsulation smds, smds static-map, smds multicast,** and **smds enable-arp commands.**

Password Recovery

This appendix explains several password recovery techniques for Cisco routers and Catalyst switches. You can perform password recovery on most of the platforms without changing hardware jumpers, but all platforms require the router to be rebooted. Password recovery can be done only from the console port physically attached to the router.

THEORY OF PASSWORD RECOVERY

There are three ways to restore access to a router when the password is lost. You can view the password, change the password, or erase the configuration and start over as if the box were new.

Each procedure follows these basic steps:

1. Configure the router to start up without reading the configuration memory (NVRAM). This is sometimes called the *test system mode, ROM mode,* or *boot mode.*

2. Reboot the system.

3. Access enable mode (which can be done without a password if you are in test system mode).

4. View or change the password, or erase the configuration.

5. Reconfigure the router to boot up and read the NVRAM as it normally does.

6. Reboot the system.

CAUTION

Some password recovery requires a terminal to issue a **BREAK** signal; you must be familiar with how your terminal or PC terminal emulator issues this signal. In ProComm, for example, the keys Alt+B will by default generate the **BREAK** signal, and in Windows Terminal you press Break or Ctrl+Break. Windows Terminal also allows you to define a function key as **BREAK**. From the terminal window, select Function Keys and define one as BREAK by filling in the characters **^$B** (Shift 6, Shift 4, and Capital B).

The following sections contain detailed instructions for specific Cisco routers. Locate your product at the beginning of each section to determine which technique to use.

PASSWORD RECOVERY TECHNIQUE #1

Following are the relevant devices:

- Cisco 2000 Series

- Cisco 2500 Series

- Cisco 3000 Series

- 680x0-Based Cisco 4000 Series

- Cisco 7000 Series Running Cisco IOS 10.0 or later in ROMs

This technique can be used on the Cisco 7000 and Cisco 7010 only if the router has Cisco IOS 10.0 ROMs installed on the RP card. It may be booting Flash Cisco IOS 10.0 software, but it needs the actual ROMs on the processor card as well.

1. Attach a terminal or PC with terminal emulation to the console port of the router. To connect a PC to the console port, attach a null modem adapter (Tandy Null Modem Adapter No. 26-1496 has been tested) to the console port, and then attach a straight-through modem cable to the null modem adapter.

2. Type **show version** and record the setting of the configuration register. It is usually 0x2102 or 0x102. If you cannot get the prompt to do a show version, look on a similar router to obtain the configuration register number or try using 0x2102.

3. Power the router down, and then up.

4. Press the Break key on the terminal within 60 seconds of the power up. You will see the > prompt with no router name. If you don't, the terminal is not sending the correct Break signal. In that case, check the terminal or terminal emulation setup.

5. Type **o/r 0x42** at the > prompt to boot from Flash or **o/r 0x41** to boot from the boot ROMs. (Note that this is the letter "o," not the numeral zero.) If you have Flash and it is intact, 0x42 is the best setting because it is the default. Use 0x41 only if the Flash is erased or not installed.

CAUTION

If you use 0x41, you can either view or erase the configuration. You cannot change the password.

6. Type **i** at the > prompt. The router will reboot but will ignore its saved configuration.

7. Answer **no** to all the setup questions.

8. Type **enable** at the Router> prompt. You'll be in enable mode and see the Router# prompt.

9. Choose one of the following three options:

To view the password, type **show config**.

To change the password (in case it is encrypted, for example), do the following:

a. Type **config mem** to copy the NVRAM into memory.

b. Type **wr term**.

c. If you have **enable secret xxxx**, perform the following:

Type **config term** and make the changes.

Type **enable secret** *<password>*.

Press Ctrl+Z.

d. If you do not have **enable secret xxxx**, then:

Type **enable password** *<password>*.

Press Ctrl+Z.

e. Type **write mem** to commit the changes.

f. To erase the config, type **write erase**.

10. Type **config term** at the prompt.

11. Type **config-register 0x2102**, or whatever value you recorded in step 2.

12. Press Ctrl+Z to quit from the editor.

13. Type **reload** at the prompt. You do not need to write memory.

PASSWORD RECOVERY TECHNIQUE #2

The relevant devices for this password recovery technique are as follows:

- Cisco 1003

- Cisco 4500

- IDT Orion-Based Cisco 3600

- Motorola 860–Based Cisco 2600

Follow these steps:

1. Attach a terminal or PC with terminal emulation to the console port of the router.

2. Type **show version** and record the setting of the configuration register. It is usually 0x2102 or 0x102.

3. Power the router down, and then up.

4. Press the Break key on the terminal within 60 seconds of the power up.

   You will see the rommon> prompt. If you don't, the terminal is not sending the correct Break signal. In that case, check the terminal or terminal emulation setup.

5. Type **confreg** at the rommon> prompt.

6. Answer **y** to the Do you wish to change configuration[y/n]? prompt.

7. Answer **n** to all the questions that appear until you reach the ignore system config info[y/n]? prompt. Answer **y**.

8. Answer **n** to the remaining questions until you reach the change boot characteristics[y/n]? prompt. Answer **y**.

9. At the enter to boot: prompt, type **2** followed by a carriage return.

   If Flash is erased, type **1**. If all Flash is erased, the 4500 must be returned to Cisco for service.

CAUTION

If you use "1," you can either view or erase the configuration. You cannot change the password.

---

10. A configuration summary is printed. Answer **no** to the Do you wish to change configuration[y/n]? prompt.

11. Type **reset** at the rommon> prompt, or power-cycle your 4500 or 7500.

12. After it boots up, answer **no** to all the Setup questions.

13. Type **enable** at the Router> prompt. You'll be in enable mode and see the Router# prompt.

14. Choose one of these three options:

To view the password, type **show config**.

To change the password (in case it is encrypted, for example), perform the following:

a. Type **config mem** to copy the NVRAM into memory.

b. Type **wr term**.

If you have **enable secret xxxx**, then perform the following:

Type **config term** and make the changes.

Type **enable secret** <*password*>.

Press Ctrl+Z.

If you do not, then perform the following:

Type **enable password** <*&ltpassword*>.

Press Ctrl+Z.

c. Type **write mem** to commit the changes.

To erase the config, type **write erase**.

15. Type **config term** at the prompt.

16. Type **config-register 0x2102**, or whatever value you recorded in step 2.

17. Press Ctrl+Z to quit from the editor.

18. Type **reload** at the prompt. You do not need to write to memory.

Password recovery procedures for Cisco Catalyst switches and older Cisco routers and communication servers can be found at www.cisco.com/warp/customer/701/22.htm.

SUMMARY

This appendix covered several password recovery techniques for Cisco routers and Catalyst switches. Recall that you can perform password recovery on most of the platforms without changing hardware jumpers, but all platforms require the router to be rebooted.

Glossary

A

AARP—AppleTalk Address Resolution Protocol. Protocol in the AppleTalk protocol stack that maps a data-link address to a network address.

AARP probe packets—Packets transmitted by AARP that determine whether a randomly selected node ID is being used by another node in a nonextended AppleTalk network. If the node ID is not being used, the sending node uses that node ID. If the node ID is being used, the sending node chooses a different ID and sends more AARP probe packets.

ABM—Asynchronous Balanced Mode. An HDLC (and derivative protocol) communication mode supporting peer-oriented, point-to-point communications between two stations, where either station can initiate transmission.

access list—List kept by routers or firewalls to control access through or to the router for a number of services (for example, to prevent packets with a certain IP address from leaving a particular interface on the router).

access method—1. Generally, the way in which network devices access the network medium. 2. Software within an SNA processor that controls the flow of information through a network.

ACK—See *acknowledgment*.

acknowledgment—Notification sent from one network device to another to acknowledge that some event (for example, receipt of a message) occurred. Sometimes abbreviated ACK. Compare to *NAK*.

active monitor—Device responsible for performing maintenance functions on a Token Ring. The active monitor is responsible for such ring maintenance tasks as ensuring that tokens are not lost and that frames do not circulate indefinitely.

adapter—See *NIC*.

address—Data structure or logical convention used to identify a unique entity, such as a particular process or network device.

address mapping—Technique that allows different protocols to interoperate by translating addresses from one format to another. For example, when routing IP over X.25, the IP addresses must be mapped to the X.25 addresses so that the IP packets can be transmitted by the X.25 network.

address mask—Bit combination used to describe which portion of an address refers to the network or subnet and which part refers to the host. Sometimes referred to simply as *mask*.

address resolution—Generally, a method for resolving differences between computer addressing schemes. Address resolution usually specifies a method for mapping network layer (Layer 3) addresses to data link layer (Layer 2) addresses.

Address Resolution Protocol—See *ARP*.

adjacency—Relationship formed between selected neighboring routers and end nodes for the purpose of exchanging routing information. Adjacency is based on the use of a common media segment. Primarily used with OSPF and NLSP.

Adminstrative Distance—Rating of trustworthiness of a routing information source. Administrative distance is often expressed as a numerical value between 0 and 255: the higher the value, the lower the truisworthiness rating.

Advanced Research Projects Agency—See *ARPA*.

advertising—A process in which routing or service updates are sent so that other routers on the network can maintain lists of usable routes.

AEP—AppleTalk Echo Protocol. Used to test connectivity between two AppleTalk nodes. One node sends a packet to another node and receives a duplicate, or echo, of that packet.

AFP—AppleTalk Filing Protocol. Presentation-layer protocol that allows users to share data files and application programs that reside on a file server. AFP supports AppleShare and Mac OS File Sharing.

agent—1. Generally, software that processes queries and returns replies on behalf of an application. 2. In NMSs, process that resides in all managed devices and reports the values of specified variables to management stations.

algorithm—Well-defined rule or process for arriving at a solution to a problem. In networking, algorithms are commonly used to determine the best route for traffic from a particular source to a particular destination.

all-routes explorer packet—Explorer packet that traverses an entire SRB network, following all possible paths to a specific destination. Sometimes called all-rings explorer packet.

ANSI—American National Standards Institute. Voluntary organization composed of corporate, government, and other members that coordinates standards-related activities, approves U.S. national standards, and develops positions for the United States in international standards organizations. ANSI helps develop international and U.S. standards relating to, among other things, communications and networking. ANSI is a member of the IEC and the ISO.

AppleTalk—Protocol used by Mac computers to communicate to other Mac computers on a common network. There have been 2 phases in the development of AppleTalk.

application—Program that performs a function directly for a user. FTP and telnet clients are examples of network applications.

application layer—Layer 7 of the OSI reference model. This layer provides services to application processes (such as email, file transfer, and terminal emulation) that are outside the OSI model. The application layer identifies and establishes the availability of intended communication partners (and the resources required to connect with them), synchronizes cooperating applications, and establishes agreement on procedures for error recovery and control of data integrity. Corresponds roughly with the transaction services layer in the SNA model. See also *data link layer, network layer, physical layer, presentation layer, session layer,* and *transport layer.*

area—Logical set of network segments (CLNS-, DECnet-, or OSPF-based) and their attached devices. Areas are usually connected to other areas via routers, making up a single autonomous system.

ARP—Address Resolution Protocol. Internet protocol used to map an IP address to a MAC address. Defined in RFC 826. Compare *RARP.*

ARPA—Advanced Research Projects Agency. Research and development organization that is part of DoD. ARPA is responsible for numerous technological advances in communications and networking. ARPA evolved into DARPA, and then back into ARPA again (in 1994).

ARPANET—Advanced Research Projects Agency Network. Landmark packet-switching network established in 1969. ARPANET was developed in the 1970s by BBN and funded by ARPA (and later DARPA). It eventually evolved into the Internet. The term *ARPANET* was officially retired in 1990.

ASCII—American Standard Code for Information Interchange. Eight-bit code for character representation (seven bits plus parity).

Asynchronous Balanced Mode—See *ABM.*

Asynchronous Transfer Mode—See *ATM.*

asynchronous transmission—Term describing digital signals that are transmitted without precise clocking. Such signals generally have different frequencies and phase relationships. Asynchronous transmissions usually encapsulate individual characters in control bits (called start and stop bits) that designate the beginning and end of each character. Compare *synchronous transmission.*

ATM—Asynchronous Transfer Mode. International standard for cell relay in which multiple service types (such as voice, video, or data) are conveyed in fixed-length (53-byte) cells. Fixed-length cells allow cell processing to occur in hardware, thereby reducing transit delays. ATM is designed to take advantage of high-speed transmission media such as E3, SONET, and T3.

ATM Forum—International organization jointly founded in 1991 by Cisco Systems, NET/ADAPTIVE, Northern Telecom, and Sprint that develops and promotes standards-based implementation agreements for ATM technology. The ATM Forum expands on official standards developed by ANSI and ITU-T, and develops implementation agreements in advance of official standards.

ATP—AppleTalk Transaction Protocol. Transport-level protocol that provides a loss-free transaction service between sockets. The service allows exchanges between two socket clients in which one client requests the other to perform a particular task and to report the results. ATP binds the request and response together to ensure the reliable exchange of request-response pairs.

AURP—AppleTalk Update-Based Routing Protocol. Method of encapsulating AppleTalk traffic in the header of a foreign protocol, allowing the connection of two or more discontiguous AppleTalk internetworks through a foreign network (such as TCP/IP) to form an AppleTalk WAN. This connection is called an AURP tunnel. In addition to its encapsulation function, AURP maintains routing tables for the entire AppleTalk WAN by exchanging routing information between exterior routers.

authentication—In security, the verification of the identity of a person or process.

B

B channel—Bearer channel. In ISDN, a full-duplex, 64-kbps channel used to send user data. Compare to *D channel*, *E channel*, and *H channel*.

backbone—Part of a network that acts as the primary path for traffic that is most often sourced from, and destined for, other networks.

bandwidth—1. Difference between the highest and lowest frequencies available for network signals. 2. Also used to describe the rated throughput capacity of a given network medium or protocol.

bandwidth reservation—Process of assigning bandwidth to users and applications served by a network. Involves assigning priority to different flows of traffic based on how critical and delay-sensitive they are. This makes the best use of available bandwidth, and if the network becomes congested, lower-priority traffic can be dropped. Sometimes called *bandwidth allocation*.

Banyan VINES—See *VINES*.

Basic Rate Interface—See *BRI*.

Border Gateway Protocol—Interdomain routing protocol that replaces EGP. BGP exchanges reachability information with other BGP systems. It is defined by RFC 1163.

binary—Numbering system characterized by ones and zeros (1 = on; 0 = off).

BOOTP—Bootstrap Protocol. Protocol used by a network node to determine the IP address of its Ethernet interfaces to affect network booting.

Bootstrap Protocol—See *BOOTP*.

BRI—Basic Rate Interface. ISDN interface composed of two B channels and one D channel for circuit-switched communication of voice, video, and data. Compare *PRI*.

bridge—Device that connects and passes packets between two network segments that use the same communications protocol. Bridges operate at the data link layer (Layer 2) of the OSI reference model. In general, a bridge will filter, forward, or flood an incoming frame based on the MAC address of that frame.

Bridge-Group Virtual Interface (BVI)—Integrated Routing and Bridging (IRB) provides the capability to route between a bridge group and a routed interface using a concept called Bridge-Group Virtual Interface (BVI). The BVI is a virtual interface within the router that acts like a normal routed interface that does not support bridging, but represents the corresponding bridge group to routed interfaces within the router.

broadcast—Data packet that will be sent to all nodes on a network. Broadcasts are identified by a broadcast address. Compare *multicast* and *unicast*. See also *broadcast address*.

broadcast address—Special address reserved for sending a message to all stations. Generally, a broadcast address is a MAC destination address of all ones. Compare *multicast address* and *unicast address*. See also *broadcast*.

broadcast domain—Set of all devices that will receive broadcast frames originating from any device within the set. Broadcast domains are typically bounded by routers (or in a switched network, by virtual LANs) because routers do not forward broadcast frames.

broadcast storm—Undesirable network event in which many broadcasts are sent simultaneously across all network segments. A broadcast storm uses substantial network bandwidth and, typically, causes network time-outs.

brouter— Concatenation of *bridge* and *router*. Used to refer to devices that perform both bridging and routing functions.

bursty—Communications characterized by sudden high traffic loads followed by low traffic periods.

bus topology—Linear LAN architecture in which transmissions from network stations propagate the length of the medium and are received by all other stations. Compare *ring topology, star topology,* and *tree topology.*

C

cable range—Range of network numbers that is valid for use by nodes on an extended AppleTalk network. The cable range value can be a single network number or a contiguous sequence of several network numbers. Node addresses are assigned based on the cable range value.

caching—Form of replication in which information learned during a previous transaction is used to process later transactions.

call setup time—Time required to establish a switched call between DTE devices.

carrier—1. Electromagnetic wave or alternating current of a single frequency, suitable for modulation by another, data-bearing signal. 2. Circuit provider.

CCITT—Consultative Committee for International Telegraph and Telephone. International organization responsible for the development of communications standards. Now called the ITU-T. See *ITU-T.*

CDDI—Copper Distributed Data Interface. Implementation of FDDI protocols over STP and UTP cabling. CDDI transmits over relatively short distances (about 100 meters), providing data rates of 100 Mbps using a dual-ring architecture to provide redundancy. Based on the ANSI Twisted-Pair Physical Medium Dependent (TPPMD) standard. Compare *FDDI.*

Challenge Handshake Authentication Protocol—See *CHAP.*

CHAP—Challenge Handshake Authentication Protocol. Security feature supported on lines using PPP encapsulation that prevents unauthorized access. CHAP does not itself prevent unauthorized access; it merely identifies the remote end. The router or access server then determines whether that user is allowed access. Compare to *PAP*.

circuit—Communications path between two or more points.

circuit group—Grouping of associated serial lines that link two bridges. If one of the serial links in a circuit group is in the spanning tree for a network, any of the serial links in the circuit group can be used for load balancing. This load-balancing strategy avoids data ordering problems by assigning each destination address to a particular serial link.

classful network—Network that uses traditional IP network addresses of class A, class B, and class C.

classless network—Network that does not use the traditional IP network addressing (class A, class b, and class c), but defines the network boundary using a prefix value that indicates the number of bits used for the network portion.

client—Node or software program (front-end device) that requests services from a server.

client/server computing—Term used to describe distributed computing (processing) network systems in which transaction responsibilities are divided into two parts: client (front end) and server (back end). Both terms (*client* and *server*) can be applied to software programs or actual computing devices. Also called *distributed computing (processing)*. Compare *peer-to-peer computing*.

client/server model—Common way to describe network services and the model user processes (programs) of those services. Examples include the nameserver/nameresolver paradigm of the DNS and fileserver/file-client relationships such as NFS and diskless hosts.

CO—central office. Local telephone company office to which all local loops in a given area connect and in which circuit switching of subscriber lines occurs.

coding—Electrical techniques used to convey binary signals.

common carrier—Licensed, private utility company that supplies communication services to the public at regulated prices.

congestion—Situation caused by traffic in excess of network or device capacity.

congestion avoidance—Mechanism by which an ATM or frame-relay network controls traffic entering the network to minimize delays. To use resources most efficiently, lower-priority traffic is discarded at the edge of the network if conditions indicate that it cannot be delivered.

connectionless—Term used to describe data transfer without the existence of a logical connection between the two devices. Compare *connection-oriented*.

connection-oriented—Term used to describe data transfer that requires the establishment of a logical connection betweeen the two communicating processes. See also *connectionless*.

console—A Port on a device in which a DTE device can be connected to enter commands directly into it.

convergence—Speed and capability of a group of internetworking devices running a specific routing protocol to agree on the topology of an internetwork after a change in that topology.

count to infinity—Problem that can occur in routing algorithms that are slow to converge, in which routers continuously increment the hop count to particular networks. Typically, some arbitrary hop-count limit is imposed to prevent this problem.

CSMA/CD—Stands for carrier sense multiple access with collision detection. Media-access mechanism wherein devices ready to transmit data first check the channel for a carrier. If no carrier is sensed for a specific period of time, a device can transmit. If two devices transmit at once, a collision occurs and is detected by all colliding devices. This collision subsequently delays retransmissions from those devices for some random length of time. CSMA/CD access is used by Ethernet and IEEE 802.3.

CSU—channel service unit. Digital interface device that connects end-user equipment to the local digital telephone loop. Often referred to together with DSU as CSU/DSU.

custom queuing—A method of queuing that is used to guarantee bandwidth for traffic by assigning queue space to each protocol.

D

D channel—1. Delta channel. Full-duplex, 16-kbps (BRI) or 64-kbps (PRI) ISDN channel. Compare B channel, E channel, and H channel. 2. In SNA, a device that connects a processor and main storage with peripherals.

DARPA—Defense Advanced Research Projects Agency. U.S. government agency that funded research for and experimentation with the Internet. Evolved from ARPA, and then, in 1994, back to ARPA. See also *ARPA*.

DAS—1. Dual attachment station. Device attached to both the primary and the secondary FDDI rings. Dual attachment provides redundancy for the FDDI ring: If the primary ring fails, the station can wrap the primary ring to the secondary ring, isolating the failure and retaining ring integrity. Also called a Class A station. Compare *SAS*. 2. Dynamically assigned socket. Socket that is dynamically assigned by DDP upon request by a client. In an AppleTalk network, the sockets numbered 128 to 254 are allocated as DASs.

data flow control layer—Layer 5 of the SNA architectural model. This layer determines and manages interactions between session partners, particularly data flow. Corresponds to the session layer of the OSI model. See also *data-link control layer, path control layer, physical control layer, presentation services layer, transaction services layer,* and *transmission control layer.*

data link layer—Layer 2 of the OSI reference model. Provides transit of data across a physical link. The data link layer is concerned with physical addressing, network topology, line discipline, error notification, ordered delivery of frames, and flow control. The IEEE divided this layer into two sublayers: the MAC sublayer and the LLC sublayer. Sometimes simply called *link layer.* Roughly corresponds to the data-link control layer of the SNA model.

datagram—Logical grouping of information sent as a network layer unit over a transmission medium without prior establishment of a virtual circuit. IP datagrams are the primary information units in the Internet. The terms *cell, frame, message, packet,* and *segment* are also used to describe logical information groupings at various layers of the OSI reference model and in various technology circles.

data-link control layer—Layer 2 in the SNA architectural model. Responsible for the transmission of data over a particular physical link. Corresponds roughly to the data link layer of the OSI model. See also *data flow control layer, path control layer, phys-*

ical control layer, presentation services layer, transaction services layer, and *transmission control layer.*

DCE—1. Data communications equipment (EIA expansion). 2. Data circuit-terminating equipment (ITU-T expansion). Devices and connections of a communications network that constitute the network end of the user-to-network interface. The DCE provides a physical connection to the network, forwards traffic, and provides a clocking signal used to synchronize data transmission between DCE and DTE devices. Modems and interface cards are examples of DCE. Compare *DTE.*

DDP—Datagram Delivery Protocol. AppleTalk network layer protocol responsible for the socket-to-socket delivery of datagrams over an AppleTalk internetwork.

DDR—Dial-on-demand routing. Technique whereby a router can automatically initiate and close a circuit-switched session as transmitting stations demand.

DECnet—Group of communications products (including a protocol suite) developed and supported by Digital Equipment Corporation. DECnet/OSI (also called *DECnet Phase V*) is the most recent iteration and supports both OSI protocols and proprietary Digital protocols. Phase IV Prime supports inherent MAC addresses that allow DECnet nodes to coexist with systems running other protocols that have MAC address restrictions.

DECnet Routing Protocol (DRP)—Proprietary routing scheme introduced by Digital Equipment Corporation in DECnet Phase III. In DECnet Phase V, DECnet completed its transition to OSI routing protocols (ES-IS and IS-IS).

default route—A route inserted into the routing table to direct unknown packets to a device that may know where to send the packets. With no default route, unknown packets are typically dropped as being unroutable.

demarc—Demarcation point between carrier equipment and CPE.

demultiplexing—The separating of multiple input streams that have been multiplexed into a common physical signal back into multiple output streams. See also *multiplexing.*

designated router—OSPF router that generates LSAs for a multiaccess network and has other special responsibilities in running OSPF. Each multiaccess OSPF network that has at least two attached routers has a designated router that is elected by the OSPF Hello protocol. The designated router enables a reduction in the number of adjacencies required on a multiaccess network, which in turn reduces the amount of routing protocol traffic and the size of the topological database.

destination address—Address of a network device that is receiving data. See also *source address*.

destination service access point—See *DSAP*.

DHCP—Dynamic Host Configuration Protocol. Provides a mechanism for allocating IP addresses dynamically so that addresses automatically can be reused when hosts no longer need them.

dial-on-demand routing—See *DDR*.

dial-up line—Communications circuit that is established by a switched-circuit connection using the telephone company network.

dialer map—An interface configuration command to configure multiple dialing destinations on a single synchronous interface.

directed broadcast—A directed broadcast sends a message to all devices within a given network or subnet range.

distance-vector routing algorithm—Class of routing algorithms that iterate on the number of hops in a route to find a shortest-path spanning tree. Distance-vector routing algorithms call for each router to send its entire routing table in each update, but only to its neighbors. Distance-vector routing algorithms can be prone to routing loops, but are computationally simpler than link-state routing algorithms. Also called the Bellman-Ford routing algorithm. See also *link-state routing algorithm*.

DNS—Domain Name System. System used on the Internet for translating names of network nodes into addresses.

DoD—Department of Defense. U.S. government organization that is responsible for national defense. The DoD has frequently funded communication protocol development.

DSAP—destination service access point. SAP of the network node designated in the Destination field of a packet. Compare *SSAP*. See also *SAP (service access point)*.

DTE—data terminal equipment. Device at the user end of a user-network interface that serves as a data source, destination, or both. DTE connects to a data network through a DCE device (for example, a modem) and typically uses clocking signals generated by the DCE. DTE includes such devices as computers, routers, and multiplexers. Compare *DCE*.

dual attachment station—See *DAS*.

dual counter-rotating rings—Network topology in which two signal paths, whose directions are opposite each other, exist in a token-passing network. FDDI and CDDI are based on this concept.

dual-homed station—Device attached to multiple FDDI concentrators to provide redundancy.

dual homing—Network topology in which a device is connected to the network by way of two independent access points (points of attachment). One access point is the primary connection, and the other is a standby connection that is activated in the event of a failure of the primary connection.

dynamic routing—Routing that adjusts automatically to network topology or traffic changes. Also called *adaptive routing*. Requires that a routing protocol be run between routers.

E

E channel—echo channel. 64-kbps ISDN circuit-switching control channel. The E channel was defined in the 1984 ITU-T ISDN specification, but was dropped in the 1988 specification. Compare *B channel, D channel,* and *H channel*.

E1—Wide-area digital transmission scheme used predominantly in Europe that carries data at a rate of 2.048 Mbps. E1 lines can be leased for private use from common carriers. Compare *T1*.

E3—Wide-area digital transmission scheme used predominantly in Europe that carries data at a rate of 34.368 Mbps. E3 lines can be leased for private use from common carriers. Compare *T3*.

EEPROM—electrically erasable programmable read-only memory. EPROM that can be erased using electrical signals applied to specific pins.

EIA—Electronic Industries Association. Group that specifies electrical transmission standards. The EIA and TIA have developed numerous well-known communications standards, including EIA/TIA-232 and EIA/TIA-449.

encapsulation—Wrapping of data in a particular protocol header. For example, upper-layer data is wrapped in a specific Ethernet header before network transit. Also, when bridging dissimilar networks, the entire frame from one network can simply be placed in the header used by the data link layer protocol of the other network. See also *tunneling*.

EPROM—erasable programmable read-only memory. Nonvolatile memory chips that are programmed after they are manufactured and, if necessary, can be erased by some means and reprogrammed. Compare *EEPROM* and *PROM*.

Ethernet—Baseband LAN specification invented by Xerox Corporation and developed jointly by Xerox, Intel, and Digital Equipment Corporation. Ethernet networks use CSMA/CD and run over a variety of cable types at 10, 100, and 1000 Mbps. Ethernet is similar to the IEEE 802.3 series of standards.

excess rate—Traffic in excess of the insured rate for a given connection. Specifically, the excess rate equals the maximum rate minus the insured rate. Excess traffic is delivered only if network resources are available and can be discarded during periods of congestion. Compare *insured rate* and *maximum rate*.

F

FDDI—Fiber Distributed Data Interface. LAN standard, defined by ANSI X3T9.5, specifying a 100-Mbps token-passing network using fiber-optic cable, with transmission distances of up to 2 km. FDDI uses a dual-ring architecture to provide redundancy. Compare *CDDI* and *FDDI II*.

FDDI II—ANSI standard that enhances FDDI. FDDI II provides isochronous transmission for connectionless data circuits and connection-oriented voice and video circuits. Compare *FDDI*.

Fiber Distributed Data Interface—See *FDDI*.

fiber-optic cable—Physical medium capable of conducting modulated light transmission. Compared with other transmission media, fiber-optic cable is more expensive but is not susceptible to electromagnetic interference. Sometimes called *optical fiber*.

File Transfer Protocol—See *FTP*.

filter—Generally, a process or device that screens network traffic for certain characteristics, such as source address, destination address, or protocol, and determines whether to forward or discard that traffic based on the established criteria.

firewall—A device that controls access to a private or public network.

Flash memory—Nonvolatile storage that can be electrically erased and reprogrammed so that software images can be stored, booted, and rewritten as necessary. Flash memory was developed by Intel and is licensed to other semiconductor companies.

flash update—Routing update sent asynchronously in response to a change in the network topology. Compare *routing update*.

flat addressing—Scheme of addressing that does not use a logical hierarchy to determine location.

flow—Stream of data traveling between two endpoints across a network (for example, from one LAN station to another). Multiple flows can be transmitted on a single circuit.

flow control—Technique for ensuring that a transmitting entity does not overwhelm a receiving entity with data. When the buffers on the receiving device are full, a message is sent to the sending device to suspend the transmission until the data in the buffers has been processed. In IBM networks, this technique is called *pacing*.

forwarding—Process of sending a frame toward its ultimate destination by way of an internetworking device.

fragment—Piece of a larger packet that has been broken down to smaller units. In Ethernet networks, also sometimes referred to as a frame containing less than the legal limit of 64 bytes.

fragmentation—Process of breaking a packet into smaller units when transmitting over a network medium that cannot support the original size of the packet.

frame—Logical grouping of information sent as a data link layer unit over a transmission medium. Often refers to the header and trailer, used for synchronization and error control, that surround the user data contained in the unit. The terms *cell*, *data-*

gram, *message*, *packet*, and *segment* are also used to describe logical information groupings at various layers of the OSI reference model and in various technology circles.

frame forwarding—Mechanism by which frame-based traffic, such as HDLC and SDLC, traverses a network.

Frame Relay—Industry-standard, switched data link layer protocol that handles multiple virtual circuits using a form of HDLC encapsulation between connected devices. Frame Relay is more efficient than X.25, the protocol for which it is generally considered a replacement. See also *X.25*.

FTP—File Transfer Protocol. Application protocol, part of the TCP/IP protocol stack, used for transferring files between network nodes. FTP is defined in RFC 959.

full duplex—Capability for simultaneous data transmission between a sending station and a receiving station. Compare *half duplex* and *simplex*.

full mesh—Term describing a network in which devices are organized in a mesh topology, with each network node having either a physical circuit or a virtual circuit connecting it to every other network node. A full mesh provides a great deal of redundancy, but because it can be prohibitively expensive to implement, it is usually reserved for network backbones. See also *mesh* and *partial mesh*.

G

gateway—1. In the IP community, an older term referring to a routing device. Today, the term *router* is used to describe nodes that perform this function. 2. A special-purpose device that performs an application layer conversion of information from one protocol stack to another. Compare *router*.

Gb—gigabit. Approximately 1,000,000,000 bits.

Get Nearest Server—See *GNS*.

gigabit—Abbreviated Gb. See *Gb*.

GNS—Get Nearest Server. Request packet sent by a client on an IPX network to locate the nearest active server of a particular type. An IPX network client issues a

GNS request to solicit either a direct response from a connected server or a response from a router that tells it where on the internetwork the service can be located. GNS is part of the IPX SAP. See also *IPX* and *SAP* (Service Advertisement Protocol).

H

H channel—high-speed channel. Full-duplex ISDN primary rate channel operating at 384 Kbps. Compare *B channel, D channel,* and *E channel.*

half duplex—Capability for data transmission in only one direction at a time between a sending station and a receiving station. Compare *full duplex* and *simplex.*

handshake—Sequence of messages exchanged between two or more network devices to ensure transmission synchronization before sending user data.

hardware address—See *MAC address.*

HDLC—High-Level Data Link Control. Bit-oriented synchronous data link layer protocol developed by ISO. HDLC specifies a data encapsulation method on synchronous serial links using frame characters and checksums.

header—Contains control and other information required to get the user data to its final application. Compare *trailer.*

hello packet—Multicast packet that is used by routers using certain routing protocols for neighbor discovery and recovery. Hello packets also indicate that a client is still operating and network-ready.

holddown—State into which a route is placed so that routers will neither advertise the route nor accept advertisements about the route for a specific length of time (the *hold-down period*). Holddown is used to flush bad information about a route from all routers in the network. A route is typically placed in holddown when a link in that route fails.

hop—Passage of a data packet from one network node, typically a router, to another. See also *hop count.*

hop count—Routing metric used to measure the distance between a source and a destination. RIP uses hop count as its sole metric. See also *hop* and *RIP.*

host—Computer system on a network. Similar to *node*, except that host usually implies a computer system, whereas *node* generally applies to any networked system, including access servers and routers. See also *node*.

host address—See *host number.*

host number—Part of an address that designates which node on the subnetwork is being addressed. Also called a *host address*.

HTML—Hypertext Markup Language. Simple hypertext document formatting language that uses tags to indicate how a given part of a document should be interpreted by a viewing application, such as a Web browser.

HTTP—Hypertext Transfer Protocol. The protocol used by Web browsers and Web servers to transfer files, such as text and graphics files.

hub—1. Generally, a term used to describe a device that serves as the center of a star-topology network and connects end stations. Operates at Layer 1 of the OSI model. 2. In Ethernet and IEEE 802.3, an Ethernet multiport repeater, sometimes called a *concentrator*.

hybrid network—Internetwork made up of more than one type of network technology, including LANs and WANs.

Hypertext Transfer Protocol—See *HTTP.*

I

IANA—Internet Assigned Numbers Authority. Organization operated under the auspices of the ISOC as a part of the IAB. IANA delegates authority for IP address-space allocation and domain-name assignment to the InterNIC and other organizations. IANA also maintains a database of assigned protocol identifiers used in the TCP/IP stack, including autonomous system numbers.

ICMP—Internet Control Message Protocol. Network layer Internet protocol that reports errors and provides other information relevant to IP packet processing. Documented in RFC 792.

IEEE—Institute of Electrical and Electronics Engineers. Professional organization whose activities include the development of communications and network standards. IEEE LAN standards are the predominant LAN standards today.

IEEE 802.2—IEEE LAN protocol that specifies an implementation of the LLC sublayer of the *data link layer*. IEEE 802.2 handles errors, framing, flow control, and the network layer (Layer 3) service interface. Used in IEEE 802.3 and IEEE 802.5 LANs. See also *IEEE 802.3* and *IEEE 802.5*.

IEEE 802.3—IEEE LAN protocol that specifies an implementation of the physical layer and the MAC sublayer of the data link layer. IEEE 802.3 uses CSMA/CD access at a variety of speeds over a variety of physical media. Extensions to the IEEE 802.3 standard specify implementations for Fast Ethernet. Physical variations of the original IEEE 802.3 specification include 10Base2, 10Base5, 10BaseF, 10BaseT, and 10Broad36. Physical variations for Fast Ethernet include 100BaseTX and 100BaseFX.

IEEE 802.5—IEEE LAN protocol that specifies an implementation of the physical layer and MAC sublayer of the *data link layer*. IEEE 802.5 uses token passing access at 4 or 16 Mbps over STP or UTP cabling and is functionally and operationally equivalent to IBM Token Ring. See also *Token Ring*.

IETF—Internet Engineering Task Force. Task force consisting of over 80 working groups responsible for developing Internet standards. The IETF operates under the auspices of ISOC.

IGP—Interior Gateway Protocol. Internet protocol used to exchange routing information within an autonomous system. Examples of common Internet IGPs are IGRP, OSPF, and RIP.

Institute of Electrical and Electronics Engineers—See *IEEE*.

insured rate—The long-term data throughput, in bits or cells per second, that an ATM network commits to support under normal network conditions. The insured rate is 100 percent allocated; the entire amount is deducted from the total trunk bandwidth along the path of the circuit. Compare *excess rate* and *maximum rate*.

Integrated Services Digital Network—See *ISDN*.

interface—1. Connection between two systems or devices. 2. In routing terminology, a network connection on the router. 3. In telephony, a shared boundary defined by common physical interconnection characteristics, signal characteristics, and meanings of interchanged signals. 4. Boundary between adjacent layers of the OSI model. 5. A port on a device.

Internet—Largest global internetwork, connecting tens of thousands of networks worldwide and having a "culture" that focuses on research and standardization based on real-life use. Many leading-edge network technologies come from the Internet community. The Internet evolved in part from ARPANET. At one time called the DARPA Internet, not to be confused with the general term *internet*.

Internet protocol—1. Any protocol that is part of the TCP/IP protocol stack. 2. The network-layer protocol used by routers to forward packets through a network. See *IP*. See also *TCP/IP*.

internetwork—Collection of networks interconnected by routers and other devices that functions (generally) as a single network.

Internetwork Packet Exchange—See *IPX*.

internetworking—General term used to refer to the industry devoted to connecting networks together. The term can refer to products, procedures, and technologies.

InterNIC—Organization that serves the Internet community by supplying user assistance, documentation, training, registration service for Internet domain names, network addresses, and other services. Formerly called *NIC*.

interoperability—Capability of computing equipment manufactured by different vendors to communicate with one another successfully over a network.

IP—Internet Protocol. Network layer protocol in the TCP/IP stack offering a connectionless internetwork service. IP provides features for addressing, type-of-service specification, fragmentation and reassembly, and security. Defined in RFC 791. IPv4 (Internet Protocol version 4) is a connectionless, best-effort packet switching protocol. See also *IPv6*.

IP address—32-bit address assigned to hosts using TCP/IP. An IP address belongs to one of five classes (A, B, C, D, or E) and is written as four octets separated by periods (dotted decimal format). Each address consists of a network number, an optional subnetwork number, and a host number. The network and subnetwork numbers together are used for routing, whereas the host number is used to address an individual host within the network or subnetwork. A subnet mask is used to extract network and subnetwork information from the IP address. CIDR provides a new way of representing IP addresses and subnet masks. Also called an *Internet address*.

IP datagram—Fundamental unit of information passed across the Internet. Contains source and destination addresses along with data and a number of fields that define such things as the length of the datagram, the header checksum, and flags to indicate whether the datagram can be (or was) fragmented.

IPv6—IP version 6. Replacement for the current version of IP (version 4). IPv6 includes support for flow ID in the packet header, which can be used to identify flows. Formerly called IPng (IP next generation).

IPX—Internetwork Packet Exchange. NetWare network layer (Layer 3) protocol used for transferring data from servers to workstations. IPX is similar to IP and XNS.

IPXWAN—IPX wide-area network. Protocol that negotiates end-to-end options for new links. When a link comes up, the first IPX packets sent across are IPXWAN packets negotiating the options for the link. When the IPXWAN options are successfully determined, normal IPX transmission begins. Defined by RFC 1362.

ISDN—Integrated Services Digital Network. Communication protocol, offered by telephone companies, that permits telephone networks to carry data, voice, and other source traffic that is all digital.

ITU-T—International Telecommunication Union Telecommunication Standardization Sector (ITU-T) (formerly the Committee for International Telegraph and Telephone ([CCITT]). An international organization that develops communication standards. See also *CCITT*.

K

Kb—kilobit.

KB—kilobyte.

kbps—kilobits per second.

kBps—kilobytes per second.

keepalive interval—Period of time between each keepalive message sent by a network device.

kilobit— 1,024 bits of data (often approximated as 1,000 bits). Abbreviated Kb.

kilobits per second—Abbreviated kbps. See *Kbps*.

kilobyte—1,024 bytes (often approximated as 1,000 bytes). Abbreviated KB.

kilobytes per second—Abbreviated kBps. See *KBps*.

L

LAN—local-area network. High-speed, data network covering a relatively small geographic area (up to a few thousand meters). LANs connect workstations, peripherals, terminals, and other devices in a single building or other geographically limited area. LAN standards specify cabling and signaling at the physical and data link layers of the OSI model. Ethernet, FDDI, and Token Ring are widely used LAN technologies. Compare *MAN* and *WAN*.

LAPB—Link Access Procedure Balanced. Data link layer protocol in the X.25 protocol stack. LAPB is a bit-oriented protocol derived from HDLC. See also *HDLC* and *X.25*.

LAPD—Link Access Procedure on the D channel. ISDN data link layer protocol for the D channel. LAPD was derived from the LAPB protocol and is designed primarily to satisfy the signaling requirements of ISDN basic access. Defined by ITU-T Recommendations Q.920 and Q.921.

LAT—local-area transport. A network virtual terminal protocol developed by Digital Equipment Corporation.

Latency—1. Delay between the time a device requests access to a network and the time it is granted permission to transmit. 2. Delay between the time a device receives a frame and the time that frame is forwarded out the destination port.

leased line—Transmission line reserved by a communications carrier for the private use of a customer. A leased line is a type of dedicated line.

link—Network communications channel consisting of a circuit or transmission path and all related equipment between a sender and a receiver. Most often used to refer to a WAN connection. Sometimes referred to as a line or a transmission link.

Link Access Procedure Balanced—See *LAPB*.

Link Access Procedure on the D channel—See *LAPD*.

link layer—See *data link layer*.

link-layer address—See *MAC address*.

Link state advertisement—Advertisement packet used by link-state protocols that contains information about neighbors and path costs. Used by the receiving routers to maintain their routing tables.

link-state routing algorithm—Routing algorithm in which each router broadcasts or multicasts information regarding the cost of reaching each of its neighbors to all nodes in the internetwork. Link-state algorithms create a consistent view of the network and are therefore not prone to routing loops, but they achieve this at the cost of relatively greater computational difficulty and more widespread traffic (compared with distance-vector routing algorithms). Compare *distance-vector routing algorithm*.

LLC—logical link control. Higher of the two data link layer sublayers defined by the IEEE. The LLC sublayer handles error control, flow control, framing, and MAC-sublayer addressing. The most prevalent LLC protocol is IEEE 802.2, which includes both connectionless and connection-oriented variants.

load balancing—In routing, the capability of a router to distribute traffic over all its network ports that are the same distance from the destination address. Good load-balancing algorithms use both line speed and reliability information. Load balancing increases the use of network segments, thus increasing effective network bandwidth.

local-area network—See *LAN*.

local loop—Line from the premises of a telephone subscriber to the telephone service POP.

local traffic filtering—Process by which a bridge filters out (drops) frames that contain source and destination MAC addresses that are located on the same interface on the bridge, thus preventing unnecessary traffic from being forwarded across the bridge. Defined in the IEEE 802.1 standard.

loop—Route where packets never reach their destination but simply cycle repeatedly through a constant series of network nodes.

loopback test—Test in which signals are sent and then directed back toward their source from some point along the communications path. Loopback tests are often used to test network interface usability.

M

MAC—Media Access Control. Lower of the two sublayers of the *data link layer* defined by the IEEE. The MAC sublayer handles access to shared media, such as whether token passing or contention will be used. See also *data link layer* and *LLC*.

MAC address—Standardized *data link layer* address that is required for every device that connects to a LAN. Other devices in the network use these addresses to locate specific devices in the network and to create and update routing tables and data structures. MAC addresses are six bytes long and are controlled by the IEEE. Also known as a *hardware address*, *MAC-layer address*, or *physical address*. Compare *network address*.

MAC address learning—Service that characterizes a learning switch in which the source MAC address of each received packet is stored so that future packets destined for that address can be forwarded only to the switch interface on which that address is located. Packets destined for unrecognized broadcast or multicast addresses are forwarded out every switch interface except the originating one. This scheme helps minimize traffic on the attached LANs. MAC address learning is defined in the IEEE 802.1 standard.

MAC-layer address—See *MAC address*.

MAN—metropolitan-area network. Network that spans a metropolitan area. Generally, a MAN spans a larger geographic area than a LAN, but a smaller geographic area than a WAN. Compare *LAN* and *WAN*.

Management Information Base—See *MIB*.

mask—See *address mask* and *subnet mask*.

MAU—media attachment unit. 1. Device used in Ethernet and IEEE 802.3 networks that provides the interface between the AUI port of a station and the common medium of the Ethernet. The MAU, which can be built into a station or can be a separate device, performs physical layer functions including the conversion of digital data from the Ethernet interface, collision detection, and injection of bits onto the network. 2. Sometimes referred to as a media access unit, also abbreviated MAU, or as a transceiver. 3. In Token Ring, a MAU is known as a multistation access unit, and is usually abbreviated MSAU to avoid confusion.

maximum rate—Maximum total data throughput allowed on a given virtual circuit, equal to the sum of the insured and uninsured traffic from the traffic source. The uninsured data might be dropped if the network becomes congested. The maximum rate, which cannot exceed the media rate, represents the highest data throughput the virtual circuit will ever deliver, measured in bits or cells per second. Compare *excess rate* and *insured rate*.

Mb—megabit. Approximately 1,000,000 bits.

MB—megabyte. Approximately 1,000,000 bytes.

MBS—maximum burst size. In an ATM signaling message, burst tolerance is conveyed through the MBS, which is coded as a number of cells. The burst tolerance together with the SCR and the GCRA determine the MBS that can be transmitted at the peak rate and still be in conformance with the GCRA.

Mbps—megabits per second.

media—Plural of medium. Various physical environments through which transmission signals pass. Common network media include twisted-pair, coaxial, and fiber-optic cable, and the atmosphere (through which microwave, laser, and infrared transmission occurs). Sometimes called *physical media*.

Media Access Control—See *MAC*.

media access unit—See *MAU*.

megabit—Abbreviated Mb. See *Mb*.

megabits per second—Abbreviated Mbps. See *Mbps*.

megabyte—Abbreviated MB. See *MB*.

mesh—Network topology in which devices are organized in a manageable, segmented manner with many, often redundant, interconnections strategically placed between network nodes. See also *full mesh* and *partial mesh*.

message—Application layer (Layer 7) logical grouping of information, often composed of a number of lower-layer logical groupings such as packets. The terms *datagram*, *frame*, *packet*, and *segment* are also used to describe logical information groupings at various layers of the OSI reference model and in various technology circles.

metric—See *routing metric*.

MIB—Management Information Base. Database of network management information that is retrieved by a network management protocol such as SNMP. The value of a MIB object can be changed or retrieved using SNMP commands, usually through a GUI network management system. MIB objects are organized in a tree structure that includes public (standard) and private (proprietary) branches.

MSAU—multistation access unit. Wiring concentrator to which all end stations in a Token Ring network connect. The MSAU provides an interface between these devices and the Token Ring interface of a router. Sometimes abbreviated MAU.

MTU—maximum transmission unit. Maximum packet size, in bytes, that a particular interface can handle.

multicast—Single packets copied by the network and sent to a specific subset of network addresses. These addresses are specified in the Destination Address Field. Compare *broadcast* and *unicast*.

multicast address—Single address that refers to multiple network devices. Synonymous with group address. Compare *broadcast address* and *unicast address*. See also *multicast*.

multiplexing—Scheme that allows multiple logical signals to be transmitted simultaneously across a single physical channel. Compare *demultiplexing*.

multistation access unit—See *MSAU*.

multivendor network—Network using equipment from more than one vendor. Multivendor networks pose many more compatibility problems than single-vendor networks. Compare *single-vendor network*.

N

NAK—negative acknowledgment. Response sent from a receiving device to a sending device indicating that the information received contained errors. Compare to *acknowledgment*.

name resolution—Generally, the process of associating a name with a network address.

name server—Server connected to a network that resolves network names into network addresses.

NAT—Network Address Translation. Only globally unique in terms of the public internet. A mechanism for translating private addresses into publically usable addresses to be used within the public internet. An effective means for hiding actual device addressing within a private network. Also known as *Network Address Translator*.

NAUN—nearest active upstream neighbor. In Token Ring or IEEE 802.5 networks, the closest upstream network device from any given device that is still active.

NBP—Name Binding Protocol. AppleTalk transport-level protocol that translates a character string name into the DDP address of the corresponding socket client. NBP enables AppleTalk protocols to understand user-defined zones and device names by providing and maintaining translation tables that map names to their corresponding socket addresses.

neighboring routers—In OSPF, two routers that have interfaces to a common network. On multiaccess networks, neighbors are dynamically discovered by the OSPF Hello protocol.

NetBEUI—NetBIOS Extended User Interface. Enhanced version of the NetBIOS protocol used by network operating systems such as LAN Manager, LAN Server, Windows for Workgroups, and Windows NT. NetBEUI formalizes the transport frame and implements the OSI LLC2 protocol.

NetBIOS—Network Basic Input/Output System. API used by applications on an IBM LAN to request services from lower-level network processes. These services might include session establishment and termination, and information transfer.

NetWare—Popular distributed NOS developed by Novell. Provides transparent remote file access and numerous other distributed network services.

NetWare Link Services Protocol—See *NLSP*.

NetWare Loadable Module—See *NLM*.

network—Collection of computers, printers, routers, switches, and other devices that are able to communicate with each other over some transmission medium.

network address—Network layer address referring to a logical, rather than a physical, network device. Also called a *protocol address* or *logical address*. Compare *MAC address*.

Network Address Translation—See *NAT*.

network administrator—Person responsible for the operation, maintenance, and management of a network.

network analyzer—Hardware or software device offering various network troubleshooting features, including protocol-specific packet decodes, specific preprogrammed troubleshooting tests, packet filtering, and packet transmission.

Network Basic Input/Output System—See *NetBIOS*.

network byte order—Internet-standard ordering of the bytes corresponding to numeric values.

network interface—1. Boundary between a carrier network and a privately owned installation. 2. A port on device used to communicate across a network.

network interface card—See *NIC*.

network layer—Layer 3 of the OSI reference model. This layer provides connectivity and path selection between two end systems. The network layer is the layer at which routing occurs. Corresponds roughly with the path control layer of the SNA model. See also *application layer*, *data link layer*, *physical layer*, *presentation layer*, *session layer*, and *transport layer*.

network management—Generic term used to describe systems or actions that help maintain, characterize, or troubleshoot a network.

network number—Part of an address that specifies the network to which the host belongs.

NFS—Network File System. As commonly used, a distributed file system protocol suite developed by Sun Microsystems that allows remote file access across a network. In actuality, NFS is simply one protocol in the suite. NFS protocols include NFS, RPC, XDR, and others. These protocols are part of a larger architecture that Sun refers to as ONC.

NIC—1. network interface card. Board that provides network communication capabilities to and from a computer system. Also called an adapter. 2. Network Information Center. Organization whose functions have been assumed by the InterNIC. See *InterNIC*.

NLM—NetWare Loadable Module. Individual program that can be loaded into memory and can function as part of the NetWare NOS.

NLSP—NetWare Link Services Protocol. Link-state routing protocol based on IS-IS.

node—1. Endpoint of a network connection or a junction common to two or more lines in a network. Nodes can be processors, controllers, or workstations. Nodes, which vary in routing and other functional capabilities, can be interconnected by links and serve as control points in the network. *Node* is sometimes used generically to refer to any entity that can access a network and is frequently used interchangeably with *device*. 2. In SNA, the basic component of a network and the point at which one or more functional units connect channels or data circuits.

nonextended network—AppleTalk Phase 2 network that supports addressing of up to 253 nodes and only one zone.

nonseed router—In AppleTalk, a router that must first obtain, and then verify, its configuration with a seed router before it can begin operation. See also *seed router*.

non-stub area—Resource-intensive OSPF area that carries a default route, static routes, intra-area routes, interarea routes, and external routes. Non-stub areas are the only OSPF areas that can have virtual links configured across them, and are the only areas that can contain an ASBR. Compare *stub area*.

NOS—network operating system. Generic term used to refer to what are really distributed file systems. Examples of NOSs include LAN Manager, NetWare, NFS, VINES, and Windows NT.

Novell IPX—See *IPX*.

NTP—Network Time Protocol. Protocol built on top of TCP that assures accurate local time-keeping with reference to radio and atomic clocks located on the Internet. This protocol is capable of synchronizing distributed clocks within milliseconds over long time periods.

NVRAM—nonvolatile RAM. RAM that retains its contents when a unit is powered off.

O

octet—8 bits. In networking, the term *octet* is often used (rather than *byte*) because some machine architectures employ bytes that are not 8 bits long.

ODI—Open Data-Link Interface. Novell specification providing a standardized interface for NICs (network interface cards) that allows multiple protocols to use a single NIC.

Open Shortest Path First—See *OSPF.*

Open System Interconnection—See *OSI*.

Open System Interconnection reference model—See *OSI reference model.*

OSI—Open System Interconnection. International standardization program created by ISO and ITU-T to develop standards for data networking that facilitate multivendor equipment interoperability.

OSI Presentation Address—Address used to locate an OSI Application entity. It consists of an OSI Network Address and up to three selectors, one each for use by the transport, session, and presentation entities.

OSI reference model—Open System Interconnection reference model. Network architectural model developed by ISO and ITU-T. The model consists of seven layers, each of which specifies particular network functions such as addressing, flow control, error control, encapsulation, and reliable message transfer. The lowest layer (the physical layer) is closest to the media technology. The lower two layers are implemented in hardware and software, whereas the upper five layers are implemented only in software. The highest layer (the application layer) is closest to the user. The OSI reference model is used universally as a method for teaching and understanding network functionality. Similar in some respects to SNA. See *application layer, data link layer, network layer, physical layer, presentation layer, session layer,* and *transport layer.*

OSPF—Open Shortest Path First. Link-state, hierarchical IGP routing algorithm proposed as a successor to RIP in the Internet community. OSPF features include least-cost routing, multipath routing, and load balancing. OSPF was derived from an early version of the IS-IS protocol.

OUI—Organizational Unique Identifier. Three octets assigned by the IEEE in a block of 48-bit LAN addresses.

P

packet—Logical grouping of information that includes a header containing control information and (usually) user data. Packets are most often used to refer to network layer units of data. The terms *datagram, frame, message,* and *segment* are also used to describe logical information groupings at various layers of the OSI reference model and in various technology circles.

packet internet groper—See *ping.*

PAP—Password Authentication Protocol. Authentication protocol that allows PPP peers to authenticate one another. The remote router attempting to connect to the local router is required to send an authentication request. Unlike CHAP, PAP passes the password and host name or username in the clear (unencrypted). PAP does not itself prevent unauthorized access but merely identifies the remote end. The router or access server then determines whether that user is allowed access. PAP is supported only on PPP lines. Compare *CHAP.*

parallel transmission—Method of data transmission in which the bits of a data character are transmitted simultaneously over a number of channels. Compare *serial transmission.*

partial mesh—Network in which devices are organized in a mesh topology, with some network nodes organized in a full mesh, but with others that are only connected to one or two other nodes in the network. A partial mesh does not provide the level of redundancy of a full mesh topology but is less expensive to implement. Partial mesh topologies are generally used in the peripheral networks that connect to a fully meshed backbone.

Password Authentication Protocol—See *PAP*.

path control layer—Layer 3 in the SNA architectural model. This layer performs sequencing services related to proper data reassembly. The path control layer is also responsible for routing. Corresponds roughly with the network layer of the OSI model. See also *data flow control layer, data-link control layer, physical control layer, presentation services layer, transaction services layer,* and *transmission control layer.*

payload—Portion of a cell, frame, or packet that contains upper-layer information (data).

peer-to-peer computing—Peer-to-peer computing calls for each network device to run both client and server portions of an application. Also describes communication between implementations of the same OSI reference model layer in two different network devices. Compare *client-server computing.*

permanent virtual circuit—See *PVC*.

PHY—1. Physical sublayer. One of two sublayers of the FDDI physical layer. 2. Physical layer. In ATM, the physical layer provides for the transmission of cells over a physical medium that connects two ATM devices. The PHY is comprised of two sublayers: PMD and TC.

physical address—See *MAC address.*

physical control layer—Layer 1 in the SNA architectural model. This layer is responsible for the physical specifications for the physical links between end systems. Corresponds to the physical layer of the OSI model. See also *data flow control layer, data-link control layer, path control layer, presentation services layer, transaction services layer,* and *transmission control layer.*

physical layer—Layer 1 of the OSI reference model. The physical layer defines the electrical, mechanical, procedural, and functional specifications for activating, maintaining, and deactivating the physical link between end systems. Corresponds with the physical control layer in the SNA model. See also *application layer, data link layer, network layer, presentation layer, session layer,* and *transport layer.*

ping—packet internet groper. ICMP echo message and its reply. Often used in IP networks to test the reachability of a network device.

PLP—packet level protocol. Network layer protocol in the X.25 protocol stack. Sometimes called *X.25 Level 3* and *X.25 Protocol*. See also *X.25*.

point-to-multipoint connection—One of two fundamental connection types. In ATM, a point-to-multipoint connection is a unidirectional connection in which a single source end-system (known as a root node) connects to multiple destination end-systems (known as leaves). Compare *point-to-point connection*.

point-to-point connection—One of two fundamental connection types. In ATM, a point-to-point connection can be a unidirectional or bidirectional connection between two ATM end-systems. Compare *point-to-multipoint connection*.

Point-to-Point Protocol—See *PPP*.

poison reverse updates—Routing updates that explicitly indicate that a network or subnet is unreachable, rather than implying that a network is unreachable by not including it in updates. Poison reverse updates are sent to defeat large routing loops.

port—1. Interface on an internetworking device (such as a router). 2. In IP terminology, an upper-layer process that receives information from lower layers. Ports are numbered, and many are associated with a specific process. For example, SMTP is associated with port 25. A port number of this type is called a well-known address. 3. To rewrite software or microcode so that it will run on a different hardware platform or in a different software environment than that for which it was originally designed.

POST—power-on self test. Set of hardware diagnostics that runs on a hardware device when that device is powered up.

PPP—Point-to-Point Protocol. Successor to SLIP that provides router-to-router and host-to-network connections over synchronous and asynchronous circuits. Whereas SLIP was designed to work with IP, PPP was designed to work with several network layer protocols, such as IP, IPX, and ARA. PPP also has built-in security mechanisms, such as CHAP and PAP. PPP relies on two protocols: LCP and NCP.

presentation layer—Layer 6 of the OSI reference model. This layer ensures that information sent by the application layer of one system will be readable by the application layer of another. The presentation layer is also concerned with the data structures used by programs and therefore negotiates data transfer syntax for the application layer. Corresponds roughly with the presentation services layer of the SNA model. See also *application layer, data link layer, network layer, physical layer, session layer,* and *transport layer.*

presentation services layer—Layer 6 of the SNA architectural model. This layer provides network resource management, session presentation services, and some application management. Corresponds roughly with the presentation layer of the OSI model.

PRI—Primary Rate Interface. ISDN interface to primary rate access. Primary rate access consists of a single 64-Kbps D channel plus 23 (T1) or 30 (E1) B channels for voice or data. Compare to *BRI.*

priority queuing—Routing feature in which frames in an interface output queue are prioritized based on various characteristics such as protocol, packet size, and interface type.

PROM—programmable read-only memory. ROM that can be programmed using special equipment. PROMs can be programmed only once. Compare *EPROM.*

protocol—Formal description of a set of rules and conventions that governs how devices on a network exchange information.

protocol address—See *network address.*

protocol stack—Set of related communications protocols that operates together and, as a group, address communication at some or all of the seven layers of the OSI reference model. Not every protocol stack covers each layer of the model, and often a single protocol in the stack will address a number of layers at once. TCP/IP is a typical protocol stack.

proxy—Entity that, in the interest of efficiency, essentially stands in for another entity.

proxy Address Resolution Protocol—See *proxy ARP.*

proxy ARP—proxy Address Resolution Protocol. Variation of the ARP protocol in which an intermediate device (for example, a router) sends an ARP response on behalf of an end node to the requesting host. Proxy ARP can lessen bandwidth use on slow-speed WAN links.

PVC—permanent virtual circuit. Virtual circuit that is permanently established. PVCs save bandwidth associated with circuit establishment and tear down in situations where certain virtual circuits must exist all the time. In ATM terminology, called a *permanent virtual connection*. Compare *SVC*.

Q

QoS—quality of service. Measure of performance for a transmission system that reflects its transmission quality and service availability.

queue—1. Generally, an ordered list of elements waiting to be processed. 2. In routing, a backlog of packets waiting to be forwarded over a router interface.

queuing delay—Amount of time that data must wait before it can be transmitted onto a statistically multiplexed physical circuit.

R

RAM—random-access memory. Volatile memory that can be read and written by a microprocessor.

random-access memory—See *RAM*.

RARP—Reverse Address Resolution Protocol. Protocol in the TCP/IP stack that provides a method for finding IP addresses based on MAC addresses. Compare *ARP*.

reassembly—The putting back together of an IP datagram at the destination after it has been fragmented either at the source or at an intermediate node.

redirect—Part of the ICMP and ES-IS protocols that allows a router to tell a host that using another router would be more effective.

Redistribution—Allowing routing information discovered through one routing protocol to be distributed in the update messages of another routing protocol. Sometimes called route redistribution.

redundancy—1. In internetworking, the duplication of devices, services, or connections so that, in the event of a failure, the redundant devices, services, or connections can perform the work of those that failed. 2. In telephony, the portion of the total information contained in a message that can be eliminated without loss of essential information or meaning.

Request For Comments—See *RFC.*

RFC—Request For Comments. Document series used as the primary means for communicating information about the Internet. Some RFCs are designated by the IAB as Internet standards. Most RFCs document protocol specifications such as Telnet and FTP, but some are humorous or historical. RFCs are available online from numerous sources.

ring—Connection of two or more stations in a logically circular topology. Information is passed sequentially between active stations. Token Ring, FDDI, and CDDI are based on this topology.

ring topology—Network topology that consists of a series of repeaters connected to one another by unidirectional transmission links to form a single closed loop. Each station on the network connects to the network at a repeater. Although logically a ring, ring topologies are most often organized in a closed-loop star. Compare *bus topology, star topology,* and *tree topology.*

RIP—Routing Information Protocol. IGP supplied with UNIX BSD systems. The most common IGP in the Internet. RIP uses hop count as a routing metric.

RMON—remote monitoring. MIB agent specification described in RFC 1271 that defines functions for the remote monitoring of networked devices. The RMON specification provides numerous monitoring, problem detection, and reporting capabilities.

ROM—read-only memory. Nonvolatile memory that can be read, but not written, by the microprocessor.

route map—Method of controlling the redistribution of routes between routing domains.

route summarization—Consolidation of advertised network numbers in OSPF and IS-IS. In OSPF and EIGRP, this causes a single summary route to be advertised to other areas by an area border router.

routed protocol—Protocol that can be routed by a router. A router must be able to interpret the logical internetwork as specified by that routed protocol. Examples of routed protocols include AppleTalk, DECnet, and IP.

router—Network layer device that uses one or more metrics to determine the optimal path along which network traffic should be forwarded. Routers forward packets from one network to another based on network layer information contained in routing updates. Occasionally called a *gateway* (although this definition of *gateway* is becoming increasingly outdated).

routing—Process of finding a path to a destination host. Routing is very complex in large networks because of the many potential intermediate destinations a packet might traverse before reaching its destination host.

routing metric—Number or cost associated with a link used by routing algorithms to determine that one route is better than another. This information is stored in routing tables and sent in routing updates. Metrics include bandwidth, communication cost, delay, hop count, load, MTU, path cost, and reliability. Sometimes referred to simply as a *metric*.

routing protocol—Protocol that accomplishes routing through the implementation of a specific routing algorithm. Examples of routing protocols include IGRP, OSPF, and RIP.

routing table—Table stored in a router or some other internetworking device that keeps track of routes to particular network destinations and, in some cases, metrics associated with those routes.

Routing Table Maintenance Protocol—See *RTMP*.

routing update—Message sent from a router to indicate network reachability and associated metric information. Routing updates are typically sent at regular intervals and after a change in network topology. Compare *flash update*.

RPF—Reverse Path Forwarding. Multicasting technique in which a multicast datagram is forwarded out of all but the receiving interface if the receiving interface is the one used to forward unicast datagrams to the source of the multicast datagram.

RSVP—Resource Reservation Protocol. Protocol that supports the reservation of resources across an IP network. Applications running on IP end systems can use RSVP to indicate to other nodes the nature (bandwidth, jitter, maximum burst, and so forth) of the packet streams they want to receive. Also known as *Resource Reservation Setup Protocol*.

RTMP—Routing Table Maintenance Protocol. Apple Computer's proprietary routing protocol. RTMP establishes and maintains the routing information that is required to route datagrams from any source socket to any destination socket in an

AppleTalk network. Using RTMP, routers dynamically maintain routing tables to reflect changes in topology. RTMP was derived from RIP.

RTP—1. Routing Table Protocol. VINES routing protocol based on RIP. Distributes network topology information and aids VINES servers in finding neighboring clients, servers, and routers. Uses delay as a routing metric. 2. Rapid Transport Protocol. Provides pacing and error recovery for APPN data as it crosses the APPN network. With RTP, error recovery and flow control are done end-to-end rather than at every node. RTP prevents congestion rather than reacts to it. 3. Real-Time Transport Protocol. One of the IPv6 protocols. RTP is designed to provide end-to-end network transport functions for applications transmitting real-time data, such as audio, video, or simulation data, over multicast or unicast network services. RTP provides such services as payload type identification, sequence numbering, time stamping, and delivery monitoring to real-time applications.

S

SAP—1. service access point. Field defined by the IEEE 802.2 specification that identifies the upper layer process and is part of an address specification. Thus, the destination plus the DSAP define the recipient of a packet. The same applies to the SSAP. 2. Service Advertising Protocol. IPX protocol that provides a means of informing network clients, via routers and servers, of available network resources and services.

SAS—single attachment station. Device attached only to the primary ring of an FDDI ring. Also known as a Class B station. Compare *DAS*. See also *FDDI*.

SDLC—Synchronous Data Link Control. SNA data link layer communications protocol. SDLC is a bit-oriented, full-duplex serial protocol that has spawned numerous similar protocols, including HDLC and LAPB.

secondary station—In bit-synchronous data link layer protocols such as HDLC, a station that responds to commands from a primary station. Sometimes referred to simply as a *secondary*.

seed router—Router in an AppleTalk network that has the network number or cable range built in to its port descriptor. The seed router defines the network number or cable range for other routers in that network segment and responds to configuration queries from nonseed routers on its connected AppleTalk network, allowing those routers to confirm or modify their configurations accordingly. Each AppleTalk network must have at least one seed router.

segment—1. Section of a network that is bounded by bridges, routers, or switches. 2. In a LAN using a bus topology, a *segment* is a continuous electrical circuit that is often connected to other such segments with repeaters. 3. Term used in the TCP specification to describe a single transport layer unit of information. The terms *datagram*, *frame*, *message*, and *packet* are also used to describe logical information groupings at various layers of the OSI reference model and in various technology circles.

Sequenced Packet Exchange—See *SPX*.

serial transmission—Method of data transmission in which the bits of a data character are transmitted sequentially over a single channel. Compare *parallel transmission*.

server—Node or software program that provides services to clients.

service access point—See *SAP*.

Service Advertising Protocol—See *SAP*.

session—1. Related set of connection-oriented communications transactions between two or more network devices. 2. In SNA, a logical connection enabling two NAUs to communicate.

session layer—Layer 5 of the OSI reference model. This layer establishes, manages, and terminates sessions between applications and manages data exchange between presentation layer entities. Corresponds to the data flow control layer of the SNA model.

shortest-path routing—Routing that minimizes distance or path cost through application of an algorithm.

simplex—Capability for transmission in only one direction between a sending station and a receiving station. Broadcast television is an example of a simplex technology. Compare full duplex and half duplex.

single-vendor network—Network using equipment from only one vendor. Single-vendor networks rarely suffer compatibility problems. See also *multivendor network*.

sliding window flow control—Method of flow control in which a receiver gives transmitter permission to transmit data until a window is full. When the window is full, the transmitter must stop transmitting until the receiver advertises a larger window.

TCP, other transport protocols, and several data link layer protocols use this method of flow control.

SLIP—Serial Line Internet Protocol. Standard protocol for point-to-point serial connections using a variation of TCP/IP. Predecessor of PPP.

SMI—Structure of Management Information. Document (RFC 1155) specifying rules used to define managed objects in the MIB.

SNA—Systems Network Architecture. Large, complex, feature-rich network architecture developed in the 1970s by IBM. Similar in some respects to the OSI reference model, but with a number of differences. SNA is essentially composed of seven layers. See *data flow control layer, data-link control layer, path control layer, physical control layer, presentation services layer, transaction services layer,* and *transmission control layer.*

Snapshot routing—Method of gathering routing information during an *active time,* taking a snapshot of the information and using that routing information for a configured length of time (referred to as the *quiet time*).

SNMP—Simple Network Management Protocol. Network management protocol used almost exclusively in TCP/IP networks. SNMP provides a means to monitor and control network devices, and to manage configurations, statistics collection, performance, and security.

socket—1. Software structure operating as a communications end point within a network device (similar to a port). 2. Addressable entity within a node connected to an AppleTalk network. Sockets are owned by software processes known as *socket clients*. AppleTalk sockets are divided into two groups: SASs—which are reserved for clients, such as AppleTalk core protocols—and DASs—which are assigned dynamically by DDP upon request from clients in the node. An AppleTalk socket is similar in concept to a TCP/IP port.

socket number—Eight-bit number that identifies a socket. A maximum of 254 different socket numbers can be assigned in an AppleTalk node. This is commonly referred to as a port in the IP world.

source address—Address of a network device that is sending data.

spanning tree—Loop-free subset of a Layer 2 (switched) network topology.

spanning-tree algorithm—Algorithm used by the Spanning-Tree Protocol to create a spanning tree. Sometimes abbreviated as STA.

Spanning-Tree Protocol—Bridge protocol that uses the spanning-tree algorithm, enabling a learning switch to dynamically work around loops in a switched network topology by creating a spanning tree. Switches exchange BPDU messages with other bridges to detect loops, and then remove the loops by shutting down selected switch interfaces. If the primary link fails, a standby link is activated. Refers to both the IEEE 802.1 Spanning-Tree Protocol standard and the earlier Digital Equipment Corporation Spanning-Tree Protocol upon which it is based. The IEEE version supports switch domains and allows the switch to construct a loop-free topology across an extended LAN. The IEEE version is generally preferred over the Digital version. Sometimes abbreviated as STP.

SPF—shortest path first algorithm. Routing algorithm that iterates on length of path to determine a shortest-path spanning tree. Commonly used in link-state routing algorithms. Sometimes called *Dijkstra's algorithm*.

split-horizon updates—Routing technique in which information about routes is prevented from exiting the router interface through which that information was received. Split-horizon updates are useful in preventing routing loops.

spoofing—1. Scheme used by routers to cause a host to treat an interface as if it were up and supporting a session. The router spoofs replies to keepalive messages from the host in order to convince that host that the session still exists. Spoofing is useful in routing environments such as DDR, in which a circuit-switched link is taken down when there is no traffic to be sent across it in order to save toll charges. 2. The act of a packet illegally claiming to be from an address from which it was not actually sent. Spoofing is designed to foil network security mechanisms, such as filters and access lists. See also *watchdog spoofing*.

SPX—Sequenced Packet Exchange. Reliable, connection-oriented protocol that supplements the datagram service provided by network layer (Layer 3) protocols. Novell derived this commonly used NetWare transport protocol from the SPP of the XNS protocol suite.

SQE—signal quality error. In Ethernet, transmission sent by a transceiver back to the controller to let the controller know whether the collision circuitry is functional. Also called *heartbeat*.

SSAP—source service access point. The SAP of the network node designated in the Source field of a packet. Compare to *DSAP*. See also *SAP*.

standard—Set of rules or procedures either widely used or officially specified.

star topology—LAN topology in which end points on a network are connected to a common central switch by point-to-point links. A ring topology that is organized as a star implements a unidirectional closed-loop star, instead of point-to-point links. Compare *bus topology*, *ring topology*, and *tree topology*.

static route—Route that is explicitly configured and entered into the routing table, by default. Static routes take precedence over routes chosen by dynamic routing protocols. A floating static route is a manually-entered route that can be overwritten by a dynamically learned address.

stub area—OSPF area that carries a default route, intra-area routes, and inter-area routes, but does not carry external routes. Virtual links cannot be configured across a stub area, and they cannot contain an ASBR. Compare to *non-stub area*.

subnet—See *subnetwork*.

subnet address—Portion of an IP address that is specified as the subnetwork by the subnet mask.

subnet mask—32-bit address mask used in IP to indicate the bits of an IP address that are being used for the subnet address. Sometimes referred to simply as *mask*.

subnetwork—1. In IP networks, a network sharing a particular subnet address. Subnetworks are networks arbitrarily segmented by a network administrator in order to provide a multilevel, hierarchical routing structure while shielding the subnetwork from the addressing complexity of attached networks. Sometimes called a *subnet*. 2. In OSI networks, a collection of ESs and ISs under the control of a single administrative domain and using a single network access protocol.

Supernetting—Aggregating IP network addresses advertised as a single classless network address. For example, given four Class C IP networks—192.0.8.0, 192.0.9.0, 192.0.10.0 and 192.0.11.0—each having the intrinsic network mask of 255.255.255.0, one can advertise the address 192.0.8.0 with a subnet mask of 255.255.252.0.

SVC—switched virtual circuit. Virtual circuit that is dynamically established on demand and is torn down when transmission is complete. SVCs are used in situations where data transmission is sporadic. Called a *switched virtual connection* in ATM terminology. Compare *PVC*.

synchronous transmission—Term describing digital signals that are transmitted with precise clocking. Such signals have the same frequency, with individual characters encapsulated in control bits (called start bits and stop bits) that designate the beginning and end of each character. Compare *asynchronous transmission*.

T

T1—Digital WAN carrier facility. T1 transmits DS-1-formatted data at 1.544 Mbps through the telephone-switching network, using AMI or B8ZS coding. Compare *E1*.

T3—Digital WAN carrier facility. T3 transmits DS-3-formatted data at 44.736 Mbps through the telephone switching network. Compare *E3*.

TACACS—Terminal Access Controller Access Control System. Authentication protocol, developed by the DDN community, that provides remote access authentication and related services, such as event logging. User passwords are administered in a central database rather than in individual routers, providing an easily scalable network security solution.

TCP—Transmission Control Protocol. Connection-oriented transport layer protocol that provides reliable full-duplex data transmission. TCP is part of the TCP/IP protocol stack.

TCP/IP—Transmission Control Protocol/Internet Protocol. Common name for the suite of protocols developed by the U.S. Department of Defense in the 1970s to support the construction of worldwide internetworks. TCP and IP are the two best-known protocols in the suite.

Telnet—Standard terminal emulation protocol in the TCP/IP protocol stack. Telnet is used for remote terminal connection, enabling users to log in to remote systems and use resources as if they were connected to a local system. Telnet is defined in RFC 854.

throughput—Rate of information arriving at, and possibly passing through, a particular point in a network system.

Time To Live—See *TTL*.

timeout—Event that occurs when one network device expects to hear from another network device within a specified period of time but does not. The resulting timeout usually results in a retransmission of information or the dissolving of the session between the two devices.

token—Frame that contains control information. Possession of the token allows a network device to transmit data onto the network.

token bus—LAN architecture using token passing access over a bus topology. This LAN architecture is the basis for the IEEE 802.4 LAN specification.

token passing—Access method by which network devices access the physical medium in an orderly fashion based on possession of a small frame called a token. Contrast with *circuit switching* and *contention*.

Token Ring—Token-passing LAN developed and supported by IBM. Token Ring runs at 4 or 16 Mbps over a ring topology. Similar to IEEE 802.5.

TokenTalk—Apple Computer's data-link product that allows an AppleTalk network to be connected by Token Ring cables.

topology—Physical arrangement of network nodes and media within an enterprise networking structure.

totally stubby area—An area that does not accept external autonomous system (AS) routes and summary routes from other areas internal to the autonomous system. Instead, if the router needs to send a packet to a network external to the area, it sends it using a default route.

traceroute—Program available on many systems that traces the path a packet takes to a destination. It is mostly used to debug routing problems between hosts. There is also a traceroute protocol defined in RFC 1393.

traffic management—Techniques for avoiding congestion and shaping and policing traffic. Allows links to operate at high levels of utilization by scaling back lower-priority, delay-tolerant traffic at the edge of the network when congestion begins to occur.

trailer—Control information appended to data when encapsulating the data for network transmission. Compare *header*.

transaction services layer—Layer 7 in the SNA architectural model. Represents user application functions, such as spreadsheets, word-processing, or electronic mail, by which users interact with the network. Corresponds roughly with the application layer of the OSI reference model. See also *data flow control layer, data-link control layer, path control layer, physical control layer, presentation services layer,* and *transmission control layer.*

transmission control layer—Layer 4 in the SNA architectural model. This layer is responsible for establishing, maintaining, and terminating SNA sessions, sequencing data messages, and controlling session level flow. Corresponds to the transport layer of the OSI model. See also *data flow control layer, data-link control layer, path control layer, physical control layer, presentation services layer,* and *transaction services layer.*

Transmission Control Protocol—See *TCP.*

transparent bridging—Bridging scheme often used in Ethernet and IEEE 802.3 networks in which bridges pass frames along one hop at a time based on tables associating end nodes with bridge ports. Transparent bridging is so named because the presence of bridges is transparent to network end nodes.

transport layer—Layer 4 of the OSI reference model. This layer is responsible for reliable network communication between end nodes. The transport layer provides mechanisms for the establishment, maintenance, and termination of virtual circuits, transport fault detection and recovery, and information flow control. Corresponds to the transmission control layer of the SNA model. See also *application layer, data link layer, network layer, physical layer, presentation layer,* and *session layer.*

trap—Message sent by an SNMP agent to an NMS, console, or terminal to indicate the occurrence of a significant event, such as a specifically defined condition or a threshold that was reached.

tree topology—LAN topology similar to a bus topology, except that tree networks can contain branches with multiple nodes. Transmissions from a station propagate the length of the medium and are received by all other stations. Compare *bus topology, ring topology,* and *star topology.*

TTL—Time To Live. Field in an IP header that indicates how long a packet is considered valid.

tunneling—Architecture that is designed to provide the services necessary to implement any standard point-to-point encapsulation scheme.

U

UDP—User Datagram Protocol. Connectionless transport layer protocol in the TCP/IP protocol stack. UDP is a simple protocol that exchanges datagrams without acknowledgments or guaranteed delivery, requiring that error processing and retransmission be handled by other protocols. UDP is defined in RFC 768.

unicast—Message sent to a single network destination. Compare *broadcast* and *multicast*.

unicast address—Address specifying a single network device. Compare *broadcast address* and *multicast address*.

URL—universal resource locator. Standardized addressing scheme for accessing hypertext documents and other services using a browser.

V

VINES—Virtual Integrated Network Service. NOS developed and marketed by Banyan Systems.

virtual circuit—Logical circuit created to ensure reliable communication between two network devices. A virtual circuit is defined by a VPI/VCI pair and can be either permanent (PVC) or switched (SVC). Virtual circuits are used in Frame Relay and X.25. Sometimes abbreviated *VC*.

W

WAN—wide-area network. Data communications network that serves users across a broad geographic area and often uses transmission devices provided by common carriers. Frame Relay, SMDS, and X.25 are examples of WANs. Compare *LAN* and *MAN*.

watchdog packet—Used to ensure that a client is still connected to a NetWare server. If the server has not received a packet from a client for a certain period of time, it sends that client a series of watchdog packets. If the station fails to respond to a predefined number of watchdog packets, the server concludes that the station is no longer connected and clears the connection for that station.

watchdog spoofing—Subset of spoofing that refers specifically to a router acting especially for a NetWare client by sending watchdog packets to a NetWare server to keep the session between client and server active. Useful when the client and server are separated by a DDR WAN link.

watchdog timer—1. Hardware or software mechanism used to trigger an event or an escape from a process unless the timer is periodically reset. 2. In NetWare, a timer that indicates the maximum period of time a server will wait for a client to respond to a watchdog packet. If the timer expires, the server sends another watchdog packet (up to a set maximum).

Weighted fair queuing—A queuing method that prioritizes interactive traffic over file transfers in order to ensure satisfactory response time for common user applications.

X

X.25—ITU-T standard that defines how connections between DTE and DCE are maintained for remote terminal access and computer communications in PDNs. X.25 specifies LAPB, a data link layer protocol, and PLP, a network layer protocol. Frame Relay has to some degree superseded X.25.

Z

ZIP—Zone Information Protocol. AppleTalk session layer protocol that maps network numbers to zone names. ZIP is used by NBP to determine which networks contain nodes that belong to a zone.

zone—In AppleTalk, a logical group of network devices.

zone multicast address—Data-link-dependent multicast address at which a node receives the NBP broadcasts directed to its zone.

Index

CISCO CERTIFIED INTERNETWORK EXPERT

Cisco's CCIE certification programs set the professional benchmark for internetworking expertise. CCIEs are recognized throughout the internetworking industry as being the most highly qualified of technical professionals. And, because the CCIE programs certify individuals—not companies—employers are guaranteed any CCIE with whom they work has met the same stringent qualifications as every other CCIE in the industry.

To ensure network performance and reliability in today's dynamic information systems arena, companies need internetworking professionals who have knowledge of both established and newer technologies. Acknowledging this need for specific expertise, Cisco has introduced three CCIE certification programs:

WAN Switching

ISP/Dial

Routing & Switching

CCIE certification requires a solid background in internetworking. The first step in obtaining CCIE certification is to pass a two-hour Qualification exam administered by Sylvan-Prometric. The final step in CCIE certification is a two-day, hands-on lab exam that pits the candidate against difficult build, break, and restore scenarios.

Just as training and instructional programs exist to help individuals prepare for the written exam, Cisco is pleased to announce its first CCIE Preparation Lab. The CCIE Preparation Lab is located at Wichita State University in Wichita, Kansas, and is available to help prepare you for the final step toward CCIE status.

Cisco designed the CCIE Preparation Lab to assist CCIE candidates with the lab portion of the actual CCIE lab exam. The Preparation Lab at WSU emulates the conditions under which CCIE candidates are tested for their two-day CCIE Lab Examination. As almost any CCIE will corroborate, the lab exam is the most difficult element to pass for CCIE certification.

Registering for the lab is easy. Simply complete and fax the form located on the reverse side of this letter to WSU. For more information, please visit the WSU Web page at www.engr.twsu.edu/cisco/ or Cisco's Web page at www.cisco.com.

CISCO CCIE PREPARATION LAB

REGISTRATION FORM

Please attach a business card or print the following information:

Name/Title: _____

Company: _____

Company Address: _____

City/State/Zip: _____

Country Code (_____) Area Code (_____) Daytime Phone Number _____

Country Code (_____) Area Code (_____) Evening Phone Number _____

Country Code (_____) Area Code (_____) Fax Number _____

E-mail Address: _____

Circle the number of days you want to reserve lab: 1   2   3   4   5

Week and/or date(s) preferred (3 choices):

_____

_____

_____

Have you taken and passed the written CCIE exam?   Yes   No

List any CISCO courses you have attended:

Registration fee: _____ $500 per day × _____ day(s) = Total _____

Check Enclosed (Payable to WSU Conference Office)

Charge to: _____   MasterCard or Visa exp. date _____

CC# _____

Name on Card _____

Cardholder Signature _____

Refunds/Cancellations: The full registration fee will be refunded if your cancellation is received at least 15 days prior to the first scheduled lab day.

Wichita State University
University Conferences
1845 Fairmount
Wichita, KS 67260
Attn: Kimberly Moore
Tel: 800-550-1306
Fax: 316-686-6520

PACKET

Packet magazine serves as the premier publication linking customers to Cisco Systems, Inc. Delivering complete coverage of cutting-edge networking trends and innovations, *Packet* is a magazine for technical, hands-on users. It delivers industry-specific information for enterprise, service provider, and small and midsized business market segments. A toolchest for planners and decision makers, *Packet* contains a vast array of practical information, boasting sample configurations, real-life customer examples, and tips on getting the most from your Cisco Systems' investments. Simply put, *Packet* magazine is straight talk straight from the worldwide leader in networking for the Internet, Cisco Systems, Inc.

We hope you'll take advantage of this useful resource. I look forward to hearing from you!

Jennifer Biondi
Packet Circulation Manager
packet@cisco.com
www.cisco.com/go/packet